The Complete Job Search Guide for Latinos

Murray A. Mann

and

Dedication

This book is dedicated to the Latino pathfinders who persevered, pioneered, and paved the roads less traveled to make our career journeys a little easier. We applaud and recognize your efforts and sacrifice . . . gracias y bien hecho.

To our readers, we have dedicated our efforts to offer career management tools and resources that will help you to successfully navigate the challenges of 21st-century job search and career advancement processes. We hope we have achieved our goal.

To our families, thank you for encouraging and supporting our commitment to making a difference in this world. The development of this book, as well as other projects over the years, has often interrupted the time dedicated to family. We appreciate your love and understanding as we work to fulfill our mission.

Acknowledgments

Collaboration, teamwork, and the support of our *familias* have served as a foundation for Latino career success. We wrote *The Complete Job Search Guide for Latinos* book with the assistance of our *career familia*, drawing on their experiences, insights, insider tips, and industry knowledge. The whole is truly greater than the sum of its parts. We especially thank our colleagues Pat Kendall, president of Advance Résumé Concepts, and Pat Criscito, president of ProType, Ltd. and a Barron's author. Without their assistance and mentorship, this book would never have been possible.

Sincere appreciation goes to the following contributors and support team: Barron's team of Wayne Barr, Anna Damaskos, and Veronica Douglas; Arnold Boldt, Arnold-Smith Associates; Mary H. Castanuela; Mary Devo, Intern, Global Career Strategies Group; Mary Douglas; Christine Edick, A Career Coach 4 U; Wendy Enelow, Wendy Enelow Enterprises; Louise Garver, Career Directions, LLC; Sally Gelardin, Ed.D, Gelardin Family Lifeworks; Gay Anne Himebaugh-Rodriguez, Seaview Résumé Solutions; Graciela Kenig, Graciela Kenig & Associates; Norberto Kogan, Kogan Group; Abe Tomás Hughes II and Maria Elena Medina, Hispanic Alliance for Career Enhancement; Michael Martinez-Mann, Student Intern, Global Career Strategies Group; Linda Matias, National Résumé Writers Association and Career Strides; Don Orlando, The Mclean Group; Adela Pena, University of Illinois at Chicago; Mario Perales, Translator, Global Career Strategies Group; Geralynn Reyes, Careers By Design; Evelyn U. Salvador, Creative Image Builders, Inc.; John Suarez, Success Stories Inc.; Barbara A. Susman, Susman and Associates; Vivian VanLier, Advantage Resumes and Career Services; Deborah Wile-Dib, Executive Power Coach; Susan Britton Whitcomb, Career Masters Institute; Larry Uribe, Partner Solutions Group and Global Career Strategies Group; Ana Maria Vasquez; Maricela Zapian, Student Intern, Global Career Strategies.

All inquiries should be addressed to:
Barron's Educational Series, Inc.
250 Wireless Boulevard
Hauppauge, New York 11788
www.barronseduc.com

International Standard Book No. 0-7641-2869-8

Library of Congress Catalog Card No. 2005042595

Library of Congress Cataloging-in-Publication Data

Mann, Murray A.
   The complete job search guide for Latinos / by
   Murray A. Mann, Rose Mary Bombela-Tobias.
      p.   cm.
   Includes bibliographical references and index.
   ISBN 0-7641-2869-8
   1. Job hunting—United States. 2. Hispanic
Americans—Employment. 3. Vocational guidance—United
States. I. Bombela-Tobias, Rose Mary. II. Title

HF5382.75.U6M36   2005   2005042595
650.14′089′68073—dc22

PRINTED IN THE UNITED STATES OF AMERICA
9 8 7 6 5 4 3 2 1

About the Authors

Murray A. Mann and Rose Mary Bombela-Tobias have been featured nationally in electronic and print media, including *60 Minutes* and more than twenty Latino and mainstream publications, four books, and several career-related Web sites. The authors speak nationally on career management, present diversity training seminars for employers, and have assisted thousands of job seekers to reach their goals.

Murray Mann's background includes more than 25 years of human resources management. In addition to being principal of Global Career Strategies Group, an international career management and diversity consulting firm, Murray serves on the board of directors of the National Résumé Writer's Association, is a diversity advisor to Parachute, inspired by Richard Bolles' worldwide best-selling book *What Color Is Your Parachute*, and is an active member of Career Masters Institute. In addition, Murray was a founding board member of the Hispanic Alliance for Career Enhancement (HACE) and has held leadership roles with numerous Latino and other multicultural organizations.

Nationally recognized executive, management consultant, journalist, and public speaker, Rose Mary Bombela-Tobias is a first-generation Latina. Rose Mary was the first Latino in Illinois to be appointed to the Governor's Cabinet as director of the Department of Human Rights. She also served as assistant director of the Illinois Department of Central Management Services, assistant director of the Illinois Department of Personnel, and vice president/executive director of Central States SER, Jobs for Progress, Inc. Additionally, Rose Mary pioneered and managed the Illinois Business Enterprise Program for Minorities, Females, and Persons with Disabilities.

Contents

Contents

Chapter 1

Why Do We Need a Book on Latino Career and Job Search Strategies?

For many years, being a Latino in the United States has meant being nearly invisible. We were the hidden workforce that took on jobs others did not want in order to support our families. This invisibility has been changing over several decades, making the Latino workforce a major driving force in the U.S economy.

Why the change? Statistics reported by the U.S. Census tell the story:

- The Latino community is now the largest minority group in the country, accounting for 13 percent of the total population.

- Latinos are the youngest population, with an average median age of 26.

- Latino buying power will be more than $700 million annually in 2005.

As the nation's workforce ages, Latinos are becoming an integral part of the future success of this country. It is to everyone's advantage to make the entry into the workforce a successful one. Before that can happen, there are issues that need to be addressed.

The Latino middle class is the fastest growing segment of the United States. Yet, the percentage of Latinos in the managerial ranks of corporate America is lower than that of any other minority group. As a result, Latinos are often left without role models to follow in their drive to succeed. Their questions are often left unanswered. How do you find employment in a tight labor market? How can you leverage your bilingual and/or bicultural skills in your job search? Are there special resources available for Latinos to help them navigate the workplace?

Our goal in writing this book is to help fill the gap in *experiencia e información* (experience and information) that exists. This book provides the entry-level and mid-career professional with concrete building blocks that can be used to create a path for full employment and a successful career.

In addition to offering more opportunity, the changing workforce also brings more challenges. The global marketplace is changing corporate America. Downsizing, outsourcing, and increased use of technology are all contributing to major shifts. Many of the jobs that our parents and grandparents used as entry jobs are gone or fast disappearing. New skills are being required, as is advanced education.

With increased global competition, it is even more important to learn how to stand out in an interview and conduct a job search using all the resources and strengths that come with being Latino. In this book, we address a broad range of job opportunities and career paths. Not everyone wants to be a corporate executive officer and invest the time and energy that such a position requires. We encourage you to pick and choose from the resources in this book to get the information you need to lay your own path to success.

CAREER VERSUS A JOB

To many Latinos the idea of a career is foreign. To earlier generations, a career meant keeping your job with the same employer for years and years. In our countries of origin, one could become a professional—a doctor, a lawyer, an engineer—but limited educational opportunities and the lack of a strong middle class preempted the idea of a career for others. If you were not lucky enough to become a professional, you simply took whatever work was available in order to survive.

Today the situation has changed. Increased opportunities, expanded lifecycles, and the desire for satisfaction and enjoyment in the workplace make moving haphazardly from job to job a losing proposition. Many Latinos have moved out from the shadows, moved forward and left us directions on how to build the careers of the future.

PUTTING YOUR HOUSE IN ORDER

Building a home from scratch can be a very difficult, sometimes frustrating, job. You need an architect to draw up the blueprint and a contractor to handle the day-to-day details. You also need construction tools and materials: hammers, nails, wood, drywall, and so on. Eventually, the pieces of the plan start falling into place. Delays and design changes are all part of the process. In the end, a well-designed and properly constructed house is a thing of beauty.

In your career, you are the architect who must create the blueprint for your success. You are also the general contractor who is the driving force in completing the job. This might seem like an overwhelming task, but remember, you are not alone. Your "consultants"—your teachers, mentors, career coaches, and friends—can help you along the way by providing support and advice.

As you begin your job search, it is important to get your house in order. The career path you design will show you which skills need to be developed and which contacts need to be made. Then, as new career opportunities develop or other changes occur, you can adjust your plan. The ultimate goal is to develop a career that satisfies your needs and aspirations.

CAREER MAPPING

The Difference Between Getting a Job and Having a Career You Love!

Think about it! If you're in New York and you want to get to Los Angeles, a map is a handy thing to have. Without a map, you might eventually end up in L.A., but your trip could take much longer than necessary, and (most likely) it will be a miserable trip. Sound familiar?

Just as companies that use a business plan as a "road map" find the path easier to negotiate, people who use a "career map" have a much better chance of reaching their destination. Think of your job search as a series of steps that when properly completed, will yield spectacular results.

In essence, career mapping separates each stage of your journey into manageable parts, thus making it easier for you to achieve success during each phase of the search. Rigid career mapping is not possible. New opportunities arise and roadblocks crop up. With this in mind, career planning must be seen as a continual evolution.

By eliminating jobs that are not a good fit for you, you'll actually spend less time on your job and career development. It is similar to a carpenter's advice: measure twice, cut once. What you devote to this all-important first step of your job search or career change is directly proportional to the amount of success you will achieve.

Compare the maps in Figures 1.1 and 1.2.

How to Use This Book

Foundation

The information, techniques, and recommendations in this book are the culmination of our more than fifty combined years of experience in the job search, human resources, and civil rights arenas. In addition, we have conducted more than one hundred interviews with CEOs, diversity managers, hiring officials, human resources staff, professional associations, employees, applicants, recruiters, career management practitioners, and students. We made a consistent effort to reach out to Latinos in these areas—not only to gain their special insight into the barriers and successes of Latino candidates but also to solicit their contributions on the topic of Latino job search.

This book is designed to resonate with the Latino reader. Each chapter contains information on job search techniques with additional information unique to the Latino job seeker. All topics may not be relevant to each reader, but if any of the cultural or language issues ring a bell with you, use the material to your best advantage.

Another goal of *The Complete Job Search Guide for Latinos* is to reach out to the employer community and others interested in learning more about the special challenges of working with Latino candidates. The sharing of information will help open the lines of communication and understanding between the two worlds.

- *Career Management Toolkit* Assessment exercises help you embark on each stage of your job search.

- *Latino and Business Perspectives* present an overview of the dynamics of the twenty-first-century career environment.

- *Latino Profiles, Anecdotal Brief Stories*, and *Advice from Experts, Professionals, or Students* demonstrate real-life practical applications of job search tactics recommended in this book.

- *Sample Résumés, Marketing Letters, and Career Communication Scripts* (written by Latino career professionals) cover many employment sectors and situations. The documents also include the strategies used in their development.

- *How-to Implementation Checklists* provide step-by-step instructions to assist you in successfully navigating your job search.

- In the appendices, you'll find *Comprehensive Resource Lists* that cover each phase of the job search process.

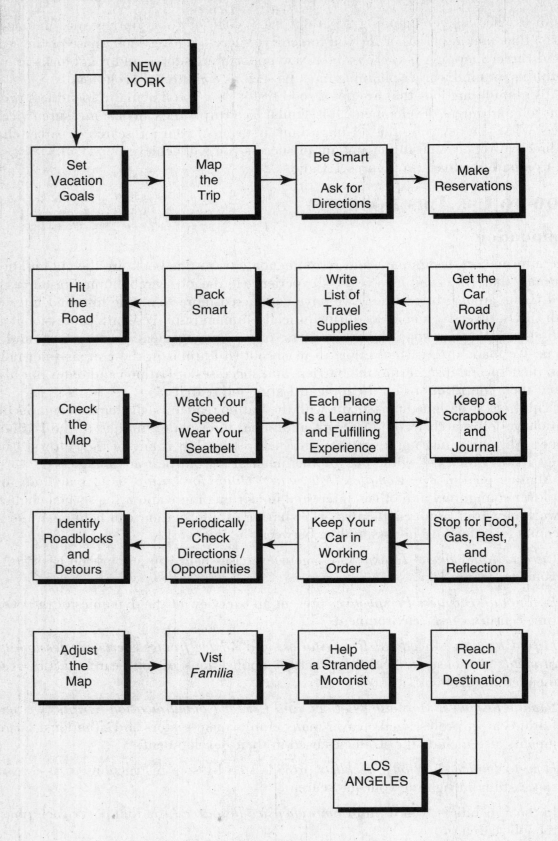

Figure 1.1. Road Trip.

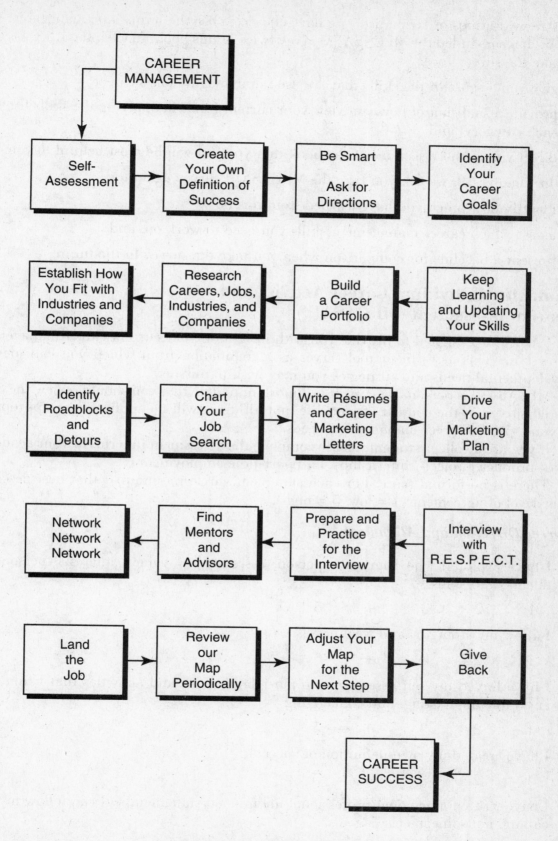

Figure 1.2. Career Map.

Are we Latinos or Hispanics? We have chosen to use the terms interchangeably.

We have included the MI CASA™ survey twice in this book. In Chapter 1, we ask you to take the survey to:

■ give you a sense of the skills that are used in managing one's career;

■ provide a snapshot of how you view your current levels in applying the skills listed in each category; and

■ direct you to those sections of the book that you feel will be most helpful to you.

In Chapter 19, we ask you take the MI CASA™ survey again to:

■ identify how much you have learned from this book;

■ assess which career management skills you need to work on; and

■ present a baseline for comparison when you take the survey in the future.

Managing Individual Career Activity and Search Assessment (MI CASA™)

MI CASA™ is designed to provide you with insight on your current career management know-how. This assessment tool serves as a foundation from which you can identify developmental needs and strategies you may wish to pursue.

MI CASA™ is personal survey. It is important to note that you should review the completed survey in the context of your life; not all items will be applicable or appropriate to your specific career management needs.

If you are a college student, please complete the assessment in terms of your academic work product, projects, internships, and part-time employment.

There is no formal score. For each statement, circle the number that best describes your level of agreement (1 = low, 5 = high).

Career Direction and Alignment

■ I have explored who I am as a person, assessing my values, interests, personality, talents, and skills.

    1   2   3   4   5

■ I know my strengths and weaknesses.

    1   2   3   4   5

■ I have linked my self-assessment to job-related tasks and activities that I find most enjoyable, interesting, and challenging.

    1   2   3   4   5

■ I have created my own definition of success.

    1   2   3   4   5

■ I have written a personal/professional life mission statement, so I can follow my own calling, not someone else's goals.

    1   2   3   4   5

■ I have clearly visualized myself at the height of my career.

    1   2   3   4   5

■ I have linked my personal values with my career goals.

    1   2   3   4   5

■ I have clear short- and long-term career goals.

    1   2   3   4   5

■ I have evolved a personal career brand that is a combination of my authentic strengths and values, work reputation, and unique promise of value to employers.

    1   2   3   4   5

■ I have created an action or business plan to implement my career goals.

    1   2   3   4   5

■ I am implementing my career action or business plan.

    1   2   3   4   5

■ I am the most powerful person influencing my career direction.

    1   2   3   4   5

■ My overall career direction and alignment is excellent.

    1   2   3   4   5

Behavioral Characteristics

■ I believe in myself as someone with something special/unique to give.

    1   2   3   4   5

■ I am aware of my biological, psychological, cultural programming, and the impact they have on my attitude, behavior, and the results that I am getting in my life.

    1   2   3   4   5

■ I know my dominant workplace behavioral styles (director, relater, socializer, thinker, passive).

    1   2   3   4   5

■ I know my main conflict management style (competitor, accommodator, avoider, compromiser, conciliator).

    1   2   3   4   5

■ My boss/colleagues/customers would currently rate my workplace attitude as very positive.

    1   2   3   4   5

■ My current enthusiasm toward my job and life is great.

    1   2   3   4   5

■ I adapt well to changes in the workplace and/or help make changes without complaints.

    1   2   3   4   5

■ I practice techniques that help reduce anxiety and stress.

    1   2   3   4   5

■ I work well under stress.
    1   2   3   4   5

■ I see problems as challenges and opportunities.
    1   2   3   4   5

■ I am willing to take risks to accomplish tasks and/or advance my career.
    1   2   3   4   5

■ I am the most powerful person influencing career behaviors.
    1   2   3   4   5

Communication

■ I have good verbal communication skills.
    1   2   3   4   5

■ I have good writing skills.
    1   2   3   4   5

■ I would do well on a test for Spanish verbal communication skills.
    1   2   3   4   5

■ I would do well on a test for Spanish writing skills.
    1   2   3   4   5

■ I am aware of the messages I send through nonverbal communication (body language, eye contact).
    1   2   3   4   5

■ I am good at reading the nonverbal cues of others.
    1   2   3   4   5

■ I am an active listener (understand the facts presented, not judgmental, not defensive, not thinking of what I am going to say next).
    1   2   3   4   5

■ I am skilled at providing helpful feedback.
    1   2   3   4   5

■ When receiving negative feedback, I handle it in a constructive and positive manner.
    1   2   3   4   5

■ I am comfortable speaking one-on-one with my coworkers.
    1   2   3   4   5

■ I am comfortable speaking one-on-one with my boss.
    1   2   3   4   5

■ I am comfortable speaking one-on-one with my customers.
    1   2   3   4   5

■ I have strong presentation skills to a group.
    1   2   3   4   5

■ Diplomacy is one of my greatest strengths.
    1   2   3   4   5

■ I have good problem solving skills.

    1   2   3   4   5

■ I deliver excellent customer service.

    1   2   3   4   5

■ I am comfortable in one-on-one negotiations.

    1   2   3   4   5

■ I am skilled in group negotiations.

    1   2   3   4   5

■ When I speak, people pay attention to my ideas and opinions, and I see them later used or implemented.

    1   2   3   4   5

■ When it is appropriate, I don't have a problem with expressing a viewpoint different from management's.

    1   2   3   4   5

■ I am the most powerful person influencing my communication skills.

    1   2   3   4   5

■ I rate my overall communication skills as excellent.

    1   2   3   4   5

Job Skills and Performance

■ I am knowledgeable and skilled at performing my job.

    1   2   3   4   5

■ I have a clear understanding of my supervisor's expectations for my performance.

    1   2   3   4   5

■ I am willing to sign my name on any task I complete.

    1   2   3   4   5

■ I deliver a high-quality and timely work product.

    1   2   3   4   5

■ I have feelings of ownership with respect to my company's welfare and output.

    1   2   3   4   5

■ I display a strong work ethic with high energy, focus, dedication, and purpose.

    1   2   3   4   5

■ My boss knows that I can be counted on to "pitch in."

    1   2   3   4   5

■ I am a team player; I contribute to the team through actions and words.

    1   2   3   4   5

■ I effectively use workplace resources (people and information) to improve my knowledge, skills, and performance.

    1   2   3   4   5

■ I communicate well with coworkers of different backgrounds.

    1   2   3   4   5

■ I understand the four basic types of power and how and when to use each (personal, position, knowledge, perceived).

    1   2   3   4   5

■ I have good time management skills.

    1   2   3   4   5

■ I know how to get and have achieved career-advancement visibility in my organization.

    1   2   3   4   5

■ My bilingual skills are an asset to the company.

    1   2   3   4   5

■ My cultural background and experiences are assets to my employer.

    1   2   3   4   5

■ I am the most powerful person influencing my job performance.

    1   2   3   4   5

■ I rate my current overall job performance as excellent.

    1   2   3   4   5

Corporate Culture

■ I know the organization's customs and values.

    1   2   3   4   5

■ I practice workplace behaviors, style, and communication expected by my company.

    1   2   3   4   5

■ I am aware of the unwritten rules of the organization.

    1   2   3   4   5

■ I deal well with office politics.

    1   2   3   4   5

■ I know what management characteristics are valued in my company.

    1   2   3   4   5

■ I understand the dynamics of my being (ethnicity/culture/gender) in my place of work.

    1   2   3   4   5

■ I know how to manage the process by which my background (ethnicity/culture/gender) is evaluated.

    1   2   3   4   5

■ I know the issues and concerns that are key to my organization's success.

    1   2   3   4   5

■ I am the most powerful person influencing my ability and success to navigate the workplace environment and culture.

    1   2   3   4   5

■ My overall skills at navigating the workplace culture are excellent.

    1   2   3   4   5

Networking

■ I have a personal network (or support system).

    1   2   3   4   5

■ I have a strong professional network.

    1   2   3   4   5

■ I have a strong workplace network.

    1   2   3   4   5

■ I effectively network with people of my background (ethnicity/culture/sex) in the workplace.

    1   2   3   4   5

■ I effectively network with people of a different background (ethnicity/culture/sex) in the workplace.

    1   2   3   4   5

■ I have a good mentor(s) with a background (ethnicity/culture/sex) similar to my own.

    1   2   3   4   5

■ I have a good mentor(s) with a background (ethnicity/culture/sex) different from mine.

    1   2   3   4   5

■ I know and fulfill my responsibilities as a mentee.

    1   2   3   4   5

■ I am a good mentor to someone.

    1   2   3   4   5

■ I have colleagues in positions similar to mine in other divisions within my company, or at other companies, with whom I regularly interact to exchange ideas and keep abreast of issues pertinent to my job.

    1   2   3   4   5

■ I belong to in-house and external professional organizations and attend their meetings with enough regularity to know the other members.

    1   2   3   4   5

■ I share my knowledge and experience with others.

    1   2   3   4   5

■ I keep in touch with my network contacts through notes, phone calls, lunches, and planned meetings.

    1   2   3   4   5

■ I am the most powerful person in making my networking a success.
    1   2   3   4   5

■ I rate my overall networking skills as excellent.
    1   2   3   4   5

Dealing with Stereotypes, Discrimination, Racism, and Sexual Harassment

■ I understand my own prejudices and stereotypes.
    1   2   3   4   5

■ I have strong cross-cultural communication and management skills.
    1   2   3   4   5

■ I am effective at managing the prejudicial behavior of others.
    1   2   3   4   5

■ I build bridges that link work and personal cultures that allow me to be authentic in both worlds and help educate others.
    1   2   3   4   5

■ I know my company's nondiscrimination policies and procedures.
    1   2   3   4   5

■ I know the workplace discrimination legal protections afforded me and how to exercise my rights.
    1   2   3   4   5

■ I know the antidiscrimination legal protections under immigration employment laws and regulations afforded me.
    1   2   3   4   5

■ I rate my overall knowledge of and willingness to exercise my antidiscrimination rights on the job as excellent.
    1   2   3   4   5

Job Search Management

■ I know what steps are necessary to conduct a successful job search.
    1   2   3   4   5

■ I am comfortable marketing my skills and abilities to employers.
    1   2   3   4   5

■ I know how to market the value of my skills and abilities.
    1   2   3   4   5

■ I know how to market the value of being a (my ethnicity/culture/gender).
    1   2   3   4   5

■ I have a high-quality current résumé available for job search, promotions, or career assignment opportunities.
    1   2   3   4   5

■ I have high-quality cover letters and career marketing letters available for job search, promotions, or career assignment opportunities.
    1   2   3   4   5

■ I maintain a career portfolio that documents my accomplishments, contributions, and work products.
    1   2   3   4   5

■ I know how to research industries and companies.
    1   2   3   4   5

■ I know how to tap into the "hidden" job market.
    1   2   3   4   5

■ I know the steps for successful job search networking and am willing to network myself into a job.
    1   2   3   4   5

■ I know how to work with the college/alumni career offices and professional association employment services.
    1   2   3   4   5

■ I know how to work with recruiters and headhunters.
    1   2   3   4   5

■ I know how to market myself to employers in ways that will get me an interview.
    1   2   3   4   5

■ I know how to tap into Latino professional associations and Latino friendly sources as part of my job search.
    1   2   3   4   5

■ I know how to use the Internet in my job search.
    1   2   3   4   5

■ I know how to use traditional and diversity career fairs in my job search.
    1   2   3   4   5

■ I know the types of job interviews and how they work.
    1   2   3   4   5

■ I know how to conduct pre–job interview research on companies and specific jobs.
    1   2   3   4   5

■ I understand the interview process, including types of interviews, testing, and background checks.
    1   2   3   4   5

■ I know how to prepare for a successful job interview.
    1   2   3   4   5

■ I am comfortable marketing myself (skills, abilities, contributions) during a job interview.
    1   2   3   4   5

■ I know how to deal with interview anxiety.
    1   2   3   4   5

■ I know how to execute my interview plan to get the employer to call me back/hire me.
    1   2   3   4   5

■ I know how to make a great first impression and manage my body language.
    1   2   3   4   5

■ I know how to "read" the interviewer and respond accordingly.
    1   2   3   4   5

■ I know how to close the interview and ask for the job.
    1   2   3   4   5

■ I know how to follow up after a job interview.
    1   2   3   4   5

■ I know how to prepare my references.
    1   2   3   4   5

■ I know how to accept, negotiate, or reject a job offer.
    1   2   3   4   5

■ I actively pursue my own continuing education, training, and development.
    1   2   3   4   5

■ I actively participate in company-sponsored training and development.
    1   2   3   4   5

■ I am assertive with my employer regarding training, development, and career-advancing work assignments.
    1   2   3   4   5

■ I am the most powerful person in my job search.
    1   2   3   4   5

■ I rate my overall job search skills as excellent.
    1   2   3   4   5

MI CASA Follow-up

■ I will review and reflect on my MI CASA™ survey answers.
    1   2   3   4   5

■ I will complete the MI CASA™ survey again after reading this book.
    1   2   3   4   5

■ I will complete the MI CASA™ survey periodically throughout my career.
    1   2   3   4   5

Chapter 2

You Are the Master of Your Own Destiny

Follow your visions and your dreams, for they are the children of your soul and the blueprints of your ultimate achievements.

—Author unknown

Myth: Latinos cannot achieve career success because our cultural scripting produces self-imposed barriers to setting significant goals and realizing our dreams.

Truth: More Latinos are realizing success in all fields and at all levels of the career ladder. Their experiences provide us with a variety of road maps to follow.

Reality 1: All people, not just Latinos, are children of their upbringing and cultural scripting. Unless we understand the impact of our personal histories, we cannot make the best career decisions.

Reality 2: You are the most powerful person in your life and career. You have the ability to harness your power to take advantage of greater workplace opportunities that have been created by rapid Hispanic population growth and removal of many external barriers to Latino employment.

In this chapter we will explore the following:

■ The definition of career success

■ The role of personal culture: Latinos and Latinas

■ Twelve factors that contribute to Latino career success

WHAT IS CAREER SUCCESS?

We have a favorite story that we use in presentations on career success that summarizes the complexities of culture, lifestyle, and goals. The story is about a fisherman of modest means in a newly discovered resort area in Mexico. One day the fisherman is spotted fishing in the bay by a visiting American businessman. The businessman asks the fisherman what he does all day. The man replies that he fishes a little in the morning and spends the rest of the day with his wife and family. The businessman (eyeing his glistening mound of fish) tells the fisherman that he ought to organize the other fishermen and build a plant for processing the catch. Then, if he works even harder, he could develop local markets, build more plants, and eventually (working 18-hour days) create an international marketplace for his fish. "What would happen next?" asked the fisherman. "Well," the businessman replied, "then you could relax and spend time with your family."

This story illustrates that success means different things to different people. Not everyone wants to be CEO of a Fortune 500 company and invest the time that kind of position requires. For many early immigrants to the United States, simply being able to find a job and provide for family was "success." Later, success expanded to include getting an education. Now Latinos look at success as building a career rather than simply getting a job.

The available opportunities are limitless. Your success can come in many forms. Perhaps you are interested in moving up the corporate ladder, or you want to start your own business and build it into one of the Top 100 Latino Businesses. For others success is not measured in dollars and cents or titles. Your number one priority may be job satisfaction and being able to spend time with your family. For some Latinos, success means a public service career, educating children, or staying home to raise a family.

No matter how you define success, the need to work and earn a living is a reality that we all must face. This book is designed to provide an instruction manual to achieve whatever level of success you desire. The road maps and checklists we've included will help you make inroads in the market you seek. In addition, we show you how to prepare for the rise and fall of the economic marketplace with skills that will transition you from one position to another.

Making the most of your experience while maximizing your earning potential in a position that you enjoy is the career success that we embrace.

THE ROLE OF PERSONAL CULTURE: LATINOS AND LATINAS

Most of us move through our busy lives without giving much thought to how our culture influences us. We are busy attending school, earning a living, or raising our families. Yet our cultural background can have a major influence on how we face the events and relationships in our lives.

As we look at our culture, it is equally important to recognize that we are not all alike. We call ourselves Latinos, Hispanics, Chicanos, and so on. We come from different backgrounds and countries of origin. We come from Puerto Rico, Mexico, Guatemala, Bolivia, Cuba, and all the other countries of Latin, Central, and South America, in addition to Spain and Portugal. We speak Spanish, Portuguese, and English. Some are new immigrants, whereas others have roots in the United States dating back for generations. We are different geographically and come from different backgrounds.

Still, there are common cultural issues for Latinos in the United States that have an impact on the employment arena. Many of the cultural traits attributed to Latinos are positive, giving us one of the best reputations in the country as responsible, reliable workers. Others are attributes that can potentially limit Latino achievement in the workplace.

Graciela Kenig, president of Kening & Associates and founder of Careers for Latinos.com, says that, in her diversity training sessions for Latino managers and employees, many participants report experiencing an "ah ha" revelation when they recognize themselves in the real-life examples she presents. She said, "The biggest reason is that people do not realize how much of their work ethic and behavior comes from culture." The relationships we develop with those we work with, our leadership style, and the way we react to those in authority all have a basis in culture.

Some of the common issues identified by Kenig and others are

■ Cultural modesty: hesitancy to promote accomplishments

■ Communication styles: oral and written

■ Lack of knowledge of corporate culture and behavior

■ Family orientation

■ Trust

Understanding that these issues do not affect all Latinos, we will look at some of the most common issues and offer recommendations and insights on how you can address those that affect you.

Twelve Characteristics of Latino Career Success

We all want to be successful in our careers. How we actually achieve success is the question because there is still a lack of Latino role models.

In the course of developing this book, we interviewed several successful Latinos and asked for opinions on a variety of topics, including the characteristics needed for success. We compiled their answers, added our own experiences, and created twelve factors for a successful career—a career that successfully coexists with a fulfilled life, uses your talents and skills to their full potential, and maximizes your opportunities and growth.

The following are twelve characteristics you must master if you want to achieve career success.

1. Know Yourself

The key to being fulfilled lies in the ability to know yourself. What are your interests, values, knowledge, skills, abilities, contributions, accomplishments, uniqueness, and worthiness? With our close family ties, there are often many outside influences attempting to dictate who you should be, what you should do, and where you should go. It is not always easy to move against the tide and strike out on a new path. In this book, we will help you assess your talents and skills so you can develop your own career path. We encourage you to create a new bond with *la familia* that values their support while allowing you to grow and succeed.

Rey Gonzalez, vice president for corporate diversity at Exelon Corporation, the nation's largest utility company, says it is equally important to understand where you come from. He says he was lucky to have parents and grandparents who taught him about his culture and instilled pride in his roots. He believes that this knowledge helped him climb the corporate ladder. When working with youth, he says, "I can see it in their eyes when they don't have that sense of pride." He added, "Know who you are, your parents' history, your grandparents' history. Look at the courage they had in coming to this country by themselves not knowing anybody, not having any contacts and in some cases with no education. They allowed us to pursue the American dream. We have a strong foundation from which we came."

2. Develop a Goal That Inspires You

There is no getting around it. In order to get anywhere, you need to know where you are going. In the story about Alice in Wonderland, Alice, who is lost, asks the Cheshire Cat for directions. The Cat asks where she is going. She replies she does not know. The Cheshire Cat responds, well, if you do not know where you are going, then it doesn't matter which way you go.

To be successful, you must develop a vision of what you want to accomplish in your life and career. You need to articulate this vision not just in broad terms, but also with clarity. Edward Rivera, a principal with Kittleman & Associates, LLC, a leading executive search firm in the nonprofit arena, believes your goal must also inspire passion. He said, "Research has show that 80 percent of success is keyed to desire. You can be picking grapes or running a corporation, but if you are passionate about it you will be a success." A saying in Spanish sums it up: *Querer es Poder*—"Where there is a will, there is a way."

You must also feel free to dream big. Don't be self-limiting. It is time to drop the "minority mentality" that keeps some Latinos tied to limiting stereotypes. You have the ability to achieve in whatever field you chose. After you set a goal, you can plot your career road map to reach that milestone and then move on to the next one.

Another aspect of success is having what Earl Nightengale calls "a worthy ideal." Gabriel Najera, managing partner of the Management Development Group, explained that there is no shame in any goal—no matter how small—as long as it is what *you* want to do and it provides value. "On the other hand," he asks, "can a drug dealer be deemed a success?" This is where you apply the concept of a worthy ideal to the mix. If the business is not honorable and does not add value to *la familia* or to the community, then you/it cannot be described as a success.

3. Believe in Your Personal Power

Yasmin Davidds-Garrido, motivational speaker and author of *Empowering Latinas: Breaking Boundaries, Freeing Lives*, always expresses the following quote in her presentations.

Personal power comes from within and when you embrace it, you feel as though there is nothing in the world that you cannot handle. It helps you recognize that everthing in your life is a choice, and it reinforces the truth that you have complete control over each and every one of those choices. While we may not have control over the events that occur in our lives, we have control over how we react to these events. You, alone, are in control of your destiny.

Tu eres el aquitecto de tu propio destino. (You are the most important person in your career.) After you envision your goal, you must take action to make it a reality. However, many of us are frozen in mid-step, allowing the demons of inadequacy to overcome us. Aliana Apodaca, owner and principal trainer of Positive Directions and nationally known speaker on Latina women and leadership observed that "As soon as we settle on a vision, our insecurities pop up, and we have to overcome our programming of self-doubt, but we must learn to walk on fire and keep our commitment to the vision."

Your personal power fuels your career power. If you can focus on developing positive energy that supports your talents, accomplishments, beliefs, values, and ability to succeed, nothing can hold you back. Sometimes we all need a little reinforcement, but your commitment to yourself and your vision must remain resolute.

Another issue that can limit your belief in yourself is your humility. As a child, I remember my aunt telling me not to look very long in the mirror because the devil would appear over my shoulder. This story was told to keep Latino children from becoming too vain. We are taught not to brag about our efforts and to let our work speak for itself. Holding back can be a disadvantage in our competitive society, but you can choose to speak honestly about yourself and build your personal power. Later in this book, we will show you how to work with these two issues in a culturally comfortable way.

4. Learn to Dance in Both Worlds

Having a successful career means adapting and making changes to accommodate your employer. You must dress, speak, and act according to the culture of your work environment. For some Latinos, this sounds like a cop-out, giving up your culture for success in the workplace. But adapting your style to the workplace does not mean giving up your cultural identity. What is important is learning to build a cultural bridge connecting one environment to the other that we can walk on and help others to cross.

Growing up in the inner city of Chicago, a friend's daughter in high school complained about the pressure she was receiving from other friends because she was using correct grammar, not slang and shopping in more upscale stores. Her mother had to assure her that being Latina did not mean that you had to be poor and uneducated. She explained that in our countries of origin and here in the United States we have many people who are educated and achievers.

Ray Suarez, award winning Senior Correspondent for "The News Hour with Jim Leher" on PBS and a founding member of the Chicago Chapter of the National Association of Hispanic Journalists, has been building cultural bridges throughout his broadcasting career. Suarez advises that you "negotiate with yourself to what is your version of authenticity. You can balance cultural integrity with earning a living and taking care of your family. Bring to bear those cultural and personal aspects that add to who you are at work, at home, and in the neighborhood. Remember that in many cases your culture is marginal to the purpose at hand—being an accountant, mechanic, or reporter. Keep your eyes open to the culture of the organization, not swallow it whole, constantly assess what gives you value and how much you are willing to work with."

Ambition and dreams of a better life fueled our immigration here. There is no shame in pursuing that dream even further. If pursuing that dream means we must adapt our workplace style, it is a small price compared to the sacrifice that our parents made in leaving family behind and working in menial jobs to build a future for their family. Or the sacrifices you may have made to be in this country, work, go to school, earn a living, support your family, or be there for your siblings.

Christian Sandoval, Hispanic marketing manager with National City Bank, also reminds us that you are actually educating your employer about the Latino culture. He said, "You do not have to carry a machete in the workplace, but know your culture and share your culture gently."

5. Create Opportunities and Be Prepared to Take Advantage of Them

In the Latino culture, fate plays a big hand: *lo que Dios quiere* (what God wills) is a common refrain. It does not matter what you do, the fatalists say, you are not the master of your own destiny. Regardless, you are the most important person in your career development. You need to take the initiative and create your own opportunities.

"Okay, but I am just not lucky," you might say. "Good things do not happen for me." Learn to look at the glass half full and not half empty. In a special study, a group of persons who considered themselves lucky and another group who considered themselves unlucky were presented with a special project. They were asked to count the number of letters in a newspaper article. Those who were lucky finished in less time because they saw a notice in the paper that said, "Stop counting." Those from the unlucky group never saw it. Why? The unlucky ones were closed to additional input, but the lucky ones were open to new information.

Adopt a *Sí se Puede* (can do) attitude. Take the initiative to learn about your company, your school, your friends, and your network. The importance of networking cannot be emphasized enough. Be sure to read the chapters devoted to networking in this book. Then after your networking has opened the door for a new phase of your career, you must take the next step forward.

Moving forward can be a difficult and scary proposition. The FEAR (False Expectations Appear Real) factor weighs heavily on us. Will I be a success or failure? Am I qualified for the position? What will my friends and colleagues say about me? No one can guarantee success, but failure should not be feared either. We learn only through failure. Expand your comfort zone each day. Every experience is a learning opportunity. Look at the risks you have taken already to get to where you are. It is time to put that preparation to use.

Finally, remember that if you do not move forward, you leave no space for other Latinos to come after you. Part of success is reaching back behind you to help the next person move upward.

6. Persistence and Success Go Together

One of the analogies we often use in presentations is the classic story of the tortoise and the hare. As you may recall, the rabbit (who is faster and stronger than the turtle), stops to rest before finishing the race, thinking he has the turtle beat. But the turtle continues at his slow pace and crosses the finish line ahead of the sleeping rabbit.

This story perfectly illustrates that the fastest or brightest do not always finish first. Persistence plays an important part of the process. Never give up. You are the one with the power to determine your fate. No career path is without obstacles. You must not let obstacles become excuses.

Kathy was a talented artist in Puerto Rico. Her teacher recognized her talent and submitted her name for a scholarship to the Julliard School for the Arts. To her surprise, she was accepted and excitedly told her parents. But her mother questioned the value of an art degree and told Kathy she would be better off in secretarial school. Kathy turned down the scholarship and went to secretarial school. Kathy Ortiz, now assistant dean of student services at Olive Harvey Community College in Chicago said, "My dream of a college degree still came true. I simply used my secretarial skills to earn my way through college and graduate school."

Kathy is one of those people who did not let circumstance get in her way. Her dream of a college education became a reality because she was persistent.

7. Build Your Personal Career Brand

In the changing marketplace, the competition for jobs is intense. One way to gain an advantage over the competition is to develop your own personal career brand. It allows you to leverage your authentic strengths and values to help distinguish you from other job seekers.

The development of a personal career brand is more than a marketing strategy. It serves as a tool to empower you on your way to success. If you build a clear vision of what you stand for—what sets you apart from others and the value you bring to the job—then you enter the job market with renewed confidence and strength.

Your personal reputation or brand is what lets people know what they can expect from you.

If you don't build your personal career brand yourself, others may label you as Chuy's sister, Javier's assistant, the Latino in the marketing department, the guy with the Spanish accent, and so on. Do any of these labels paint a compelling picture of who you are and the unique promise of value you offer?

In Chapter 3, you will learn how to build your own personal career brand and use it to give yourself a personal and professional boost.

8. Make Learning a Lifelong Process

An important strategy on the road to career success is being prepared to take advantage of opportunities. As a professional, you must keep abreast of the newest developments in your profession as well as advancements in technology. Think how many career professionals were forced to learn about computers, email, and other technologies or risk losing their jobs.

If you make learning a lifelong process, you will never be caught flat-footed in the employment game. In today's job market, advanced credentials are key. David Gomez, president of David Gomez, Inc., a nationally recognized recruiting firm, said "We are at the crossroads of some major educational issues; our parents needed a high school diploma, we needed a college degree, and now applicants need a postgraduate degree and/or a specialty to be successful in corporate America."

Another important aspect of lifelong learning is how your continued advancement reflects on you. Ana Hart, multicultural community relations manager with Tyson Foods, Inc., reminds us that "When a company hires you, they are investing in you. They will look to see if their investment is working out." Your commitment to professional and personal development will be seen as a positive move.

Yet it is not just keeping up with changing skills requirements, expanding your expertise, or credentialing that makes learning key. It is also the ability to expand your mind and learn new ideas.

9. Be Flexible

It is important to keep your options open. If there is one lesson we must learn it is that change is inevitable. The best career plan will be interrupted by unexpected twists and turns. While we emphasize persistence in reaching our goals, sometimes we need to recognize that change is necessary and good. If you are offered a great opportunity, or if you see another road to success that meets your criteria and is a worthy ideal, then sometimes you need to be flexible and change.

Maria Pesquiera was working as a recruiter at a national not-for-profit organization recruiting mentors for one of their programs. She considered herself an activist and organizer. Yet, Maria also had a talent for writing. She was approached to take a position as the fund development director for a local Mexican-American arts museum. She was concerned about her lack of experience in fundraising, but with support from her future boss and her career familia *she accepted the opportunity anyway. During her ten-year tenure she helped raise the museum's budget from under $1 million to more than $4 million a year.*

The question is when do you need to accept or reject a choice? Only you can provide that answer. We can all look back to the path not taken and say "I should have done this" or "I should have done that." It is in the moment that you need to keep your antennae up, look to your options, and remember to confirm that the opportunity fits with your goals.

10. Create a Strong Support System

One of the most important steps in building your career success is developing a strong support system. Your support system can be composed of family, friends, former teachers, colleagues, mentors, and employers. The list is endless. This network of support can play many roles, providing among other things

- Information
- Contacts
- Advice
- Resources
- A sympathetic ear

It is valuable because no one can find success alone. Yes, you must do the hard work yourself, but in the end you need your own cheering team that will give you the energy and impetus to succeed. We Latinos have a hidden treasure in our built-in support system—*la familia*: Perhaps it was the *tío* who hired you as you worked your way through school or your cousin who lent you her best blouse for your first professional interview. This family of support needs to expand and grow into a career *familia*—a network that will help you in your career.

As you move upward in your career, your need for a support system continues to grow. As an individual, you can be self-sufficient and achieve certain career success. But after you become a manager, you will need to use different attributes, be more flexible, and access a broader network. Your advancement is now tied into accomplishing through a group, with a need for information and support from superiors, colleagues and other outside sources.

One of the hardest parts of building a support system is investing time to develop and nurture your network. In the helter-skelter of our busy days, it does not always seem important to take the time to keep in contact with those not directly involved in our day-to-day lives. But the time invested will pay big dividends in the long run.

11. Know When to Let Go

One of the hardest lessons in life is knowing when to let go. Some people may see this with a negative spin, but it can be a freeing and empowering position.

As a leader and manager, it is important to recognize that you cannot control everything yourself. You must learn to let go and let others help you do your job. Trying to do it all yourself can lead to burnout and stress.

For example, changes happen in the workplace that can transform a comfortable, positive situation into one that is not workable. Rather than hanging on, it is important to recognize the change, let go, and move on. You can also outgrow your job and need to move on to continue your career growth.

Finally, mistakes are a fact of life. Too many of us have the tendency to beat ourselves over the head when we make a mistake. There are enough bumps and bruises in life without inflicting our own damage. You must learn to accept your mistakes, use them as learning experiences, and move on.

There are many stories of people who have started a job and found out two weeks later that it was not a good match. There they sit bored, unhappy, and stressed. They are not performing to their maximum potential and are cheating themselves and their employer. Sometimes they sit there for years before making a move. Why? It could be displaced loyalty or fear of the unknown, but there are many different factors. Staying in an uncomfortable work environment is not the path to career success. You must take control of your career and let go of a job (or a losing situation) and move on.

Your *abuela* may believe that suffering is good for the soul. But nothing is gained by hanging on when the situation has no remedy.

12. Remember to Give Back to Your Community

It is said that the true measure of a person's worth is based on whether he or she has made a difference in the lives of others. You can do this by taking the time to give back to your community. The many pioneers who came before you opened the doors for others to follow by breaking into the upper spheres of their professions. You can do the same.

Giving back to the community was an important "success trait" mentioned by many of the people we interviewed for this book. One of the things not often realized, said Rey Gonzalez of Exelon, is that giving back often adds to your own value. Gonzalez shared that his own career was enhanced when he took on leadership roles in the community, which gave him greater visibility and enhanced his networking opportunities.

There are many ways to give back to the community, and nonprofit organizations are always looking for able bodies to help them in their work. If organized activities are not for you, there are other ways to give back. For example, you could mentor a coworker, provide tutoring, or participate in your company's Latino employee group. But remember that authenticity counts here, too. Aliana Apodaca of Positive Directions warned, "People don't want to know how much you know until they know how much you care." You must be sincere in your efforts. If all Latinos took the time to give back, we could add to our Latino brand: a giving, caring community.

YOU ARE THE MASTER OF YOUR OWN DESTINY CHECKLIST
TÚ ERES EL ARQUITECTO DE TU PROPIO DESTINO

Making the most of your experience while maximizing your earning potential in a position that you enjoy is the career success that we embrace for *The Complete Job Search Guide for Latinos*.

☐ Life and career success can only be defined by you for you.

☐ Taking the time to develop your definition of success is essential to achieving career satisfaction.

Twelve Factors of Latino Career Success

Know Yourself

☐ Evaluate your interests, values, knowledge, skills, abilities, contributions, accomplishments, uniqueness, and worthiness.

☐ Understand your cultural programming, if any, and how to transform those gifts into career assets.

☐ Embrace your attributes, family history, and culture.

☐ Craft your combined attributes into a foundation to launch or grow your career.

Develop a Goal That Inspires You

Develop a vision of what you want to accomplish in life and your career:

☐ Arouse your passion and desire to be successful at whatever you do.

☐ Allow your goals to be courageous to drive your career forward. Your objectives should not be self-limiting.

☐ Make sure your goals, no matter how large or small, contribute value to others.

Believe in Your Personal Power

☐ Trust that you are the most important person in your career.

☐ Embrace your personal power to fuel your career power.

☐ Activate your career power so you can be proactive in your job search, manage the process, and respond well, rather than react, to the events you cannot control.

☐ Learn to adapt and transform any self-limiting cultural scripting into power centers.

Learn to Dance in Both Worlds

☐ Recognize that adapting to an employer's workplace culture is neither selling out nor changing your cultural identity.

☐ Build a cultural bridge that crosses from one environment to the other so that we can walk on and help others to cross.

☐ Know your culture and share it gently.

Create Opportunities and Be Prepared to Take Advantage of Them

☐ Initiative and networking create opportunities.

☐ Preparation and practice are often the difference to career success.

☐ Keep your attitude positive and picture yourself as lucky.

☐ Use tested strategies to overcome any job search FEARs (False Expectations Appear Real) you may have.

Persistence and Success Go Together

☐ Remember that it is not the fastest or brightest job seeker but the prepared and judiciously persistent candidate who generates an interview and secures employment.

☐ Recognize that job search roadblocks are only minor detours and that you can find an alternative route or outwit or avoid the obstacle altogether.

☐ Work smarter and use the increasing number of Latino-specific, diversity-friendly, networking-generated, and skills-focused access doors to employers.

Build Your Personal Career Brand

☐ If you do not develop a personal career brand, others will label you.

☐ Paint a compelling picture of who you truly are and the unique promise of value you offer.

☐ Building your reputation or personal career brand increases your confidence and job search power.

Make Learning a Lifelong Process

☐ Lifelong learning maintains and enhances your employability and upward mobility.

☐ Continuous professional and personal development improves your career staying power, agility, and marketability.

☐ Your commitment to self-improvement validates an employer's return on investment (ROI) in you.

Be Flexible

☐ Keep your job search and career options open.

☐ Be open, adaptable, and accommodating to different approaches and opportunities.

☐ Be willing to weigh job offers and career opportunities on how they fit into your career goals and plan. Don't just look at the money.

Create a Strong Support System

☐ Grow your career *familia*, a network of people who will be there for you in the various capacities that aid your job search.

☐ Nurture your network by maintaining contact, being thankful, and giving back where you can.

Know When to Let Go

☐ Being willing to let go should not be seen as a negative. It is often liberating, empowering, and leads to career success.

You Are the Master of Your Own Destiny

☐ You may have accepted a job that turned out to be the wrong fit, or your work situation may sour to the breaking point. Choose to move on.

☐ Your duties may have changed, or you may be required to adopt a team approach to be more productive and so give up some control. Recognize that it is time to let go.

☐ Learn to accept your mistakes and use them as learning experiences. Leave them behind.

Remember to Give Back to Your Community

☐ Appreciate the Latinos who were among the first in their career fields who blazed a trail for you to follow.

☐ Helping Latinos who are your colleagues or coming up behind you opens up even more opportunities for other Latinos.

☐ Giving back adds to your own value and helps build your personal career brand.

☐ Leadership and volunteer positions offer professional development opportunities that may not be available in the workplace.

Chapter 3

Self-Evaluation and Building Your Personal Career Brand

Authentic Self + Work Reputation + Unique Professional Image = HireVisibility

One of the twelve characteristics of Latino career success is the ability to combine personal strengths with work identity and reputation—in short, your personal career brand.

If you don't build your personal career brand, others will label you. The fact is that you're giving your power to other people to categorize and define you from their perspective. As we mentioned in Chapter 2, you might be identified as Chuy's sister, Mr. Johnson's assistant, the brown one, or the Latino in the business department. You may be described solely as your job title or job description. Is this how you want to be identified? No matter what kind of work you do or where you are in your career, do you want to be known as the Cadillac, Lexus, or Volvo of employees or as a four-cylinder basic performance vehicle?

Peter Montoya, CEO of Peter Montoya, Inc., and author of *The Brand Called You*, says, "Personal branding lets you control how other people perceive you. You're telling them what you stand for—but in a way that's so organic and unobtrusive that they think they've developed that perception all by themselves."

Debra Dib, certified career management coach, described personal branding in the following context: "If you had a sick child and your doctor recommended a certain brand of medication, you would use that brand. If you were hosting an important event and wanted the best refreshments, you would purchase brand name products. If you wanted to buy a major appliance, you would likely purchase a major brand after researching reputations and service records."

Dib adds "Brands have reputations built on quality and benefit to the consumer. They have performed well in the past and are expected to do so in the future. There is a trust factor involved in purchasing a branded 'known quantity.'"

Employers place the same value on hiring candidates who project a compelling personal career brand.

Myth: Many of us have been taught that if we work hard and do a good job, our careers will work out just fine.

Truth: In the twenty-first century, job searching is about personal marketing. You are the product, and the employer is the consumer. A clear and compelling career brand helps employers perceive the benefits of your product, giving you an advantage in the job market.

Reality 1: Successful job seekers are those who leverage their true strengths, individuality, and value into a convincing reputation so employers see them as the solution to the company's hiring needs.

Reality 2: Building a personal career brand is not about bragging. It is about embracing authenticity and giving yourself permission to be you. When you develop and live your personal career brand, you are able to execute your job search confidently and effectively.

In this chapter, you will learn how to

- Accurately assess your employment value
- Empower yourself to present your assets to employers
- Develop an authentic personal career brand

The value of brands and branding is a very important concept in marketing.

According to Ginger Zumaeta, vice president for advertising and promotion at NBC 5/Telemundo in Chicago:

- Latinos tend to stick with brands they know and trust
- Ninety-four percent of Latinos are likely to buy a brand that provides the best customer service
- Eighty-five percent of Latinos are willing to pay for quality and prefer to buy a more trusted brand versus a less expensive unfamiliar brand

Suppose you have been a loyal purchaser of Allstate Insurance because you trust their brand. Now you want to work for the company. Allstate will place the same value on you as a potential employee, if you project a compelling personal career brand.

According to William Arruda, the leading expert in personal career branding and CEO of Reach Communications Consultancy, just as it is with corporate and product brands, your personal brand is your promise of value. It distinguishes you from your peers, your colleagues, and your job search competitors. And it allows you to expand your career success.

Personal branding is not about building a special image for the outside world; it is about understanding your unique combination of rational and emotional attributes—your strengths, skills, values, and passions—and using these attributes to differentiate yourself and guide your career decisions. So, whether you are an employee of a company, a senior executive, or the president of your own business, managing your brand is critical to achieving your professional goals. When you have built and nurtured a winning brand, you'll reap the many benefits.

THE BENEFITS OF SELF-EVALUATION AND CREATING A PERSONAL CAREER BRAND

Personal Benefits

1. Helps you understand yourself better
2. Allows you to embrace your values, knowledge, skills, abilities, contributions, achievements, uniqueness, and worthiness

3. Strengthens your personal power, allowing you to remain honest to yourself, be more flexible, exercise control of your career, and shape how you are perceived by employers
4. Gives you permission to express your value to employers
5. Prepares you for the job search
6. Increases your confidence and ability to conduct a successful job interview
7. Guides you in making well-founded career decisions
8. Improves your value and employability
9. Attracts and opens employment and career-building opportunities
10. Leads to better, more interesting jobs and assignments
11. Enables you to persist and weather the tough times
12. Empowers you

Employment Benefits

1. Paints a compelling concise picture of who you are and the unique promise of the value you offer
2. Establishes the critical great first impression that makes you stand out as a top candidate who must be considered
3. Allows employers to learn about you through others, which generates more credibility
4. Clearly positions you as the best candidate to get the job done
5. Makes others aware of your expertise
6. Increases your continuing visibility and presence in the workplace, in the community, and within your network
7. Promotes you from the status of an "employee" to one of a talented player or leader
8. Differentiates you from your peers and other applicants
9. Moves you to the top of the applicant pool
10. Makes you the pursued, not the pursuer
11. Provides employers with tangible reasons to hire you
12. Creates in the employer's mind a compulsion to hire you

Unearthing and Communicating Your Personal Career Brand

Arruda reminds us that a successful personal career brand is authentic. It must be uncovered, strengthened, and nurtured. It is not a gimmick or slogan. It is the process of identifying, clarifying, and communicating who you are and your unique value. Arruda adds that "the best career advice I received was from the CEO of a Fortune 100 company I worked for; he said, 'Be yourself.'"

Arruda and Dib stress that competency, contributions, and accomplishments are the building blocks of branding. They are the quantifiable results of your knowledge, skills, and abilities. Susan Britton Whitcomb, CEO of Career Coach Academy and Career Masters Institute, adds that the "essence of career branding is all about image and connection. You must project an image of your authentic self, focus on the advantages you offer in getting the job done, and make employers aware of those advantages."

We have compiled and adapted their recommendations into the checklist starting on page 31.

PERSONAL CAREER BRAND CASE STUDY

The following case study is for one of Murray Mann's former students.

Lisseth Sesatty—Strategic financial partner who builds corporate value and winning organizational infrastructures that consistently deliver multimillion-dollar savings.

Lisseth Sesatty is currently a tax coordinator for the global tax department at a top multinational corporation in the United States, which oversees tax operations of three Latin American countries and a leading country in the European Union.

Lisseth is known for her personal career brand, not her job title, leading to her fast-track advancement during the two and one-half years she has spent with her current employer. Her career goal is to become a chief financial officer for a Fortune 500 corporation.

Lisseth has grown her brand through the following steps:

- She confirmed her passion for accounting as a student at Tec de Monterrey University in Mexico and the University of Oregon.

- Exceptional professors instilled in her a global vision, not just in her area of specialization, but also in her perspective on life.

- She found mentors who encouraged her to become active in student professional organizations and recommended her for internships to hone her accounting, organizational management, and leadership skills.

- Lisseth began building a career portfolio to document her skills, abilities, contributions, and achievements and to build her brand.

- In Mexico, she successfully competed in the Arthur Andersen Nationwide Team Competition. She led her team in developing a comprehensive business plan for Anderson based on actual data.

- She interned for Counterclaim, Inc., a small business company in Eugene, Oregon, and for General Electric in Mexico, where she saved G.E. more than $1 million.

- With an evolving personal career brand, Lisseth received job offers in Europe, Latin America, the Middle East, and the United States. She chose a one-year internship with her current employer because it offered international taxation experience and an opportunity to develop expertise in worldwide finance.

- Lisseth immediately attracted brand supporters and champions in her supervisor and the head of the global tax department. She not only saved the company millions of dollars but also identified operational changes to improve teamwork between corporate and Latin American operations—resulting in improved productivity, increased efficiency, and enhanced product quality.

- Lisseth's brand championed documented achievements, advertised her contributions, and gave her assignments to raise her visibility to those that mattered in the corporation.

- Lisseth was one of the few interns from her group selected to advance to the position of tax accountant and then the only intern to become tax coordinator.

- She is now in demand for special projects, has been offered professional development assignments, and serves as a worldwide multilingual trainer on taxation, operations, diversity, coaching, and team building.

- The multinational corporation is underwriting Lisseth's masters of science in taxation and juris doctorate in taxation law.

- Lisseth continues to build network relationships through company-sponsored activities, industry associations, and Latino professional associations.

BUILDING YOUR PERSONAL CAREER BRAND CHECKLIST

☐ Know yourself. Understand your values, personality, knowledge, skills, abilities, passions, uniqueness, and worthiness.

☐ Assess your abilities through testing. There are numerous assessment tools to help you identify your personality type, strengths, values, and career orientation. Appendix H contains sources of free and fee-based tests.

Examples: The Keirsey (*www.keirsey.com*) or Meyer's Briggs personality profile; Mazemaster or StrengthsFinder Profile; and the MAPP (Motivational Appraisal of Personal Potential) Career Analysis or Princeton Review Career Quiz.

☐ Perform your own appraisal.

Examples: Conduct a SWOT (Strengths, Weaknesses, Opportunities, and Threats) analysis as they relate to your career goals. Reread your performance evaluations from the past couple of years and ask yourself what they are really saying about you. Are there adjectives that are consistently used among all the reviews?

☐ Brainstorm. Make a list of all the things you are good at.

Examples: Some ideas for brands include conflict management, sales training, best-practice systems, marketing for service professionals, and customer service.

☐ Identify your passion.

Example: Using your brainstormed list of what you're good at, circle those items you are most passionate about. Narrow the list to one or two items.

☐ Determine the advantages of your passion and best attributes.

Example: If you are great at conflict management, the advantages to recipients (employers) of your brand might be greater cooperation among team members, which leads to enhanced productivity, new ideas, less employee turnover, and the like.

Note at least three distinct advantages for your brand.

☐ List your contributions and accomplishments.

Examples: Use your Career Management Toolkit's Primary and Industry-Specific Questionnaires for Developing Your Career Marketing Documents. (See Chapter 19.)

☐ Assess your reputation quotient.

Example: Listen to what others are saying about you. When people introduce you or talk about you to others, they often make some powerful personal career brand state-

Self-Evaluation and Building Your Personal Career Brand

ments and use adjectives that clearly describe you. Pay attention the next time you are being introduced.

☐ Become self-observant and reflect on the following questions honestly:

- How do people respond to my presence?
- Are people glad to see me in meetings or do they sigh with relief when I leave?
- Do people listen to me?
- Do they want to hear what I have to say or are they glad when I stop talking?
- What do I see and hear from others in daily conversation that gives me ideas about who I am to them and how they feel about me?

☐ Give yourself permission to create and promote your personal career brand.

Examples: Use the power of the R.E.S.P.E.C.T. model in Chapter 14 to empower your career-building efforts. For some of us, it means starting with your family by asking them what they see as your greatest strengths and accomplishments. Their acknowledgment of your qualities acts as a blessing for you to embrace your gifts. Then work your way outward by asking your friends, peers, supervisors, employees, friends, mentors, and coaches.

☐ Create awareness. Look for opportunities to make the right people aware of your brand. Get on the radar screen. The best brand in the world is useless unless people are aware of it.

Examples: You can get your name out there by participating in company or association meetings, requesting to work on high-profile projects, serving on projects where you'll be seen by a number of people (i.e., handing out name tags at a trade show meeting), copying your boss's boss on significant emails/memos, and suggesting time-saving/money-saving ideas to your immediate employer.

☐ Check the employment opportunities for your emerging brand. Is there a need for what you offer? Are companies hiring in that area?

Example: Check with your network or Internet search engines.

☐ Determine the best approach for positioning your brand.

Example: To demonstrate your unique value, be best, first, or most at whatever you do. Are you the best at creating product marketing strategies, are you the first one to have mastered how to use new office technology, are you the most accomplished, award-winning sales professional in your company/industry?

☐ Branding can be accomplished through verbal and visual means.

Examples:

- Verbal branding includes sound bites and success stories.
- Visual branding is accomplished through your actions, attitude, and attire—live and breathe your brand!

☐ Refine your product benefits into a three-point marketing message that conveys your unique strengths. This is a critical sound bite in your branding campaign.

Example: "I excel at the 3 Rs of sales: research, relationships, and revenue. I exhaustively research client needs, build relationships based on serving those needs, and have a track record of increasing revenue as a result."

☐ Prepare brief brand statements. You must be succinct in expressing your unique promise of value. If your brand promise is too complicated to be expressed in a few sentences, it will not be effective.

Examples: Include success stories and sound bites to create a comfortable yet compelling two-minute introduction. Read the sample script in Chapter 13. Consider using a tagline that helps people remember you in a unique and favorable light such as: "My colleagues call me 'Mr. FedEx' because I always deliver projects on time!"

☐ Practice.

Example: Rehearse so that you deliver your sound bites naturally, without appearing as though you're reading a telemarketing script.

☐ Build a support group.

Example: Recruit a person or two who will respectfully and selflessly support you in your commitment to shaping and enhancing your ideal image. Mentors and career coaches can be ideal supporters.

☐ Enlist brand champions.

Example: If you develop your career network and build relationships with them, you will create a career *familia* of brand cheerleaders, advertisers, promoters, and marketers.

☐ Periodically evaluate your brand to ensure its significance.

Example: Use your career *familia*, annual performance review, and job market research to determine whether your personal career brand is relevant to the current job market.

☐ Maintain your brand.

Examples:

- Be consistent in every task you perform at work and in your communications with every person.
- Nurture two-way relationships with peers, supervisors, managers, mentors, career *familia*, and new contacts.
- Ensure positive measured visibility of your brand attributes.
- Evolve your brand.

Example: To remain relevant to their target audiences, all strong brands evolve with the times. We now have AOL Latino and *People En Español* magazine. If your customer base alters, technology changes, or opportunities requiring additional skills arise, you also must grow with the times.

Whitcomb reminds us that personal career branding will contribute to the positive chemistry you want to create with employers. Being labeled by others will weaken that chemistry.

Enjoy the process of creating and communicating a clear and compelling brand!

Chapter 4

Invest in Your Career Portfolio to Maximize Your Hire-Ability Net Worth

Career portfolios are extraordinarily powerful vehicles for driving your job search and career success.

Career portfolios present a three-dimensional picture of Brand You. They are a visual representation of your values, abilities, direct and transferable skills, capabilities, knowledge, qualities, accomplishments, and contributions—portraying your assets and potential. They are a collection of data, documents, and objects that can be presented in a variety of formats—Master Portfolio, Brand You, Targeted Marketing, Internet, Targeted Job Interviewing, Bilingual, Special Skills or Interests, and Educational and Learning. Remember *El que no enseña, no vende.*(If you don't show your wares, you can't sell.)

- A *master portfolio* provides a solid foundation for making career decisions (*and putting your house in order*). It is *the* source for building your targeted portfolios.

- *Targeted portfolios* are critical tools in executing a successful job search. These portfolios document the claims you make in your résumé and interview and demonstrate your value to the employer. Targeted portfolios can give you a decisive edge over your competition.

The very act of organizing your personal career portfolio brings clarity to your career direction. The process requires reflection and analysis. When you sequence the documents in your portfolio you begin thinking more broadly about your collection of talents. You also think more deeply about who you are. As a result, you become empowered in your job search and career management.

Myth: Career portfolios are a lot of work and provide little return on my investment of time since most employers do not have the time to review them.

Truth: Strategically presented career portfolios are evaluated by recruiters and hiring officials.

Reality 1: A *master portfolio* makes crafting your career marketing materials easier.

Reality 2: A well-conceived *targeted portfolio* can be the difference in networking yourself into a job interview and being offered the position after the interview.

WHY ARE CAREER PORTFOLIOS WORTH THE EFFORT?

Master Portfolio

■ Creates a personal database from which you can assess your values and assets, construct your career management plan, and develop and evolve your personal career brand

■ Helps you map a specific job search, prepare for a performance review, seek a promotion or career assignments, and apply for educational opportunities

■ Assists you in crafting your résumé, cover letters, and other career-marketing documents

■ Is customizable to prepare your targeted career portfolios

■ Fosters the habit of documenting your accomplishments, contributions, and results

■ Monitors your career development

Ana Graf Williams, Ph.D., author of *Creating Your Career Portfolio: At a Glance Guide*, emphasizes that the twenty-first-century job market requires proactive career management tools to separate you from the competition. Employers are more demanding and more selective than ever. Whether you are applying for a job, going through a performance appraisal or review, or targeting a job promotion, a career portfolio gives you the edge you need.

Targeted Job Search Portfolio

■ Helps you prepare for and conduct interviews with confidence

■ Draws attention to Brand You and the key information you want to convey

■ Showcases your assets and potential value for the position you are applying for

■ Sets you apart from your competition as a premier candidate for the position

■ Matches your skill sets with the needs of the employer

■ Focuses the interview conversation on the points you want to make

■ Validates the claims you make in your résumé with tangible proof and enhances your credibility

■ Establishes a positive emotional connection for the employer with your intangibles (i.e., soft skills, working ethic, personality, and corporate culture fit)

Jose Gomez, Jr., of corporate diversity for Brinker International, is a strong proponent of using career portfolios. When Jose first changed careers from the not-for-profit sector to the private sector, he used his targeted job search portfolios to demonstrate how his transferable skills were strategic assets that the employer needed to achieve its business goals in Hispanic markets.

TYPES OF CAREER PORTFOLIOS

We strongly recommend that you develop at least a master career portfolio and one job search portfolio.

Master Career Portfolio

This portfolio can be likened to a central file cabinet that organizes all of your career-related documents, providing easy access to the right folders needed for your career management and job search. This file is basically for use by you and your career coaches. We recommend that you keep it in both paper and digital formats. When extracting items, leave original documents in the portfolio and use only copies for your purposes.

Targeted Job Search Portfolios

1. **Personal Career Brand or Brand You Portfolio** allows you to focus on building and evolving your personal career brand. It becomes the canvas on which you paint the portrait of Brand You. You will also use the portfolio to extract your branding statements for your career marketing documents, performance evaluations, and "living your brand."

2. **Targeted Marketing Portfolio** is designed and compiled based on the requirements of an industry, individual company, or specific job opening. This portfolio is most effective for networking your way into an interview. You can now offer more than a résumé to your career *familia*, networking contacts, and the people that they refer you to. See Chapter 14 to learn how to introduce your targeted marketing portfolio.

3. **Internet Portfolio** is the marketing portfolio restructured for the Internet. See Chapter 7 to learn how to build an e-folio or e-résumé. Web portfolios allow you to:

   - *Push your job search*—You can email a link, part of or the complete portfolio, to employers. You should also list your URL on paper career marketing documents.

   - *Pull employers to you*—The Internet portfolio can also attract employers and recruiters to you. Use the build-it-and-they-will-come philosophy. Many headhunters, job search firms, and company recruiters use the Internet to identify potential candidates.

4. **Targeted Job Interview Portfolio** distinguishes you from other interviewees and can be the deciding factor in securing the job offer. It demonstrates your professionalism, interest, and understanding of the employers needs. It substantiates the skills and accomplishments you present in your résumé and interview, supplies examples of your ability to meet the requirements of the specific position, and highlights your potential value to the employer. See Chapter 14 to learn how to introduce your portfolio at the interview.

5. **Special Skills and Interest Portfolios** document specific skill sets or areas of expertise (i.e., technical, leadership, soft skills), volunteerism, and hobbies. These are used when applying for a specific assignment, nonprofit volunteer position, or membership in a special interest organization.

6. **Bilingual Portfolio** documents your Spanish, Portuguese, and/or other language competencies. It also provides evidence of how, where, and when you have used these language skills (i.e., translating, customer support). It can be a stand-alone folder or a component of other career portfolios.

7. **Educational or Learning Portfolio** is designed to document your college, continuing education, professional development, and personal learning activities. It is most often used to assist you, academic advisors, and your career *familia* to assess and guide the learning side of your career growth.

SAMPLE TARGETED JOB INTERVIEW PORTFOLIO FOR MARISOL TORRES

Table of Contents

Target Position: Regional Director of Hispanic Markets—Hyatt Hotels

Contents

MASTER CAREER PORTFOLIO CHECKLISTS FOR EACH TYPE OF PORTFOLIO

Personal Information

- ☐ Birth certificate
- ☐ Social Security card
- ☐ Driver's license (copy)
- ☐ Any other licenses (including business, professional, and technical)
- ☐ Work authorization papers
- ☐ Passport/citizenship papers
- ☐ Additional personal information needed to complete employment applications and hiring documents (i.e., emergency contacts, physician information, medical insurance)

Latino Career Management Toolkit

- ☐ MI CASA™ Survey
- ☐ Personal and career styles assessments (i.e., Myers-Briggs, PSI, Strong)
- ☐ Primary questionnaires for developing your career marketing documents
- ☐ Industry-specific questionnaires for developing your career marketing documents
- ☐ Branding analysis
- ☐ S.T.A.R. story sheets and cards
- ☐ Written career business plan
- ☐ Personal life mission statement/professional philosophy—short description of the guiding principles that drive you and give you purpose
- ☐ Résumés—master, targeted, text, curriculum vitae, and any other versions

Education—Professional Development—Certifications—Licensures

- ☐ Schools attended (all—high school, technical, college, university, private, etc.) with school addresses and names of faculty references
- ☐ Transcripts (all)
- ☐ Diplomas, certificates, Continuing Education Units (CEUs)
- ☐ Professional licenses
- ☐ Relevant course descriptions and syllabi
- ☐ Course work product—papers, thesis, presentations, research, case studies, hands-on practicum, simulations, and projects (on team projects, identify your role)—and written instructor comments and grades
- ☐ Assessments, test results, appraisals, and grade reports

- ☐ Awards, honors, Dean's List (if so which or how many semesters?), honor society memberships—Describe in detail each award, what activity you engaged in to win the award, how competitive the award was, and when you received it
- ☐ Scholarships—Describe in detail each award, what activity you engaged in to win the award, how competitive the award was, and when you received it
- ☐ Internships, apprenticeships, cooperative education, work study, community learning, and special projects
- ☐ Workshops, seminars, conferences attended including brochures, descriptions, and completion certificates (if available)
- ☐ In-service and company sponsored training including brochures, descriptions, completion certificates (if available)
- ☐ Independent learning (things you've learned on your own or taught yourself)
- ☐ Special training (private institute, business, professional association, student group, volunteer organization, etc.)
- ☐ Military training

Work-Related Activities

Provide details and any documentation to support the following:

- ☐ Jobs/contracts held (title, description of all duties, supervisor, phone, address)
- ☐ Performance evaluations, appraisals, supervisor memorandum or comments, emails, thank you letters, and handwritten notes complimenting you on a job well done
- ☐ Accomplishments
- ☐ Contributions
- ☐ Major projects completed/participated in
- ☐ Work product and writing samples including
    - ☐ Memorandum
    - ☐ Reports
    - ☐ Papers
    - ☐ Presentations
    - ☐ Graphs/charts
    - ☐ Photographs
    - ☐ Team meeting reports
    - ☐ Evaluation reports
    - ☐ Minutes of meetings
    - ☐ Briefing notes
    - ☐ Guidance notes to staff on policies and procedures
    - ☐ Samples of brochures and flyers made

Besides print samples, you can also include CD-ROMs, videos, and other multimedia formats. (Do not use proprietary documents! You can fictionalize some of your work product.)

☐ Awards

☐ Special recognitions from supervisors or customers for work performed

☐ Clippings from employee newsletter relating to you

☐ Publications, reports, published articles

☐ Training materials

☐ Attendance records

☐ Organization charts

☐ Customer surveys

☐ Documentation of accomplishments

☐ Computer-related items

Other Activities

List and provide any documentation of positions, roles, participation, and skills used or learned.

☐ Professional, volunteer, social organizations (all)

☐ Leadership positions held along with list of responsibilities and accomplishments

☐ Volunteer activities—work performed and results

☐ Presentations and speeches

☐ Hobbies or interests (documents, summaries, photos, etc.)

☐ Participation in team sports

☐ Public speaking or performances

☐ Awards

☐ Travel

References

☐ Master reference list including names of managers, supervisors, mentors, professional colleagues, clients, teachers, peers, coworkers, or friends who can vouch for your character or accomplishments. Ask permission to list someone as a reference or a referral source, and be sure individual is willing to speak about your strengths, abilities, and experience.

☐ Reference list format

☐ Full names, titles, addresses, phone/email

☐ Professional or personal relationship to you

☐ Summary of what the reference will say about your skills, abilities, attributes, achievements, and contributions

Personal Qualities or Strengths

Use your Career Management Toolkit to identify the following attributes. You should include the name of the skill area; the performance or behavior, knowledge, or personal traits that contribute to your success in that skill area; your background and specific experiences that demonstrate your application of the skill.

☐ Skill sets

☐ Transferable skills

☐ Personal characteristics

☐ Interests

☐ Values

Also, don't forget the activities that you might be taking for granted! Consider, for example,

☐ Strengths (personal qualities that will help you contribute to an employer)

☐ Teamwork and people skills, problem solving, budgeting, planning and organization, time management, energy, discipline, motivation, persistence, responsibility, dependability, and so on

☐ Contributing to your family (teaching, caring for siblings, cooking—all require planning, responsibility, dependability)

☐ Helping your friends or work on extracurricular projects (may require teamwork, problem solving skills, teaching skills, people skills)

☐ Raising a family and/or running a household (requires budgeting, organization, time management skills, adaptability)

☐ Keeping fit and healthy; being a member of a sports team (requires energy, discipline, motivation, persistence, teamwork)

TARGETED JOB INTERVIEW PORTFOLIO CHECKLIST

You can bring two versions of your interview portfolio—one for your reference and the other with copies of any documents you plan to leave with the interviewer (never leave originals). Portfolios are often maintained in a professional-looking and manageable organizer. Remember that every item you bring with you is a reflection of your personal career brand.

Example:

☐ Three-ring zipper binders with documents in clear sheet protectors

☐ Table of contents

☐ Dividers, if necessary, to organize for easy reference

Invest in Your Career Portfolio to Maximize Your Hire-Ability Net Worth

Your portfolio for reference before and during the interview should include:

- [ ] Correspondence sent to and received from the employer

- [ ] Job posting and research on the position

- [ ] Company research

- [ ] Résumé—with notations related to the position (Your résumé may be used by the interviewer as a basis for asking some questions.)

- [ ] Interview-specific S.T.A.R. stories (see Chapter 13)

- [ ] Your two-minute verbal biography and personal career brand statement tailored for the interview (see Chapter 13)

- [ ] Responses to questions you expect to be asked (see Chapter 14)

- [ ] Questions you have prepared to ask at the interview (see Chapter 14)

- [ ] Documentation of achievements listed in your résumé that are related to position you are being interviewed for (see master portfolio checklist for types of documentation). Do not use proprietary documents. You can fictionalize some of your work product.

- [ ] Performance reviews

- [ ] Writing samples

- [ ] Salary history (if requested)

- [ ] Photocopies of related diplomas, certificates, CEUs, and licenses

- [ ] References—targeted reference list (see Chapter 8), master reference list and each reference on an individual page (you can select based on information gathered during your interview)

- [ ] Letters of recommendation

- [ ] Additional information to complete applications and other employment-related documents

Your portfolio of documents you may wish to provide the employer during the interview is often no larger ten to twenty documents. Remember that you can always refer to your review portfolio if other documents are needed. This version may include

- [ ] Résumés for interviewers

- [ ] Refined documentation of achievements listed in your résumé that are related to position

- [ ] Selective performance reviews

- [ ] Selective writing samples

- [ ] Salary history (if requested)

- [ ] Photocopies of related diplomas, certificates, CEUs, and licenses

- [ ] References list

- [ ] Letters of recommendation

BILINGUAL PORTFOLIO CHECKLIST

Your bilingual portfolio can be a stand-alone binder or a section of one of the other portfolio assets. It should include

☐ Résumé

☐ Spanish, Portuguese, and other language career-marketing letters

☐ Documentation of achievements listed in your résumé that are related to position

☐ Writing samples in English and Spanish (Do not use proprietary documents. You can fictionalize some of your work product.)

☐ Listing of how, when, and where you have used bilingual skills in work, academic, or volunteer settings

☐ Listing of Spanish coursework, training, and formal assessments of your language proficiencies

☐ Performance evaluations covering your use of bilingual skills

☐ Documentation of bilingual special pay or related compensation

☐ Letters of recommendation regarding your bilingual skills

Chapter 5

Making the Most of Your Education

Part 1: Traditional College and University

Trabaja para más Valer; Estudia para más Saber.
(Work to increase your value; study to increase your knowledge.)

College can be a lot of fun. It is an opportunity to explore new freedom and activities—the freedom that comes with adulthood, the socialization on and off campus, and the intellectual stimulation that education provides. If you are lucky enough to attend school full-time and live on campus, college can be a tremendous growing experience. Yet, for most Latinos, the ability to attend a four-year college and live on campus is not a reality due to economic hardship, poor educational foundation, family constraints, and a lack of guidance from high school counselors. Even so, more Latinos are pursuing advanced degrees and pushing aside myths about Latinos and higher education.

Myth: Latinos do not value education and are interested only in getting a job and earning money. Colleges and universities do not offer Latino students assistance or development opportunities outside the classroom, and Latinos do not take advantage of the programs available to them.

Truth: Latinos are attending colleges and universities in greater numbers than ever before. Twenty-two percent of 18–24 year old Latinos are enrolled in higher education compared to only 16 percent in 1980 according to the National Center for Education Statistics (NCES).

Reality 1: Compared to other ethnic groups, Latinos are much more likely to enroll in two-year colleges. The Pew Hispanic Center (PHC) in a 2002 study reported that 40 percent of Latinos age 18–24 enrolled in college attend a two-year school as compared to about 25 percent of both white and African American students in the same age group.

Reality 2: Graduation rates for Latinos from colleges and universities have been increasing rapidly from associate through doctorate degrees. The NCES reports that the number of bachelor degrees awarded rose by 105 percent, which is faster than any other racial group.

Reality 3: Latinos who take advantage of academic and nonacademic resources turn college into a more complete career-building program. They are more competitive for twenty-first-century career opportunities. Employers are looking to hire new graduates or students not solely on their grades. They are also looking for those who have developed the beginnings of their personal career brand as illustrated by coursework and projects that document professional skills, personal development initiatives, membership in professional or other student organizations, leadership success, short- or long-term volunteer activities, and evidence of the ability to balance work and be successful in class.

High enrollment rates show that Latinos are placing increased value on a college education. While the statistics are improving for enrollment in community colleges, colleges, and universities, and the number of degrees awarded is rising, the graduation rate for Latinos still lags behind other groups. By age 29, approximately 37 percent of white high school graduates have received a bachelor's degree compared to 21 percent of African Americans and only 16 percent of Latinos according to a 2002 PHC study.

There is disagreement on the reasons for the differing graduation rates, but part-time attendance, the selection of schools, support, and guidance have all been identified as key factors. So, it is especially important that you carefully examine the educational options open to you to ensure that you select the best school for you and take full advantage of the support systems available.

In this chapter, we will examine these issues and look at

- Educational options
- The importance of curriculum choices
- Hispanic student support systems
- Services offered by career placement offices
- Strategies to maximize your educational experience

THE OPTIONS: COMMUNITY COLLEGES, UNIVERSITIES, GRADUATE SCHOOLS

Community Colleges

Community colleges are a favorite option for Latinos due to their open admissions policy. They are open to anyone who wants to learn regardless of heritage, wealth, or previous academic experience. They are much less restrictive and more affordable than a four-year institution. The average tuition is less than half that of a state or private four-year school. The 1,173 community colleges are usually conveniently located and accessible.

Students interested in earning a bachelor's degree can use the community college as a bridge to a four-year institution. You can pick up academic skills you might have missed in high school and take basic courses such as history or math to build up your grade point average (GPA) and successfully transition to a four-year school. Many community colleges are working out dual enrollment programs to help ease the transition, such as the one between El Paso Community College and the University of Texas at El Paso (UTEP). The program allows students to use services, classes, and expertise on both campuses at the same time. Briane Carter, Director of Career Services at UTEP says, "The program is designed to make a seamless transition to the university. Our goal is to keep as many students in school as we can."

Making the Most of Your Education

If your community college does not have a dual enrollment program and you are interested in pursuing a four-year degree, you must make a visit to the community college Transfer Center a priority. Students should begin planning for their transfer process during their freshman year. The transfer center is usually a part of the Academic Advising Office and provides potential transfer students with the necessary tools to ensure a smooth transition to their selected school of higher education.

The transfer center typically offers a variety of resources such as information on academic majors, admission processes, articulation agreements, certificate and major sheets, financial aid, and scholarship resources.

Community colleges also offer

- Associate degrees
- Professional certificates
- English as a Second Language (ESL) classes
- General Educational Development (GED) classes
- Personal development courses
- Credential programs
- Work-related courses
- Information technology classes
- Welfare-to-work programs

Community colleges pride themselves on being responsive to the needs of their local communities and serve as major educational learning centers for some professions. The American Association of Community Colleges reports that 65 percent of new healthcare workers get their training at community colleges.

While community colleges have some definite advantages, if you are pursuing a bachelor's degree you must be aware of some of the disadvantages as well.

COMMUNITY COLLEGE

Advantages	Disadvantages
Open admissions policy	Academic standards less stringent
More affordable	Fewer scholarships available
Teaching staff readily available	Fewer full-time teaching staff
Credit and noncredit classes	Transfer of credits not always accepted and must transfer to complete bachelor's degree
More diverse student population	Fewer student organizations
Evening class schedule available	Less student support services available
Located in community setting	Commuter campus lifestyle

Colleges and Universities

The terms "college" and "university" are often used interchangeably. Both offer under-graduate degrees, but universities offer more graduate programs, tend to be larger than colleges, and offer more research opportunities. Both universities and colleges offer a wide range of programs and services including the opportunity to live on campus. For our purposes, we will use the terms interchangeably.

As you compare different colleges and universities, trying to decide where to attend, you should consider some important factors that can have an impact on which educational experience would be best for you.

- Does the school have a reputation for specializing in the area of study that interests you?

- Are there Latino faculty and staff on board?

- Are there on-campus Latino support services?

- What Latino student organizations are available?

- Is the school located in a part of the country you want to live in?

- How big is the school? What is the average class size?

- What type of financial aid is available?

- What types of residence facilities are available?

Each one of these factors can have an impact on your choice. Most important, be sure to visit the campus of the college that interests you. Talk to the students and look up for-mer students to get a feel for the school. Then consider your decision. Is the Ivy League what you want, or is a mid-sized state institution or the small campus life your ideal?

Ganas (desire) is also an important part of your choice. Limitations are often self-imposed. However, there are also some external limitations such as admission standards, finances, and time that can impact your decision. There are, just as often, ways to make the reality come true. If you cannot enter the school of your choice the first time around, it is always easier to transfer later in your academic career if your grades are up to par. Finan-cial aid is also available to help make academic goals come true. But whatever your goal, it is important to look at each choice and see the pros and cons of the college experience.

One of the largest and oftentimes unexpected challenges that Latino students face when they opt to attend college away from home is culture shock. It can be a very trau-matic experience for some.

Latinos often come from very homogenous communities surrounded by an extended family network. Some Latinos have never been far from their neighborhoods and travel-ing far from home can be a very stressful experience, leading to a feeling of isolation. On campus, students are confronted with an Anglo dominant culture. The students and pro-fessors look differently, speak, act, and even dress differently. Academic expectations are different and the rules of conduct have changed with very little coaching available for the newly arrived student.

Part of this culture shock can include being looked at and treated differently. Some-times this different treatment can turn into discrimination.

COLLEGE AND UNIVERSITY

Advantages	Disadvantages
Academic standards higher	More competition in gaining admission
Financial aid and scholarships available	More expensive than community college
More full-time teaching staff	Professors less accessible
Bachelor's and advanced degrees	Class schedules not always conducive to part-time attendance
More curriculum choices	Classes sometimes large
Latino professional student organizations and support services available on campus	Larger student body, easy to get lost in the crowd
Residential "dorm" facilities available	Means moving away from family setting

Leonard Ramirez, director of the LARES program at the University of Illinois Chicago says, "Latino students have often been sheltered from the worst of discrimination by their parents and community. So, when they hit the outside world, it may be the first time they have ever encountered discrimination." (See Chapter 17 on discrimination.)

In addition, some students may feel conflicted if they had to overcome opposition from family members to go away to school. Latino students are often not prepared to confront these issues.

Henry Ingle, Ph.D., professor of communication technology at UTEP, received his undergraduate degree from a local college. He said he faced family resistance when he left his small Texas hometown to attend graduate school at Syracuse University in New York. He said, "It is a tough decision for students to leave their home environment and it requires a tremendous amount of adaptability to survive." He added that the discipline and determination he learned at home allowed him to succeed.

Pursuing a college education is not an easy task.

There are often sacrifices to be made in whatever choice you make. After you have made your decisions, you must work to make your college career a success. The first step is to make and extend your school network into a college *familia*. The development of your professional brand and network begins here. You need to make the campus your home.

Beatrice Jamaica, manager of college and high school outreach at HACE, a career development organization, says her experience working with students has shown her that Latino students often do not know how to work the college experience to their advantage. She advises students to avoid the following traps.

1. Latino students don't want to bother anyone and don't want to cause any trouble. This can cause problems in communicating with faculty and staff. Example: A student may work during the professor's hours but needs to ask a question. Suggestion: Approach the teacher after class, explain the problem, and ask for a different appointment time.
2. Students need to connect with fellow students. Example: It is much better to find out the professor is a jerk the first week (and drop the class), than to wait until midterm when it is too late.

3. Students need to learn to be creative. Example: If you cannot change a bad professor, then try to audit a good professor's class and learn.
4. Students need to develop good communication and networking skills. Suggestion: Be sure to attend activities and meet people on and off campus to practice your networking skills.
5. Be assertive. Students need to learn their options and understand how college life works. Suggestion: Find a mentor on campus—a professor, counselor, or graduate student—who can help you navigate the system.

Beatrice Jamaica is a networking success story herself. As a junior in high school, she became pregnant and had to leave home and support herself and her daughter. Beatrice worked part-time, and with the help of her support network, she graduated and was later recruited to Cornell University. With persistence and the support of her college familia, *she graduated and moved on to graduate school at the University of California in Santa Barbara. She has devoted more than 15 years to giving students advice and support during their university experience.*

Graduate School

Even though higher numbers of Latinos are actively pursuing four-year degrees, the numbers of Latinos moving into graduate-level education are still small. According to a PHC study, Latinos have the lowest rates of graduate school enrollment of any major racial/ethnic group. Only 1.9 percent of 25- to 34-year-old Latino high school graduates are enrolled in graduate school compared to 3.8 percent of whites and 3 percent of African Americans. These low numbers have an impact on Latino career achievement because advanced credentials open the door to some of the nation's best-paid and most influential careers.

For those who do attend graduate school, the result can be financially lucrative. The U.S. Census Bureau reports that the average holder of a bachelor's degree will earn $2.1 million over 40 years; a master's degree earns $2.5 million; doctorates earn $3.4 million; and a professionally degreed person will earn $4.4 million.

The choice of graduate schools is especially important to your career. Many schools have strong ties to important local, regional, and national industries. These ties can translate into employment opportunities for their graduates. As discussed in previous chapters, the acquisition of an advanced degree is becoming a must in the corporate world for advancement. The right degree from a recognized school can give your career a real boost.

Martin Castro, a partner at Sonnenschein Nath & Rosenthal, a leading law firm, relates his experience choosing a law school. "After graduation I applied to 11 or 12 law schools. My advisors and I boiled it down to two. The University of Wisconsin had a very aggressive diversity program and offered free tuition, free room and board, and a $10,000 annual stipend. But the University of Michigan was the best law school in the country at that time, and there is a certain imprimatur that going to a school like Michigan brings especially for a person of color. It was one of the best decisions I ever made. It took me 10 years to pay off my debt, but by going to Michigan I was able to intern at Baker & McKenzie, one of the largest firms in the country, and eventually made partner."

Information on researching colleges, universities, and graduate schools are listed in the Appendix. You should also review magazines such as *Latina Style*, *Hispanic*, and *U.S. News and World Report* that list the best schools for Latinos and Latinas. As you research which graduate school is right for you, keep in mind that many now offer online programs. These online programs offer maximum flexibility as far as scheduling goes, but they require increased discipline to stay on track and complete your assignments on time.

Bottom line: Attend the best graduate school you can. Its value is not only in the education you receive but in the contacts and career networking relationships you cultivate.

CURRICULUM CHOICES

For some of you, there is no question in your mind as to what course of study you want to take. Rose Mary says she knew from the age of five that she wanted to be a journalist like Lois Lane and hang out with interesting people like Superman. But for others, the path is not as clear. Whatever the course of your study, it is important to make sure that

- Your class schedule leads to a degree
- You take advantage of learning opportunities in and out of the classroom
- You graduate with a higher GPA, even if it takes more time
- You translate your course of study into career opportunities

There are multiple sources with information about the "hottest" and "best" careers for the future, and some students may base their curriculum choices on those. It is good to know what the outlook is for your particular choice; perhaps it was an area you were not aware existed. But the "show me the money" career path is not the route for personal success. The best course of study is one that interests you.

Andres Garza, director of career services career centers at the University of Illinois Chicago (UIC) relates that one student he worked with was floundering and close to dropping out of school. His parents were pushing him into medical school. He hated it but was afraid to tell his parents. With support from a counselor at the Latin American Recruitment and Educational Resources (LARER) Program at UIC he addressed his parents and changed his major to history. The student finished his degree and is working as a teacher in a local high school.

Self-evaluation and experimentation are good ways to narrow your choices. Then, as you design your program, be sure to seek out advice from the career placement office or other advisors to make sure you are getting the educational foundation you need to make you more marketable in the future.

LATINO STUDENT SUPPORT SYSTEMS

There are more support systems available to students than ever before. The services offered cover everything from financial support to academic support and student life. Unfortunately, these programs are often underutilized by Latino students. Proper use of the services can make the difference between success and failure.

Teresa Nuno, director of planning and development at First 5 LA says, "I came in with a handicap in writing and math, but I found they had tutorials at the university and I took them. A college professor told me I was working twice as hard as the regular student. I needed to in order to catch up. My drive came from having a goal for myself . . . a force so strong inside me it kept me focused no matter the cost."

Remember, these support services are covered by your tuition. You are not asking for special favors; you paid for them. Don't let anyone intimidate you or keep you from getting the help you need.

Dean of Minority Student Services

The dean of minority student services works with Latino students as well as other underrepresented groups. The dean's office offers academic, personal, financial, and (on certain campuses) career services. The office focuses on facilitating academic excellence, developing leadership skills, and promoting graduation rates among minority students. The dean often reports to the vice chancellor or president.

Student Advisors

Student advisors generally provide academic support for students. They will help you navigate through college life and provide support with career decision making. Student advisors help track all your credit hours to make sure you graduate.

Latino Services Centers

Many campuses have Latino services centers. These centers offer a multitude of services such as academic support (including tutoring), special academic programs, part-time employment opportunities, and social activities. Some centers are structured programs such as LARES at the University of Illinois Chicago; others are student run and operated. These centers offer a less formal environment and provide a social connection for students. Some students describe these centers as a home away from home.

Student Associations

There is no better way to get involved in campus life than to join one of the student associations. There is usually one to fit any criteria: general umbrella organizations as well as social-, service- and curricula-oriented associations. On campus you will also find student chapters of many professional associations. These chapters offer students a way to better understand the profession and gain valuable insights and contacts for future career opportunities. Several Hispanic professional associations also have active college chapters such as the Association of Latino Professionals in Finance and Accounting (ALPFA) for finance, the Society of Hispanic Professional Engineers (SHPE) for engineers, and the Latino Social Workers Organization (LSWO) for Latino social workers. Participation in these organizations can also help build leadership and communication skills.

Ivan Roman, executive director of the National Association of Hispanic Journalists (NAHJ), explained that the association has begun forming student chapters because it realized that Hispanic students needed help in finding mentors to jumpstart their careers. The NAHJ plans to start eight to ten chapters on campuses nationwide.

Latino Student Organizations

Latino student organizations provide forums where Latino students can meet and connect in a more relaxed setting. These organizations usually have a supportive faculty member as a sponsor who serves as an unofficial advisor or mentor to the members.

Latino Sororities and Fraternities

The development of Latino sororities and fraternities grew out of the fact that Latinos were not always welcomed into the regular Greek organizations. Latino sororities and fraternities provide an opportunity for their members to participate in the Greek experience while maintaining close ties to their own ethnic background. An advantage of the sorority and fraternity system is the tradition of a network of former members that can be used for future networking contacts. (See Appendix B.)

Individual Faculty

One of the best sources of support for any student is a faculty member who has taken a personal interest in a student. As an official or unofficial advisor or mentor, the faculty member can provide advice on curriculum selection, graduate programs, and job hunting tips among other things. These relationships are developed over time. If you have a favorite professor or find someone whose opinion you value, approach him/her and ask for advice—this is a good way to open up the lines of communication.

No one has to make it through school alone. We encourage you to use the support services available and to participate in one or more student activities. If you have trouble contacting these resources, check with other students who have used them and ask for their help. Keep in mind that your active participation will broaden your network of contacts and help in the development of leadership skills, which are widely sought in the marketplace today. It is also important to not restrict your activity to Latino-based organizations. Limiting yourself to only one group closes doors to contacts and experiences that can prepare you for the multicultural workplace.

CAREER PLACEMENT SERVICES

The career placement office can be the most valuable resource on campus. Its sole purpose is to help you with career related concerns. But a much broader spectrum of services is available including

- Advice on selecting a major

- Help in locating internships

- Information on part-time employment

- Assistance with résumés and cover letters

- Resources for interview preparation

- Information and assistance with graduate schools

- Research on companies and employers

- Organized networking sessions with professionals in your field

- Work with on-campus recruiters

■ Help in planning your future

■ Sponsoring traditional and diversity career fairs

With this array of services it is amazing that career placement centers are not overflowing with waiting students. But too often, students wait until they need the services at the end of the senior year before entering the door. The earlier you contact the career placement office staff, the better for you. As a known quantity, you will help yourself "stand out" from the crowd and help others understand your vision and create opportunities for you. As they say in West Texas, "dale gas" get moving.

STRATEGIES TO MAXIMIZE YOUR EDUCATIONAL EXPERIENCE

Information on the college experience is provided to encourage you to take full advantage of services that can help you with your job search after graduation. Without the benefit of professional role models, many Latinos do not know how to use their college years to jumpstart their careers. Abe Tomas Hughes, chairman of the board for Hispanic Alliance for Career Enhancement (HACE) and a Cornell and Harvard Business School grad, says students need help. "Just because Latinos make it to the Ivy League does not mean they know what they are doing," he said. "No one has ever told students you have to start in your freshman year to lay the groundwork for your career."

The combination of leadership skills and academic achievement with the right network can make finding a job a lot easier at graduation. The following strategies were developed in conjunction with Sally Gelardin, Ed.D., instructor and women's studies portfolio evaluator at universities in the San Francisco Bay area, to help you polish your skills and develop your college *familia*.

We encourage students to participate in a new dynamic career management program called The Parachute Express. The Parachute Express bus will be visitng more than 100 college campuses and communities to offer two-day programs on all aspects of the job search process. Students will take away real skills and career marketing tools such as networking business cards to accelerate their job search activities. Parachute, inspired by the best selling career book *What Color Is Your Parachute?* by Richard Bolles, was founded to help people manage their careers and lives.

Freshman Year

Stop at the career services center.

❑ Participate in the pre-orientation program. It is an opportunity to meet with advisors, register for classes, learn about campus resources, and meet your peers.

❑ Get help in picking a major. The career center has information on a wide variety of career fields. Even if you have written something down on paper, if there is any doubt in your mind, a little exploration can turn up an option you never thought of before.

❑ Do a self-assessment. The tools available will help you look inside yourself and take stock of your interests and values. The assessment will not tell you what major or job to pursue, but it will give you information to help you find your own answers.

❑ Get help finding a part-time job. The center will often have listings of vacancies on and off campus.

Find the Latino service center.

❑ If you need tutorial help in any subject area, now is the time to get it. Do not wait until you are lost in an educational sinkhole. If the Latino service center is not available, check with the regular student service center.

❑ Acquaint yourself with the services they offer for future reference.

Begin developing your college *familia.*

❑ If you've visited the previously listed centers, then you have started the job.

❑ Get to know your fellow students.

❑ Look for an association, organization, sorority, or fraternity that interests you. Think about joining.

❑ Create a study group.

Sophomore Year

Expand your job search knowledge.

❑ Do not isolate yourself. By getting involved in curricula-oriented associations, you can do career exploration while you are building your network. Some professional associations sponsor conferences and welcome student participation, often at a discounted rate.

❑ Begin to learn job search strategies. The Job Juggler, an online, self-paced course, helps students to gain job search skills, so that when they graduate, they will be "job ready" (view *www.jobjuggler.net*). In addition, *JobWeb.com* (sponsored by the National Association of Colleges and Employers [NACE]) is a web site of career development and job search information for college students and new college graduates.

Use the career services center.

❑ Arrange informational interviews to help you continue your exploration of career choices. These can also lead to internships or other opportunities.

❑ Get help with your résumé and cover letter (in preparation for internship opportunities).

❑ Sign up for work study—in an area of interest to you, if possible

Explore study-abroad opportunities.

❑ Explore the possibilities of studying abroad.

❑ Immerse yourself in another language and culture to attain a world view that is vital to success in the global marketplace.

❑ Your study in another country may lead to intern or work opportunities in that country when you graduate from college. Be aware that employers like to have students who can stay a couple of years.

Keep in touch with your faculty advisor.

❑ You've made it past the first-year hurdle. Create a communication flow between you and your advisor.

Junior Year

Find a mentor.

❑ Most students will have selected a major course of study by now. Look for a favorite professor or someone in your career area who can help and advise you. These relationships can last long beyond your college career.

Yolanda Rodriguez Ingle, Ph.D., assistant vice president, office of institutional advancement/alumni relations at UTEP, says she might not have gotten her doctorate from Claremont without her mentors. She waited until the last minute to apply because she was worried about her qualifications. But when she found out that her application was being considered because of her connection to the Tomas Rivera Institute where she worked, she says she was insulted and walked away from the table. But her mentors helped her understand her opportunity, and one even walked with her to turn in her application.

Gain some job experience.

❑ Use the career services center to help you find opportunities for internships, co-op programs, or volunteer activities.

❑ Think strategically. If you are working part-time or looking for an internship, think of how you can turn it into a career networking opportunity. For example, if you are studying Italian, apply for work in an Italian restaurant or a consulate office. These positions might provide job leads or contacts later.

Doris Salomon, community affairs director for the Midwest and East Coast at BP America, says she used internships to achieve her career goal. "When I was writing my Masters thesis I made sure I interned at then-Senator Paul Simon's office, because I knew I wanted to work in Latino politics. I went to work at the Congressional Hispanic Caucus Institute through the networking contacts I made at Senator Simon's office."

Senior Year

Use the career services center.

❑ Update your résumé and cover letter.

❑ Get some help with your job search. Be sure to take advantage of the alumni network. They can provide leads and seasoned advice on your search.

❑ Attend career fairs. Use the Keys to Driving Your Career Fair Success Checklist included in Chapter 9 to maximize your job fair experience.

❑ Practice your interviewing skills with mock interviews.

❑ Set up appointments with the on-campus recruiting program.

❑ Get information on graduate schools, and ask for help with your application.

In the end, you are the driver of your own career search. You must light your own flame. But it is the wise driver who understands the rules of the road and follows the road map to success.

MAKING THE MOST OF YOUR EDUCATION: TRADITIONAL COLLEGE AND UNIVERSITY CHECKLIST

Community College, Universities, Graduate Schools

Community colleges are the favorite stop for Latinos due to their open admission policy.

☐ See if a dual enrollment program with a local university is available.

☐ Take basic courses such as math or history to build up your grade point average.

☐ Look into special training and certificate programs, if you are not interested in a four-year degree.

☐ Consider an Associates degree if you are not interested in a four-year degree.

Colleges and Universities

Before enrollment

☐ Check out the reputation of the school in the area of study that interests you.

☐ Find out what Latino student organizations and support are available.

☐ Find out what type of financial aid is available.

☐ Decide whether you are interested in a large or small school experience.

Graduate Schools

☐ Investigate ties to local, regional, and national industries.

☐ Look into online graduate programs.

☐ Ask about financial aid programs.

☐ Attend the best graduate school you can.

Curriculum Choices

☐ Use the career placement center to help you determine your degree interest.

☐ Make sure your class schedule leads to a degree.

☐ Take advantage of learning opportunities in and out of the classroom.

☐ Graduate with a higher GPA, even if it takes more time.

☐ Translate your course of study into career opportunities.

☐ Experiment with different courses of study to help narrow your career interests.

Hispanic Student Support Systems

☐ Know who the dean of minority student services is and introduce yourself.

☐ Visit and use the Latino services center, if one is available.

☐ Join a student association.

☐ Consider joining a Latino student association, sorority, or fraternity.

☐ Learn the services the career placement services offers.

☐ Don't wait until senior year to use the career placement service; go your freshman year.

Avoid Student Traps

☐ Do not worry about bothering people; ask for help.

☐ Connect and network with fellow students.

☐ Find the correct professor for you, even if you have to monitor a class.

☐ Work on your communication and networking skills.

☐ Find a mentor on campus to help you navigate the system.

☐ Develop your college *familia*.

Gain Work Experience

☐ Find out who is in charge of work study programs.

☐ Ask the career placement center about internship programs.

☐ Learn about study-abroad programs.

☐ Attend the career fairs.

☐ Visit with on-site recruiters.

☐ Join a student chapter of a professional association to do career exploration.

Chapter 6

Making the Most of Your Education

Part 2: Lifelong Learning

A close friend recently shared a conversation he had with his grandchild about music. He was recounting the feelings he remembered about how he had saved all his money to buy his first record album. "But grandpa" the child asked, "What is a record?" This story is funnier depending on your perspective and age. Although, it does point out the incredible and fast-paced changes taking place in technology today. If you are one of those people who is stuck with a stack of VHS tapes in a world of DVDs, then you know what we mean. Soon even the DVDs will be obsolete when newer technologies are introduced.

It is the same way with our education. Whether you are still attending school or graduated several years ago, the world of knowledge keeps increasing exponentially. History books cannot keep up with the march of time, accepted business practices of a few years ago are dropped, and changing tax law requires continual study by accountants and lawyers. Nothing stays the same.

In Chapter 2 we listed lifelong learning as one of the characteristics necessary for success. It is true. As a professional in today's marketplace, you must work to keep current on industry and market changes if you want to progress and thrive. Many industries require continuing education to keep licenses and certifications current. It is in your best interest to make learning a lifelong habit for your professional and personal growth. According to the American Association for Adult and Continuing Education, lifelong learning contributes to human fulfillment and positive social change.

In this chapter we will look at the different avenues available to continue your learning process.

Myth: Continuing education is only for those who need a GED, ESL, or have lost their job.

Truth: On-going learning is a necessity to staying employed and for career advancement at levels of the twenty-first century workplace.

Reality 1: Participation in continuing and professional education has been steadily increasing. Approximately one-third of adults participated in some kind of education classes according to a recent report by the Education Statistics Service Institute of the U.S. Department of Education.

Reality 2: Hispanics are less likely than either whites or African Americans to enroll in personal and professional development courses.

CONTINUING EDUCATION

After you have adopted a lifelong learning mentality, the idea of exploring new ideas and developing your skill sets is a natural. The pursuit of learning is not just job-related but also important to the development of yourself as a creative, energetic person who is open to new experiences. Gloria Gutierrez, assistant director of marketing and customer liaison for the U.S. Department of Commerce Census Bureau, says, "I have taken classes because I wanted to not because it was a career interest." She adds, "I studied criminal justice even though I had no thought of becoming a parole officer, but because it was an area that interested me. It keeps you fresh and evolving and that is a good thing." Learning takes on a whole different flavor when you are not pressured about your grade point average. You are free to agree or disagree with your instructor and create your own learning curve.

In addition, you can continue your career road-mapping process with continuing education. A degree in one subject area does not automatically mean that you are ready to achieve your career goal. You may need to take a few more credit hours to be ready to make your next career move. On the other hand, the Department of Labor reports that the average person will change careers several times during his/her work history. Taking classes in an area of interest could open up a whole new career path for you.

Continuing education classes are offered in many different locations, including community colleges, colleges and universities, and local community organizations. The cost for attending the classes is usually affordable.

SKILLS-CENTERED LEARNING

Skills-centered learning provides value-added benefits both to you and your employer. As an employee, you will improve your marketability by increasing your expertise and skills. The employer will see a return on investment that added skills bring to the workplace. These skills can be both hard and soft.

Top executives and managers have long recognized the need to expand their knowledge base through executive training and development. These programs offer classes in subjects including leadership skills, organizational behavior, ethics, and budget analysis. The courses vary from one day to several weeks and are usually paid for by the employer. The return on investment is considered well worth the cost.

Not only can top-level management benefit from these types of courses, but mid-level managers and line staff can also grow their careers and skills by attending these types of programs. Developing management, communication, and finance skills makes good sense no matter what career you choose. If a similar type of program is not currently available in your area, you can approach your local educational institution to see what curriculum is offered and to get some assistance in designing your own program. Be sure to ask for tuition reimbursement from your employer, if it is available.

Local community colleges are a good source for updating and learning the hard skills needed in today's marketplace. Word processing, data processing, and spreadsheets are all part of the technology used in offices around the country. If you fall short in any of these or other skill set areas necessary for your field, it is up to you to follow through and find a class that can help you. The digital world is here, and you do not want to be left behind.

PROFESSIONAL CONTINUING EDUCATION UNITS

The Continuing Education Unit (CEU) is a nationally recognized method of quantifying the time spent in the classroom during professional development and training. The CEU was developed by a national task force on continuing education formed by the Bureau of Education in 1968. Any organization that offers professional development education and training programs may potentially award CEUs. Each CEU stands for ten hours of instruction.

The following are frequently asked questions about CEUs identified by the International Association for Continuing Education and Training (IACET).

What is the difference between a CEU and a professional development hour (PDH)?
One CEU is equal to ten PDH units.

Are all CEUs the same?
The national standard for instructional time is the same, but not all awarding agencies are accredited by the International Association for Continuing Education and Training (IACET). Accreditation is not mandatory to award CEUs.

Why would I need to obtain CEUs?
The CEU offers a permanent record of training and continuing education for individuals who need to submit proof of their continuing education to state licensing boards, employers, and so on.

Who keeps track of CEUs?
The awarding agency will monitor the awarding of CEUs and should provide a form to register your training hours. Each agency should keep a database of CEUs awarded.

Are CEUs recognized by state licensing agencies for professional development?
It is important to contact each state licensing agency to find out their standards. Some states currently have mandatory continuing professional competency requirements for each profession.

Do CEUs count towards attainment of a bachelor's or master's degree?
No, CEUs are awarded only for professional development and training and are not related to academic credit.

PROFESSIONAL CERTIFICATIONS

A professional certification provides recognition of a standard of excellence in your chosen profession. A certification shows employers, clients, and associates that you are a committed professional who has shown the initiative to be held to a higher standard of knowledge and skill.

Certifications are awarded by various accrediting institutions:

- Colleges and universities
- Professional associations
- Community colleges
- Not-for-profit agencies
- For-profit organizations
- Government agencies

Before signing up for a certification program, you need to check with each provider to ensure that it is accredited by a recognized authority in each professional field. Individual certification procedures vary by profession. Some require testing; others require review of professional product, demonstrated training hours, and so on. The number of professional certifications available is varied and growing every year as professional groups unite to provide certification standards for their profession.

As part of your ongoing career development it is important to consider getting a professional certification. Some of the benefits of certification include

- Job advancement—certification gives you a competitive edge for promotion and hiring
- Professional skills—by studying for and fulfilling certification requirements, you solidify and enhance your skill level
- Salary—certification can enhance your earning power over those who have no certification
- College credit—many colleges and universities offer course credit for certain certification programs
- Esteem—attaining certification demonstrates to you, your employer, and clients that you value yourself as a professional
- Brand—certification adds to your professional brand

The time and effort in getting your professional certification can pay off with big dividends. As Juan Andrade, president of the U.S. Hispanic Leadership Institute, observed, "We have potential, we have abilities that need to be developed and discovered. We need to engage ourselves in activities that will cultivate them because somewhere down the road they will become useful to you."

SPANISH CONVERSATION AND WRITING

Our culture and language expertise are critical assets needed by today's employers. As pointed out earlier, U.S. companies are pushing to service and expand their markets locally and globally. They are not likely to be competitive unless they understand the culture and language of their customers. As Latinos, we offer potential employers the specific additional skills their companies need to be competitive.

Not only is fluency in Spanish and English a required or desired skill in job postings, but it is also one that is worthy and demanding of extra compensation and economic rewards. Bilingual pay is becoming increasingly common for professional and direct service positions. More managers and supervisors with bilingual/bicultural skills are being hired and compensated to administer target markets, service Latino sectors, and/or supervise Spanish-speaking employees. Frank Casillas, national board of directors of SER, Jobs for Progress, and former Assistant Secretary of the U.S. Department of Labor, said, "With the rapid growth of the Hispanic population in this country and the changing workforce, anyone hired in a supervisory position today will undoubtedly come in contact with non-English speaking employees and consumers and will have to know how to work with them."

As mentioned earlier, a survey conducted by the authors showed that 58 percent of the Latino job seekers surveyed said that being bilingual had helped them in their job search. So, if you are currently fluent, you have an advantage over others who may not be. Fluency often fluctuates according to whether you are a recent immigrant or second or third generation. But it is a talent that, if developed, can bring big returns both professionally and culturally.

Ruben was working for a major retail company in a major market with a large Hispanic population. He felt his lack of Spanish skills was a hindrance to his upward mobility, so he enrolled in a Spanish language course in Mexico. His patience and efforts paid off when he was promoted to vice president of corporate affairs.

The growing Hispanic market has sparked a similar growth in Spanish language schools. You can find classes ranging from beginner to conversational to strictly work-related. Course schedules are also flexible with day and night classes and special four- to six-week intensive seminars in and out of the country.

Whatever course you choose, we have one more bit of advice: *practicar* (practice) is key.

MAKING THE MOST OF YOUR EDUCATION: LIFELONG LEARNING CHECKLIST

Continuing Education

☐ The pursuit of learning is not just job-related but also important to the development of you as a creative and energetic person who is open to new experiences.

☐ Take classes in a subject that interests you. It can open up a whole new career.

☐ Check out community colleges, colleges and universities, and local community organizations to learn about their continuing education class schedule.

☐ Ask your employer if the company reimburses for classes.

Skills-Centered Learning

☐ Ask yourself if your skills are up-to-date.

☐ Determine which added skills would increase your marketability.

☐ If the type of program you want is not available, contact your local educational institution and see about designing your own program.

☐ Your employer will see a return on investment with your added skills.

Professional Continuing Education Units

☐ CEUs stand for time spent in the classroom during professional development and training services.

☐ Each CEU stands for ten hours of instruction.

☐ Make sure you register your training hours with the agency awarding the CEUs.

Professional Certifications

☐ Consider obtaining a professional certification that recognizes a standard of excellence in your chosen profession.

☐ Your certification shows employers, clients, and associates that you are a committed professional.

☐ Before signing up for a certification program, make sure the provider is accredited by a recognized authority.

Working on Your Certifications

☐ Provides a competitive edge for promotion and hiring

☐ Enhances your skill level

☐ Boosts your earning power over those who have no certification

☐ Counts for college credit in some cases

☐ Adds to your personal brand

Spanish Conversation and Writing

☐ Fluency in Spanish and English is required in many job postings.

☐ Bilingual pay options are becoming more common.

☐ Bilingualism is particularly useful in companies that target the Latino population.

☐ Classes in Spanish are offered in community colleges, universities, private organizations, and local community organizations.

☐ Course schedules vary from single sessions to four- to six-week intensive seminars.

Chapter 7

H.I.S.P.A.N.I.C. Résumés Generate Job Interviews

Myth: Résumés should be generic so that they can be used for many kinds of jobs. The résumé should list my job descriptions so that employers will know what my responsibilities were.

Truth: Generic résumés don't work. Companies receive hundreds of résumés a day. The employer's strategy is to narrow down the best "match" candidates through the process of elimination by assessing your skills, abilities, and accomplishments, not a list of your responsibilities.

Reality 1: In the twenty-first-century job search, résumés are marketing tools designed to launch you past the screening process, generate an interview, and serve as a guide for a successful interview.

Reality 2: H.I.S.P.A.N.I.C. résumés successfully answers the infamous WIFM ("What's in it for me?") question asked by every employer. Translated: "Why should I meet with you? Can you do the job? Can you do it better than most anyone else?"

H.I.S.P.A.N.I.C. résumés are persuasive career marketing tools that set you apart from the competition in today's tough job market. They are dynamic and honest portraits of Brand You and are crafted to be read from the hiring official's perspective. Companies are seeking employees to satisfy some kind of need: the need to be more competitive, expand business, make or save money, improve productivity, save time, attract or retain customers, build relationships, solve problems, and so on.

EIGHT KEY FACTORS OF A H.I.S.P.A.N.I.C. RÉSUMÉ

H **High-impact summaries of measurable achievements.** Your résumé should focus on contributions, core competencies, and skills, with emphasis on what you can accomplish and how you can contribute to the bottom line.

I **Illustrate your capabilities.** Examples of personal and work attributes—like detail orientation, communication abilities, team working skills, and the ability to multitask—should be added to the résumé in context to illustrate your competence and ability to contribute to the bottom line.

S **Strategically aim toward your job target.** Your résumé should demonstrate your ability to perform the job by focusing on relevant keyword skills and industry buzzwords. If you are seeking employment in more than one industry, or at more than one level, prepare different versions of your résumé.

P **Professional in appearance.** A good résumé should be eye-appealing and have plenty of white space to invite readability and emphasize critical points. The format should also be well organized and designed in a style that is appropriate for the job target.

A **Actively advocate and sell your candidacy.** A professional profile or qualifications summary at the beginning of the résumé is crucial to advocating your candidacy and capturing readers' interest. It provides a quick overview of your experience and expertise and establishes who you are, what you can do, and how you can benefit the organization.

N **No errors.** In résumé writing, attention to detail reflects your professionalism and commitment to excellence. To ensure accuracy, the résumé should be proofed several times (by yourself and others) for typos, correct grammar use, formatting consistency, and readability. Even one typo can doom your résumé to the recycling bin.

I **Internet savvy and keyword loaded.** The résumé-processing systems used by the majority of employers search for keywords to determine whether you are a match for job vacancies. Without the proper keywords, your résumé will sit unnoticed in a company's database. To ensure that your résumé has the proper keywords, research your job target to determine the most important hard skills, soft skills, work experience, and industry terminology for your field.

C **Compelling and inviting.** If you do a good job of writing and formatting your résumé—stressing the proper keywords and accomplishments and making readability a priority—hiring officials are much more likely to see you as a "must" interview.

BASIC RÉSUMÉ TYPES

Deciding which type of résumé is best for you can be a difficult task. These are the basics:

Chronological: The chronological résumé is the standard, traditional format. It focuses on employment history and presents your work experience in reverse chronological order. This type of résumé is ideal if your job listings are impressive, your employment history is linear, and your current position is directly related to your career path. Because of their straightforward nature, chronological résumés are typically favored by recruiters and hiring managers.

Functional: Functional résumés focus on transferable skills and de-emphasize individual positions, job duties, and employment dates. Functional styles are frequently used by job seekers who have "holes" in their work history or want to make a career change. Their use should be carefully weighed, as some employers consider them less credible than traditional résumés with a blow-by-blow employment history.

Combination: For many job seekers, the best approach is a combination résumé with a functional summary *and* a chronological work history. This strategy is advantageous for most job seekers and allows employers to quickly see how your background qualifies you for the position. A combination résumé also provides additional flexibility if you have multiple objectives, as the summary can be keyword-loaded and "slanted" toward the skills you want to emphasize.

Other Types of Résumés: Until recently, résumés were paper documents designed to be viewed by human beings. These days, the definition for *résumé* has expanded to include many genres:

❑ Traditional word processed files

❑ ASCII résumés for pasting into email

❑ "Federal" résumés for government jobs

❑ Scanable résumés for electronic scanning

❑ Plain text résumés for online posting

❑ Web-hosted résumés and portfolios

Resources and additional information on electronic résumé formats is included in Appendices E and F.

Figure 7.1 shows Marisol Torres' résumé in a scannable (word processed) format; Figure 7.2 shows Marisol's résumé in ASCII/plain text; and Figure 7.3 shows Marisol's Web portfolio.

Twelve-Step Résumé Writing Checklist

The following instructions are adapted from Barron's *How to Write Better Résumés and Cover Letters* and *e-Résumés: A Guide to Successful Online Job Hunting* by Pat Criscito. We strongly recommend that you follow the advice in these books to craft your H.I.S.P.A.N.I.C. résumé.

1. Focus on Your Target

Write your job target at the top of a piece of paper. This can become your objective statement, should you decide to use one, or it may become the first words in your profile. An objective isn't required on a résumé, but if you use one, make sure it is precise. For example, "A marketing management position with an aggressive international consumer goods manufacturer" is better than "A position that utilizes my education and experience to mutual benefit."

2. Outline Your Education Qualifications

List all relevant education or training, focusing on what relates to your job target (i.e., type of degree, dates, significant projects, courses, honors, recognitions, awards, scholarships, volunteer work, leadership positions, student organizations, social groups, activities, GPA, studies abroad, language training and usage). List all relevant vocational, technical, occupational, and military training, as well as professional development and continuing education units, workshops, seminars, in-services, corporate training programs, conferences, and conventions.

3. Review Job Description / Job Target

Get your hands on a written description of the job you are pursuing. Use the Internet resource links listed in Appendix G. If this is not possible, go to your local library and ask for a copy of *The Dictionary of Occupational Titles* (Jist, 1999) or the *Occupational Outlook Handbook* published annually by the U.S. Bureau of Labor Statistics. These references offer occupational titles and job descriptions for everyone from abalone divers to zoo veterinarians. Your local library may have Job Scribe, a software program with more than 3,000 job descriptions.

Other places to look for job descriptions include your local government job service agencies, professional and technical organizations, recruiters, associates, newspaper advertisements, and online job postings.

4. Develop Keyword Strategy

In the current (electronic) job market, most résumés are searched for keywords, so it's important to build job-specific keywords into your résumé. In short, keywords are the nouns or short phrases that describe the essential knowledge, abilities, and skills required to do the job.

The job descriptions you found earlier are great sources for keywords. You can be certain that nearly every noun and some adjectives in a job posting or advertisement are keywords.

5. Catalog Your Jobs

Start with your present position and work backward. List the title of every job you've held, along with the name of the company, the city and state, and the years you worked there. You can list years only (1996–present) or months and years (May 1996–present), but be consistent. It helps to put each job on a separate sheet of paper.

6. Detail Your Duties

Under each position, make a list of your job responsibilities and projects. Incorporate phrases and keywords from the job target description wherever they apply. You don't have to worry about writing great sentences yet or narrowing your list at this point.

7. Inventory Your Accomplishments and Contributions

Look at each job you've held and think about how you contributed in a way that was above and beyond the call of duty. Did you exceed sales quotas by 150 percent each month? Did you save the company more than $100,000 by developing a new procedure? Accomplishments show potential employers what you have done in the past, which translates into what you might be able to do for them in the future. Quantify your accomplishments whenever possible. Numbers are always impressive.

8. Delete Nonrelevant Data

Now that you have the words on paper, go back to each list and determine which items are most relevant to your target job. Cross out those things that don't relate, including entire jobs (like flipping hamburgers in high school if you're an electrical engineer with ten years of experience). Remember, your résumé is just an enticer, a way to get your foot in the door. It isn't intended to be all-inclusive.

9. Write in a Clear and Compelling Manner

Your writing should be clear, action-oriented, well organized, and compelling. Use the duties you listed under each job to create sentences, combining related items to avoid short, choppy phrases. Remember to structure the sentences so they're interesting to read. Never use personal pronouns (*I, my, me*). Instead, begin sentences with active verbs such as *planned, organized,* and *directed.* Make your sentences positive, brief, and accurate.

10. Rearrange and Rewrite

You're almost done! Return to the sentences you've written and review the order they are in. Put a number 1 by the most important description of what you did for each job. Then place a number 2 by the next most important duty or accomplishment, and so on until you've numbered each sentence. Keep related items together so the reader doesn't jump from one concept to another. Rewrite as needed to make the words flow smoothly.

11. Focus on Relevant Qualifications

Give some thought to anything else that might qualify you for your job target. This could include licenses, certifications, affiliations, or personal interests or activities, if relevant. For example, if you want a job in sports marketing, mentioning the fact that you are a triathlete would benefit your candidacy.

12. Include a Profile

Add a qualifications profile or summary at the top of your résumé—four or more sentences that provide an overview of your qualifications. This is a great place to include personal traits or special skills that might have been difficult to get across in job descriptions. This profile section should focus on skills and attributes that qualify you for the job.

The Career Management Toolkit located in Chapter 20 includes questionnaires that will help you apply the twelve-step process for developing your résumé. Review the résumé samples at the end of this chapter. We have included several résumé-writing resources in Appendix F.

H.I.S.P.A.N.I.C. Résumé Checklist

☐ Is my résumé focused on a specific job target or theme?

☐ Is my résumé crafted to be read from the hiring official's perspective? Does it address the employer's needs?

☐ Does my résumé emphasize my quantifiable/qualifiable accomplishments and skills?

☐ Does my résumé illustrate how I can handle the job—that I have positive work attitudes, solid interpersonal skills, and a willingness to go above and beyond what is expected?

☐ Does my résumé contain a Professional Profile or Qualifications Summary that communicates my personal career brand—who I am, what I can do, and the value I bring to an organization?

☐ Is my résumé inviting to read? Does the layout look professional? Is there adequate white space? Are the fonts readable? Is the résumé printed on quality paper?

☐ Does my résumé contain keywords that highlight specific industry and job-related skills?

☐ Does my résumé demonstrate soft and transferable skills such as verbal and written communication, organization, leadership, planning, aptitude for learning, adaptability, creativity, resourcefulness, problem solving, and work ethic?

☐ Does my résumé include plenty of active verbs (*managed, coordinated, planned, implemented, directed, initiated, conducted, completed, recommended, . . .*)?

☐ Is my writing clear, action-oriented, and well organized?

☐ Are my claims believable and backed up by examples and measurable results?

☐ Have I (and others) proofread my résumé for typos, grammar, consistent formatting, and readability?

☐ Have I tested the plain text or ASCII version of my résumé to ensure its Internet functionality?

☐ Will my résumé pass a fifteen- to sixty-second initial screening?

☐ Will my résumé pass the recruiter's or hiring official's detailed scrutiny?

☐ Does my résumé provide the framework for an exceptional interview?

SAMPLE RÉSUMÉS

The following pages feature sample résumés written by professional résumé writers from all over the United States. A full list of contributors is in the Appendix.

Résumé #1

TORRES (SALES DIRECTOR/HOSPITALITY INDUSTRY)
Word processed version of Marisol Torres' résumé, pages 74–75

Strategy/Approach: To showcase Marisol's strong qualifications and experience, I used a combination résumé (chronological work history and qualifications summary) with accomplishments listed under each job description to demonstrate her history of success. To optimize keyword matches during electronic processing, keywords were used throughout the résumé. The format is also computer-scannable, which makes it ideal for faxing.

Pat Kendall, NCRW, JCTC, Advanced Résumé Concepts

Résumé #2

TORRES (ASCII Version)
ASCII/plain text version of Marisol Torres' résumé, pages 76–77

Strategy/Approach: This is the ASCII version of Marisol's résumé that is used for e-mailing and online posting. This plain text format lacks the typical formatting enhancements found in word processed résumés and is universally compatible with all systems.

Information on how to create and use ASCII résumés is included on the book's Web site: *www.jobsearchguideforlatinos.com.*

Pat Kendall, NCRW, JCTC, Advanced Résumé Concepts

Résumé #3

TORRES (Web Version)
Web portfolio for Marisol Torres' résumé, page 78

Strategies/Approach:
- **Specific job target:** Marisol's job target (sales director/hospitality) is prominently displayed. This reinforces her candidacy more effectively than a generic entry page with no job target. The three supporting skills listed under the job target (i.e., event planning, community relations, and marketing) summarize the wide range of Marisol's qualifications.
- **Employer quote:** The quote is excerpted from a letter of recommendation and "proves" that she can contribute to the bottom line.
- **Bilingual skills:** Including a link to Marisol's language capabilities on the entry page (as opposed to burying them in the résumé) positions her bilingual skills as a desirable qualification.
- **Alternate formats:** If an employer wants to view the résumé in another format (printable Word document, PDF, or plain text version), alternatives are immediately accessible through the download links under the main screen. Offering multiple formats ensures compatibility with employers' systems and file preferences.
- **Reference links:** Marisol's letters of recommendation are immediately accessible and lend instant validation to her capabilities and accomplishments.

Pat Kendall, NCRW, JCTC, Advanced Résumé Concepts

Résumé #4

SALAZAR (OD Executive)
Solana Salazar's résumé, pages 79–80

   Strategy/Approach: Ms. Salazar has a strong organizational development back-ground. We wanted to highlight the depth of her corporate experience by showing the progression from departmental management to strategic leadership, with a strong emphasis on her contributions to create an educational culture in a global company.

John Suarez, MA, Success Stories INK

Résumé #5

NUNEZ (Human Resources)
Mariela Nuñez' résumé, pages 81–82

   Strategy/Approach: Mariela Nuñez is a human relations executive whose company was undergoing a merger. Her position was eliminated in the process. To distinguish her from the competition, I created a format that emphasizes her accomplishments in a Chal-lenge—Action—Results format. This résumé was effective in landing Mariela a new posi-tion and was the winning entry in the Best Résumé Competition (Human Resources Executive Category) at the Professional Association of Résumé Writers and Career Coaches' annual conference.

Louise Garver, CPRW, JCTC, CMP, CEIP, MCDP,
Career Directions, LLC

Résumé #6

ROCA (MBA Candidate)
Alicia Roca's résumé, pages 83–84

   Approach/Strategy: Alicia wants a senior leadership position with a company that trades in Central and South America. She had already decided on an MBA program but had no sense of how to get the best return on her investment in her education. I wrote this résumé to go far beyond the school's requirement for such a document. I wanted them to see Alicia as a top-notch potential student who would graduate near the top of her class and reflect well on the school—and go elsewhere if they didn't extend attractive financial assistance. Alicia expects to graduate from AUM in 2006.

Don Orlando, The McLean Group

Résumé #7

ACOSTA (PA/Nursing)
Yanina Acosta's résumé, pages 85–86

   Approach/Strategy: My approach was to highlight Ms. Acosta's recently acquired skills as a physician's assistant, while minimizing her varied and highly productive twenty-year nursing career. Reverse type on the categories adds visual interest to the page. Quotes in the side margin further validate Ms. Acosta's skills and qualifications.

Gay Anne Himebaugh-Rodriguez, Seaview Résumé Solutions

Résumé #8

VALENCIA (Science/Executive)
Victor Valencia's résumé, pages 87–88

Approach/Strategy: Victor Valencia was targeted for the position of senior science and technology manager with a leading company in computer industry. The résumé was crafted to underscore the combined technical expertise, business acumen, and personal career brand (*Spearheading Innovative Technology Solutions that Drive Change in a Career Spanning 14 Years*) the employer was seeking.

The client insisted on limiting the résumé to two pages. To improve readability, we formatted the document into distinct categories, added bold typeface to highlight Victor's quantifiable and leadership achievements, and used plain typeface for additional supporting information. Victor's résumé is a compelling first read and template for a successful interview.

Murray Mann, Global Career Strategies

Résumé #9

RODRIGUEZ (Federal)
Richard Rodriguez's résumé, pages 89–90

Approach/Strategy: It is important to understand the federal hiring process and write an effective federal application package—résumé and knowledge, skills, and abilities (KSAs) statements. The federal résumé should include "keywords and skills" and "government-type language" that come directly from the vacancy announcement and must be result-oriented.

In addition to technical expertise, job seekers should emphasize interpersonal and communication skills as well as leadership competencies. The Office of Personnel Management (OPM), defines five leadership competencies that are "the underlying characteristics—such as traits, skills, knowledge, or abilities—which result in, or contribute to, successful job performance." The five competencies are leading change, leading people, business acumen, results driven, and building coalitions/communication.

USAJobs, *www.usajobs.opm.gov*, allows job seekers to create a résumé suitable for most federal job vacancies, stores it, and allows the registered user to create a job search agent that will regularly send emails on available jobs.

Geralynn Reyes, Careers By Design

Résumé #10

CARILLO (Controller)
Iván Carillo's résumé, pages 91–93

Approach/Strategy: Ivan had extensive experience working for international companies in various financial positions and wanted to bring that experience to an American company doing business in South America. We focused on his financial management and business development background, making certain to quantify his achievements and fiscal accountability in each position. His fluency in Spanish, English, and Portuguese were critical to his ability do business in Latin America.

Pat Criscito, ProType, Ltd.

Résumé #11

ORTIZ-RIVERA (Teacher)
Wanda Ortiz-Rivera's résumé, pages 94–95

   Approach/Strategy: Wanda Ortiz-Rivera was completing her Ed.D. in Spanish with an emphasis in Bilingual Education. She was applying for a newly created administration tenure track position of Master Teacher. We structured the résumé to match the school district's requirements in a reader-friendly format with topic headers and keywords from the job description. Wanda's experience was leveraged into an "interviewable" résumé that delivers a consistent message, with carefully chosen phrases that are written to the employer's perspective.

Linda Matias, NCRW, CareerStrides

Résumé #12

GUTIERREZ (Administration/Accounting)
Sonia Gutierrez's résumé, page 96

   Approach/Strategy: Sonia wishes to progress in her career and use more of her bookkeeping and accounting abilities. We have thus included "accounting specialist" in the "target." Key words and phrases are bolded to capture attention; her bilingual skills are very marketable in the healthcare industry in Southern California (and other communities with a large Latino population). We emphasize her goal orientation and sense of responsibility by indicating at the top of the résumé that she has consistently demonstrated an exemplary work ethic while concurrently managing her education and family responsibilities.

Vivian VanLier, Advantage Résumé & Career Services

Résumé #1 (by Pat Kendall)

MARISOL TORRES

www.careerfolio.com/marisoltorres

123 River Road • (503) 555-9055
Bend, Oregon 97999 • mtorres@email2.org

SALES DIRECTOR / HOSPITALITY

Qualifications

Successful in maximizing sales through multiple marketing channels, including direct mail, telemarketing, community relationship building, local / regional advertising, event planning, and Web marketing.

- **Big Picture Manager** – Solid experience with sales force management, budget development, long- and short-range planning, and corporate compliance.

- **PR Savvy** – Accustomed to playing a highly visible role in community networking, partnership management, and event planning.

- **Dynamic Leader / Team Leader** – Positive and enthusiastic with broad experience in staff recruiting, hiring, training, development, and performance management. Well-developed presentation skills and enthusiasm for leading weekly sales meetings.

- **Computer Literate** – Advanced experience with computer applications such as MS Word, Excel, PowerPoint, Photoshop, Dreamweaver, and FrontPage.

Experience

ZERCO ENTERPRISES, INC. – Bend, Oregon
Sales Director / Operations (2003–Present)
Manage marketing and sales for retirement community with five facilities (112 units each). Hire, train, supervise, and motivate sales force. Develop and manage annual budget. Coordinate the in-house production of sales and marketing tools.

- Expanded sales 17% by focusing new business development on the local Hispanic market.
- Generated higher-than-average resident satisfaction, retention, and profit levels.
- Planned and coordinated multiple startups. Opened two new facilities and planned full-scale (2-day) marketing events with entertainment and food service for 675-750 guests.
- Established Human Resources department and assumed full responsibility for recruiting, hiring, training, development, retention, and HR compliance.

WELLINGTON CORPORATION – Vancouver, Washington
General Manager / Retirement Community (2000–2003)
Coordinated startup operations for upscale retirement community. Managed relationship building, sales, advertising, and marketing. Developed targeted strategies for sales promotions, marketing events, and community networking.

- Hired, trained, and motivated sales team that consistently exceeded sales goals by 10% or more.
- Developed targeted sales and marketing tools that are still in use today.
- Planned and organized full-scale onsite promotional events.
- Oversaw direct mail campaigns, telemarketing, Web marketing, media advertising, trade show representation, and public relations.

Continued

MARISOL TORRES • PAGE 2

Experience

HOSPITALITY LTD. CORPORATION – Portland, Oregon
Marketing Director / Retirement Community (1998–2000)
Hired to rebuild and expand sales operation. Recruited, supervised, and trained sales team. Implemented short- and long-range marketing plans; conducted tours, planned media events, and functioned as high-profile community representative.

- Developed aggressive resident retention programs that contributed to record profits.
- Created Web site and launched online marketing campaign to boost sales.
- Designed and produced collateral materials, promotional tools, and marketing aids.
- Planned and executed onsite promotional events from concept through execution.

Education

PORTLAND COMMUNITY COLLEGE – Portland, Oregon
B.S. Business Administration (1997)

PROFESSIONAL DEVELOPMENT
- Hospitality Plus Marketing Program
- Dale Carnegie Human Relations
- The Winning Spirit
- Over the Top Profit Performance
- Sales and Marketing Power

Affiliations

International Association of Hispanic Meeting Professionals
Bend Chamber of Commerce, Committee Chair
U.S. Hispanic Chamber of Commerce
Portland Hispanic Chamber of Commerce, Board of Directors
Hispanic Public Relations Association

Personal

Speak and write fluent Spanish.
References provided on request.

Résumé #2 (by Pat Kendall)

MARISOL TORRES

123 River Road
Bend, Oregon 97999
(503) 555-9055
www.careerfolio.com/marisoltorres
mtorres@email2.org

SALES DIRECTOR / HOSPITALITY

::: Qualifications :::

Successful in maximizing sales through multiple marketing channels,
including direct mail, telemarketing, community relationship building, local
/ regional advertising, event planning, and Web marketing.

Big Picture Manager - Solid experience with sales force management, budget
development, long- and short-range planning, and corporate compliance.

PR Savvy - Accustomed to playing a highly visible role in community
networking, partnership management, and event planning.

Dynamic Team Leader - Positive and enthusiastic with broad experience in
staff recruiting, hiring, training, development, and performance management.
Well-developed presentation skills and enthusiasm for leading weekly sales
meetings.

Computer Literate - Advanced experience with computer applications such as
MS Word, Excel, PowerPoint, Photoshop, Dreamweaver, and FrontPage.

::: Experience :::

ZERCO ENTERPRISES, INC. - Bend, Oregon
Sales Director / Operations (2003-Present)
Manage marketing and sales for retirement community with five facilities
(112 units each). Hire, train, supervise, and motivate sales force. Develop
and manage annual budget. Coordinate the in-house production of sales and
marketing tools.
* Expanded sales 17% by focusing new business development on the local
Hispanic market.
* Generated higher-than-average resident satisfaction, retention, and profit
levels.
* Planned and coordinated multiple startups. Opened two new facilities and
planned full-scale (2-day) marketing events with entertainment and food
service for 675-750 guests.
* Established Human Resources department and assumed full responsibility for
recruiting, hiring, training, development, retention, and HR compliance.

WELLINGTON CORPORATION - Vancouver, Washington
General Manager / Retirement Community (2000-2003)
Coordinated startup operations for upscale retirement community. Managed
relationship building, sales, advertising, and marketing. Developed targeted
strategies for sales promotions, marketing events, and community networking.
* Hired, trained, and motivated sales team that consistently exceeded sales
goals by 10% or more.
Developed targeted sales and marketing tools that are still in use today.
* Planned and organized full-scale onsite promotional events.

* Oversaw direct mail campaigns, telemarketing, Web marketing, media advertising, trade show representation, and public relations.

HOSPITALITY LTD. CORPORATION – Portland, Oregon
Marketing Director / Retirement Community (1998-2000)
Hired to rebuild and expand sales operation. Recruited, supervised, and trained sales team. Implemented short- and long-range marketing plans; conducted tours, planned media events, and functioned as high-profile community representative.
* Developed aggressive resident retention programs that contributed to record profits.
* Created Web site and launched online marketing campaign to boost sales.
* Designed and produced collateral materials, promotional tools, and marketing aids.
* Planned and executed onsite promotional events from concept through execution.

::: Education :::

PORTLAND COMMUNITY COLLEGE – Portland, Oregon
B.S. Business Administration (1997)

PROFESSIONAL DEVELOPMENT
* Hospitality Plus Marketing Program
* Dale Carnegie Human Relations
* The Winning Spirit
* Over the Top Profit Performance
* Sales and Marketing Power

::: Affiliations :::

International Association of Hispanic Meeting Professionals
Bend Chamber of Commerce, Committee Chair
U.S. Hispanic Chamber of Commerce
Portland Hispanic Chamber of Commerce, Board of Directors
Hispanic Public Relations Association

::: Personal :::

Speak and write fluent Spanish.
References provided on request.

Résumé #3 (by Pat Kendall)

CareerFolio MarisolTorres

MTorres@EMail2.org

sales director / hospitality

event planning ▫ community relations ▫ marketing

▫▫ qualifications

Successful in maximizing sales through multiple marketing channels, including direct mail, telemarketing, community relationship building,.local / regional advertising, event planning, and Web marketing.

▫ **Big Picture Manager** – Solid experience with sales force management, budget development, long- and short-range planning, and corporate compliance.

▫ **PR Savvy** – Accustomed to playing a highly visible role in community networking, partnership management, and event planning.

▫ **Dynamic Team Leader** – Positive and enthusiastic with broad experience in staff recruiting, hiring, training, development, and performance management. Well-developed presentation skills and enthusiasm for leading weekly sales meetings.

▫ **Computer Literate** – Advanced experience with computer applications such as MS Word, Excel, PowerPoint, Photoshop, Dreamweaver, and FrontPage.

▫▫ affiliations

▫ International Association of Hispanic Meeting Professionals
▫ Bend Chamber of Commerce, Committee Chair
▫ U.S. Hispanic Chamber of Commerce
▫ Portland Hispanic Chamber of Commerce, Board of Directors
▫ Hispanic Public Relations Association

▫▫ personal

Speak and write fluent Spanish.
References provided on request.

123 River Road
Bend, Oregon 97999
(503) 555-9055
mtorres@email2.org

Solana Salazar

41 Harpers Road • Belleville, Illinois 62221
(618) 555-1333 (H) • (314) 555-1334 (W)
solanasal@aol.com

Organizational Development Executive

Strategic Planning...Culture Change...Performance Improvement
Transformational Learning...Training Management...Curriculum Design/Delivery

- Performance Management/Organizational Feedback Systems
- Needs Assessment/OD Interventions
- Master Trainer/Facilitator/Instructional Designer
- Train-the-Trainer/Self-Directed Work Teams
- Corporate Value Alignment/Integration
- Diversity Awareness; Fluent in Spanish and English; Working knowledge of German

Demonstrated expertise planning, implementing, and managing large-scale change and continuous learning programs in multi-cultural organizations. Successful track record aligning education, training and development initiatives with strategic business objectives and market-driven performance indicators. Especially skilled at building consensus among senior management for critical buy-in and top-down participation of new programs.

Pioneered enterprise-wide team projects involving multiple business units, requiring high degree of employee involvement, empowerment, and accountability. Credited with orchestrating first-time training, leadership, train-the-trainer, and orientation programs benchmarked against world-class leaders in productivity, customer service, and quality.

Career Highlights

RALSTON PURINA COMPANY, St. Louis, Missouri, 1994 to Present
Comprises two business units - Pet Products (26 manufacturing facilities) and Battery Products (34 manufacturing facilities). Leading producer of pet food in the US and Canada.

Director, Organizational Development *(1999 to Present)*: Challenged with creating and implementing the company's first integrated global education, training, and development plan. Provided the vision and spearheaded the strategic planning of infrastructure, technical and human resources, budgeting, design/implementation teams, and curriculum development to create a transformational learning organization with widespread use of intranet technology.

- Created an Organizational Learning Board of top executives and representatives from all business units to design training, create action plans, administer budgets, develop recommendations, and serve as liaison to specific departments.
- Developed and launched a corporate university called the Universal Learning Institute to serve corporate education, training and development goals in areas of orientation, diversity, communication, and specific job skills.
- Earned the prestigious Business Excellence Award for the design and implementation of a new associate orientation program: "Ambassadors Making a Difference".
- Led the self-assessment for employee education, training, and development component of Malcolm Baldrige National Quality Award criteria.

Career Highlights
(cont.)

RALSTON PURINA COMPANY, St. Louis, Missouri, 1994 to Present
Comprises two business units - Pet Products (26 manufacturing facilities) and Battery Products (34 manufacturing facilities). Leading producer of pet food in the US and Canada.

Business Development Manager *(1994 to 1999)*: Recruited to master plan, oversee, and facilitate the switch to multi-functional teams for 100-person Pet Products department. Assessed needs, assigned technical trainers, and developed training for associates, customer clusters, and regional teams. Provided vision, strategic plan, and ongoing tactical support for new team-oriented business philosophies.

- Designed and implemented a four-tier training certification program for individuals and teams linked to company compensation system. Redesigned pilot program with greater emphasis on strengthening customer partnerships.
- Analyzed and planned new recruiting and employee orientation strategies. Created multi-functional research team comprised of business unit representatives. Grew departmental program into a first-ever, three-day company-wide program with support and participation from CEO and other senior management.
- Laid the foundation for a core curriculum projected to be finalized and phased into future continuing education programs. Introduced a university internship program, later replicated by corporate HR and utilized on a larger scale.
- Developed training programs involving leadership, business communication, customer focus, domain expertise, and team concepts. Recruited and developed staff members to become functional trainers for J.I.T. and outsourced programs.

Previous background: Regional Manager of Business Development, The Impact Group, St. Louis, 1992 to 1994; Manager of HR, Training & Development, BCBS Plan Services, Barcelona, Spain, 1990 to 1992; Owner/Training & Development Director, Proact, Inc./PDP International, Germany, 1984 to 1990

Education/Professional Development

Ed.M. in Psychology: Boston University
M.A. in Communication: Utah State University
B.A. in Communication: Utah State University

- Meyers-Briggs Type Indicator: Professional Qualifying Program
- Leading and Training Multi-Cultural Teams: BCBS Plan Services International
- Certified Master Trainer: Team Concepts, Productivity Development Systems
- Certified Zenger-Miller Trainer: FrontLine Leadership and Working Programs
- Certified Master Trainer: Life Orientations Theory & Practice

References On Request

Résumé #5 (by Louise Garver)

MARIELA NUÑEZ
589 Brighton View
Providence, RI 02864

(401) 555-5555   marielanz@aol.com

CAREER PROFILE

Bilingual Human Resources Executive and proactive business partner to senior operating management to guide in the development of performance-driven, customer-driven and market-driven organizations. Demonstrated effectiveness in providing vision and counsel in steering organizations through accelerated growth as well as in turning around under-performing businesses. Diverse background includes multinational organizations in the medical equipment and manufacturing industries. Bilingual (English and Spanish).

Expertise in all generalist HR initiatives:

Recruitment & Employment Management ... Leadership Training & Development ... Benefits & Compensation Design ... Reorganization & Culture Change ... Merger & Acquisition Integration ... Union & Non-Union Employee Relations ... Succession Planning ... Expatriate Programs ... Long-Range Business Planning ... HR Policies & Procedures.

PROFESSIONAL EXPERIENCE

MARCONE MANUFACTURING COMPANY, Providence, RI
Vice President, Human Resources (1996–Present)

Challenge: Recruited to create HR infrastructure to support business growth at a $30 million global manufacturing company with underachieving sales, exceedingly high turnover and lack of cohesive management processes among business entities in U.S. and Asia.

Actions: Partnered with the President and Board of Directors to reorganize company, reduce overhead expenses, rebuild sales and institute solid management infrastructure.

Results:
- Established HR with staff of 5, including development of policies and procedures; renegotiated cost-effective benefit programs that saved company $1.5 million annually.
- Reorganized operations and facilitated seamless integration of 150 employees from 2 new acquisitions within parent company.
- Reduced sales force turnover to nearly nonexistent. Upgraded quality of candidates hired by implementing interview skills training and management development programs. Results led to improved sales performance.
- Recruited all management personnel, developed HR policies, procedures and plans, and fostered team culture at newly built Malaysian plant with 125 employees.
- Initiated business reorganization plan, resulting in consolidation of New York and Virginia operations and $6.5 million in cost reductions.

BINGHAMTON COMPANY, New York, NY
Director, Human Resources & Administration (1993–1996)

Challenge: Lead HR and Administration function supporting 1,600 employees at $500 million manufacturer of medical equipment. Support company's turnaround efforts, business unit consolidations and transition to consumer products focus.

Actions: Established cross functional teams from each site and provided training in team building to coordinate product development efforts, implement new manufacturing processes and speed products to market. Identified cost reduction opportunities.

MARIELA NUÑEZ • PAGE 2

Director, Human Resources & Administration continued...

Results:
- Instituted worldwide cross-functional team culture that provided the foundation for successful new product launches and recapture of company's leading edge in a competitive environment.
- Led flawless integration of 2 operations into single, cohesive European business unit, resulting in profitable business turnaround.
- Restructured and positioned HR organization in the German business unit as customer-focused partner to support European sales and marketing units.
- Initiated major benefit cost reductions of $3 million in year one and $1 million annually while gaining employee acceptance through concerted education and communications efforts.

ARCADIA CORPORATION, New York, NY
Director, Human Resources (1989–1993)

Challenge: HR support to corporate office and field units of an $800 million organization with 150 global operations employing 4,500 people.

Actions: Promoted from Assistant Director of HR to lead staff of 10 in all HR and labor relations functions. Established separate international recruitment function and designed staffing plan to accommodate rapid business growth. Negotiated cost-effective benefits contracts for union and non-union employees.

Results:
- Oversaw successful UAW, Teamsters and labor contract negotiations.
- Established and staffed HR function for major contract award with U.S. government agency.
- Introduced incentive plans for field unit managers and an expatriate program that attracted both internal and external candidates for international assignments in the Middle East.
- Managed HR issues associated with 2 business acquisitions while accomplishing a smooth transition and retention of all key personnel.
- Restructured HR function with no service disruption to the business while saving $500,000 annually.

EDUCATION

M.B.A., Cornell University, New York, NY
B.A., **Business Administration**, Amherst College, Amherst, MA

AFFILIATIONS

Society for Human Resource Management
Human Resource Council of Rhode Island

Alicia Roca

1220 Plymouth Street, Montgomery, Alabama 36100
aliciarocade@yahoo.com — 334.555.5555 (home) — 334.555.6666 (cell)

WHAT I CAN BRING TO AUBURN'S MBA PROGRAM:

❑ **Dedication** to use critical thinking skills to help me master new concepts ❑ **Skill** to organize not only deadlines, but the time required to meet them ❑ **Ability** to help people *want* to succeed ❑ **Proficiency** to make thought "visible" in writing and speaking

RELEVANT EXAMPLES OF BUSINESS-RELATED PROBLEMS SOLVED:

IN THE PRIVATE SECTOR

❑ **Export Documentation Assistant** *with additional duties as an* **Assistant Cotton Broker**, Mid-Atlantic Cotton, Inc., Montgomery, Alabama   January 2003 – Present

Mid-Atlantic is a world-wide cotton broker with annual sales, for my division alone, approaching $65M.

What I am responsible for...

Examining international letters of credit, completing wire transfers and payments, collecting A/R of more than $600K monthly, coordinating between our Brazilian office and worldwide agents, translating calls and documents, maintaining sales and purchase records.

Sample contribution to my employer...

Stepped in smoothly, without supervision, when a Chilean buyer had difficulty meeting payment schedules. Worked with an overseas bank to restructure the buyer's letter of credit. *Outcomes:* New arrangement protected our grower, yet kept the buyer as a valued customer. Very experienced co-worker approved my work virtually without change—**even though I had never solved such problems before.**

❑ **Administrative Assistant**, Jacob Carlberg, The Jewel, Inc., Montgomery, Alabama
                                                September 2002 – December 2002

The Jewel is a retail dealer in precious stones and jewelry. Our customers are elite buyers from across the nation. Annual sales are about .5M.

What I was responsible for...

Made daily deposits, did basic bookkeeping, helped inventory our stock of more than 2,000 items, drafted original correspondence and ordered office supplies.

❑ **Receptionist**, Longfield & Terrier, Montgomery, Alabama   April 2002 – August 2002

This corporate law firm's 16 attorneys have a statewide clientele.

What I was responsible for...

Maintained daily records of payments received, calculated fax charges, and compiled the weekly report of packages send by our firm.

Alicia Roca 334.555.5555– 334.555.6666

Sample contribution to my employer...

Overhauled the manual system we were using to track 35+ express packages a day. *Outcomes:* **Designed an Excel spreadsheet** to track data and translate it into information we could use. Cost reports completed in 30 minutes. **Done without spending an extra dime.**

IN THE UNIVERSITY CLASSROOM

Took on the work of two other team members when it became clear that we might not meet a project deadline just few weeks away. *Outcomes:* Not only made the closing date, but helped our group get a high grade. In the oral defense of this project, fielded probing questions from peers and a professor with years of experience.

EDUCATION

- ❑ BS, **Business Administration** (with emphasis in **Finance**), University of Tarpon Springs, Tarpon Springs, Florida   December 2003
  Earned this degree while working up to 20 hours a week and carrying a full academic load.

COMPUTER SKILLS

- ❑ Proficient in Excel, Word, proprietary sales, purchasing, and invoice software suite, and Internet search protocols
- ❑ Working knowledge of PowerPoint and Access.

PROFESSIONAL AFFILIATIONS

- ❑ Charter member, Vice President, and first elected President, Tarpon Springs of the Financial Management Association   Since January 2001

  Helped **build this chapter from the ground up** when no one wanted the leadership role. Sought out students we could serve best and listened carefully to their needs. Persuaded a faculty member to sponsor us. *Outcomes:* Membership grew to be larger than many similar, well-established groups. Made us more visible by guiding a new tutoring program serving nearly 50 students.

LANGUAGE SKILLS:

- ❑ Read, write, speak, and **think** in fluent Spanish.

SERVICE TO MY COMMUNITY:

- ❑ Volunteer, Montgomery Cancer Center, Montgomery, Alabama   May 2003 – Present
  Contribute at least 60 hours a year helping patients get the treatment they need.

- ❑ Volunteer, Refugee and Immigration Services, Catholic Social Services, Tarpon Springs, Florida   January 2001 – April 2001
  Guided clients through the intimidating maze of immigration paperwork and phone calls needed to help them maintain legal status in this country.

AFFILIATIONS

Association of Latino Professionals in Finance and Accounting

Résumé #7 (by Gay Anne Himebaugh-Rodriguez)

94576 Jasmine View
Santa Ana, CA 92705
(714) 693-6611
yanina77@aol.com

Yanina P. Acosta
PA-C, RNP, BSN, PHN

What others are saying
about Yanina Acosta:

"Yanina works hard and
effectively. Her attention to
the whole patient is
outstanding/remarkable. Her
fund of knowledge and
clinical judgment are superb.
She relates well to all of us
here at Smith."

—Supervising Physician

"Excellent documentation
and updating of problem lists
and immunizations. She's
also always on time and
ready. Attention to detail.
Enthusiasm, knowledge."

—Office Manager

"Overall she's excellent
and has great patient rapport."

—Patient Advocate

"Very conscientious and
caring..."

—Nursing Supervisor

"High adherence to medical
standards."

—ER Supervisor

"Very cooperative."

—Charge Nurse

"High level of consideration
for patients and their needs."

—Colleague Practitioner

PERSONAL PROFILE

Exceptional Certified Physician Assistant. Knowledgeable and passionate about her
profession... Accustomed to providing quality health care in a quality environment...
Conscientious... Professional... Thorough... Caring... Outstanding background in education,
training, public speaking, personnel development and leadership. Bilingual... Both spoken and
written English and Spanish proficiency.

Areas of Expertise

Family Medicine
Patient Education

Medical/Legal Consulting
Trauma and Life Support

Health Care Maintenance
Presentations

EDUCATION

B.S., Physician Assistant, University of Southern California, Los Angeles, CA
Nurse Practitioner Development, University of Southern California, Los Angeles, CA
B.S., Nursing, California State University, Fullerton, CA
Public Health Certificate, California State University, Fullerton, CA
Vocational Education Teaching Credential, Nursing, California State University at Long Beach

Specialty Classes

- How to be an Expert Witness, University of California, Irvine Extension
- Medical/Legal Consulting, Salinger Management Institute
- Risk Management in the Emergency Department, Cigna Loss Control Services, Inc.

AWARDS and HONORS

- Recruited by Chroma Pharmaceuticals as a spokesperson for their migraine division
- Voted Practitioner of the Year by peer health care providers at Smith Medical
  Associates
- Graduated Suma Cum Laude, USC School of Family Medicine, Physician Assistant
  Program

PROFESSIONAL EXPERIENCE

Paul Johnson, MD, Santa Ana, CA   5/03 – Present
Endocrinology: Nurse Practitioner (part time)
- Assist physician with management of patients with Diabetes, Thyroid and Lipid disorders
- Educate patients and families on all health care matters

Doctors Medical Group, Garden Grove, CA   2/03 – Present
Family Practice Team Leader and Urgent Care Center: RN (per diem)
- Supervise and coordinate 20+ professional and administrative staff members
- Perform patient assessment and triage.

Garden Grove Medical Center, Garden Grove, CA   11/02 – Present
Surgical Services: per diem RN
- Provide direct patient care in pre-operative ambulatory care unit
- Monitor post anesthesia recovery unit, GI lab and cardiology non-invasive procedures
- Interview, assess and prepare pre-operative and pre-procedural patients
- Perform procedural conscious sedation induction, monitor and recovery

Smith Medical Associates, Santa Ana, CA   1/97 – 11/02
Family Practice Primary Care Physician Assistant
- Provide Pediatric-to-Geriatric health care
- Perform histories and physicals, minor surgical procedures, and well-women / well-baby
  exams.
- Provide health care maintenance
- Member of Medical Standards Committee

Garden Grove Medical Center, Garden Grove, CA   3/75 – 8/97

Emergency Department Staff Nurse (5/83-8/97)
Critical Care and Emergency Department (9/79-5/83)

- Assisted physicians in attending to patients' immediate needs
- Coordinated and assisted with patient triage
- Performed intake histories and physicals
- Operated paramedic base station radio (MICN)
- Acted as relief charge nurse and Base Station Coordinator
- Served as Hospital Quality Improvement Representative
- Participated as member of Hospital Float Pool and Hospital IV Therapy Team

Staff RN ICU/CCU (12/76-9/79)

- Directed patient care for general category critical patients
- Acted as Relief Nursing Supervisor of 141-bed hospital

Head Nurse [33 bed unit medical floor] (3/75-12/76)

- Supervised 15 employees involved in patient care

Relief Nursing Supervisor [hospital wide] (3/75-12/76)

Mobile Intensive Care Nurse/Emergency Department (3/75-12/76)

Independent Medical/Legal Consultant, Expert Witness (part-time)   5/89 – Present

- Provide expert testimony for cases in litigation
- Review documents, perform research, provide attorney consultation

EDUCATOR

Speaker for Chroma Pharmaceuticals on migraines and asthma   Present

Hospital Staff and Community Educator, *Garden Grove Medical Center*   9/84 – 8/97

- Conceived, planned and implemented community education program entitled "Basics of Babysitting"
- Taught classes on basic childcare, first aid and safety
- Educated hospital staff and community in Basic Cardiac Life Support
- Worked directly with fire department paramedics to maintain their clinical skills

Clinical Instructor, *Vocational Nursing School of California, Van Nuys, CA*   7/82 – 4/83

- Taught 15 vocational nursing students during hospital clinical experience

Theory Instructor, *School of Medical Studies, Anaheim, CA*   6/81 – 6/82

- Planned and presented theory content of nursing curriculum for vocational nursing students

CURRENT LICENSES, CERTIFICATIONS, and CREDENTIALS

- Physician Assistant - Active - State of California
- Registered Nurse Practitioner - Active - State of California
- Registered Nurse - Active - State of California
- Public Health Nurse Certificate
- American Heart Association
  - Basic Cardiac Life Support Provider
  - Advanced Cardiac Life Support Provider
  - Pediatric Advanced Life Support

PROFESSIONAL MEMBERSHIPS

- California Academy of Physician Assistants (CAPA)
- American Academy of Physician Assistants (AAPA)

Victor Valencia, Ph.D.

7979 N. Richmond
Chicago, IL 60616

valenciaphd@comcast.net

Residence: 773.337.7321
Cellular: 773.642.2164

SENIOR SCIENCE AND TECHNOLOGY MANAGER

CTO / PROJECT MANAGER / INTELLECTUAL PROPERTY / BUSINESS DEVELOPMENT

Spearheading Innovative Technology Solutions that Drive Change in a Career Spanning 14 Years

Technically sophisticated and business-savvy management professional with a solid record in building new technology start-ups, state-of-the-art operations, cross-functional teams, IP assets, and organizational expansion to achieve competitive market advantages. Adept in spearheading technological innovations, global teaming, new product delivery, and commercialization. Record of success delivering simultaneous large-scale, mission-critical projects on time and under budget. Recognized industry pioneer with 2 patents, 11 patent applications, 36 invention disclosures and 27 periodical articles / conference papers. Bilingual: English / Spanish proficient. Ph.D. Physical Science.

Representative industries served:

- Medical Devices
- Printing and Imaging
- Surface Mount Technology (SMT)

- Displays
- Packaging
- Nanotechnology

- RFID
- Coating
- Fuel Cells and Batteries

TECHNOLOGY / MANAGEMENT EXPERTISE

- Ground-Breaking Research Programs
- R&D Lab Management
- Full Life Cycle Project Management

- SBIR Management
- Strategic / Operational Planning
- New Product Development

- Quality / Reliability / Performance
- Competitive Benchmarking
- Technical Staffing

CAREER PROGRESSION

SUPER CAPACITOR TECHNOLOGY INC – Chicago, IL and Guadalajara, Mexico
Designer and manufacturer of the world's leading supercapacitors.
Chief Technical Officer / Business Development Manager / Regional Sales Manager

1998 - Present

Recruited to SCT in 1998 as a key member of the start-up management team to orchestrate commercialization of supercapacitor technology transfer from CSIRO. Upon building successful technology operations in Mexico, transferred to U.S. to launch the North American business enterprise. Contracted with global customers and vendors. 12 Direct reports: 1 Senior Scientist, 4 Scientists, 3 Research Engineers and 4 Technicians.

HIGHLIGHTS OF ACCOMPLISHMENTS:

- **Captured the company's first multi-million dollar sales order with the global leader in class 12 GPRS PC modems.** Research team formulated an electrolyte that exceeded the design specifications by 15%. SCT won 100% of the business. No competitors could meet specifications driving them from this market.

- **Piloted SCT's full life cycle, solution-focused business model in U.S.** A technology liaison initiates business contact, generates design win, and oversees contract manufacturer to insure quality product delivery.

- **Chaired IP Asset Management Team that leveraged one of the industry's most viable portfolios.** Team included senior management, key scientists, and IP Attorney.

- **Captured 60%+ market share** for supercapacitors used in GPRS modems worldwide. Secured additional clientele include the world's most recognized CPU and leading digital still camera manufacturers.

- **Reduced prototype failure rates from 85% to almost 0%** via innovative performance testing / packaging technologies. **Dramatically improved product yields and lifetimes.** Patent pending.

- **Achieved 80% cost reduction** designing and equipping two state-of-the-art research and coating laboratories.

- **Invented** novel thin film coating formulations, techniques and testing processes.

Victor Valencia, Ph.D.

CAREER PROGRESSION, CONTINUED

ADVANCED RESEARCH INSTITUTE – Los Alamos, NM   1995 - 1997
Principal Research Investigator / Senior Scientist (Ultracapacitors)
Project Manager (Advanced Battery)

HIGHLIGHTS OF ACCOMPLISHMENTS:
- **Managed** SBIR project.
- **Led research team** that developed advanced battery technologies for the USAF.
- **Achieved greater control** of process and 100 times increase in throughput by inventing novel method of depositing capacitive material onto a substrate.

VANGUARD TECHNOLOGIES – Houston, TX   1992 - 1995
Senior Research Scientist (Lithium Ion Batteries)

HIGHLIGHTS OF ACCOMPLISHMENTS:
- **Developed formulations** for thin polymer electrolytes with emphasis on conductivity, coatability and UV or E-Beam cross-linking resulting in greater uniformity of coatings and longer battery life.
- **Performed full IP analysis** of competitive products and manufacturing technologies. Evaluated carbon materials and methods of particle size reduction.

PATENTS AND PUBLICATIONS

Patent	9,876,543	Cathode-active material blends of $Li_x Mn_2 O_4$. **Cited in 36 other patents.**
Patent	9,123,456	System and method for impregnating a moving porous substrate with active materials to produce battery electrodes.
Patents Pending	11	Supercapacitor performance and manufacturing technology.
Invention Disclosures	36	Various materials and process improvements focused on Li Polymer batteries. Some disclosures incorporated as trade secrets in preference to patenting.
Periodical Articles / Papers, Posters	27	Authored / co-authored articles published in peer reviewed journals. Delivered papers, seminars, and 15 poster presentations at professional conferences.

PROFESSIONAL PROFILE

EDUCATION

PhD Physical Science
MASSACHUSETTS INSTITUTE OF TECHNOLOGY
Cambridge, MA   1989-1992
Thesis: EXAFS for Polymer Batteries. Structure conductivity in doped thin film polymer membranes. Funded by USDOE and Energy, Inc.

BSc. (Hons) Applied Chemistry
INSTITUTO DE TECNOLOGÍCO
Monterrey, Mexico   1986-1988

BTech HD Physical Sciences
INSTITUTO TECNOLOGÍCO
Monterrey, Mexico   1983-1986

AFFILIATIONS

Diversity Committee
American Association for The Advancement of Science (AAAS)

Regional Chair
The Society of Mexican American Engineers and Scientists, Inc. (MAES)

Member
Society of Hispanic Professional Engineers (SHPE)

Member
Latino Alumni of MIT (LAMIT)

ADDITIONAL TECHNOLOGY SKILLS

Manufacturing Science, Supercapacitors, Materials Engineering, Electrical Engineering, Quality Control, Electrochemistry, Competitive Analysis, Reverse Engineering, Advanced Polymers, Device Testing, Batteries, Packaging Processes, Selection and Design, Anticipatory Failure Determination

COMPUTER SKILLS

Operating Systems: Windows, Mac, UNIX

Office Software: Word, Excel, Project, PowerPoint, Outlook

Programming Languages: Basic, Visual Basic, C/C++, HP Interface Basic-HPIB

Richard E. Rodriguez
El Morro Street, San Juan, PR 00901
Home: (555) 123-4567

Social Security Number: xxx-xx-xxxx
Citizenship: United States

Veterans Status: VEOA
Reinstatement Eligibility: N/A

OBJECTIVE: Human Resources Specialist (GS-201-13/14)

SUMMARY OF QUALIFICATIONS

Human Resource Management: Motivated leader; possess comprehensive knowledge and skill in administration, analysis, and implementation of human resources policies and programs. Researches and recommends options and/or solutions on complex human resources issues to management officials.

- Serves as **HR Consultant** to management and staff to plan, organize and evaluate and improve HRM services to provide the most efficient service to internal and external customers.
- High level of **technical competency** in the following areas: EEO/Diversity; Labor Management and Employee Relations; HR Policy and Program Development; Position Management and Classification; and Recruitment and Placement.
- **Secret Clearance:** Handles sensitive information in accordance with security policies.

Recruitment: Dynamic recruiter; results-oriented and successful in coordinating highly effective recruitment initiatives throughout Puerto Rico to attract and retain highly qualified talent.

- Implements innovative recruitment strategies that link to agency mission and identified workforce needs through the use of a variety of recruitment sources.
- Leads and coordinates outreach and marketing efforts with colleges, universities, professional associations and interest groups, unions, state and local governments.

Communication and Interpersonal Skills: Effective communicator; makes clear and convincing oral presentations; listens to others, and seeks to gain a clear understanding of issues. Interacts with customers/clients (internal or external) to assess their needs, provide information, resolve problems, and satisfy demands and expectations.

- **Bilingual:** Skillful in oral and written communications in both English and Spanish languages. Conducts presentations, interviews and translates materials.
- **Team Leader:** Inspires successful team and individual effort to consistently meet departmental goals. Exercises good judgment, flexibility, and resourcefulness to resolve problems and coordinate the work of others to ensure short and long-term project goals and objectives are met.

PROFESSIONAL EXPERIENCE

Human Resources Specialist (GG-0301-12/3)
U.S. CUSTOMS & BORDER PROTECTION
33 South King Street, San Juan, PR
Supervisor: Helen Ramirez (787) xxx-xxxx

4/01 – 10/04
40 hours/week
Salary: $61,942/year

Provide guidance and assistance to employees, supervisors and/or general public about employee benefits. Announce vacancies of all levels in the organization. Conduct orientation to new hires. Coordinate and participate in ranking panels for rating of applicants. Draft position descriptions and crediting plans for new positions within the field office.

- Promote Special Hiring Authorities' initiatives with high-ranking managers to develop recruitment strategies (e.g., hiring individuals with disabilities).
- Work closely with the EEO Specialist in providing support to management when complaints of discrimination arise. Ensure compliance with EEO requirements within the agency is met.

Yeoman (Personnel Specialist)
US COAST GUARD
100 McArthur Causeway, Miami Beach, FL
Supervisor: John Smith (305) xxx-xxxx

5/96 – 11/00
40 hours/week
Salary: $35,000/year

Coordinated and assisted in administering policies related to members' compensation, training, recognition, disciplinary actions, leave and all human resources services. Advised management on personnel issues.
- Advised and counseled members on benefits available (e.g., leave, health insurance, retirement, awards, educational programs, and any other entitlement available to service members).
- Prepared statistical reports and personnel management information entries for 200+ members.

Equal Opportunity Specialist (Internship)
City of Carolina, Equal Opportunity Office
3443 Camino Del Rio, Carolina, PR
Supervisor: Roberto Diaz (787) xxx-xxxx

8/95 – 12/95
20 hours/week
Salary: N/A

Reviewed and ensured that all government contractors' employment policies and practices were in compliance with EEO and Labor laws. Processed and investigated complaints of discrimination and conducted visits to worksites to interview workers as part of the investigations.
- Assessed legal decisions related to EEO programs.
- Analyzed findings of investigations and presented them to supervisors for further action.
- Advised management of under-represented segments of the population for affirmative action initiatives.

EDUCATION

NOVA SOUTHEASTERN UNIVERSITY, Ft. Lauderdale, FL 33139
Degree: Master of Arts in Human Resources Management (2002)

UNIVERSITY OF PUERTO RICO, Rio Piedras Campus, San Juan, PR 00901
Degree: Bachelor of Arts in Labor Relations (1995)

ACHIEVEMENTS AND AWARDS

- U.S. CUSTOMS SERVICE, Outstanding Performance Award (September 2003)

- U.S. CUSTOMS SERVICE, Outstanding Performance Award (June 2001)

- U.S. COAST GUARD, Commendation for Superior Achievement (October 2000)

- U.S. COAST GUARD, Good Conduct Medal (May 1999)

REFERENCES available upon request.

IVÁN CARILLO

CONTACT	Address: 1234 Key Drive • Apartment 123 • Miami, Florida 33131 Phone: (305) 555-1234 • E-mail: icarillo@protypeltd.com.ar

PROFILE

- Experienced controller and financial analyst with the vision to define and strength to implement successful business strategies.
- Proven expertise in valuation, forecasting, financial statement analysis, and IT solutions.
- Effective communicator with strong negotiation and relationship management skills.
- Multi-culturally sensitive professional with extensive contacts in Mercosur countries—Argentina, Brazil, Chile, Uruguay, and Paraguay—and in North America, Spain, and Belgium.

EXPERIENCE

DIRECTOR OF NEW BUSINESS DEVELOPMENT (PARTNER), 2000 – present
Playcorp, Ltd., Mico & Associates, Argentina, Brazil, and Chile
Developed new business opportunities and formed corporate alliances within the Mercosur territory for the company's five divisions—Playcorp Sponsorships, Playcorp Associates, Playmusic, Playcorp POS, and PromoHouse. Performed due diligence and evaluated the economic and strategic values of proposed new ventures.
- Wrote business plans and successfully sourced funds from banks, retirement funds, sponsors, and strategic partners.
- Evaluated and won $3.5 million in new business for the partnership in the first year.

FINANCIAL DIRECTOR (PARTNER), 1999 – 2000
Procobro SA, Heran Services Argentina SA, Buenos Aires, Cordoba, Argentina
Formed a partnership with a Belgian group (Heran Services Belgium NV), a law firm (Nicholson & Cano), and a bank director to build a company specializing in debt collection for banks and large service companies. Participated in the development of strategic action plans as a member of the Board of Directors. Wrote and executed the business plan and managed all administrative, financial, and IT functions. Recruited personnel to staff the firm. Sourced and implemented the computer network and applications. Made presentations to prospective clients, developed proposals, and negotiated contracts.
- Built the company from the ground up, achieving breakeven within seven months with an initial investment of $500,000.
- Managed a portfolio of $54.6 million in debt within the first five months, with $3.5 million per month of regular collections; achieved a 96.4 percent success rate.
- Achieved a recovery ratio of 2 percent in cash per month and 12.6 percent in monthly payments (12 to 24 installments of refinanced old debt) in a recession economy.

FINANCIAL MANAGER, 1995 – 1999
Director of Administration and New Business, SA San Miguel
Brazil, Argentina, Uruguay (1998 – 1999)
Analyzed and negotiated the purchase of McDonald SA and Rubifrut, Ltd., two fruit-producing companies belonging to the McDonald's family. Lived in Brazil for seven months, in Argentina for two months, and in Uruguay for three months in order to acquire an in-depth understanding of each market.
- Analyzed global operations that required an annual expenditure of $42 million from the companies.
- The successful purchase helped to diversify production and export of various fruits for SA San Miguel and significantly increased their sales.

Adjunct Faculty, Universidad dé Austral and Universidad Católica Argentina
Buenos Aires, Argentina (1997 – 1999)
- Developed and taught courses in corporate finance, capital markets, enterprise development, project management, valuation methods, and accounting for managers.
- Designed the learning environment to meet educational development requirements, adapting teaching style to accommodate both individual and group learning styles.
- Formulated, developed, and reviewed curriculum materials to meet university standards and lesson objectives, incorporating experiential learning wherever possible.
- Documented and completed training records; provided remedial instruction and counseled students.

EXPERIENCE
(continued)

Financial Advisor, Bank of Boston NA
Buenos Aires, Argentina (1998 – 1999)
Provided financial advice to the Director of Institutional Relationships, Dr. Enrique Morad. Evaluated the economic viability of the Bank of Boston Foundation, institutional relationships, human resources, and marketing. Analyzed costs, proposed strategic solutions for the future, and restructured each of the areas.
  • Decreased annual spending by $1 million through administrative staff cutbacks.

Financial Analyst, Miguens Bemberg Holding SA
Argentina and Brazil (1998 – 1999)
Served as the principal financial analyst on a Bank of Boston venture with Molinos Río de la Plata SA and Sadia, two of the main players in the Latin American food industry. The aim of the project was the construction of a "cold chain" necessary for the preservation, handling, and distribution of perishable foodstuffs throughout the Mercosur, which involved an investment of $34 million.

Financial Consultant, Mico & Associates SA, Comunicacion Publicitaria
Buenos Aires, Argentina (1998 – 1999)
Hired to evaluate the possibility of a merger between this advertising company (with annual billings of $9 million) and a Dutch agency, as well as a strategic alliance with Playcorp, Ltd., the Brazilian leader in event sponsorships and partnerships.

Financial Manager, MBP International SA, MB Holding SA
Argentina and Chile (1995 – 1998)
Represented an equity fund formed by investment funds of Argentinean origin (Miguens Bemberg Holdings SA) and Australian origin (Ellerstina SA) belonging to Kerry Packer. Searched for potential acquisitions and performed quantitative and qualitative analyses of the ventures. Evaluated businesses valued at $168 million and personally negotiated with the companies or their investment bankers. Managed $10 million per month in liquid investments, including fixed terms, common investment funds, stocks, options, and bonds traded on the markets of Buenos Aires, New York, and Luxembourg. Responsible for the realization of capital contributions.
• Audited the operations and financial functions of the 54 restaurants of Burger King Southern Cone in Argentina, Chile, Uruguay and Paraguay with $46 million in annual sales. Responsible for strategic planning, including marketing campaigns, strategic alliances, and new point-of-sale programs.
• Principal analyst and negotiator for the equity fund's $80 million investment in Grainco SA, which was dedicated to the purchase of land for the construction of national entertainment centers and shopping malls.
• Created the monthly financial packages for the administration of SA San Miguel SACIFYA, a world leader in the production and export of fresh lemons and their derivatives. The company billed $110 million annually and showed a net profit of $8+ million. Helped to prepare the company for an initial public offering made through BBV Banco Frances SA as the main underwriter of $170 million for 15 percent of the stock. Key member of the team responsible for the acquisition of Citrus Trade Famailla SA for $23 million.
• Collaborated with the English mining group, Branckote Mining Company, in the analysis and setup of the Esquel-based mining company, El Desquite SA, requiring an investment of $20 million.
• Main financial analyst in the bid for the 40-year lease of Dock 4 of Puerto Madero in the central commercial business district of Buenos Aires, which resulted in $37.5 million of construction business over four years.

ASSISTANT, INVESTMENT BANKING DEPARTMENT, 1993 – 1995
Scotiabank Quilmes SA, Buenos Aires, Argentina
Assisted the Regional Director and three senior investment bankers in the preparation of sales books, handouts, presentations, market surveys, market research, and rating of the department's operations. Closed $76 million in business over two years. Administered the computer network of the department and resolved problems with workstations.

ASSISTANT, INVESTMENT BANKING DEPARTMENT, 1992 – 1993
Bullrich Mercado de Capitales SA, Buenos Aires, Argentina
Assisted bank officials with the preparation of presentations and sales books for their respective businesses. Maintained the computer network and purchased all supplies for the department.

IVÁN CARILLO

EDUCATION

BACHELOR OF ARTS, BUSINESS ADMINISTRATION (1997)
Universidad Católica Argentina, Buenos Aires
- Specialization in Banking Organizations and Accounting
- Editor and writer for the campus monthly newspaper

PROFESSIONAL DEVELOPMENT
- Mergers, Acquisitions, and Restructuring, IESE-IAE
- Business Appraisals, CEMA, University of Chicago
- Competitive Strategies for Small and Medium-sized Companies, Arthur Andersen
- Mergers and Acquisitions, Asociacion de Bancos Privados Argentinos
- Debt Collection, Asociacion de Bancos Privados Argentinos
- Capital Markets, Asociacion de Bancos Privados Argentinos
- Liabilities and Bonds, Instituto Tecnico de Mercado de Capitales
- Advertising Strategies, Camara Argentina de Publicitarios

LANGUAGES

Spanish: Native tongue
English: Highly proficient, writing and speaking (PET, FIST Certificate, TOEFL, TSE, TWE)
Portuguese: Fluent speaking, proficient writing
French: Working knowledge (5 years Aliance Francaise)

COMPUTERS

Operating Systems: Proficient in Windows, Macintosh, and Imac environments
Applications: CorelDraw, PhotoShop, Microsoft Office (Word, Excel, PowerPoint, Access, Outlook, and Internet Explorer applications)

Résumé #11 (by Linda Matias)

| **WANDA ORTIZ-RIVERA** | 2 Fir Lane
Smithtown, New York 11787 | Home: (631) 555-2118
Email: wrivera@email.com |

TEACHING PROFILE

Dedicated tenured teacher with the desire to instill in children the passion to be lifelong learners. Set curriculums that facilitate learning and feelings of success. Create an interactive, hands-on teaching style that builds on students' strengths to expand learning and self-awareness. Highlights of Qualifications:

- **Enthusiastic Educator:** Ability to consistently individualize instruction based on students' interest and needs.
- **Motivator:** Stimulate students' need for learning by establishing an active learning environment through positive feedback and reinforcement.
- **Team Contributor:** Foster strong inter-teacher cooperation and exchange of ideas with social workers, psychologists, faculty members and parents.

EDUCATION AND CERTIFICATION

Columbia University, Teachers College, New York, NY
Spanish with an Emphasis in Bilingual Education, Ed.D (expected 2004)

Columbia University, Teachers College, New York, NY
Ed.M. in Spanish, Emphasis in Bilingual/Bicultural Education, 1998

Dowling College, Oakdale, NY
Master of Business Administration, 1992
Bachelor of Art, Natural Science and Math, Minor: Spanish Literature, 1991

New York State Certification, N-6 with an Extension in Bilingual Education
ESL Teaching Certification and Spanish Teaching Certification

TEACHING EXPERIENCE

Brentwood Union Free School District, Brentwood, NY   **2001-Present**

<u>Third Grade, Dual Language Teacher, Solo Model (2002-Present)</u>
<u>Kindergarten Teacher, 2-Teacher Model – Spanish Component, (2001-2002)</u>
Recruited to provide a supportive and student-centered approach to learning. Recognized as a visionary leader and active participant in the school community.

- Set realistic and challenging goals; complement school curriculum with innovative classroom instruction in order to meet the needs of various learners; assess individual performance levels and adopt different approaches to maximize results for LEP and EP student population.
- Consistently complement curriculum through nontraditional methods in teaching; teaching style reflects a continual effort to innovate and inspire students.
- Collaborate with fellow members of the SIT Committee and coached teachers on how to respond to student challenges; offered advice, support, and encouragement.

Continued...

WANDA ORTIZ-RIVERA

...Professional Experience Continued...

John F. Kennedy, Portchester School District, Portchester, NY   **1994-2001**

<u>Bilingual Resource Teacher (1998-2001)</u>
Designed, created, and implemented innovative teaching curriculums for kindergarten through fourth grade that successfully mainstreamed bilingual students. Encouraged parental involvement in their children's education by facilitating interactive workshops. Performed evaluations and assessments for referral and mainstreaming.

- Interacted with Title 1 teachers to integrate reading, math, science, and social studies into learning curriculums that touch upon mainstream topics and ideas.
- Utilized knowledge of CALPS and BICS to proactively engage students in the learning process.
- Administered school-wide ESL testing, documented findings and reviewed results with central staff and parents.

<u>Bilingual First Grade Teacher, 1994-1998</u>
Encouraged parental involvement through regular communication, presentations, and parent-teacher conferences. Served as a liaison between the student, parents, teachers and administrators.

- Instructed and independently designed lesson plans; assumed full charge for classes.
- Initiated a reading program integrating different reading methodologies and workshops.

OF NOTE

COMMITTEES

- Served on Committee of Special Education (CSE) to determine the future status of bilingual students.
- Assisted in writing grants and proposals for state and federal funding.

HONORS

Fellowship Award, Multicultural Studies, Emphasis Bilingual/Education, 1994

Member, Kappa Delta Pi, 1995-1997

Honor Student, National Dean's List, 1987-1993

Awarded by Columbia University and Fundacion Jose Ortega Y Gasset – Madrid, Spain
Presented Methodologies of Teaching Reading to Bilingual Students

Selected by college President and faculty to represent student body at Mediterranean XIII Conference in Murcia, Spain, 1990

Selected as a Language Translator and Interpreter, Dowling College Symposium for Dr. Camilo Jose Cela, 1989 Nobel Prize Winner In Literature, 1990

RESEARCH

Bilingual/Bicultural Classroom – Teacher's Reflective Practice

Résumé #12 (by Vivian VanLier)

SONIA GUTIERREZ
SoniaG@email.com

55123 Hydrangea Lane
Studio City, California 91604

Residence (818) 555-1234
Mobile (818) 555-5554

ADMINISTRATIVE/ACCOUNTING SPECIALIST
Strengths in Bookkeeping and Accounting Support • Staff Training and Supervision

- Highly motivated professional with over **8 year's progressive experience** in diverse industries, and **special expertise in medical settings**.
- Possesses a **strong work ethic** as demonstrated by managing full-time employment concurrent with high school/college studies and family responsibilities, consistently maintaining a **verifiable record of punctuality and low absenteeism**.
- **Learns quickly** and **demonstrates flexibility** in accepting new challenges. **Works well independently** and/or collaboratively as a team member. **Proactive in identifying problems and taking corrective actions and streamlining procedures** to increase operational efficiency.
- **Natural communicator** who gets along well with public and all levels of co-workers.
- **Computer Literate:** Experience in Windows, WordPerfect, Microsoft Word, Excel, Quicken, and QuickBooks

Bilingual English/Spanish

PROFESSIONAL EXPERIENCE

CLINICA MEDICO VAN NUYS, Van Nuys, CA
Administrative Assistant • 2001 to Present
Provide wide variety of clerical and administrative support services, including answering busy phones, directing calls, greeting visitors, maintaining office supply and equipment inventories, reconciling invoices and providing diligent follow-up on pending contracts.
- Instituted tracking system to monitor high-volume of incoming UPS and Fed Ex shipments. Developed procedural manual for administrative operations; trained and supervised new team members.

ALL VALLEY BUILDERS, Canoga Park, CA
Administrative / Accounting Assistant • 1999 to 2001
Developed and oversaw office procedures for large construction company specializing in home remodels.
- Created policy/procedure manual; designed and implemented use of various forms and logs.
- Placed recruitment ads, screened applicants, trained new hires and provided field support for staff.
- Summarized employee time sheets for staff in excess of 100.
- Provided accounting support; reconciled invoices and accounts.

WEST VALLEY HEALTH CLINIC, Woodland Hills, CA
Administrative / Accounting Assistant • 1996 to 1999
Registered patients, verified insurance coverage, scheduled diagnostic procedures and ensured availability of test results for follow-up visits.
- Provided translation services for Spanish speaking patients.
- Opened and closed office.
- Performed data entry, processed cash payments and assisted billing department with billing, collections and Medicare and Medi-Cal matters.

EDUCATION

LOS ANGELES VALLEY COLLEGE, Valley Glen, CA • Major: Business—*currently attending*

Chapter 8

L.A.T.I.N.O. Career-Marketing Letters Generate Even More Job Interviews

Myth: Recruiters and hiring officials do not read cover letters and other career marketing communications.

Truth: A strategically written marketing letter can be the deciding factor for an applicant securing an employment interview. The added effort sets you apart from other applicants who submit a generic letter or only a résumé.

Reality 1: In a recent study by the Society of Human Resources Management (SHRM), more than two-thirds of human resource managers view well-written, personalized cover letters as advantageous to a job applicant. Nearly half believe that they are more important than or just as important as résumés.

Reality 2: A poorly written letter can abruptly end an applicant's candidacy.

L.A.T.I.N.O. CAREER-MARKETING LETTER

123 Job Search Drive • Career Management, USA • (444) SUC-CESS • Email: MarketYourSelf.com

Dear Latino Job Seeker:

As a **Senior Career Marketing Tool**, I understand that communicating your *Personal Career Brand* is a key step in career success. My current goal is to assume expanded responsibilities in job search where I can apply a life-long record of delivering strong performance results.

The scope of my experience includes all forms of career-marketing correspondence:

Broadcast / Cold Call	Networking	Bilingual or Spanish Version
Advertisement Response	Résuletter	Reference
Targeted: Company/Industry	Confirmation	Acceptance/Rejection of Job
Targeted: Position	Thank You	Scannable / FAX
Recruiter / Headhunter	Follow-up	ASCHII / Plain Text

My contributions include:

- Forging strategic partnerships with stand-alone résumés to advertise target-specific job seeker attributes and demonstrate strong communication skills.
- Securing millions of employment interviews by successfully navigating the hiring process to position users as a premier candidate.
- Productively following-up interviews with strategic communications that sway employers to hire my clients.

I have enclosed my résumé in anticipation that you may be interested in adding an impact player to your team. I would welcome a personal interview to explore employment opportunities with your company. Thank you for your time and consideration.

Sincerely,

L.A.T.I.N.O. Career-Marketing Letter

L.A.T.I.N.O. Cover Letter

Enclosure

KEY STRENGTHS OF A L.A.T.I.N.O. CAREER-MARKETING LETTER

L.A.T.I.N.O. career-marketing letters are persuasive career-marketing tools that set you apart from the competition in today's tough job market. They are dynamic and honest portraits of Brand You and are crafted to be read from the hiring official's perspective.

L.A.T.I.N.O. career-marketing letters:

L **Link to a specific audience.** Cover letters are situation-dependent. Your target may be a particular job, reader, employer, or industry. To be successful, tailor your message to inspire the reader to consider your résumé carefully.

A **Are a complement to, not a repetition of, your résumé.** The cover letter allows you to personalize your application. Using your letter to focus on information that will immediately appeal to the employer gives you an opportunity to impress the reader that you took the time to research the company's needs.

T **Ties your personal career brand to the employer's buying (hiring) motivators.** Your cover letter should project your ability to satisfy the employer's need to be more competitive, expand business, make or save money, improve productivity, save time, attract or retain customers, build relationships, or solve a specific problem.

I **Imparts information that might not be appropriate on a résumé.** Cover letters are a great way to provide the additional information that some employers request (i.e., problem–solution scenarios, salary requirements, salary history, references).

N **Nails down your written communication skills.** Employers prefer applicants who demonstrate good communication skills. If the position requires bilingual candidates, be sure to send your letter in both English and Spanish.

O **Orchestrates an invitation to an interview.** Leverage the L.A.T.I.N. portion of your letter by concluding with a compelling statement and a request for an interview.

TYPES OF CAREER-MARKETING LETTERS

Job seekers use a variety of career-marketing letters, including the following:

Broadcast letter: The purpose of this letter is to inquire about possible openings and generate (if not a job interview) at least an initial informal interview. Its structure is similar to the letter of application, but instead of addressing specific position requirements, it focuses on your qualifications and interests in broader, more general terms. Like the ad-response/target position letter, it will be most effective if it reflects knowledge of the organization and communicates your ability to contribute to the operation. Your letter should be organized as follows:

❑ Use a referral name if you have one (whether inside or outside the company). Be sure to get permission to use this name.

❑ Ask to be considered for existing or anticipated openings suited to your qualifications.

❑ Let the employer know why you are attracted to the organization and indicate the area or job function that interests you most.

❑ Highlight your qualifications as they relate to your stated job target.

❑ Request an opportunity to meet with someone to discuss your interests and qualifications further.

Ad-response/target position letter: This type of letter is written in response to an advertised position or specific job opening. The goal here is to get your résumé read and generate a job interview. In order to be successful, you must demonstrate that your qualifications match the requirements of the position. If possible, get a copy of the position description, study it carefully for keywords, and focus on these keyword skills in your letter and résumé. Your letter should be organized as follows:

❑ Identify the position that you are applying for, mention how you learned about the job, and use the name of a referral if you have one (whether inside or outside the company). Be sure to get permission to use this name.

❑ Describe your qualifications as they relate to the position requirements, providing evidence of your related experiences and accomplishments.

❑ Let the employer know that you have the personal qualifications and motivation to perform well in the position.

❑ Indicate your availability for an interview.

Thank-you/follow-up letter: This is one of the most important, yet least used forms of correspondence. It can be used to strengthen your candidacy, establish goodwill, and express appreciation. When sending a thank-you letter after a job interview, try to mail the letter within twenty-four hours.

❑ Make this letter brief and concise.

❑ Restate your qualifications and interest in the position. Express your sincere appreciation for the interview.

❑ Think of the thank-you letter as a sales letter in disguise, so don't be afraid to put some "sell" into it.

❑ Send thank-you letters to everyone who assists you during your job search, no matter how small a role they play.

Letters to recruiters/headhunters: As more employers use the professional screening services of recruiters, you might want to send a few letters to recruiters that specialize in your field. You must include the following specific information in a cover letter to a recruiter:

❑ The type of position or positions you are targeting

❑ The industry or industries that interest you most

❑ Your expected salary (a range is always better than a set amount)

❑ Your geographic preferences

❑ If relevant, your willingness to relocate or work abroad

❑ A brief note that your search is confidential (unless it isn't)

OTHER TYPES OF CAREER-MARKETING LETTERS

Until recently, career-marketing letters were limited to cover sheets and after-interview thank-you letters. These days, the definition for *career-marketing letters* has expanded to include a wide range of letters:

- Networking to request informational interview, contacts, and job leads
- Scannable format for faxing
- ASCII cover letters for pasting into email
- Follow-up to check the status of your résumé, application, or interview
- Confirmation of an interview
- Bilingual or Spanish version of your letter when applying for positions that require Spanish language skills
- RésuLetter, a shortened résumé in letter format
- Reference letters that support your application or candidacy
- Professional Reference List with contact information and a summary of your relationship with the person
- Career-marketing business cards, an abbreviated version of your RésuLetter
- Acceptance of job offer
- Withdrawal from consideration
- Declining a specific job offer

Figure 8.1 shows Marisol Torres' ad-response letter in a scannable (word processed) format; Figure 8.2 shows the same letter in ASCII/plain text format for emailing; and Figure 8.3 shows Marisol's reference sheet.

SIX-STEP COVER LETTER BLUEPRINT

While the specific words and strategies will vary from one situation to the next, the template in this section provides a model for structuring your cover letter. These instructions are adapted from *Jumpstart Your Job Search in a Weekend* (Prima Publishing) by one of our team members, Pat Kendall (*www.jumpstartyourjobsearch.com*). Information on how to create ASCII cover letters is also included on our book's Web site: *www.jobsearchguideforlatinos.com*.

1. First Paragraph

Explain why you are writing and which position (or job target area) interests you. Focus on critical keywords, compatible skills, and your ability to produce the desired results.

Your LatPro.com posting for AREA SALES MANAGER/HISPANIC MARKETS interests me, as I have a proven track record in regional sales management in Latino and general markets. The accompanying résumé outlines my ten-year career.

2. Second Paragraph

Outline primary qualifiers (whether experience, education, or acquired skills) needed for the job. This paragraph should emphasize keywords and tangible (hard) skills.

As you will note, I have progressive management experience in highly competitive national and international environments. As territory director for Consumer Brands, Inc., I supervised sales operations and made numerous bottom-line contributions:

3. Bullet Points

Use bullets to showcase accomplishments, special projects, or capability statements that were introduced in the second paragraph.

- *Coordinated seven successful product launches in five years.*
- *Built sales teams that exceeded marketing objectives by a minimum of 34 percent.*
- *Expanded market share by 46 percent.*

4. Fourth Paragraph

Describe secondary qualifiers (soft skills, supporting experience, and transferable skills).

In the past five years, I've provided effective sales training and leadership for established and startup companies.

5. Closing Paragraph

Your letter should close with an assertive call to action (when applicable), or it should project confidence in your ability to contribute at an above-average level. In addition, saying thank-you is always a nice touch.

I am confident that I can make similar contributions as a member of your team and look forward to describing my background in more detail. Thank you for your consideration.

6. Optional Postscript

Use a postscript (PS) to highlight a critical skill or to mention the URL (Web address) for your HTML résumé. It's a well-known fact that the PS is one of the hot spots in a letter. (The postscript is almost always read.)

PS: Details of my management performance and a synopsis of my training program are included on my Web résumé: www.careerfolio/richortega

L.A.T.I.N.O. CAREER-MARKETING LETTERS PROJECT VALUE

One of the best ways to get employers' attention in the introductory paragraph of your cover letter is to focus on critical keywords (i.e., "qualifying skills," "knowledge," and "expertise"). If you focus attention on relevant qualifications from the beginning, employers will be motivated to continue reading.

Even better, explain how you can improve their bottom-line. The following before and after samples illustrate this concept. The before examples fail to mention the candidate's potential contributions. The after examples are rich with keyword-heavy value statements.

Before: Your Saludos.com posting for a marketing intern interests me, as I believe that I have the skills you need.

After: As a recent graduate with a Bachelor of Science degree in business administration, I've received solid training in all aspects of marketing research, product positioning, and statistical analysis.

Before: I would like to apply for a sales management position with your company.

After: My ten-year career in sales and record of success in account penetration and market share development qualify me for a key position on your management team.

Before: I would like to work for ABC Company as a sales representative and believe that my proven experience will benefit your company.

After: As an award-winning sales representative with a broad knowledge of electronics products, I have the ability to increase your company's sales volume and market share.

Before: My seventeen years of experience may interest you as you search for a senior-level candidate to lead your new company.

After: With seventeen years of management success in highly competitive national and international markets, I can do much to contribute to your company's startup and expansion efforts.

The Career Management Toolkit in Chapter 19 includes questionnaires that will help you apply the six-step process for developing your career-marketing letters. In addition, review the career marketing samples at the end of this chapter. We have included several letter writing resources in Appendix F.

L.A.T.I.N.O. CAREER-MARKETING LETTER CHECKLIST

- Is my career-marketing letter tailored to a specific job target, reader, theme, or purpose?

- Is my career-marketing letter crafted to be read from the hiring official's perspective? Does it address the employer's needs and appeal to the reader's hiring motivators?

- Does my career-marketing letter supplement my résumé with a personalized sales pitch and present the additional information the reader needs?

- Does my career-marketing letter illustrate how I can handle the job? That I have positive work attitudes, solid interpersonal skills and a willingness to go above and beyond what is expected?

L.A.T.I.N.O. Career-Marketing Letters Generate Even More Job Interviews

■ Does my career-marketing letter tie into my personal career brand—who I am, what I can do, and the value I bring to the needs of the specific reader?

■ Is my career-marketing letter inviting to read? Does the layout look professional? Is there adequate white space? Are the fonts readable? Is the résumé printed on quality paper?

■ Does my career-marketing letter contain keywords that highlight specific-industry and job-related skills?

■ Does my career-marketing letter demonstrate position-related soft and transferable skills such as verbal and written communication, organization, leadership, planning, aptitude for learning, adaptability, creativity, resourcefulness, problem solving, and work ethic?

■ Does my career-marketing letter include plenty of active verbs (*managed, coordinated, planned, implemented, directed, initiated, conducted, completed, recommended,* . . .)?

■ If necessary, have I responded to an employer's request for specific information (salary requirements, salary history, and references) by presenting the information in a way that markets me as a top candidate?

■ Where appropriate, have I addressed my career-marketing letter to the correct individual and/or clearly referenced the specific position I am applying for?

■ Is my writing clear, action-oriented, and well organized?

■ Does my career-marketing letter nail down my written communication skills?

■ If applying for a bilingual position, have I written a second career-marketing letter that demonstrates my Spanish language skills?

■ Have I (and others) proofread my career-marketing letter for typos, grammar, consistent formatting, and readability?

■ Have I tested the plain text or ASCII version of my career-marketing letter to ensure its Internet functionality?

■ Will my career-marketing letter pass a fifteen- to sixty-second initial screening?

■ Have I closed my career-marketing letter seeking action by the reader or indicating how I would follow up?

■ Does my career-marketing letter inspire the recipient to take the next step—carefully read my résumé, identify me as a top candidate, and set up an interview?

CAREER-MARKETING LETTER SAMPLES

Figures 8.1 through 8.10 are sample career-marketing letters written by professional résumé writers from all over the United States. A full list of contributors is in Appendix BB.

Career-Marketing #1

TORRES (Ad Response Version—Professional)
Word processed version of Marisol Torres' cover letter, page 108.

Strategy/Approach: Marisol's cover letter was built around keywords that were extracted from the online job posting (i.e., hotel sales, marketing, new business, community alliances and networks, relationship building, customer service, team building). It focuses on her first-hand knowledge of the local market and ability to make bottom-line contributions.

Pat Kendall, NCRW, JCTC, Advanced Résumé Concepts

Career-Marketing #2

TORRES (ASCII Version)
ASCII/plain text version of Marisol Torres' cover letter, page 109.

Strategy/Approach: This version of Marisol's cover letter is designed specifically for cutting and pasting into email or online forms for electronic processing.

Pat Kendall, NCRW, JCTC, Advanced Résumé Concepts

ASCII Cover Letters

Here is one way to respond to an advertised job online:

1. Paste ASCII cover letter into email window.
2. Paste ASCII résumé after cover letter.
3. Add a URL (live link to Web résumé, if you have one) to the cover letter.

ASCII cover letters have the following subtle (but significant) characteristics that distinguish them from traditional cover letters:

Formatting: Instead of bullets, use asterisks (or other standard keyboard symbols) to break up large blocks of text, and emphasize specific points or accomplishments. ASCII text cannot be bolded, italicized, or underlined and specific fonts and sizes are not recognized. When opened, ASCII files assume the user's default settings and type styles.

Address: A street address is unnecessary. Unless you have a specific contact name, drop the salutation and simply start with the first line of the cover letter.

No date: The email system dates the letter automatically.

Space for signature: Extra spaces for the signature are eliminated because the letter is not signed.

Résumé reference: The résumé should be referred to as being "attached" or "pasted below" instead of being "enclosed."

Subject line: The subject line is one of the most critical parts of an emailed cover letter. Be sure to reference the job number/announcement number in the subject line. In other situations, type your job target or most critical keywords into the subject line.

When forwarding an unsolicited résumé to employers and recruiters, be sure to use the subject line to reference your job target/job title.

Career-Marketing #3

TORRES (Reference Version)
Marisol Torres' references marketing letter, page 110.

    Strategy/Approach: Marisol's cover letter was built around keywords extracted from the online job posting (i.e., hotel sales, marketing, new business, community alliances and networks, relationship building, customer service, team building). It focuses on her first-hand knowledge of the local market and ability to make bottom-line contributions.

Pat Kendall, NCRW, JCTC, Advanced Résumé Concepts

Career-Marketing #4

MARTINEZ (Broadcast/Cold Call Version—Entry Level)
Michael Martinez' broadcast letter, page 111.

    We included this letter to demonstrate that you can write an honest and powerful career-marketing document regardless of your age or experience. This letter was actually written for a high school senior who was seeking a part-time job. The letter presented Michael's proven skills and maturity and resulted in numerous interviews and job offers.

Murray Mann, Global Career Strategies

Career-Marketing #5

DIAZ (Broadcast Version—Senior Level)
Miguel Diaz' broadcast letter—senior level, page 112.

Louise Garver, CPRW, JCTC, CMP, CEIP, MCDP,
Career Directions, LLC

Career-Marketing #6

GOMEZ (Referral, Ad-response, Combination)
Hilda Gomez' combination referral, ad-response and comparison letter, page 113.
    The salutation section of this letter contains two key components:

1. The letter is addressed to a specific recipient rather than to Whom It May Concern or a generic office. Where possible, try to identify the correct party to whom to send your letter to increase the chances it will be read.
2. The letter references the position title and source of job listing to make it easier for the recipient to process.

    The body of the letter is constructed in three parts:

1. The first paragraph of the letter mentions the referring individual's name to ensure that the letter and résumé are not passed over. Hilda reinforces this step by identifying the position of her referring source and his working knowledge of her skill sets.
2. The comparison format makes key information easy to skim and demonstrates that Hilda exceeds each listed requirement. Additionally, the chart demonstrates that the candidate researched the position.

3. The next paragraph provides additional job-related hard qualifications and soft skills that sell Hilda as the "ideal" candidate for the position.

Murray Mann, Global Career Strategies

Career-Marketing #7

BETANCOURT (Targeted Version—Senior Level)
Joaquin Betancourt's targeted letter, page 114.

Joaquin's letter was targeted to the position of senior vice president of onboard services. It was written to address three key concerns the employer had.

* A leader who could turn around its passenger services operations.
* A senior vice president who could help transition airlines' corporate culture to be more customer and employee friendly.
* Confirmation that Joaquin's hotel and resort industry skills were transferable to the position.

The letter was crafted to portray Joaquin's management philosophy, personality, and corporate fit in ways that could not be achieved in his résumé.

Murray Mann, Global Career Strategies

Career-Marketing #8

AGUILERA (Recruiter)
Ricardo Aguilera's recruiter letter, page 115.

Strategy/Approach: This letter was sent to a search firm that specializes in pharmaceutical recruitment. It highlights Ricardo's skills in outside sales, specialty sales, or other account relations management through easy-to-read bullet points.

Arnold Boldt, CPRW, Arnold-Smith Associates

Career-Marketing #9

MERCADO (Headhunter)
Ana Mercado's executive recruiter letter, page 116.

Strategy/Approach: It is customary in executive recruiter letters to include salary requirements, availability for interviews, and interest in relocation.

Don Orlando, CPRW, Mclean Group

Career-Marketing #10

ORTEGA (Thank You—After Interview)
Richard Ortega's thank-you letter, page 117.

Strategy/Approach: In addition to saying "thank you for your time," this letter communicates Richard's enthusiasm, interest in the job, and ability to contribute and "excel" in a similar role. To reinforce the positive message, he reminds the interviewer of his successful track record with a major competitor.

Pat Kendall, NCRW, JCTC, Advanced Résumé Concepts

Career-Marketing #1 (by Pat Kendall)

MARISOL TORRES
www.careerfolio.com/maritorres

123 River Road • (503) 555-9055
Bend, Oregon 97999 • mtorres@email2.org

January 9, 2005

Marcy Woods
RE: iHispano.com posting 123456789
RTF Corporation
P.O. Box 4555
Sunriver, Oregon 97999

Dear Ms. Woods:

My proven track record in sales qualifies me for the Hotel Sales / Marketing position posted on iHispano.com. The accompanying resume outlines my related accomplishments.

As you will note, I have been very successful in achieving sales and revenue goals in the Bend / Sunriver market. I have consistently ranked as a top producer for the past six years and am well equipped to:

- Expand sales by identifying and capitalizing on new business opportunities.
- Aggressively target the untapped Hispanic market.
- Cultivate and manage community alliances and business networks.
- Build top-producing teams that consistently exceed sales and revenue goals.

My success can be attributed to two factors: The ability to build long-term relationships and a solid commitment to excellent customer service.

I am confident that I can make immediate contributions to your operation and would appreciate an opportunity to describe my capabilities during a personal interview. Thank you for your time and consideration.

Sincerely,

Marisol Torres

Career-Marketing #2 (by Pat Kendall)

SAMPLE COVER LETTER - *In ASCII Format for e-Mailing*
(Includes URL to Web Resume)

Subject Line: iHispano.com posting 123456789 - Hotel Sales / Marketing Specialist
----

Your iHispano.com posting for Hotel Sales / Marketing Specialist interests me, as I have a proven track record in regional sales management and goal attainment. The accompanying resume (pasted below in ASCII format and online at www.careerfolio.com/maritorres) outlines my related accomplishments.

As you will note, I have been very successful in achieving sales and revenue goals in the Bend / Sunriver market. I have consistently ranked as a top producer for the past six years and am well equipped to:

* Expand sales by identifying and capitalizing on new business opportunities.
* Aggressively target the untapped Hispanic market.
* Cultivate and manage community alliances and business networks.
* Build top-producing teams that consistently exceed sales and revenue goals.

My success can be attributed to two factors: The ability to build long-term relationships and a solid commitment to excellent customer service.

I am confident that I can make immediate contributions to your operation and would appreciate an opportunity to describe my capabilities during a personal interview. Thank you for your time and consideration.

Sincerely,

Marisol Torres

Resume
Marisol Torres
etc., etc., etc.
----

www.careerfolio.com/maritorres

Career-Marketing #3 (by Pat Kendall)

MARISOL TORRES

www.careerfolio.com/maritorres

123 River Road • (503) 555-9055
Bend, Oregon 97999 • mtorres@email2.org

PROFESSIONAL REFERENCE LIST

Reference Known	Relationship	Years
Roberta Kramer VP Sales GHY Corporation LTC 4560 Richards Drive Bend, Oregon (555) 556-5555	**Current Supervisor** Ms. Kramer has been my direct supervisor for the past two years. She can attest to my ability to develop new business and exceed sales and profit goals. I worked as a key member of her marketing and sales team.	Two
Howard Lee (555) 556-5555 6789 Main Street Sunriver, Oregon (555) 555-4555 hlee@wwwmail.com	**Former Supervisor** Among other projects, I worked closely with Mr. Lee on a large sales campaign targeting the Hispanic market. Mr. Lee can attest to my keen understanding of local market conditions, trends, and consumer motivators.	Four
Georgia Winston (555) 555-5555 12345 Hanford Lane Bend, Oregon (505) 555-6788 georgiawin@www.com	**Former Supervisor** I worked with Ms. Winston to plan and manage dozens of marketing and sales development projects. Ms. Winston has witnessed my ability to win large accounts, resolve problems, and work independently.	Four

MICHAEL MARTINEZ

123 London Street • Northern, IL 60099 • (847) 444-2222 • mmartinez@isp.com

Dear :

As a child my playground was most often the family restaurant. I learned early on that success depends on a strong commitment to customer satisfaction, quality and a constant focus on the bottom line. My recent experience includes retail management roles in book, video, and game product store environments.

The range of my experience spans:

Retail Store Operations Management
P & L Responsibility / Budgeting/ A-P / A-R
Solutions-Focused Customer Service
Shift Supervision / Opening and Closing
Primary / Peripheral Sales
Inventory Control / Purchasing / Loss Prevention

Merchandising / Creative Product Display
External Marketing / Publicity
Special Events Coordination
Editor / Author Monthly Catalog
Solid Communication / Teambuilding Skills
Strong PC and Database Skills

My contributions include:

- **Editor, author, creative designer for a 20-page monthly book catalog** including writing feature articles and book / product synopsis.

- **Redesigned product displays** resulting in a **50% increase in sales** in targeted merchandise sales.

- **Awarded 35 recognitions for customer service and peripheral sales**; personally exceeded all other district stores in presales of select video product.

I have approached my work with a strong sense of urgency, working well under pressure and change. I am considered a team player who has a strong commitment to the people and the organization I work for.

The sum of experience has provided me with the qualifications to contribute to your company's long term success. I have enclosed my resume in anticipation that you may be interested in adding an impact player to your team. I would welcome a personal interview.

Thank you for your time and consideration.

Sincerely,

Michael Martinez

Enclosure

Career-Marketing #5 (by Louise Garver)

MIGUEL DIAZ

100 Scarborough Drive
Fullerton, California 96889
(316) 675-8334
mdiaz@cox.net

As Director of Operations for a nationwide retail organization, I successfully innovated and introduced operational, merchandising, customer service and employee training programs.

- **RESULTS: Sales climbed $25 million annually and the gross profit margin increased by 13 full points within the first year.**

As Regional Manager, I reversed a store-closing trend and turned a non-producing region into a highly profitable operation.

- **RESULTS: Under my management, the region achieved the highest sales volume throughout the entire company comprised of 52 regions.**

As Store Manager, I provided superior customer service increasing average sale by 50%.

- **RESULTS: Recognized for significantly increasing store sales, margins and profits to record heights.**

Beginning with a concept, I have created and implemented sales and marketing strategies designed to achieve bottom-line results. Equally important has been my success in recruiting, developing and directing teams of well-qualified management and sales personnel. By creating proactive business cultures encouraging employee participation in the decision-making process and rewarding individual contributions, I have built profitable operations.

If you need a management professional with my talents, may we meet to discuss the value I would to your operations?

Very truly yours,

Miguel Diaz

HILDA GOMEZ

2222 South Campbell, Chicago, Illinois 60622 ▪ HGomez@isp.com ▪ 555-456-9999

March 1, 2005

Ms. Lori Dominguez
Senior Human Resources Consultant
Advocate Healthcare
111 South Wacker Drive
Chicago, Illinois 60606

Re: Customer Service Supervisor, AHC Bulletin 11236

Dear Ms. Dominguez:

Doctor Jaime Rosado (from your Logan Square Medical Center) suggested that I contact you about securing a *customer service supervisor* position with Advocate Healthcare. I provided administrative support to Dr. Rosado during his residency at the Latin American Community Medical Center. Dr. Rosado can attest to my ability to provide quality customer service and staff assistance in a multi-physician office.

The comparison below summarizes how my experience meets your requirements:

Your Requirements	*My Qualifications*
Five years of customer service experience in a medical or hospital billing office.	Seven+ years of experience in medical office environments and solid skills in billing and claims management. Three years of experience in supervisory roles.
Experience with Microsoft Office, billing software, ICD-9 coding, and general office technologies.	Certified in MS Office, Genesis Solutions, Misys, and MedRec+. Medical Coding Certificate - thoroughly familiar with ICD-9 and CPT requirements. Office Administration Certificate.
Bilingual in English and Spanish.	Proficient in speaking, reading, writing, and translating business and medical English and Spanish.

Additionally, I have first-hand experience with claims processing and proven ability to resolve billing problems, handle patient inquiries, verify insurance coverage, submit bills, and follow-up on claims and denials. I have a strong work ethic, excellent interpersonal communications, a commitment to exceptional service, and well-developed teambuilding and supervisory skills.

Please review the enclosed résumé for details of my background and experience. If you have questions or would like to schedule an interview, you may reach me at 555-917-2345 (days) or 555-436-9999 (evenings).

Thank you for you consideration.

Sincerely,

Hilda Gomez

Résumé Enclosed

Career-Marketing #7 (by Murray Mann)

JOAQUIN BETANCOURT

501 Private Beach Drive
Newport Beach, CA 92659

JBentancourt@isp.com

Home/Fax: 949.000.1001
Cell: 949.000.2002

[Date]

John E. Smith
Major Airlines
30 Rockefeller Plaza, Suite 1000
New York, NY10112

RE: Senior Vice President of Onboard Services

Dear Mr. Smith:

Building corporate value, total quality guest environments, and workplaces that reflect a company's mission are my professional passion and expertise.

In January 2000, I was recruited by Multinational Hotels, Inc. to serve as Senior Vice President for Inter-American Operations and play a key role in the corporation's $ 4 billion start-up. We envisioned and created an environment which thrives on the improvement process and the breakthrough ideas that result from never accepting a formula just because "everyone else is doing it." Today, Multinational is the largest international hotel and leisure operations enterprise and is recognized by guests, trade publications and the airline industry as the "World's Best Global Hotel Company."

I bring to the position of Senior Vice President of Onboard Services, 20 years of proven strategic and tactical leadership in the hospitality industry. My strengths in operations management and complex negotiations are measured in multi-million dollar revenue increases, earnings gains, reduced operating costs, and more competitive and sustainable market advantages. These core proficiencies are critical to meeting Major Airlines financial, operating, market, superior customer service, and employee relations goals.

My team has successfully implemented innovative guest services programs that improve customer satisfaction and loyalty in collective bargaining environments. We consistently receive top approval ratings from management to front line staff. My participatory leadership style evolved from having worked through school as a doorman, busboy, server, line cook and front desk agent. I can, and still do, walk in our employees' shoes. I do not ask any one to do anything I would not do.

As a frequent flyer, I have observed and experienced the best and the worst our industry has to offer. The same traveler who steps onto a plane also stays at our hotels. Our goals are the same - to provide an enjoyable, comfortable, safe, and hassle-free experience.

I appreciate your consideration and look forward to speaking with you regarding your search.

Sincerely,

Joaquin Betancourt

Resume Enclosed

RICARDO AGUILERA

516 Creek Street ◆ Rochester, New York 14625 ◆ (585) 387-7984
E-mail: rick_aguilera@hotmail.com

November 28, 2004

Mr. Ron Recruiter
Managing Partner
Professional Recruiters, Ltd.
1234 Main Street
Rochester, New York 14699

Dear Mr. Recruiter:

Capitalizing on recent success in pharmaceutical sales, plus a ten-year proven track record in business-to-business sales, I am seeking a new professional opportunity where my talents can benefit a leading pharmaceutical firm. Accordingly, I have enclosed a résumé outlining my career.

Some points you may find relevant include:

- *Outstanding ability to build rapport with physicians and medical office staff, which leads to increased access and, ultimately, improved market share for represented drugs.*

- *Demonstrated capacity to organize and execute facilitated meetings, educational opportunities, and e-seminars for physicians and staff, which increase physician access and provide opportunities to promote drugs represented.*

- *Successful experience coordinating efforts with fellow cluster representatives and specialty reps. to collaboratively advance corporate business objectives.*

- *Bilingual fluency in Spanish and English. I am a native speaker of Spanish and am business fluent in English, having lived and worked in the US for ten years. This may be relevant in pursuing business within the growing Hispanic market, both domestically and internationally.*

I am confident that I can contribute to the bottom line success of a pharmaceutical firm in an outside sales, specialty sales, or other account relations management role that requires a dynamic, results-oriented performer. I would enjoy speaking with you or one of your clients in person to discuss how my capabilities can meet someone's current needs, and will follow up with you in the next few days to arrange such a meeting. In the meantime, feel free to contact me via phone or e-mail, should wish to speak with me sooner.

Thank you for your time and consideration. I look forward to talking with you soon.

Sincerely,

Ricardo Aguilera

Enclosure

Career-Marketing #9 (by Don Orlando)

Ana Mercado
5555 Conklin Drive
Montgomery, Alabama 36000   ✉ amma4434@aol.com   ☎ [334] 555-5555 (Home)
                                                           [334] 555-6666 (Pager)

March 24, 2004

Alice Hathaway
Principal
Hathaway & Associates
1800 Century Park West
Suite A
Los Angeles, California 90067-1507

Dear Ms. Hathaway:

I would like to be the BayArea Rapid Transit's "productivity multiplier." Your client calls that position Manager of Labor Relations. The difference is more than semantic.

For more than three years, I've been bringing management and employees – including union workers – closer together. My résumé includes at least eight examples of payoffs I've achieved. Those outcomes have meant better productivity, stronger team work, and enduring capabilities. I have built a culture in which people are rewarded for finding and fixing problems of every kind. In short, I guide people in profitable directions and *have them believe it is their own, good idea*. If that approach and track record appeal to you, I'd like to join BART's human resources team.

My organization has always rewarded me for my success. Now, however, I'm ready to relocate. That's why I am submitting this confidential application. I would be pleased to consider any position with a base salary of $55K with the customary benefits, perks, and severance. As a next step, I'd like to hear about your client's special HR needs. May I call in a few days to set a convenient time?

Sincerely,

Ana Mercado

One enclosure: Résumé

C O N F I D E N T I A L

Career-Marketing #10 (by Pat Kendall)

RICHARD ORTEGA

5555 Market Avenue
San Antonio, Texas 97054

Cell (555) 777-6555
rortega@careerfolio.com

February 12, 2005

Sandra Kenney
New Horizons Marketing Inc.
3455 S.W. Corporate Way
San Antonio, Texas 97033

Dear Ms. Kenney:

Thank you for giving me the opportunity to interview for the position of assistant marketing manager at New Horizons Marketing.

Your hospitality on Tuesday was truly appreciated! Now that I've seen your operation and met your staff, I'm even more confident that my marketing experience and long-term interests are a good match for this position.

As we discussed, my successful track record at Littleton Corporation has given me the team building, strategic planning, and business development skills needed to excel in this role.

I am genuinely excited about joining your marketing team and working with you to tackle the challenges that lie ahead. I appreciate your consideration and look forward to hearing from you once a hiring decision has been made.

Sincerely,

Richard Ortega

Chapter 9

Twenty-first-Century Job Search Strategies with Some Salsa and Merengue

GENERAL CAREER NETWORKING FOR LATINO JOB SEEKERS

According to Richard Nelson Bolles, author of *What Color Is My Parachute*, "Networking is one of the most important—if not the *most* effective—methods that job-seekers need to master to be truly successful in your job-search." Let's examine some of the truths, myths, and realities facing Latino job seekers in today's job market.

Myth: Latinos are not good networkers.

Truth: Because the majority of jobs are filled through networking and referrals, Latinos should add Latino-specific and Latino-receptive employer contacts to their career network to improve their chances of securing interviews.

Reality 1: Latinos *are* adept networkers through family, social, and other cultural experiences.

Reality 2: Many Latinos need to expand their networking skills beyond their cultural comfort zones.

Statistics indicate that the majority of jobs are not advertised or publicly announced but are filled through word-of-mouth or networking (i.e., the "hidden job market"). In addition, as the job level increases, so does the likelihood that the position will be filled through networking or other alternatives.

The focus of Chapters 9–11 is to identify the who, why, and how of successful Latino career networking and job search. One of the advantages of being in the job market now is that there are so many resources available to help you in your search. So, do not put your eggs all in one basket, but use all the sources listed to help make your job search a success. In this chapter, we will provide you with basic information on

- Where the jobs are
- How to research companies that are Latino friendly
- Where to find published job openings
- How to tap into the hidden job market
- Tips on job search networking
- Career fairs

- How to make contact with potential employers
- Secrets of an effective Internet job search
- How to use the telephone effectively
- Follow-up strategies that generate interviews

We have also compiled a comprehensive list of job search and career networking resources available to Latinos—both on and off the Web. You will find the resources organized by subject area in Appendices A–T.

WHERE THE JOBS ARE

There is almost no excuse for not finding current and potential job vacancies. According to the Bureau of Labor Statistics (BLS), there were 114.1 million nonfarm private sector workers in fiscal year 2001 as follows:

- Small businesses with fewer than 500 workers employed 57.1 million.
- Large firms employed 56.9 million.
- Smaller firms with fewer than 100 employees employed 40.9 million.

The BLS predicts that these hiring trends will continue throughout the decade.

Major Corporations and Businesses

Industry leaders report that corporate profits, corporate investments, and productivity are all up. Many companies that avoided hiring in recent years are now finding themselves understaffed as business continues to pick up. BLS projects that total employment will increase 15 percent between 2000 and 2010, or 2.2 million new jobs every year. Only one-third of these jobs will be created by major employers; the rest will be created by small and mid-sized companies.

Small Business

The U.S. Small Business Administration defines small business as an independent business having fewer than 500 employees. This represents more than 99.7 percent of all employers. Approximately 89 percent of the nation's 5.6 million employers have fewer than twenty workers. Small business employers

- Consistently employ more than 50 percent of all private sector employees
- Pay 44.5 percent of total U.S. private payroll
- Employ 39 percent of high-tech workers (e.g., scientists, engineers, and computer workers)
- Generate 70 to 80 percent of new net jobs annually

Another key to the successful job search is learning which industries are likely to experience the greatest job growth in the future. BLS forecasts the major growth areas to be in the computer, service, security, and healthcare industries. The service sector (including business, financial, and social services) will add 20 million new jobs by 2010. Aging baby boomers will have a growth effect on the healthcare industry. The BLS also predicts that the pharmaceutical and biotech industries will need more workers. In order to stay up to date on growth fields and research trends, check with your career *familia*, and your professional network.

COMPANY RESEARCH

The Internet has made researching companies so user friendly that it is available to everyone. It can be as easy as typing in a company name on *Google.com* or another general search engine or using one of the resources listed in this section. Most large and mid-sized companies post employment information, job vacancies, job descriptions, benefits, workplace philosophy, and business information on their Web sites.

Many of the large career portals, jobs sites, and Latino job search engines (*ihispano.com*, *LatPro.com*, and *Saludos.com*) provide company research instructions and Web links to appropriate sites. *Vault.com* and *Wetfeet.com* have searchable company databases. Job seekers can look up a company by name or search by industry, city, state, country, number of employees, and revenue to generate a list of potential employers. Many message boards and Web sites are available to provide the inside scoop on company culture and industry trends.

How can you find the right small employers to target? The INC 500 (*www.inc.com*) is a great starting point. You can access the entire Fortune 500 (*www.fortune.com*) list online. The list is searchable by state or key word, and each listing includes revenue and employee growth over the past five years. Other resources for identifying small emerging companies include local chambers of commerce, newspapers, regional business publications like *Crain's* newspaper (*crains.com*), and your neighborhood newspaper.

Latinos are the fastest growing segment of entrepreneurs and small business owners. The national and local Hispanic Chambers of Commerce can open employment doors not only to their membership but also to the large and small companies they do business with.

When you're planning your job search strategy, broaden your horizons and consider each and every employer in your field, regardless of size. Remember that some small firms will become large firms as new jobs are created.

PUBLISHED JOB OPENINGS

Looking through the classified section of the newspaper for job leads has become a minor thing in the new job search arena. Less than 5 percent of new hires come from these sources. The Newspaper Association of America's preliminary statistic for 2003 shows advertising revenue for employment classified advertising took a hit, dropping to $3.9 billion. This translates into a total 59 percent loss in revenue in three years. Job boards and other online advertising are gaining the major share of employment advertising.

A good source for job postings is found on the Web at sites such as *CareerBuilder.com* and other corporate career Web sites.

TAPPING INTO THE HIDDEN JOB MARKET

Despite all the hype about the multitude of job sites on the Internet and scanning the local and national newspapers, it is widely accepted that more than 75 percent of available job positions are not advertised through the media. These positions include those that will be filled by word of mouth when there is no advertised vacancy yet, but the vacancy is coming and will be advertised soon as a result of changes in companies, such as reorganization, expansion, introduction of new products or services, transfers, and expansion into new markets. It is also possible that a position may open after the receipt of a well-designed and professional résumé or when a referral has revealed a formerly unexpressed need.

Norberto Kogan, CEO of the Kogan Group and a past president of the Hispanic Alliance for Career Enhancement (HACE), observed that "Employers are constantly on the lookout for suitable candidates to replace people who retire, resign, relocate, transfer, depart and get sick to work on new projects or to add expertise in a particular area."

Successful hidden job market candidates are able to connect with the employer's network. Does this mean the employer knows them? Not necessarily. But the candidate comes "pre-recommended" by someone the employer trusts. Networking—using your contacts to connect with the employer's contacts—is the key to the hidden job market.

Job Search Networking

Personal networks and referrals account for more than half of all job placements. This trend continues to grow as companies and job search engines are flooded with oftentimes unmanageable numbers of applicants. Many find they do not have the resources or personnel to sift through the high volume of résumés received for each vacancy announcement. Coca Cola USA receives more than 100,000 Internet applications per month. The secret is to use the hidden job market and network yourself into a position. A personal referral can go a long way in opening the doors to a new opportunity.

Jose Jimenez, a recruiter with Turner Communications, says networking got him his job. He advises, "Be a constant networker. Consistently letting people know what you have accomplished in your career. Not just handing out your résumé. It is amazing how many people will remember you by your story."

Latinos have long used our networking skills to communicate to our extended family network.

Daniel Gutierrez, motivational speaker and author of Stepping into Greatness *says, "Latinos go to a lot of networking events to make friends, we make a lot of friends, but we don't go to do business." Now is the time to turn that communication talent into a resource for your job search.*

The specifics of networking are covered in Chapters 10 and 11.

Career Fairs

Even though many professionals write off career fairs as a means of finding a job, according to a recent SHRM/Career Journal Poll Search Tactics Survey, over 70 percent of human resources departments rely on job fairs to recruit employees. They are great events not only for identifying employment opportunities but also for expanding your network, honing your interview skills, learning industry information, gathering information about companies, and collecting business cards.

In recent years, niche career fairs, particularly diversity career fairs, have grown in popularity. You can also find events for people in your specific career specialty or in your specific industry. A great resource for these types of events is professional association conferences. Most of these events prominently feature workshops to assist the job seeker with hints on how to make your search successful.

We suggest getting to the career fair early and doing your homework on the companies that will be at the career fair. For more information on how to make a career fair work for you, look at the Keys to Driving Your Career Fair Success Checklist at the end of this chapter.

DIRECT CONTACT WITH POTENTIAL EMPLOYERS

Direct contact with a potential employer can be a very effective method of gaining entry into a company. But, before contacting a potential employer, you must do your research on the company to learn about its hiring strategy, diversity program, affinity groups, and other employment-related contacts. Cold calling and sending an unsolicited résumé will garner poor results. To make the most effective use of your time and to provide the employer with a greater understanding of how you can help them, use your network to find the most Latino-receptive people at the company. Then make your contact by telephone, by email, or in person. Most company recruiters say they prefer email versus regular mail.

Keep in mind that each contact is a potential interview, and present yourself in a professional manner. Your résumé, cover letter, and portfolio are your marketing tools and must be an accurate presentation of Brand You. (See Chapters 4, 7, and 8.)

Each industry is different and has its own rules for successful entree into the system. It is up to you to learn the rules of the game.

Manny Leyva, a recent University of Texas film school graduate, was stuck in the "no experience, no job" quandary. Realizing that contacts were key, Leyva posted his name at a local hangout for industry people. He offered his services as a sound technician for free. His resulting new contacts provided him with the experience he needed on his résumé for future employment opportunities. He has since worked on several movie and television productions.

THE EFFECTIVE INTERNET JOB SEARCH

The Internet has become an integral part of job searching. The numbers and kinds of job search engines and sites is growing daily as newspapers transfer their job postings online and companies and professional associations are also joining the online movement. Take advantage of the many sites available, but remember that only 6 percent of jobs are filled through online job sites.

Essential to a successful online job search is the development of keywords in your résumé. As discussed in Chapter 7, you will find keywords in job postings for the industry and job titles you are looking for. You should search major career portals, industry-specific job sites, and Latino search engines. After you have developed your keywords, then begin your search by using the specifications that meet your salary, job function, geographic and other needs.

Your best bet is to move from the more general job sites to the more specific ones. Some popular sites include

- *Monster.com*
- *Hotjobs.com*
- *Flipdog.com*

- America's Job Bank

- *CareerBuilder.com*

In Chapter 10, we discuss specific Latino job search sites and how to use them. A more complete list of job search engines and sites is listed in Appendices I and J.

One of the best things about Internet job searching is that it is active twenty-four hours a day with no vacations or holidays. Another advantage is that it allows you to do all your job search functions in one spot: research, writing, and responding to job postings. But, remember that at some point you need to go out and meet people to create networking contacts that can make a difference in your search.

For guidance on how to post your résumé, read Barron's *e-Résumés* by Pat Criscito and *e-Résumés: Everything You Need to Know*, by Susan Britton Whitcomb and Pat Kendall.

INTERNET JOB SEARCH DOS AND DON'TS

Dos	Don'ts
Do make the Internet a part of your search.	Don't forget to use your other job search and networking tools.
Do scale your search to areas you are interested in.	Don't expect the Internet to provide all your answers.
Do use keywords in your search.	Don't forget to ask for help and use the online guides in finding your keywords.
Do use all possible job sites in your search.	Don't forget to use industry-specific and Latino job sites.
Do prepare a résumé, portfolio, and cover letter in plain text and scannable.	Don't respond to a job posting you are not qualified for. You may be blacklisted.
Do post your résumé and apply for jobs.	Don't forget to follow up.

The best part of the Internet search is when it is successful!

When she moved from Germany to Connecticut, Sonia Camara de la Fuente did not have the contacts to use networking in her job search. De la Fuente reports that her posting on Monster.com *netted her a job using her marketing, technology, and language skills just fifteen miles from her home.*

USING THE TELEPHONE EFFECTIVELY

Good telephone technique is an important skill for your job search. The telephone is an important tool used to contact potential employers and, in more and more instances, for the interview process as well. When you contact the employer, you must be clear in both your message and presentation. You will have a only short window of opportunity to present yourself, your experience, your interest, and your connectivity to the company. Your goal in this conversation will be to secure an interview.

Often the most difficult part of a making a telephone contact is in getting through and around the screening systems that shield the contact source. The following chart shows some of the common telephone contact problems and their solutions.

HELPFUL TELEPHONE NETWORKING HINTS

If	Then
You have a title and first name . . .	Use it.
You have a company affiliation . . .	Use it.
You don't know the full name, title, and address of the decision maker . . .	Get it by calling the company receptionist asking for the person in charge of _____ and requesting to be connected with his/her secretary. Then ask the secretary for the correct spelling, exact title and company address.
You have a referral name from a person, book, register, company Web site . . .	Call the company and check it first because these sources are quickly outdated.
They won't see you in person . . .	Obtain two or three referrals and send your résumé anyway.
They can't think of referrals at the time . . .	Say you'll call back in a few days. By all means, do call back.
You begin to generate conversation . . .	Seize the opportunity to use your two-minute elevator speech and press quickly for a personal interview.
You ask a question . . .	Listen for an answer, don't jump in; learn to tolerate the silence.
He or she needs to call you back . . .	Leave phone number and specific times when you are available; avoid waiting by the phone all day.
The contact indicates that he or she is very busy . . .	Offer to visit at their convenience—early morning or late afternoon. If necessary, ask when you might call back to arrange an appointment at a more convenient time.
The contact will not see you. . . .	Write a gracious letter and ask the contact to call you with the steps you should take to connect with the appropriate person in the company. If you don't hear from the person in a month or so, write a nice follow-up note.
You can't get past the secretary . . .	Try calling before 8:00 A.M. or after 5:00 P.M. when secretaries are typically not there. Tell briefly why you are calling and ask the boss to call back. Busy people often come in early and stay late. They often answer their own phones at these times.
You can't get through to the person you are trying to reach . . .	Have a mutual acquaintance make a phone call on your behalf. Try writing a letter first and follow up with a phone call later on.

FOLLOW-UP STRATEGIES THAT GENERATE INTERVIEWS

Now that you have begun your networking, the next step is how to turn those networking contacts into interviews. Not every person you meet is going to have a job for you, but the broader your network, the more likely you are to run into the "right" person.

The following points can turn contacts into CONTACT:

■ Make sure you mention your job search and areas of interest to everyone you meet. A client of ours said her job lead came from a person she met at a party.

■ Circulate your résumé to friends, career *familia*, and contacts. This way they will have a résumé on hand if they need to forward it to someone.

■ Write letters to promising contacts. In each letter, express your delight in meeting him/her and remind him/her where you met. Take the opportunity to highlight your core professional competencies and successes. And don't forget to ask for an interview.

KEYS TO DRIVING YOUR CAREER FAIR SUCCESS CHECKLIST

The following suggestions will help you make the most of your career conference experience. You may only have time to follow some of this advice. **The primary key is that you are proactive by attending career conferences and networking.**

Preregistration

☐ Many diversity job fairs are *free* if you submit your résumé and complete the registration form. This will eliminate one line you will need to wait in.

Preparation

☐ Research the employers who are attending. Check exhibitor Web sites to learn more about the company, its products, services, and so on.

☐ Map a strategy for working the fair. Determine which employers are a priority for you to visit.

☐ Bring more résumés than you think you need; also bring industry-targeted versions (if you have them). See Chapter 7 for résumé writing advice.

☐ Take your career portfolio (if you have one). These portfolios should include copies of your résumés, samples of your best work, testimonials, evaluations, and a list of references. Even though most career fair interviews are fairly short, there may be opportunities for discussing your portfolio with a recruiter—either over a short break or during a second interview on-site. See Chapter 4.

☐ Think about printing networking business cards with pertinent contact information on one side and a focused mini-résumé on the other.

☐ To keep your résumés neat, carry a folder, portfolio, professional tote, or briefcase with space to keep the business cards, collected materials, and a pad of paper or electronic organizer/PDA for notes.

☐ Dress professionally as you would for an interview and wear comfortable shoes.

☐ Write and practice a thirty-second to two-minute introductory sales pitch/elevator speech/commercial about you. First impressions are critical.

Example: Hand the recruiter a copy of your résumé and be prepared to expand on it quickly! Share basic information about yourself and your career interests like this: "Hello, my name is Marisol Quinones. I have a BA in Business Administration with three years of progressive experience as an account representative with XYZ Corporation in New York. I'd like to talk with you about the senior bilingual marketing positions that your organization is recruiting for. As you can see from my résumé, I have completed the following professional education courses in. . . ."

☐ **Prepare company-specific questions** you want employers to answer. Asking good questions demonstrates your interest in working for the company.

Examples: Can you tell me more about your marketing management training program? What are the career paths in your marketing department? What are the steps in your interview and selection process?

☐ **Prepare Latino-specific questions** you want Latino, minority, or female company representatives to answer. Asking these questions will help you assess how Latino friendly the employer is, points of access to get your foot in the door, and the interview process.

Examples: Do you have a Hispanic or minority employee network? What are the best strategies I can use to improve my chances of getting an interview? Is there someone I can speak with in the business unit I am interested in to get more detailed information on position X or future employment opportunities? What is the profile of the Latino candidates who are hired and retained for this position?

and

You can ask more thorough questions and receive more informative answers on hiring. What are the steps in your interview and selection process? What interview formats do you use (i.e., panel, progressive, behavioral—see Chapter 13)?

☐ Get plenty of sleep so you are rested and energized for the fair. Eat a good meal to keep your energy up. Keep some mints with you—nothing destroys confidence faster than worrying about whether your breath is fresh.

When You Arrive

☐ Arrive early, check in, review the directory and floor plan, walk the exhibit area to get a feel for the conference, and revise your strategy if necessary.

☐ Be confident, display a winning attitude, and stay focused.

☐ Visit the career help center booths to get résumé-writing advice or interviewing tips.

During the Career Fair

☐ Start with your priority employers. Many people get stuck in the stampede at the front. Make your way to where there are representatives waiting for someone to appear.

☐ Be efficient. If you see a booth that has a lot of people at it, don't wait for your turn to talk to the recruiter—simply move on to another booth and go back later, or grab the representative's business card and call him/her after the job fair.

☐ Conduct yourself professionally at all times. Remember that you could be making impressions when you are standing in line or walking the fair.

☐ Do not assume a company does not have open positions in your field. Instead, ask what positions they have available now and anticipate in the future.

☐ Don't judge a booth by its cover. Some of the best opportunities may be at the booths that don't have the nicest looking display. If no other job seekers are present, this is a great opportunity to talk one on one with the recruiter. You also stand a better chance of being remembered.

☐ Observe recruiters from a distance or while you are waiting in line. Once you've scoped out the kind of person you're about to face, you can mentally prepare for the interview or conversation that you're about to have. Watching the job seekers in line ahead of you will give you some idea of what to expect.

☐ Make personal connections. Approach exhibitors with a smile while making direct eye contact and offering a full, firm handshake. Introduce yourself as you practiced earlier. Express your interest by demonstrating knowledge about the organization. Relate your skills, professional interests, and experiences to the specific needs of the employer. Relax and speak slowly and confidently. Listen carefully, and ask relevant questions about the company and the positions. Ask what they look for in an ideal job candidate. This is not the time to ask salary related questions. Make a human connection.

☐ Before you leave the booth, get appropriate contact information, request a business card, and ask the representative what the next step is, how to follow up, and the like.

☐ Take notes on the back of the recruiter's business card, your note pad, or electronic organizer. Write down important details about the company, including names of people who may not have had business cards. Take a few minutes after you leave each table to jot down these notes!

☐ Use the career fair to polish your interviewing skills. Pay close attention to the popular questions that you may not have anticipated, and prepare answers to those questions in future interviews.

☐ Network with other job seekers and Hispanic professional associations. Talk to others while you are standing in line to exchange job-hunting ideas, provide support, and identify employment leads.

☐ Visit the career help center booths for a résumé critique, career management advice, job search assistance, and interviewing coaching.

☐ Take a break to review the literature you have picked up and identify additional questions you may have.

☐ Before leaving the career fair, head back to the booths where you have some interest. Remind the recruiter of your interest. Thank the recruiter for his/her time, and be clear that you'll be in touch soon. Your follow-up contact demonstrates professionalism. There is a good chance that you will leave a lasting impression that will serve you well.

After the Career Fair

☐ Immediately send a thank-you note and reconfirm interest in the position and company. If possible, address the company's hiring needs, state your qualifications, and express your desire for a second interview.

☐ Send a letter(s) to the company's Hispanic Network, Equal Employment Opportunity/ Affirmative Action (EEO/AA) manager, and/or vice president of diversity as well as other contacts you have made at the company. Attach a copy of your résumé and any thank-you notes you sent to company staff.

☐ Within a week, follow up with a well-rehearsed phone call, unless you were specifically instructed not to.

Chapter 10

Latino-Specific Job Search Strategies and Resources to Access Employment Opportunities

Myth: Latino and diversity career fairs, job search engines, and professional associations are a waste of time. Employers are not serious, and the organizations are ineffective.

Truth: Employers participate in Latino-specific job fairs, Internet job search engines, and other organizations as an effective means to recruit the Latino applicant and community. Companies have realized that to remain competitive in their industries, they need to build credibility with and aggressively reach out to the Latino job seeker, not wait for them to be approached.

Reality 1: A poll by Hispanic job board *LatPro.com* and the National Society of Hispanic Professionals found that about 64 percent of job seekers got their jobs through networking or niche employment Web sites.

Reality 2: Latino-specific/Latino-receptive job search and networking resources have effectively contributed to the employment of millions of Hispanics. Our professional associations, services, programs, and employment resources continue to evolve their own brands of excellence. The majority of employers that partner with Latino job search-related organizations are legitimately hiring Hispanics or are scrutinized if they do not.

For many people the idea of networking at an event with a large number of people can be intimidating. How can you make an impact when there are hundreds of other applicants at a job fair? Or, how can you make your résumé stand out from the thousands posted daily on a job search engine?

In this chapter we will discuss

- Latino and diversity job fairs

- Latino and diversity job search engines

- Latino professional associations

- Mainstream professional associations/trade organization Hispanic subcommittees

- Unions

- Latino college and university resources for alumni and former and current students

- Hispanic search firms

■ Hispanic leadership, economic development, and employment and training organizations

■ Personal networks

We will discuss some of these and other external resources that are available to you in your job search. We will also provide you with recommendations on how to overcome your fears and come out the winner in the networking game.

Se aprende haciendo. (We learn by doing.)

LATINO AND DIVERSITY JOB FAIRS

Diversity job fairs are designed to attract minorities, women, and people with disabilities. Hispanic professional associations, company-based employee organizations, college alumni associations, campus groups, and community-based employment organizations sponsor career recruiting events (i.e., career fairs) that target Latinos.

Hispanic and diversity job fairs offer many opportunities to leverage cultural expertise and language skills. At these fairs you will be able to

■ Make Latino-friendly employer contacts

■ Meet a Latino from the company that you can follow up with

■ Ask detailed questions on company-specific access strategies and hiring processes

■ Find recruiters/headhunters who unofficially attend the fair to identify Latino candidates

■ Network with other Latinos attending the event on job search strategies

■ Take advantage of job search assistance and résumé-writing critiques available through these venues

Liza Canino was finishing up her MBA and was working at a not-for-profit agency. She attended the HACE career fair with a good résumé. She says, "my résumé spoke for me" and the Walgreen's representatives asked her to contact a recruiter. She was offered a position and turned it down because it was a poor "fit." A few months later, she was called back and offered a position as a marketing analyst, which she accepted. Liza's success was doubled when she was promoted to senior business analyst within a year.

You can learn more about Hispanic and diversity job fairs by using the following Internet and Web search strategies:

■ General search engines like Google, Lycos, and Yahoo—Use any of the following as search terms: "Diversity Job Fairs," "Hispanic Job Fairs," or "Latino Job Fairs."

■ General job search engines, including *Monster.com, CareerBuilder.com, CareerJournal. com*, and the National Association of Colleges and Employers' *JobWeb.com*

■ Hispanic and Diversity job search engines such as *Latpro.com, Saludos.com, DiversityInc.com*, and *ihispano.com*

Note: In your Web search you may substitute the word "career" for "job." Also try other word combinations with the search engines.

- Hispanic professional associations and community-based employment organizations, including Hispanic Alliance for Career Enhancement (*HACE-USA.org*), National Society of Hispanic Professionals (*NSHP.org.*), Society of Hispanic Professional Engineers (*SHPE.org*), National SER Jobs for Progress (*SER.org*), and the American GI Forum (*AmericanGIForum.org*)

- College and university diversity/Hispanic alumni associations, student services, career centers, and student organizations

- Company Web sites

An events calendar or job fair link usually appears on the preceding three sites.

LATINO AND DIVERSITY JOB SEARCH ENGINES

Hispanic and diversity job search engines are an excellent resource for identifying job listings targeted to Latino and minority candidates. These openings tend to be more viable than those found in many of the general job search engines. Companies that list vacancies on these job search sites tend to be more Latino friendly in their hiring.

Virginia Ojeda, president of Midan, Inc., and president of the Mexican American Chamber of Commerce in Chicago, stressed that "it is absolutely critical for Latinos to not only use the Internet in their job search but to be smart about it. Be sure to use Latino-based key words and Latino or diversity job sites."

After you have identified potential employment opportunities, submit your résumé and immediately follow up with the employer using appropriate contacts recommended earlier in this chapter. Send both electronic and hard copies of your targeted cover letter and résumé. See Chapter 9 for detailed Internet strategies.

You should also connect with any employer of interest that posts jobs on the site even if there is not a current vacancy that meets your needs. The company may have vacancies in the future.

Here are some popular Hispanic and diversity job search engines:

- **Hirediversity.com** has separate news channels of interest to different populations with employment listings combined in one job bank.

- **iHispano.com** is a leading career site for Hispanic and bilingual professionals with job listings, career advice, networking events, and an e-newsletter.

- **LatPro.com** is one the largest Hispanic and bilingual job sites and diversity career boards in the Americas.

- **Saludos.com** primarily lists bilingual/bicultural positions. The site offers a Career Pavilion for researching career fields, mentor profiles, career guides, job search information, résumé posting, job search agents, job fairs, and career links.

- **Telemundo.com/empleos** is a career site for Hispanics/Latinos with job listings and career advice.

- **Joblatino.com** allows job seekers to post their résumés, offers interview tips, and provides job postings by state.

Rudy S. Martinez, CEO of *ihispano.com*, offers this advice for job seekers who are utilizing job search engines: "You've got to do more than just post your résumé with a

Latino search engine. You have to become known. Refresh your profile and résumé at least once every sixty days, preferably every thirty." Martinez adds, "Some companies like Nike are receiving 30,000 résumés a month. They do not have the staff to review them all. Latino job search engines can help them sift through and make real progress on their diversity goals."

W. Pedrero, a magazine editor, writes: "By the time I came across LatPro, I had been searching for a job for more than 3 months without any success. The job market, needless to say, is downright brutal and I was beginning to lose hope. I found LatPro, applied for a position that interested me and I got an immediate response and the job! I think the service is essential and highly successful in placing Hispanics in companies where their ethnic diversity is welcome and treated as an asset, not a handicap, which I found to be the case with most other job search websites."

A comprehensive list of Hispanic and diversity job search engines, with contact information, appears in Appendix J.

HISPANIC/LATINO PROFESSIONAL ASSOCIATIONS

Hispanic professional associations can play a pivotal role in maximizing career opportunities for Latinos. Many organizations sponsor career centers, job postings, career fairs, professional development, mentoring, networking, professional and student chapters, scholarships, research, advocacy, profession-related resources, benefits programs, and social functions. The groups often maintain strategic partnerships with employers that hire from their specialized career fields.

Manny Espinoza, CPA and CEO of the Association of Latino Professionals in Finance and Accounting (ALPFA), explains that even though their main mission is to build Hispanic leadership in accounting, finance and other related fields, opportunities to build employment-related relationships with corporations have grown due to the talented, experienced Latino professionals on their membership list. In fact, Espinoza said some companies use ALPFA as their own affinity group because they do not have a large number of Latinos on board.

A few national organizations, like the Hispanic Alliance for Career Enhancement, serve as umbrella organizations for Latino professionals and often as joint venture programs with other Hispanic professional groups. HACE's Career Continuum chart (Figure 10.1) is representative of the range of services offered by Latino professional associations.

A sample list of professional associations follows:

- Association of Latino Professionals in Finance and Accounting (ALPFA)
- Coalition of Hispanic Police Associations (CHAPA)
- Hispanic National Bar Association (HNBA)
- National Association of Hispanic Federal Executives, Inc. (NAHFE)
- National Association of Hispanic Journalists (NAHJ)
- National Association of Hispanic Nurses (NAHN)
- National Association of Hispanic Real Estate Professionals (NAHREP)

- National Association of Puerto Rican and Hispanic Social Workers (NAPRHSW)
- Society of Hispanic Professional Engineers (SHPE)

A comprehensive list of Hispanic professional associations with contact information is included in Appendix K.

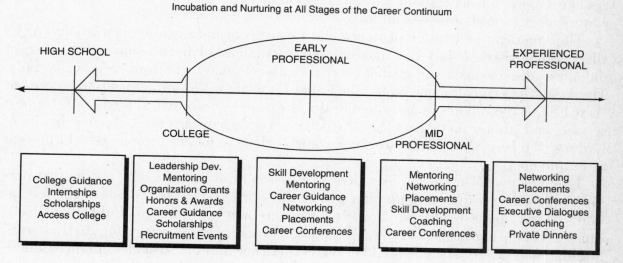

Figure 10.1. Range of Services Offered by Latino Professional Organizations.
Example provided by the Hispanic Alliance for Career Enhancement.

TRADITIONAL INDUSTRY, BUSINESS PROFESSIONAL ASSOCIATIONS/TRADE ORGANIZATIONS

Hispanic Subcommittees

As discussed in Chapter 9, a key job search resource is membership in or at least contacting mainstream professional associations. Many professional and trade organizations have diversity and Hispanic task forces, subcommittees, or caucuses that represent the concerns of the Latino membership. These special interest programs also work to increase the number of Latino professionals in their respective fields. Officers and members of the groups can become excellent connections.

One example is REFORMA, an affiliate of the American Library Association (ALA) formed in 1971. Carol Brey, president of ALA, explains that a large number of librarians are nearing retirement, and unless the new generation of librarians is expanded in the minority community, there will be a shortage of librarians in the future. REFORMA has actively sought the recruitment of more bilingual and bicultural library professionals and support staff. REFORMA also offers a job link and scholarship program for students interested in library sciences.

You can find mainstream professional associations and trade organizations on the Internet, at the library, at the college/alumni career center, and in the telephone directory.

Unions

Unions, along with companies that have collective bargaining agreements, are working to address the need for corporate competitiveness in Hispanic local and global markets and the needs of the growing Latino workforce. Labor management committees have successfully negotiated bilingual skills requirements for selected positions. It is also important to note that unions serve professionals and technical employees, office workers and laborers, teachers and teamsters, firefighters and farm workers, engineers and editors, doctors and nurses—and more.

The American Federation of Labor and Congress of Industrial Organizations (AFL-CIO) is comprised of sixty-five national and international labor unions representing 13 million working women and men of every race and ethnicity and from every walk of life. The AFL-CIO's constituency group, the Labor Council for Latin American Advancement (LACLA), is the union's main bridge to the Hispanic professional, skilled craft, support service, and laborer members. The AFL-CIO is working toward the full participation of Latinos. Ten percent of Latina working women belong to unions compared to 11 percent of Latino men.

Linda Chavez-Thompson, executive vice president of the AFL-CIO, is the first person to hold the position and the first person of color to be elected to one of the federation's three highest offices. Born to sharecropper parents in Lubbock, Texas, Chavez-Thompson began her trade union career as union secretary for the Laborers' International Union. She has used her own experience and the struggles of other Latinos to create opportunities for all Latinos.

Chavez-Thompson says, "In the past 10 years, we have made great progress to diversify not only the leadership but also their staff, to the point that we see more women and people of color not just in organizing departments, but also in education, research and all other areas."

In 2001, The American Federation of State, County, and Municipal Employees (AFSCME) implemented a Hispanic leadership and training program directed to implement job recruitment and membership recruitment, to increase union leadership ranks, and to address Latino-specific issues. The Teamsters Hispanic Caucus serves a similar function. Both unions are also active in promoting economic development and education in Latino communities.

You can contact Hispanic leadership, caucuses, stewards, and representatives by communicating directly with the unions or checking out their Web sites that are listed in Appendix R.

LATINO COLLEGE AND UNIVERSITY RESOURCES FOR ALUMNI, FORMER AND CURRENT STUDENTS

Colleges and universities offer alumni, former students without degrees, and current students a wide array of career networking resources and employment services. Key contacts include Latino-specific and diversity alumni associations, offices of student services, student centers, student associations, fraternities/sororities, faculty and staff that are discussed in Chapter 4.

Yolanda Rodriguez, Ph.D. and vice president of institutional advancement/alumni relations at the University of Texas at El Paso, relates that the president of the Dallas UTEP alumni chapter was contacted by another alumnus seeking his assistance in hiring an acquaintance. The young woman had been attending a local community college in Dallas for three years and was going nowhere. After hiring her, the president quickly realized how bright she was and heard her speak of getting a bachelor's degree. He arranged through the alumni relations office to have her attend UTEP. As a Mexican national the young woman required extra help with her enrollment. With the help of the alumni office, she gained entrance to the university and employment on campus as well.

Latino-specific and diversity college and university resources include

- Hispanic Association of Colleges and Universities (HACU)
- Latino Alumni Association Network (LAAN)
- Association of Latino Alumni (ALA)
- National Association of Latino Fraternal Organizations (NALFO)
- Offices of multicultural, minority, and Latino student services
- Hispanic/Latino student centers
- Strategic Alliance of Latino Student Associations (SALSA)
- Latino faculty and staff

Dr. Antonio Flores, president and CEO of HACU, points to the importance of organizations like HACU in advancing your career. He says HACU offers the largest and best internship program in the nation serving nearly 700 interns yearly, a faculty development program, and a special leadership program for university and college administrators who are interested in becoming presidents and CEO's of institutions of higher learning.

A comprehensive list of Hispanic/Latino college and university resources and contact information appears in Appendices A–D.

Latino/Diversity Headhunters, Search Firms, Staffing Agencies, and Recruiters

Many employers contract the services of Latino-specific and diversity-focused recruiters to target Hispanic applicants. Several jobs that would normally not be outsourced to a traditional staffing agency are listed because of the employer's need to use effective sources that can attract well qualified, bilingual/bicultural candidates.

Working with Latino and diversity firms can add significant value to your job search, if managed well. The pros and cons of using search firms are discussed in Chapter 9. *Remember that recruiters work for the employer.*

Here are a few tips to improve the likelihood that recruiters will take an interest in you and to make the most of the relationship you establish with them:

- Have marketable industry, cultural, and bilingual skills that the firm specializes in.

- Be recommended to the search firm by someone who has contracted the agency's services, a former job seeker the firm has worked with, or a networking contact who has a connection with the recruiter.

- Contact headhunters before you need them to develop the recruiter's interest and a good working relationship early. Use a strong cover letter and résumé targeted to address why the particular recruiter should be interested in you and emphasize your assets that can be sold to an employer. (See cover letter and résumé samples in Chapters 7 and 8.)

- Work only with recruiters you trust. Make use of the recruiter's expertise and seek feedback on how to improve your marketability.

Be wary of any search firm that offers services for a fee.

To check out industries of specialization and the reputability of recruiters, check with the National Association of Executive Recruiters or the Better Business Bureau.

LATINO LEADERSHIP, ECONOMIC DEVELOPMENT, AND EMPLOYMENT AND TRAINING ORGANIZATIONS

Hispanic leadership and economic development advocacy organizations work to ensure corporate responsibility and market reciprocity for the nation's Latino population. One such group is the Hispanic Association on Corporate Responsibility (HACR), a coalition of the nation's leading Hispanic organizations representing all sectors and corporate membership ranging from American Airlines through WalMart. HACR's mission is "to ensure the inclusion of Hispanics in Corporate America at a level commensurate with our economic contributions. HACR focuses on four areas of corporate economic activity and refers to them as indicators of corporate responsibility and 'Market Reciprocity.' They are: Employment, Procurement, Philanthropy, and Governance."

National Hispanic employment and training organizations with affiliates throughout the United States and local or community-based organizations provide skill development, career services, and job fairs, and host on-site recruiting events. The organizations partner with major corporations, local chambers of commerce, and area businesses to identify and fill employer needs.

You can find employment information, listings of corporate partners, and contacts at each organization's Web site or by contacting them directly. A sample list of organizations follows:

- American GI Forum
- Hispanic Association on Corporate Responsibility
- Mexican American Legal Defense Fund
- National Council of La Raza
- National Hispana Leadership Institute
- National Puerto Rican Forum, Inc.
- SER—Jobs for Progress National, Inc.
- United States Hispanic Leadership Institute

James Parsons, executive director of SER—Jobs for Progress National, Inc., says, "We like to say that we help people find jobs." SER runs fifty One-Stop centers in five states. Parsons adds that the involvement of SER affiliates in the One-Stop process is good for the community because Latinos know that if they go to a SER One-Stop for service they will be helped.

A comprehensive list of Hispanic economic development and career development organizations appears in Appendices M and O.

BACK TO PERSONAL NETWORKS

No quiero que me den, solo que me pongan cerca de donde hay. (I don't want to be given anything, just place me close to where it is.)

In Chapter 9 we stressed that personal contact is one of the key items in securing an interview. Along with the contacts at the employer level, it is very important to look to your personal connections to provide you with that extra insight you need to get that dream job.

As Latinos, we have much experience dealing with extended family networks. Now is the time to redirect that network to your advantage. Arabel Alva Rosales, an entrepreneur who leads several successful businesses including Alva Rosales & Rauthbord, LLC, a public relations and marketing firm that specializes in women and Latino markets, says, "One of the things we tend to forget is that our parents and their friends also have contacts. Expand your network to fit in the business associates of your family." She says, "We can do this by keeping them up to date with our activities through notes, phone calls, lunches, or inviting them to certain events. That way when it is appropriate or needed, they may think of us upon referring the 'right person.'" She adds, "There might be ten different applicants that have applied, but the personal contact from someone that the employer knows and trusts can make all the difference."

It is often through the family network that Latinos gain their first job. It is a "tried and true" tradition that as one person gets their foot in the door, your *primos* and *primas* (cousins) will soon follow.

Make sure you tell everyone you know that you are looking for employment and what type of position you are seeking. These personal connections can open up a wide range of potential job leads. Forward your résumé to contacts and ask them to share it with appropriate decision makers. This is also a great time to ask your contacts if you can use them as future references.

Churches often serve as a point of contact for members of the Latino community, and many companies are using the church as an outlet for communication and recruitment. Church members come from many backgrounds with wide experience at many levels of the job market. Some churches also host job recruitment events to help members secure employment.

Look at all the professional, social, religious, and economic (i.e., stores, restaurants, banks) organizations in your life as possible career networks.

Example: A young associate of ours reports that he got his job lead from his basketball league team members, many of whom were attorneys. He now works for the state attorney general's office.

The development of your personal network not only will serve you in your job search but can also become a support network after you are employed.

LATINO SPECIFIC JOB SEARCH STRATEGIES AND RESOURCES TO ACCESS EMPLOYMENT OPPORTUNITIES CHECKLIST

Latino and Diversity Job Fairs

☐ These fairs are designed to attract minorities, women, and people with disabilities.

☐ Be sure to do your research on what companies will be attending the job fair.

☐ Meet a Latino from the company that you can use for future contact.

☐ Take advantage of job search assistance and résumé writing critiques that are often available at these events.

☐ Follow the guidelines in the Keys to Driving Your Career Fair Checklist in Chapter 9.

Latino and Diversity Job Search Engines

☐ Job postings on Latino and diversity job search engines are more viable for Latino job seekers.

☐ Post your résumé and make sure to use keywords relative to your search area.

☐ Use keywords to highlight your cultural and language skills.

☐ Refresh your profile and résumé at least every sixty days.

☐ Take advantage of the résumé and other job search services offered by the search engine companies.

Hispanic/Latino Professional Associations

☐ Find a Latino professional association in your career track.

☐ Investigate to see if the association sponsors a career center.

☐ Take advantage of the professional development, mentoring, and other services offered.

☐ Consider becoming an active member or officer.

☐ Use the opportunity to add members to your career *familia*.

Traditional Industry and Business Professional Associations/Trade Organizations Hispanic Subcommittees

☐ Mainstream professional associations often have diversity or Hispanic subcommittees.

☐ One of the main purposes of these subcommittees is to increase the number of Latinos in the profession.

☐ Scholarship opportunities are often available for college students who wish to study in the particular industry or profession.

Unions

☐ Unions serve professional and technical employees, office workers, teachers, and other professional groups as well as laborers.

☐ The AFL-CIO is the largest association representing sixty-five unions and representing 13 million working men and women.

☐ The development of Hispanic leadership and training programs has opened new opportunities for Latino membership.

☐ Ten percent of working Latinas and 11 percent of working Latinos belong to unions.

Latino College and University Resources for Alumni and Former and Current Students

☐ The alumni network offers unique opportunities for former and current students to make connections and develop networking and employment opportunities.

☐ Latinos underutilize the services offered by alumni associations and offices of student services.

☐ For college students, it is important to visit the student services office and career placement office beginning in your freshman year to learn of the services they offer. Do not wait until your senior year.

☐ Become a known quantity at the career services office.

☐ The Hispanic Association of Colleges and Universities runs the largest internship program in the nation offering nearly 700 internships yearly.

☐ Participate in student associations connected to professional associations because they offer networking and employment opportunities after graduation.

☐ Make a connection with Latino faculty and staff to gain their support and potential employment connections.

Hispanic/Diversity Headhunters, Search Firms, Staffing Agencies, and Recruiters

☐ Hispanic and diversity search firms are excellent contacts in your job search because they are usually focused on searching out qualified Latino applicants.

☐ Make sure you have marketable industry, cultural, and bilingual skills that the firm specializes in before contacting them.

☐ Contact a former client or other networking contact who can recommend you to the search firm.

Latino-Specific Job Search Strategies and Resources

☐ Use a strong cover letter and résumé targeted to address why the recruiter should be interested in you and how your assets can be sold to the employer.

☐ Be wary of any search firm that offers services for a fee.

Hispanic Leadership, Economic Development, and Employment and Training Organizations

☐ Hispanic leadership and economic development organizations use their corporate contacts to ensure corporate responsibility and market reciprocity for Latinos.

☐ National employment and training organizations provide skill development, career services, job fairs, and on-site recruiting events.

☐ Local chambers of commerce offer networking opportunities and potential employment sources from their membership.

Personal Networks

☐ Look to your personal connections for employment opportunities and contacts.

☐ Remember that a personal recommendation can make the difference in securing an interview and employment.

☐ Keep in contact with your extended family contacts through notes, phone calls, lunches, and other means to keep them up to date on your job search.

☐ Be sure to tell everyone you know that you are looking for employment and what type of position you are looking for.

☐ Churches and religious-affiliated organizations can serve as points of contact for networking opportunities.

☐ Development of your personal network can transform into a support network after you are employed.

Chapter 11

Latino Job Search Strategies and Resources Available Through Employers

Myth: There are few resources at companies that will assist Latinos to secure job interviews, get hired, and achieve promotions. Reaching out to Latino-specific resources at employers does not help because Latinos do not help and support each other.

Truth: Companies are creating formal resources to expand their Latino workforce. As these companies hire more Latinos, there are also increasing numbers of individuals willing to help us successfully get past employment opportunity gatekeepers.

Reality 1: The most important part of effectively using Latino sources within a company is crafting your communication into a two-way street. Ask for advice or contacts but remember to offer your services and follow through if asked. Convey your personal career brand, seek advice, identify key company contacts, and establish collaborative relationships.

Reality 2: Not every networking encounter will be immediately productive at the moment. But the broader your base of contacts becomes, the more opportunities for connecting the right source for your job search.

FOLLOWING LESS TRAVELED JOB SEARCH ACCESS ROADS

Some of the many company-based access roads available to Latinos are so obvious that we may have overlooked them. Being willing to ask for directions may mean the difference between securing an interview or joining the thousands of applicants who crash into the résumé pile-up at a dead end sign.

Remember, we can leverage our cultural and language assets because the Latinos who came before us learned how to navigate the barriers, and ultimately, opened up avenues for access and upward mobility.

In this chapter we will discuss the following company-based resources:

- Diversity and Hispanic recruitment programs
- Offices of corporate diversity
- Diversity councils
- Equal Employment Opportunity/Affirmative Action
- Diversity/Hispanic employment programs

- Hispanic employee networks/affinity groups
- The Latino management team
- Supplier diversity programs
- Hispanic consumer programs
- Individual Latino employees at companies

WHAT KIND OF LATINO-SPECIFIC/LATINO-RECEPTIVE RESOURCES CAN EMPLOYERS PROVIDE?

The study "Diversity Recruitment Report 2003" (prepared by WetFeet, Inc.) details the extensive measures used by companies to attract and retain minority employees. According to WetFeet's findings, some companies spend as much as 70 percent of their recruiting budgets on minority recruiting activities. Other companies are establishing programs to develop potential employees as early as high school. This type of investment shows that diversity recruiting remains a critical focus for companies.

Employer-based Latino job search access roads range from formal company operations dedicated to diversity employment, minority business suppliers, and Hispanic consumers—all the way to individual frontline Latino staff.

"I think contact is everything," says Patricia L. Garza, Manager of Corporate Contributions and past co-president of the Hispanic Employee Council at Kraft Foods, Inc. "You have to make a list of the best contacts you know or can find at the company where you are applying for employment. Even if it's the Human Resource manager and you may have only met them at a job fair, you have still met them. You have to contact whoever can help you differentiate your résumé from the pile of résumés the employer receives."

It is important to remember when contacting these resources that networking is about cultivating relationships. It is not a "taking experience." Information must be shared with your contacts: let them know about you and your brand and make it a win-win situation for both of you.

What follows is a list of resources to facilitate your internal entrée into your company of choice.

DIVERSITY AND HISPANIC RECRUITMENT PROGRAMS

Offices of diversity and Hispanic recruiting, human resources department's minority recruitment programs, and individuals assigned to Hispanic recruitment are directly accountable for recruiting Latino candidates. Hiring initiatives can focus on either vacancy-based hiring strategies or long-term development of Latino talent pools.

To fill immediate and other vacancies scheduled to be filled in the near future, recruiters can be reached at direct phone numbers, locations, and email addresses. They host or participate in diversity and Hispanic job fairs, dedicated Web-based recruitment sites, and advertising. These are the people who should be among your first contacts at the company. Their mission is to recruit well-qualified Latino candidates—*Aproveche la oportunidad* (Take advantage of the opportunity).

Long-term diversity recruitment efforts are often based on relationship building with national and local organizations that promote the interests of minority groups. Companies provide scholarships, knowledge sharing, mentoring, and recruiting opportunities. They collaborate with the minority not-for-profit employment organizations, professional associations, and targeted programs at colleges and universities.

Using these networking sources can provide direct links to hiring authorities who are specifically interested in reaching Latino applicants. Deborah Prior, a recruiter with Aetna Insurance Company, tells her recruiters to search through the résumés they receive for connections to specific Hispanic organizations. She says, "You must be deliberate if you want to recruit for diversity."

OFFICE OF CORPORATE DIVERSITY AFFAIRS

The vice president of diversity manages a company's diversity practices, focusing on recruiting, succession planning, and accountability for diversity initiatives. This senior executive oversees diversity councils, employee networks, consumer markets, and supplier programs. The vice president often reports to the president of the company and the board of directors.

Offices of corporate diversity facilitate proactive and integrated approaches to ensuring diversity in all business practices. Representatives from these offices support division management in creating tailored diversity initiatives that fit business needs, and serve as recruitment and retention consultants.

DIVERSITY COUNCILS

Diversity councils typically include employees from all levels of the organization, from various functional areas, with diverse backgrounds. A senior vice president often chairs the company-wide diversity council. In large corporations, you may find additional councils operating at the business unit and at regional and local levels.

Diversity councils work to

■ Review data from cultural audits

■ Create diversity plans

■ Offer ideas and recommendations

■ Implement agreed-on changes

■ Recognize and track progress

Activities may include

■ Orientation and training programs

■ Career development systems, mentor programs, and internal job fairs

■ Policy development

■ Lunch discussion or feedback sessions

■ Recruitment and retention programs

EQUAL EMPLOYMENT OPPORTUNITY/AFFIRMATIVE ACTION OFFICE

The Equal Employment Opportunity/Affirmative Action (EEO/AA) office coordinates and monitors employers' affirmative action/equal opportunity efforts to ensure compliance with the Americans with Disabilities Act, Title VII of the 1964 Civil Rights Act, Executive Order 11246 and other relevant state and federal statutes.

EEO/AA offices typically provide the following services:

- Guidance and advice to business units, employees, and the public on a company's nondiscrimination and affirmative action policies and procedures

- Assistance with recruitment and retention activities

- Investigation and resolution of discrimination complaints

Larger companies have corporate-wide EEO/AA directors, business unit or regional EEO/AA managers, and local or facility EEO/AA officers.

FINDING DIVERSITY-FRIENDLY AND LATINO COMPANY CONTACTS ON THE INTERNET

Most large employers offer employment and diversity pages on their Web sites. These pages can provide the information you need to connect with the Latino-friendly contacts mentioned earlier.

Many company Web sites look like our fictitious corporation, Latino Friendly Company, Inc. (see Figure 11.1). In our example, review each of the highlighted words. Clicking on **Careers** should provide you with most of the information you need. You should also try clicking on **Site Map** to find any additional useful contacts.

HISPANIC EMPLOYMENT PROGRAMS

Latino-specific employment programs can be found in private, government, educational, and not-for-profit sectors. One of the earliest initiatives, the Hispanic Employment Program (HEP), was established in 1970 to focus specifically on the needs of Hispanic Americans in federal employment. Over the next two decades, the HEP evolved into a national model for all employers.

HEP has three overall objectives:

1. Eliminate discrimination practices and disparate treatment in the workplace.

2. Ensure that Hispanic Americans are represented throughout the workforce at all grade levels and occupations.

3. Provide information on employment, training, and educational opportunities to all individuals seeking such opportunities.

Every U.S. government agency has an HEP office or an HEP manager who can be contacted. The U.S. government is the largest single employer in the country. The Office of Personnel Management reports that more than 2,704,959 civilians are employed full- and part-time nationwide.

LATINO FRIENDLY COMPANY, INC.

HOME • SITE MAP • LOCATIONS • CONTACT US • CAREERS

Overview

Job Search

Submit Your Résumé

Résumé Builder

Benefits and Work/Life

Diversity

Diversity Fact Sheets

Leaders Shaping the Company

Diversity Recruiting Events

Corporate Partnerships

Supplier Diversity Program

Our Organization

University Recruiting

Corporate Directory

Diversity Fact Sheets

Explore our commitment to diversity through the following fact sheets:

Diversity Inclusion and Fact Sheet

Hispanic Fact Sheet

Diversity Inclusion and Fact Sheet

We are proud of our legacy, which distinguishes Latino Friendly Company as a corporate leader in the area of diversity and equal employment opportunity. At Latino Friendly Company, our policy, as well as our practice, is to ensure that our environment fosters an inclusive corporate culture and is free of discrimination.

As evidence of its commitment to diversity and inclusion, Latino Friendly Company:

- Established a 20 member Executive Diversity Advisory Council, consisting of representatives from major businesses and support units throughout the company, which sets the direction and guides the implementation for diversity and inclusion at Latino Friendly Company.
- Has more than 30 Diversity Business Councils operating in various business lines to address diversity and inclusion issues within their respective businesses.
- Has company-supported affinity groups of associates with common interests, that meet periodically to network and support one another's development and success.
- Has women and minority representation on the Corporate Management Council, which is responsible for the development and implementation of strategic, financial and talent plans at Latino Friendly Company.
- Minorities and women also serve as presidents for lines of business and in key markets nationwide.

Management Operating Committee.

- Ensures senior executive management develops accountable annual goals to increase diversity in their businesses and has incentive pay tied to progress in hiring, promoting and retaining minorities.
- Partners with national and local multicultural professional associations to recruit new talent and develop new business relationships. Sponsor of over 20 national minority organizations.
- Named to 20 national publications as one of the Top Companies for Minorities.

For additional information contact: **Senior Vice President of Diversity,**
Latino Friendly Company, Inc.
1 LFC Plaza, mail code 1234
Los Angeles, CA 90001
(800) 000-0000
lfcdiversity@latinofriendlycompany.com

Hispanic Fact Sheet*

We embrace Hispanic culture and take pride in serving Hispanic consumers, who have an estimated buying power of $580.5 billion. Providing increased services to Hispanic consumers is a strategic business priority for the corporation, which recognizes that this segment of the U.S. population has long been underserved by the service industry.

Here are just some of the ways we are working aggressively to apply our resources to meet the needs of individuals, families, businesses, and communities:

Serving Hispanic customers

- Throughout its markets, Latino Friendly Company staffs its business centers with **bilingual, Spanish-speaking managers, supervisors and associates**.
- Latino Friendly Company provides all communications in English and Spanish languages including automated call centers and websites.

Practicing culturally and ethnically diverse employment

- Latino Friendly Company has been named every year to *Hispanic Magazine's* **Corporate 100** list for providing the most opportunities for Hispanics and contributing to the advancement of the Hispanic community in the areas of recruitment and hiring, scholarships, minority business development and support for Hispanic organizations.
- Latino Friendly Company has been ranked by *Latina Style* magazine as one of the **top 50 companies in America** for **Hispanic women** to work.
- To increase career opportunities for Hispanics, the bank partners with the **Hispanic Alliance For Career Enhancement**, and supports the **Hispanic Scholarship Fund** with need-based scholarships. Latino Friendly Company Senior Vice President of Operations, Rose Mary Bombela, is a member of the Hispanic Scholarship Fund board of directors.
- In the 1990's, Latino Friendly Company formed an ongoing partnership with the **Hispanic Association on Corporate Responsibility** to ensure the inclusion of Hispanics in Corporate America.
- Latino Friendly Company was honored by leading woman- and minority-owned businesses as one of the premier companies promoting **multicultural business opportunities** in a survey conducted by Div2000.com, a business-to-business Internet portal that serves as an information center for multicultural businesses.

Contacts
Latin American Team Inclusion National Organization (L.A.T.I.N.O.)
Latino Friendly Company, Inc.
1 LFC Plaza, mail code 5555
Los Angeles, CA 90001
(800) 000-5555
latino@latinofriendlycompany.com

LATINO Regional Contacts
Senior Vice-President for Hispanic Affairs
Latino Friendly Company, Inc.
1 LFC Plaza, mail code 5111
Los Angeles, CA 90001
(800) 000-5111
hispanicaffairs@latinofriendlycompany.com

Supplier Diversity Program: *supplierdiversity@latinofriendlycompany.com*

Business Unit Directory: *businessunits@latinofriendlycompany.com*

Figure 11.1. Latino Friendly Company, Inc. Sample Web Site.

Kathy Ortiz, assistant dean of student services at Olive Harvey College, recounted: "When I first applied to work for the federal government, the local HEP manager helped me fill out my application. His advice helped me secure a higher rating and a position at the Department of Labor Women's Bureau."

To further improve the representation of Hispanics in the federal workforce, the U.S. Office of Personnel Management has launched a Hispanic Employment Initiative. The initiative features a nine-point plan.

1. Support and implement the White House Initiative on Educational Excellence for Hispanic Americans by matching job opportunities with curriculums of institutions serving Hispanics.

2. Provide employment information to students, faculty and members of the community.

3. Use the Presidential Management Intern Program for recruiting, converting and advancing Hispanic college graduates.

4. Participate in the Hispanic Association of Colleges and Universities Internship Program.

5. Use the Student Educational Employment Program as a tool to recruit Hispanic students.

6. Develop mentoring programs to motivate young Hispanics to pursue a federal civil service career.

7. Promote participation of Hispanic employees in career development programs.

8. Assess the need for Hispanic Employment Program managers in federal agencies.

9. Monitor the progress of recruiting and training Hispanic employees.

Both the federal program and some state-run Hispanic employment programs offer specialized applicant lists for people with bilingual skills that allow managers to bypass the traditional applicant listings to facilitate employment opportunities for Latinos with bilingual skills.

HISPANIC EMPLOYEE NETWORKS/AFFINITY GROUPS

Diversity and Hispanic employee networks (often called affinity groups) are flourishing at a growing number of companies. These are in-house organizations comprised of minority and/or Latino employees, often receiving formal corporate support for their activities. These networks play a key role in a company's recruitment, development, and retention of Hispanic employees.

For companies with a corporate-level commitment to diversity, the benefits of affinity groups have grown over time. Networks at the top-ranked employers for Latinos (according to *Fortune, Hispanic Business, Latina Style,* and other magazines) include

■ AFLAC Hispanic Association

■ Kodak's Hispanic Organization for Leadership and Advancement (HOLA)

■ Coca Cola's Latin American Forum

- Kraft Foods' Hispanic Employee Council
- Fannie Mae's Hispanic Employee Networking Group
- Ryder's Hispanic Network
- Daimler Chrysler Hispanic Employee Network
- General Mills Hispanic Employee Network
- Sears Hispanic Alliance Network
- SBC's HACEMOS
- Illinois Association of Hispanic State Employees
- Southern California Edison's Latino Employees Association for Development (LEAD)
- JP Morgan Chase's Hispanics and Latinos Group
- Sun Microsystems' Sol@Sun

These networks are often established to encourage mutually beneficial relationships for the company and its employees. Representing groups that have historically been excluded from corporate America's mainstream, networks help companies become the employer or provider of choice, while empowering individual members to build confidence and become more effective in the workplace.

Albert J. DeVeer, president of the Daimler Chrysler Hispanic Employee Network, said their group was formed to work as a resource linked directly with the company's diversity council. He explained that their organization not only provides support to other members but also partners with other functional areas. He said they serve as part of the recruitment team by providing informal referrals in response to requests. DeVeer added, "We Latinos like to build relationships as a people—we do that now as a company."

One of the issues Latinos still face is being the only Hispanic in their division, company, and so on. The lack of coworkers who are familiar with Hispanic culture can be difficult and isolating for employees.

These networks enrich their members by providing a forum for people from similar backgrounds, culture, and interests to come together to network, develop personally and professionally, identify issues of concern, and provide mutual support and advocacy. They share information, reduce feelings of isolation, address issues of common concern, and create bonds to other employees and the company. Not only are networks valuable as a source of information, but they also facilitate a supportive environment that improves the company's ability to attract, develop, retain, and advance diverse employees.

Isaias Zamarripa, director of diversity at General Mills, says that General Mills' Hispanic Employee Network provides informal networking opportunities, some even at his home in Minneapolis. He explained that these activities are key in the retention of employees in communities that do not have large Hispanic populations, where the feeling of isolation can be demoralizing.

Because it is not always possible to have all members of a Hispanic network in one place physically, some companies are developing "virtual networks" on the Internet to provide services to their employee network members.

As a job source, you can contact members of the employee network to gain inside knowledge of potential opportunities and working conditions at the company you have targeted. This is part of the research we recommend to clients before they commit to any job offers. This and other job offer recommendations will be discussed in Chapter 19.

A directory of Hispanic employee networks is provided in Appendix I.

THE LATINO MANAGEMENT TEAM

Even though the primary responsibilities for Latino corporate officers, senior executives, managers, and supervisors are company business operations, many are actively recruiting or receptive to Latino applicants from outside the company. Several of these individuals were trailblazers and among the first to reach their positions. They are familiar with the journey you are taking. Making appropriate contacts with these individuals might be your entry to the company.

SUPPLIER DIVERSITY PROGRAMS

The focus of supplier diversity programs is to increase the number of minority-owned, women-owned, and disadvantaged business enterprises (M/W/DBEs) that work to provide goods and services for a company as suppliers, contractors, and subcontractors. These programs are designed to ensure strict compliance with regulatory agency, federal, state, and local procurement regulations. Employees who are involved in these programs often work in conjunction with the diversity office and can provide the information or access you are looking for.

HISPANIC CONSUMER PROGRAMS

Another point of access to an employer is through the company's business operations dedicated to capturing and serving the Hispanic consumer market.

Many major corporations and even small companies have established Hispanic business units, increased their budgets, and hired Latino and Spanish-speaking staff to capture the U.S. Hispanic and Latin American market share. According to early 2003 studies quoted in *Hispanic Business Magazine* and *Global Insight/Univision Communications Inc.*, this focus on the Hispanic consumer is driven by the following statistics:

- Hispanic purchasing power is increasing faster than any other segment of the population and is expected to reach $700 billion by the end of 2005.

- The number of Hispanic households increased at an average rate of 3.6 percent per year from 2000 to 2002, while Hispanic consumer spending rose 8 percent.

- The U.S. Hispanic population is expected to grow from 38.5 million in 2002 to almost 56 million in 2010, with most being U.S. born.

INDIVIDUAL LATINO EMPLOYEES AT COMPANIES

There are several ways to connect with individual Latino employees in a particular company. For example, you may know someone who works at the company. Perhaps one of your contacts knows someone, or you may meet an employee or former employee during the course of your job search networking.

If you are looking for retail, service industry, academic, or other public contact jobs:

- Visit the company location and talk with Latino employees, supervisors, or managers.

- If you go to a company's human resources department, seek out Latino employees you can communicate with while you are in the building.

- Check the company's phone directory (on-site or online); then start cold calling Latino employees for information. Identify managers, target business unit staff, union stewards, and individuals.

CREATING YOUR NETWORKING RELATIONSHIP

Making the initial contact with some of the sources listed earlier can be intimidating. Keep in mind that most of the people you are contacting have been in your position at some point in their careers. In addition to their empathy, their positions in the company can be enhanced by finding new talent.

In our experience, 90 percent of the time that you ask someone for help they will come through for you. The most important thing is to make the contact as simple and efficient as possible. Remember to

- Have an agenda for your contact. Know what you want to ask or accomplish.

- Present yourself and your brand.

- Make an effort to establish a rapport.

- Keep your conversation upbeat.

- Be flexible, show consideration of the other person's time.

- Be courteous and show appreciation.

- Send a thank-you note or email within forty-eight hours.

Sending Email and Hard Copy Cover Letters to Company Contacts

If possible, always send your correspondence by email and regular mail. It is important to follow up your written communication with a phone call. Chapter 8 contains a thorough set of how-to instructions, strategies, and a gallery of letters to assist you in writing effective job search correspondence.

The following are samples of introductory correspondance:

Example 1: This unsolicited letter (opening and closing paragraphs) to a Latino-specific contact is a follow-up to a résumé submitted to the human resources department in response to an advertised vacancy.

Marisol Colon
Senior Vice-President for Hispanic Affairs
Latino Friendly Company, Inc.
1 LFC Plaza, mail code 5111
Los Angeles, CA 90001

Re: Purchasing Supervisor

Dear Ms. Colon:

Latino Friendly Company, Inc.'s Procurement Services Division advertised for a Purchasing Supervisor. As a resource management and purchasing professional with a track record of achievement in expense reduction, vendor partnership agreements and revenue enhancement, I have the credentials that meet your requirements. Additionally, I am an active member of the Hispanic Purchasing Professionals' Committee of the National Contract Management Association.

My background includes . . .

Attached are copies of the résumé and cover letter I submitted to the department of human resources. I would welcome an opportunity to discuss how my experience would contribute to the achievement of your corporation's objectives for growth and success.

Sincerely,

Example 2: This unsolicited letter (opening and closing paragraphs) is a follow-up to a Hispanic network contact.

Dear Mr. Rivera:

Jaime Díaz recommended that I contact you directly. We met at the Latino Friendly Company, Inc. recruitment booth during the National Association of Hispanic Professional's career conference. Mr. Díaz suggested the L.A.T.I.N.O. is assisting Hispanic employment at your company. I would like an opportunity to speak with you or a member of L.A.T.I.N.O. to discuss career opportunities at your corporation. . . .

These results and similar achievements are further detailed in my enclosed résumé. I look forward to hearing from L.A.T.I.N.O. soon.

or

Dear Mr. Uribe:

Alberto Gonzalez, regional vice president of the National Association of Hispanic Publications, described Latino Friendly Company, Inc. as a dynamic environment for learning about Hispanic consumer markets— and upon further research, he is not the only one who thinks so! As a junior in marketing at New York University (NYU), I am seeking a summer internship opportunity with your corporation.

Mr. Gonzalez and Jonathan Bynam, Chairman of the School of Business at NYU can attest to my skills and work ethic.

Example 3: This unsolicited letter (opening and closing paragraphs) is directed to a Latino contact listed on a company Web site.

Dear Ms. Mendez:

Your name came to my attention while researching Latino Friendly Company, Inc. on JobsLatino.com. I am seeking your guidance, as the director of diversity employment programs, on how to secure an interview for a marketing representative position with your corporation. Some of my applicable strengths and capabilities include . . .

The enclosed résumé summarizes my background and experience in the above areas. If you are interested in a highly motivated marketing representative with a proven track record of success, please contact me . . .

Making Phone Calls to Company Contacts

The telephone can be a powerful ally in your job search to identify and connect with Latino-specific or Latino-friendly contacts. The Using the Telephone Effectively section of this book (Chapter 9) contains guidelines and a problems/solutions road map to assist you in accessing company contacts.

Example 1: Cold call to identify Latino-specific or Latino-friendly contacts—Usually you will go through the company operator.

"Good morning. My name is Roberto Ruiz. I would like to get the name, title, mailing/email address and phone number for the vice president of diversity." (You can just ask for the name and phone number if it is easier for you.)

You may try for more than one contact at a time if the operator sounds comfortable with assisting you. Additionally, be prepared to be transferred to the person or office you are trying to reach.

Example 2: Getting past a secretary—Often the secretary will try to screen calls, and ask, "What is this in reference to?" Have a good response ready, but try not to provide information that will let the contact off the hook in communicating with you.

"Estrella Triana, a mutual friend, suggested that I contact Mr. Uribe directly. It's a personal matter." (This information will be conveyed to Mr. Uribe or noted on a message and could make him feel obligated to call you back.)

Example 3: Call to follow up your unsolicited letter to Latino-specific or Latino-friendly contact—If the contact picks up the phone, you should be prepared to be warm but get to the point directly. Be considerate of other people's timetables. Introduce yourself and the purpose of your call.

"Good morning, Mr. Rivera. My name is Maria Elena Ortiz. Jaime Díaz recommended that I contact you directly. I am calling to confirm that you received my correspondence and résumé. I would like to take five minutes of your time to discuss my job search with Latino Friendly Company, Inc."

If the contact is unable to talk with you or you hear tension on the other end then ask,

"Have I caught you at a bad time?" or "Can we schedule a time to meet or have a telephone conversation?" or "Is there a member of L.A.T.I.N.O. I should contact?"

If you reach the contact's voicemail, then leave a short but specific message.

"Good morning, Mr. Rivera. My name is Maria Elena Ortiz. Jaime Díaz recommended that I contact you directly. I am calling to confirm that you received my correspondence and résumé. I would like to take five minutes of your time to discuss my job search with Latino Friendly Company, Inc. I can be reached at 942-555-5555 or at my email address, meortiz1000@email.com. I am looking forward to hearing from you or a member of L.A.T.I.N.O. at your earliest convenience. Thank you."

Preparing Latino-Specific Questions to Ask Company-Based Contacts

We previously discussed the background information that you need to gather on a potential employer to determine if the position and company are the right fit for you, identify general access contacts to get your foot in the door, and prepare for the interview. We now turn to Latino-specific questions to improve your chances of landing an interview and the job. A Latino contact at the company, or knowledgeable resource from outside the company, may be open to providing you with the information you need to achieve success in your job search.

Example 1: Assessing Latino-friendly company culture—Your basic questions are "What makes your company an employer of choice for Latinos?" and "What do Latinos need to know about your company to determine if it is the right fit for them?" It is often best to ask personal questions to open dialog such as:

- What do you enjoy most about working for the company?
- Why did you apply for a job with the company?
- Why have you continued your employment with the company?
- What do you see for your future with the company?

You may need to ask follow-up questions such as:

- What is the work environment for Latinos?
- How many Latinos are in the company? At what levels? How many Latinos work in the department that you are specifically interested in?
- What characteristics do the successful Latinos in this company seem to share?
- What support systems does your company have for new Latino employees (orientation, training, mentors)?
- What support systems does your company have for the retention, development, and advancement of Latino employees (ongoing training, educational benefits, special rotations, employee networks)?
- What is the retention rate of Latinos versus others in the position for which I am interviewing?

Example 2: Identifying company access contacts/strategy—Your basic question is "What are the best strategies for Latinos to get their résumé reviewed by the right people and secure an interview with your company?" Some sample follow-up questions are:

- Who can I contact in your company to get my résumé reviewed and secure an interview (such as actual hiring official, division manager, Latino/diversity recruiters, chief diversity officer, Latino managers, or employee groups)?

- What is the best way to initiate contact and follow-up with these individuals?

- Can I use your name as the person who suggested I communicate with these contacts?

Example 3: Preparing for the interview—Your basic question is "What do I need to know about your interview process to be selected for employment?" You may need to ask follow-up questions, for instance:

- What types of interview formats are used for the position I am applying for (individual, panel, sequential, behavioral)?

- What characteristics are the interviewers looking for in a candidate for this position?

- What do the interviewers look for from Latino candidates?

- How do you test for Spanish speaking and writing proficiency?

- Should I bring my career portfolio to the interview? What should it contain?

- Do you have other recommendations for preparing for the interview and discussing my cultural and or language expertise?

LATINO-SPECIFIC JOB SEARCH STRATEGIES RESOURCES AVAILABLE THROUGH EMPLOYER'S CHECKLIST

Diversity and Hispanic Recruitment Programs

☐ Diversity and Hispanic recruitment programs are directly accountable for recruiting Latino candidates.

☐ Contact recruiting staff directly through email or telephone, or on-site to follow up on immediate and other vacancies.

☐ Ask for information on upcoming Latino job fairs and dedicated Web-based recruitment sites.

☐ These staff people should be your first contact at a company.

☐ Long-term diversity recruitment efforts are often partnered with local minority not-for-profit employment organizations, professional associations, colleges, or universities.

☐ Investigate scholarship opportunities at your local college or university offered by employers by contacting the career services office.

Office of Corporate Diversity Affairs

☐ The vice president of corporate diversity affairs manages the company's diversity practices including recruitment, succession planning, and other diversity initiatives.

☐ Contact this office to gain information on diversity councils, employee networks, consumer programs, and diversity supplier programs.

☐ Diversity councils are usually composed of employees from all levels of the organization.

☐ The EEO/AA office coordinates and monitors affirmative action and equal opportunity efforts.

☐ The EEO/AA office usually investigates complaints alleging employment discrimination, sexual harassment, and disability discrimination.

Hispanic Employment Programs

☐ Hispanic employment programs are designed to facilitate the recruitment, hiring, and retention of Hispanic employees.

☐ The Federal HEP was one of the first programs established and serves as a national model.

☐ Every U.S. government agency has a HEP office or HEP manager who can be contacted regarding employment opportunities in their agency.

☐ Specialized employment lists are often part of a HEP program that allows the manager with bilingual skills to bypass the traditional applicant listings.

Hispanic Employee Networks/Affinity Groups

☐ In-house employee networks are composed of minority and or Latino employees that receive corporate support for their activities.

☐ Contacting members of the affinity group can provide insights into the corporate culture of an organization.

☐ Network members can provide information on existing vacancies and recruitment efforts.

☐ Affinity groups are gaining in popularity in corporate America as a means of providing mutually beneficial relationships between the company and its employees.

☐ Latino management team members are often active with the affinity groups.

☐ Contacting a management team member can provide potential references and further insight into a company's operations.

Latino Supplier/Consumer Programs

☐ Both Latino supplier and consumer programs are Latino oriented.

☐ The focus of supplier diversity programs is to increase the number of minority-, female-, or disability-owned business enterprises that provide goods and services to the company.

☐ The focus of Latino consumer programs is to capture the Hispanic consumer market.

☐ Employees involved in these programs often work in conjunction with employee recruitment programs.

How to Create a Networking Relationship

☐ Prepare a script for your initial contact.

☐ Know what you want to ask or accomplish in your contact.

☐ When you present yourself, present your brand as well.

☐ Try to establish a rapport with your contact. Look for signs of common interests or conversation starters.

☐ Keep your conversation positive; do not let negative comments deflate your presentation.

☐ Show consideration of the other person's time.

☐ Always be courteous to both the contact and his/her staff.

☐ Send a thank-you note or email within forty-eight hours of your contact.

Chapter 12

Interviewing

Part 1: Culture and Language in Interviewing

Who am I anyway?
Am I my résumé?
This is a picture of a person I don't know.

What does he want from me?
What should I try to be?
So many faces all around, and here we go.
I need this job, oh God I need this job.

—Paul, an extremely talented Puertoriqueño, who was uncomfortable about discussing his accomplishments for his interview in the Broadway hit *A Chorus Line*.

Felicidades! You've done it! The good news is that you are one of the few applicants who has successfully negotiated the interview on-ramp. Your research, résumé, marketing letters, and networking have resulted in an interview with an employer you really want to work for.

The exciting news is that you now need to navigate through the rough terrain of the interviewing process. It's all in how you look at it. Unlike Paul, you are going to plan (adapt your career map to this specific interview), prepare, practice, and exercise your personal power to steer yourself into the position of receiving a job offer. And we are about to give you the directions to get there.

Myth: Latinos are not competitive in interviews due to culture and language barriers.

Truth: The key factor in successful job interviewing is communicating your value, skills, fit with the company, and ability to perform the specific job.

Reality 1: Our multicultural experiences and/or language skills are critical business assets employers are seeking. We are experienced at looking at problems from different perspectives; we can adjust our styles to different people and different situations; we think before we act; we know how it feels to be misunderstood, and we know what it takes to reverse misunderstandings; we can help resolve conflicts or problems between customers and colleagues; and we understand leadership and creative solutions within the context of diversity.

Reality 2: Many Latinos have been raised to think that speaking about yourself and your accomplishments is boastful, rude, disrespectful, and *mal educado* (not raised properly). Yet, it is disrespectful to the employer and to yourself not to provide a complete picture of what you can contribute to the company.

Interviewing is an art that can be learned. Many successful Latino interviewees use their natural storytelling talents to communicate their value to the employer in a manner that engages the listener in a continuing dialogue.

In this chapter we will explore the following:

- Purpose of the interview

- The power of R.E.S.P.E.C.T. in interviewing

- Maximizing our culture and language

Figure 12.1 illustrates how to use your culture and language in your job search plan.

THE REAL PURPOSE OF THE JOB INTERVIEW

The root of the word "interview" means between. Contrary to popular opinion, the job interview is not an interrogation. It is an exchange of information between two or more people about you, the job, and the employer.

Simply viewed, a job interview is a conversation in which two people who share complementary goals transact business. The employer who interviews you has a need: a job that needs to be competently filled. It is important for you to recognize that you are the "solution" to the employer's need. Interviews are about *oportunidad* (opportunity). Both parties get to assess whether this opportunity is a good match.

If you adopt this basic perspective, you can increase your comfort level, improve your skills, and reduce your stress when interviewing. The next sections will give you a better picture of what interviews look like.

What Interviews Look Like

Interviewers Goals

The interviewer's three primary goals are to determine if

- You can do the job

- You will do the job

- You fit into the company

The interviewer will look for indicators of

- Expertise and competence

- Motivation

- Interpersonal skills

- Decision-making skills

- Interest in the job

- Personality and likability

Your Inteview Goals

Your three primary goals are to

- Gather information about the employer, organization, and job
- Impress the interviewer with your communication skills, cultural fit, and acquired competencies that match the job
- Be offered the job

To accomplish this you should

- Research the company and vacant position
- Make a great first impression
- Engage the interviewer's interest
- Control the content and demonstrate your knowledge of the company
- Market your skills, abilities, and achievements
- Exhibit how you fit into the company's workplace culture
- Ask questions
- Show your interest and ask for the job

Types of Interviews

Informational

- Telephone
- Formal one-on-one
- Recruitment events

Screening

- Telephone
- Video conference
- Face-to-face
- One-on-one
- Group
- Computer

Selection

- One-on-one
- Sequential
- Serial

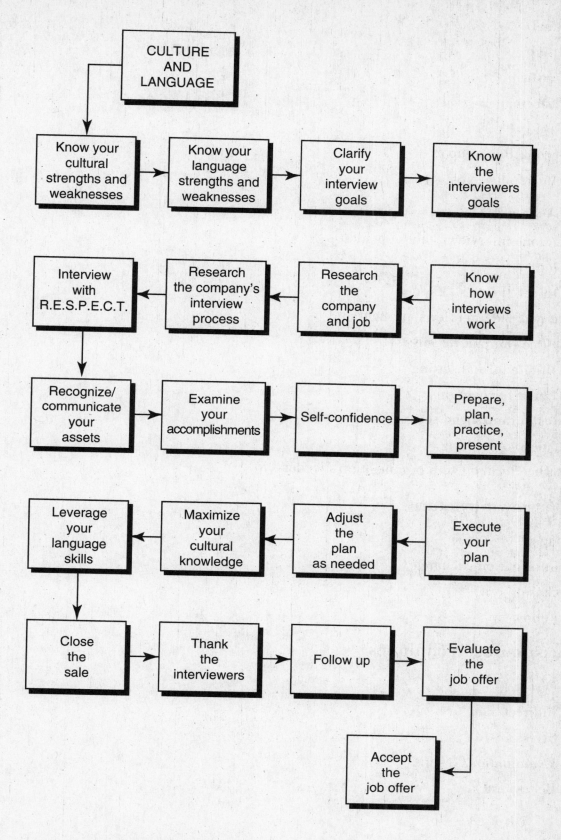

Figure 12.1. Culture and Language Interviewing Road Map.

- Panel
- Group
- Testing
- Performance
- Case
- Second follow-up
- Third follow-up

Interview Settings

Telephone interviews can be held at

- Home
- Office

Face-to-Face interviews are held at

- Office (human resources)
- Off-site formal setting
- Career fair/campus
- Restaurant/social setting
- Video conference
- Office formal (with organization's leadership)

Interview Structure

- Open
- Information exchange
- Close
- Follow-up

Questioning Techniques

- Direct
- Indirect
- Stress
- Examination/Testing
- Behavioral

THE POWER OF R.E.S.P.E.C.T. IN INTERVEWING

We developed and refined the R.E.S.P.E.C.T. interviewing model over a period of two decades when we assisted Latino clients of all backgrounds. This strategy has helped interviewees with the issues of valuing their accomplishments and presenting them in a compelling way in an interview.

The primary personal barrier to Latino success or failure in job interviews is self-promotion, verbally communicating one's accomplishments and abilities to the employer. This is the number one issue raised by the more than two hundred Latino managers, recruiters, and CEOs we interviewed and surveyed for this book. This has also been the experience of the thousands of clients we have served.

Many Latinos have been raised to believe that speaking about yourself and accomplishments is boastful, rude, disrespectful, and *mal educado*. As the *dicho* goes, *La persona no ha de ser de dichos sino de hechos* (A person is not made out of talk, but of deeds).

The elements of R.E.S.P.E.C.T. are:

Recognize
Examine
Self-confidence
Prepare
Execute
Close
Thank

Let's take a closer look at each element.

R **Recognize** that the concept of respect for Latinos is a very powerful one. The concept of respecting elders and authority figures is a theme instilled since childhood. Some see it as a negative factor in hindering our ability to present ourselves forcefully in an interview.

Self-promotion is seen as bragging. But the concept of respect used properly in an interview adds a level of authenticity and comfort for both the interviewee and the employer.

Consider the following points:

- You must respect yourself by recognizing all the skills and abilities that you bring to the employer. In highlighting your achievements, you are simply presenting a complete picture for the prospective employer to review.

- Respect for family occurs by maximizing your ability to better provide for them. There is no greater motivator.

- The employer is also shown respect when you provide a full picture of your personality and achievements so that they can make a fully informed decision and select the best candidate for the job.

You are also respecting your roots by remaining true to the traditions that have provided a base for Latinos throughout our history.

Ana Martinez earned a masters degree in accounting from Mexico. She worked for almost two years in housekeeping at a major Chicago hotel to support her family until she landed a position with a respected firm. Ana said, "I expected to be recognized for the quality of the education and work listed on my résumé. I felt that it was bad mannered and bold to say any more about my skills and abilities at the interview. It was only after I received job search coaching from the Association of Latino Professionals in Finance and Accountants that I realized that using the R.E.S.P.E.C.T. method was proper for me. Then I got the job offer."

Rays Suarez reflects that "self promotion is still an issue for many Latinos. Early in my career I explained to my mother that I had to tell my employer what benefits I could bring to a story to get the assignment. My mother responded that it was 'unbecoming' to go to your boss to tell him what you have to offer. In news and many other fields you have to toot your own horn. It is important that you calibrate how to do it."

E **Examine** your individual values, cultural assets, work-related accomplishments, contributions to the team, impact on an employer, a customer, at school, or in the community. Seek input from friends, coworkers, supervisors, and career advisors on what they see as your accomplishments. Then use the S.T.A.R. (Situation, Task, Action, and Results) technique to flesh out your achievements. This is the foundation of the success stories you will communicate in your interview.

Developing a list of specific goals is key to preparing for any interview. These goals not only indicate if the position fits into your value system but also helps you determine where you are now in you career and where you are heading according to your overall plan. Notwithstanding financial desperation, having to work in a job that you do not like is contrary to your values, nor does it move you closer to your goals. It is no fun.

Andres Garza, director of the office of career services career centers at the University of Illinois Chicago, found that "Too many people start a job search, respond to want ads, and send out résumés without really evaluating who they are and what they want in a career. The assessment is also the foundation from which you prepare for job interviews.

"By performing this self-analysis, you'll have the opportunity—perhaps for the first time in your career—to choose the position and organization that is personally satisfying and financially rewarding. Otherwise you end up applying for the wrong job and also not interviewing well."

S **Self-confidence** is a concept that for some is unattainable. For too many years, Latinos have been hounded by the "*peon*" (unskilled laborer) imagery that is modeled in modern media. But the heart of the Latino culture is a proud one composed of the best of the wealth of cultures that comprise the modern Latino.

As you navigate in the workplace you must learn to value your abilities and present yourself with *confianza* (confidence). When you learn to do both, you build personal power and begin to feel more comfortable discussing your strengths with an employer.

Doris Salomon, community affairs director for the Midwest and East Coast for BP America, is a former officer of their Latino Network, which leads an active minority outreach and mentorship program. "We address the issue of self-confidence because many Latinos are often not as sure of ourselves and the qualities that make us valuable employees. While in college, I always did internships that helped build my knowledge base and self-assurance."

P **Prepare**, plan, and practice. Your plan must be customized to each individual interview. Review your company research, match your background to the specific job opening, and develop your presentation and stories. Then *practice, practice, and practice some more* until you are comfortable and genuine in your dialogue.

Your stories need to answer these questions:

1. Can you do the job? (Do you have the skills and experience?)
2. Will you do the job? (Are you motivated to perform?)
3. How do you fit into the company? (Can you succeed in the employer's workplace culture?)

According to David Gomez, president of David Gomez, Inc., a nationally recognized executive recruitment firm, "the applicant who tailors his or her interview preparation to the individual company and job description has an advantage over other candidates. Identify which skills you have and how they fit the employer's needs. It is often not the candidate with the best qualifications who gets the job offer, but the one who is best prepared."

E **Execute** your interview plan with poise. There is a *dicho: El que no se avienta no crusa la mar* (He who does not move does not cross the sea). A plan means little without action.

To successfully manage the interview, you must observe, listen, and make a presentation. By taking your cues from the environment, the interviewers' body language, and their questions, you can respond appropriately and express what you wish to communicate, rather than miss opportunities to convey your strengths by functioning solely in a reactive mode.

Melina Hernandez, recently promoted to assistant service department manager at a Ford Motors dealership, says "As a Latina, I knew what I would have to prove at the interview for my first job as service department assistant. I was ready to show them that I had a solid knowledge of automobile technology, could work with the male mechanics, and had excellent customer service skills. I passed all of the dealership's tests. I then explained how being bilingual, bicultural, and female would make me even more valuable. Finally, I think my offer to have them try me out for a day showed my confidence and convinced the dealership to hire me."

C **Close** the transaction. It is amazing how many applicants leave the interview without "asking for the job." The interviewer is left wondering if you are truly interested in working for the company. Most hiring officials recommend that you "close the sale" by

■ Stating your interest in the position

■ Summarizing why you are qualified for the job

163

- Asking for feedback
- Clarifying the remainder of the hiring decision process

Octavio Mateo, manager of Hispanic markets and a former vice president of human resources for Citibank, said, "If you want the job and feel that you are a good match, then close the deal by saying 'I really would like the opportunity to work for you. This is why . . .' and asking 'Do my qualifications match your needs?' This gives you an opportunity to address any doubts the interviewer may have and then inquire what the next step in the process will be."

T **Thank** the interviewer(s) and the people who helped you get there. Send a letter to the interviewers, thanking them for taking the time to meet you, saying how much you enjoyed your discussion, reviewing your qualifications for the position, and letting them know how much you'd like to join their team. This not only conveys *respeto* (respect) but also reaffirms your professionalism and interest.

Send a letter showing your appreciation to the individuals who assisted you in securing the interview. It is one of the customs in networking to give back. This promotes good will and future support.

Even if you are not hired for the position, you may be considered for the next one like Teresa Nuno, director of planning and development for 5 LA. Teresa said, "When I applied to the American Red Cross I did not get the job. But later I was told by the hiring official that my interview and follow-up thank-you letter stuck in his mind, and when another position opened up where I was a perfect fit, he contacted me."

By using the power of R.E.S.P.E.C.T. when you interview, you will feel more comfortable, confident, focused, and successful. The rest of the chapter provides a variety of techniques on how to do it. Select those that work best for you.

MAXIMIZING CULTURE AND LANGUAGE IN YOUR JOB SEARCH

Our cultural and language expertise are critical assets needed by today's employers. We discussed earlier that U.S. companies are pushing to service and expand their markets locally and globally. They are not likely to be competitive unless they understand the culture and language of their customers. Latinos offer the specific skills companies need to compete successfully in a diverse marketplace.

How can you communicate your multicultural experiences and/or language skills as an asset? First, you must convince yourself that your skills are valuable. Remember: *Yo tengo valor* (I am valuable) should be your motto.

Therese Droste, a Washington, D.C.-based career columnist, suggests writing a list of benefits you bring to the workplace. Here are a few suggestions:

- My accent will be seen as an additional competence that helps me communicate better with colleagues and customers from diverse backgrounds.

- My language skills will be used to resolve cultural or language conflicts or problems between customers and colleagues.

- Being multicultural or multilingual demonstrates I can adjust my style to different people and situations.

- Being multicultural or multilingual indicates I have experienced looking at problems and opportunities from different perspectives.

- Being multicultural or multilingual indicates I think before I act.

- Being multicultural or multilingual means I know how it feels to be misunderstood, and I also know what it takes to reverse misunderstandings.

The next step is to take that list of statements and match them with positive experiences in your life in which your multilingual abilities or multicultural background helped you resolve a problem or communicate better with another person. It's similar to creating a life résumé. Yet because so many of our life experiences become distant memories, you have to ponder the past, target such situations, and write them down. Your multicultural assets must be presented in a manner that proves that you can help drive a company's business goals.

Let's say you're asked in an interview how you would deal with a problem situation with a colleague or customer. You could preface your answer with "Partly because I know how it feels to have the shoe on the other foot" and then fill in the rest with a specific example of how your background helped you solve a similar problem. Simply put, you provide the employer with an example of how you used your experience as a multilingual person to solve a past business problem or show how your skills helped you in a previous job.

After you've convinced yourself of how valuable your skills are, you will articulate them better and gain an employer's confidence.

THE POWER OF R.E.S.P.E.C.T. IN INTERVIEWING CHECKLIST

- Use the R.E.S.P.E.C.T. interviewing model to boost your interviewing power.

- Recognize that the concept of respect for Latinos is a very powerful one.
  - ❏ Respect yourself by recognizing your skills, abilities, contributions, and achievements.
  - ❏ Respect your family by maximizing your ability to provide for them.
  - ❏ Respect the employer, who needs to make a fully informed decision that you meet the company's needs and are the right person for the position.

- Examine and assess who you are and what you have to offer the employer. Develop your interview goals and build your targeted interview portfolio.

- Self-confidence is necessary to conducting a successful job interview. Valuing all that you have to offer an employer is key to empowering you to present yourself with self-assurance and poise.

- Prepare, plan, and practice for each interview. Tailor your success stories to the specific position and employer. Practice until you are comfortable and natural in your presentation.

Interviewing

- Execute your plan with poise. Observe, listen, and take cues from the environment, interviewers' body language, and their questions so that you can effectively communicate your value.

- Close the transaction. Communicate your interest in the position, summarize your qualifications, ask for feedback, and clarify the next steps in the hiring process.

- Thank the interviewer and those who helped you get there. Sending thank-you letters conveys your professionalism, promotes good will, and builds relationships.

- Maximize your culture and language in your job search.

- Identify and list the benefits of your multicultural experiences and/or bilingual skills.

- Match your list with positive experiences explaining when you used these attributes.

- Tie these stories to the requirements of the position and the needs of the employer.

Chapter 13

Interviewing

Part 2: The Twenty-first-Century Job Interview

The Constantly Changing Rules of *The Twenty-first-Century Job Interview*

The Twenty-first-Century Job Interview (TCJI) is a high-stakes, live-action activity that requires planning, strategy, preparation and practice. The goal is to create a win–win situation for all players.

Set-Up
2 to 8 (or more) players
The primary player (you) is seated on one side.
The remaining players (interviewers) are seated at the other side.
Tip: The game starts before the players ever meet.
The remaining players choose the rules for each round.
The primary player has two choices:

1. Identify the rules for each round and prepare to win

or

2. Throw the dice and lose

> — Excerpted from comments by the thousands of employers and job seekers playing *The 21ˢᵗ Century Job Interview*

According to Martita Mestey, COO of *iHispano.com*, "Just as companies are continually changing the way they do business to be competitive in the 21st century marketplace, so have their expectations of prospective employees. Job interview formats and questions keep evolving to meet employers' needs. Our employers and successful job seekers agree that conscientious preparation for each job interview is a decisive factor in securing a job offer."

HOW CAN I WIN WHEN THE RULES OF THE TWENTY-FIRST-CENTURY JOB INTERVIEW KEEP CHANGING?

Myth: Interviewing is a game of chance. There is little I can do to get ready for an interview other than know my résumé, read the job description, and pray that they will ask me questions I can answer.

Truth: You have the choice to be a fully prepared, powerful candidate for each and every interview.

Reality 1: Today it is relatively easy to research the company, position, and the specific interview process you will be participating in. The few applicants who make the effort to do so tend to be more successful.

Reality 2: Using pre-interview practice techniques discussed in this chapter can help you to be more confident in most interview settings.

In this chapter, we will cover the following topics for winning at *The Twenty-first-Century Job Interview* game:

- Types of interviews
- Interview-specific research
- Company and position review
- Questions to ask before the interview
- Research: finding out what to expect in a specific interview
- Preparation: understand, plan, deal with anxiety, and practice
- Twenty-first-century job interview checklist

TYPES OF INTERVIEWS

In Chapter 12, we provided an outline of what interviews look like. Here we describe several employment interview types and formats. The interview checklists at the end of this chapter provide several strategies you can use to be successful in each setting. As part of your pre-interview research, try to determine the interview process the employer uses.

Informational Interviews

The informational or research interview is one of the best sources for gathering information about what is happening in an industry, occupation, or company. It is an interview you initiate to speak with people working in the field. You will ask many of the questions. You must be clear that even though informational interviews are not job interviews, they are a means of preparing for and possibly securing an employment interview. Job offers are sometimes a byproduct of informational interviewing.

The informational interview is a great opportunity to

- Explore careers and clarify your career goal
- Access the most up-to-date career information
- Tap into the "hidden job market" even when there are no current job openings
- Discover employment opportunities that are not advertised or available
- Generate leads and referrals
- Expand your professional network
- Practice and build job interviewing skills
- Identify your professional strengths and weaknesses

Telephone

The telephone is most useful in informational interviewing when you want to conduct rapid networking, the contact person is not available to see you, or the individual is the stepping stone to the person you need to speak with.

Formal One-on-One

The old saying that "it is better to be seen, not just heard" is important here. You can better appeal to the interviewee's willingness to be of assistance to you when you can establish a personal rapport. By visiting the interviewee's workplace, you can also observe the work environment and be seen by others.

Recruitment Events

Career conferences, job fairs, and networking events provide opportunities to initiate and conduct informational interviews. Review the Keys to Driving Your Career Fair Success Checklist in Chapter 9 for specific suggestions.

Screening Interviews

Your first interview with an employer may be the screening interview. This is usually an interview with someone in human resources. It may take place in person or on the telephone. He/she will have a copy of your résumé in hand and will try to verify the information on it. The human resources representative will want to find out if you meet the minimum qualifications for the job and, if so, move you along to the next step.

Telephone

Increasing numbers of companies are using telephone interviews to pre-screen applicants and narrow down the list of candidates who get invited to personal interviews. Telephone interviews save companies time and money.

There are other reasons that telephone interviews might be required. For example, if the position of interest requires good telephone skills, hearing your voice and communication style on the telephone makes a lot of sense from the employer's standpoint.

The phone interview is the second step in the process for many recruiters. During a phone interview, interviewers can determine whether you are as good as you sound on paper, if you can communicate, and if you would be a good addition to the company.

The phone interview is a way for both you and the interviewer to test the waters. Think of it as a trial run for the face-to-face interview, and your objective is to win that face-to-face interview!

Some phone interviews are conducted to check that your qualifications match the job requirements, so that might only take a few minutes. A more detailed preselection interview could last twenty minutes to an hour.

The telephone interview is designed to screen people *out*, but that does not mean you cannot impress them so much that they immediately screen you *in*.

Video Conference

These interviews are becoming more common due to improved technology and reduced costs. You should treat a video conference interview like a face-to-face interview: dress as you would for a conventional interview, and address your answers to the interviewer (be aware if you are to speak to the camera or the display screen). Listen carefully to the questions and instructions. Ask the interviewer to repeat anything that you do not understand.

Face-to-Face or One-on-One

As the name suggests, this is a meeting between the candidate and one interviewer. To be successful, try to develop a rapport with the interviewer. (See Chapter 14.)

Group Interviews

The screening version of the group interview could be as simple as a presentation about the company conducting the session, followed by open discussion with question-and-answer segments. In an expanded form, several job candidates may be interviewed at once. Your interpersonal and team skills usually are assessed. Group interviewers may favor candidates who ask meaningful questions because it shows that the candidates are truly interested in the position and the company and may be worth inviting to a one-on-one interview. Being prepared for this format is one way to stand out among the other members of the group, as some candidates will arrive unprepared.

Computer

The computer interview process is rare. You may be asked to complete online questions and assessments as part of the screening process. Additionally you may be screened online by an interviewer. The latter process has been used for customer service and technical applicants who would be responding to inquiries via the Internet.

Campus

Some types of interviews are unique by their very nature. The campus interview is different from other employment interviews because a typical campus interview lasts thirty minutes or less, and the interviewer generally conducts eight to ten interviews in a day. The time pressures, fatigue, and boredom of repetitive interviewing offer some unique challenges to both the interviewer and interviewee. For example, the interviewer must be careful not to become mechanical in asking questions but to listen attentively to each candidate's responses. You should read the interviewer's frame of mind and be ready to engage him/her actively in the process. The same issues and challenges are present in interviewing at job fairs.

Selection Interviews

One-on-One

In the on-on-one interview, one person interviews each candidate and makes the hiring decision. With small employers, these interviews tend to be less formal; however, it will depend on the employer's style. The interviewer will often have a series of prepared questions, but may have some flexibility in the choices. It is important to establish rapport with the person interviewing you.

Sequential

In a sequential interview, a human resources representative or other company employees often screen applicants first. If the candidate is considered worthy of further consideration, the next higher-ranking manager then interviews the applicant. That person decides either to pass them on to a more senior manager—or to hire them. This screening procedure eliminates less-qualified applicants early, before they take a senior manager's valuable time. Sometimes, two or more lower-level interviewers compare evaluations and choose a few top applicants for interviews with the executive who will make the final choice.

Serial

In the serial interview, a human resources representative or administrative assistant screens out the obviously unqualified candidates according to specific guidelines. All candidates who meet the basic qualifications are usually interviewed by at least two other company representatives. They may be human resources specialists, department heads, managers, or other members of the operation that has the job opening.

Usually, no one interviewer can reject anyone. Each interviewer completes a written review for each candidate. When all interviews are finished, the interviewers meet, compare notes, and decide which candidates to present to the final decision maker. In this way, the hiring official can base his or her decision on the perspectives and evaluations of several managers.

Panel

In a panel interview, typically three to six members (with different roles in the organization) ask candidates questions to assess their knowledge, skills, team fit, ability to make decisions, and so on. Panel interviews can be quite intimidating because the interviewee is asked questions by several different people. In this type of interview, you should try to remain calm and establish rapport with each member of the panel.

A key to succeeding in this type of interview is to focus your attention on the person who asks you the question—at both the beginning and end of your response—while in between looking at each member of the panel, in turn. When appropriate, link your response to an answer that you have previously given. This helps the panelists connect the dots as to the value you offer to the company. If at all possible, obtain the names of the interviewers before starting; otherwise, write their names down as they are introduced. Try to address the interviewers by name (Mr. Smith or Ms. Juarez).

Group

In the selection version of the group interview, several job candidates are often interviewed at once. You may meet the staff members who will be your coworkers if you get hired. Usually one or more interviewers will ask you several questions. They will be primarily testing your ability to work in a team environment.

They want to know how you will present information to other people, offer suggestions, relate to other ideas, and work to solve a problem. For certain positions, the interviewer(s) will be trying to separate the leaders from the followers. The type of personality the employer is looking for determines the outcome of this interview. In short, your interpersonal skills will be tested.

It is difficult to prepare for this type of interview, except to remember what is being tested and to use your skills to be the best team player and/or leader you can be. If you are perceived to be acting naturally, then you will leave a positive and friendly impression.

Traditional Interviews

The traditional interview is the most common type of interview. The interview consists of a series of questions that may or may not be standardized. In addition to responding to questions, you are expected to ask questions as well. Frequently, success or failure will hinge on your ability to communicate and establish rapport rather than on the content of your answers.

Traditional interviews focus on questions such as

- Tell me about yourself?

- What are your strengths and weaknesses?

- Why are you interested in working for us?

We have provided you with fifty of the most frequently asked questions in Chapter 14.

Behavioral or Competency-Based Interview

Behavioral and competency-based interviews are the growing trend in the twenty-first century. They are rooted on the principle that a candidate's past performance is the best predictor of future performance. Competencies are patterns of behavior that go beyond education, experience, and technical knowledge. They are knowledge, measurable skills, and abilities as demonstrated by behavior; they test how you act or respond in a specific situation. They distinguish high performers from others in the same job.

The interview questions are directly linked to the essential functions of the job. They are designed to assess general core competencies such as problem-solving and decision-making abilities, conflict resolution, and competencies that are specific to your industry. For example, if you are a customer service representative, the core competencies that recruiters will be interested in will include interpersonal communication, customer satisfaction, account management, and customer retention.

The competency-based interview has interviewers ask candidates what they have done in their work, community, and other life experiences rather than have them respond to hypothetical questions about what the candidate would do in a given situation. Responses are based on actual experiences and elicit a *story* from the candidate. Interviewers ask probing questions to determine if the candidate has demonstrated the specific competency being assessed.

The major benefits of this type of interviewing are that these questions allow you to relate your answer to a real-life experience and demonstrate your personal career brand rather than giving a generic textbook answer. This enables you to reveal the most relevant information in context to the current job opportunity.

Larry Uribe, human resources consultant and a former human resources manager for Fortune 500 companies, provides the following discussion of competency-based interviews, examples of competencies, and related questions.

Competency-Based Interviews

Today, more than ever, employers are looking at candidates in terms of what "value" each candidate would bring to the organization. The employer has usually selected their "corporate brand" of core competencies that all new hires should possess in order to maintain or create the "key behaviors" culture of the organization.

Employers are using the concept of competencies in the following areas of the organization:

Skills assessment software
Job and competency software
Job postings
Employment applications
Behavioral interviewing
Training
Compensation plans
Hiring
Performance mangement
Promotions

You need to consider the impact of competencies in reference to all your employment-related activities, such as

Networking
Résumés
Cover letters
Targeted interviews
Personal and career development
Marketing "your personal brand"

The employer selects and interviews for critical and essential competencies and behavior-based performance standards that the organization determines necessary for success in the immediate job opening and future growth opportunities within the organization.

In order to effectively prepare for the various employment-related situations that could provide you an opportunity to market yourself, you need to assess what are the behaviors and competencies that the organization values and prepare all of your employment tools and resources to reflect and focus on your possession of those valued competencies.

A simple process to create a quick reference to your competencies would be to develop a written list of your competencies and along the side of this list indicate short clear statements of quantifiable (if possible) accomplishments or outcomes. Try to define the "who, what, when, where, and why" of your input in these situations and also why it will be valued by the organization. Effective marketing of competencies is accomplished only after you have thoroughly researched the valued competencies of the organization and the essential competencies for the job opening and prepared a verbal and written presentation of appropriate accomplishments that match the organization's value competencies.

Sample Core Competency Questions

Adaptability

- Tell me about a time when you changed your priorities when presented with a better alternative for the larger group.

- Describe a time when you altered your own behavior to fit the situation.

- Tell me about a time when you had to change your point of view or your plans to take into account new information provided by your boss. How did you communicate the change and what was the outcome?

Client Focus

- Give an example of how you provided service to a customer beyond their expectations. How did you identify the need? How did you respond? What were the results?

- Tell me about a time when you had to address a difficult customer service issue.

- Describe a situation in which you acted as an advocate within your organization for your client or team member's needs, where there was some organizational resistance to be overcome.

Communication

- Describe a situation you were involved in that required a multifaceted communication strategy—verbal and written.

- Give an example of a difficult or sensitive situation that required extensive persuasive communication.

- Tell me about a time when you really had to pay attention to what someone else was saying, actively seeking to understand their message. How did you use feedback to confirm your understanding?

Organizational Awareness

- Describe the culture of your organization, and give an example of how you work within this culture to achieve a goal.

- Describe the things you consider and the steps you take in assessing the viability of a new idea or initiative.

- Tell me about a time when you used your knowledge of the organization to get what you needed.

Problem Solving and Judgment

- Tell me about a situation when you had to identify the underlying causes of a problem and generate a solution.

- Tell me about a situation where you had to solve a problem or make a decision that required careful thought. What did you do?

Results Orientation

- Tell me about a specific time when you set and achieved a goal that resulted in a quantifiable result.

- Tell me about a time when you improved the way things were typically done on the job.

- Describe something you have done to improve the performance of your work unit. How was the improvement measured?

Teamwork

- Tell me about a time when you worked successfully as a member of a team.

- Describe a situation where you were successful in getting people to work together effectively.

- Describe a situation in which you were a member (not a leader) of a team and a conflict arose within the team. What did you do? What was the impact on the team?

Sample Role-Specific Competency Questions

Developing Others

- Tell me about a time when you coached someone to help them improve their skills or job performance. What did you do? What was the outcome?

- Describe a time when you provided feedback to a peer or subordinate about his/her performance.

- Give me an example of a time when you recognized that a member of your team had a performance difficulty/deficiency. What did you do?

Impact and Influence

- Describe a recent situation in which you convinced an individual or a group to do something.

- Describe a time when you went through a series of steps to influence an individual or a group on an important issue, what action you took, and the results.

- Describe a situation in which you needed to influence different stakeholders with differing perspectives.

Innovation

- Describe something you have done that was new and different for your organization, that improved performance and/or productivity.

- Tell me about a time when you identified a new, unusual, or different approach for addressing a problem or task.

- Tell me about a recent problem in which old solutions wouldn't work. How did you solve the problem? What was the effect on the organization?

Leadership

- Tell me about a time when you had to lead a group to achieve an objective.

- Describe a situation where you had to ensure that your "actions spoke louder than your words" to a team.

- Describe a situation where you inspired others to meet a common goal.

Relationship Building

- Describe a situation in which you developed an effective win–win relationship with a Latino client. How did you go about building the relationship?

- Tell me about a time when you relied on a contact in your network to help you with a work-related task or problem.

- Give me an example of a time when you deliberately attempted to build rapport with a coworker or customer.

Resource Management

- Describe a situation in which you took a creative approach to resource management to achieve a goal. What cost savings resulted?

- Tell me about a time when you had to deal with a particular resource management issue regarding people, materials, or assets.

- Describe a situation in which you established a partnership with another organization or client to achieve a mutual goal. What steps did you take to ensure the partnership experienced a win–win outcome?

Self-Management

- Describe the level of stress in your job and what you do to manage it.

- Describe a situation when you were in a high-pressure situation and continued functioning effectively.

- Describe a time when things didn't turn out as you had planned and you had to analyze the situation, revise your strategy, and return to accomplish a challenging task.

Strategic Thinking

- Describe a challenge or opportunity you identified based on your industry knowledge. How did you develop a strategy to respond to it? What measurement applied?

- Describe a time you created a strategy to achieve a long-term business objective.

- Describe a time when you analyzed a specific business situation involving customers and proposed a change in procedure.

Later in this chapter, we provide you with strategies to develop your S.T.A.R. stories where you are successful and to practice them so they feel natural and will not sound like they are being recited.

Performance Interview

In a performance interview, the interviewer asks candidates to role-play job functions to assess their knowledge and skills. This is not the same as a case interview, in that it typically is only a portion of the interview and is focused on performance or knowledge rather than critical thinking.

Case Interview

The case interview is a special type of interview commonly used by management-consulting firms and is increasingly being used in many other organizations for more senior-level positions. It helps the interviewer analyze your critical-thinking skills. If you are not familiar, do not have experience, or are not comfortable with case analysis, it can be one of the most difficult interviews to undergo.

In a case interview, you are given a problem to see how you would work it out on the spot. The problems that are presented come in many forms, but the interviewer wants to assess your analytical skills, ability to think under pressure, logical thought process, business knowledge and acumen, creativity, communication, and quantitative analysis skills.

Direct, Indirect, and Patterned Interviews

The direct interview format is one in which the interviewer maintains tight control over what is said, usually asking a series of scripted questions. In this setting, you should make sure that you emphasize your key job-related selling points.

In the indirect interview format the interviewer usually makes rather general statements or questions, such as "Tell me a little about yourself." The purpose here is to see how you deal with ambiguous situations. The interviewer is also looking for your ability to organize your thoughts and your ability to communicate your ideas precisely and effectively. Here is where you can apply your prepared responses and S.M.A.R.T. stories.

The patterned interview is a format that combines both the direct and the indirect interview style. This approach involves the interviewer noting some general areas of interest that he/she wants to cover.

Stress Interview

During the stress interview, the interviewer deliberately subjects the applicant to pressure to assess an individual's ability to deal with unexpected as well as expected stressful situations. After a candidate demonstrates that he/she can perform effectively under stress, this portion of the interview is usually ended.

These interviews are not frequently used, and the *technique must be validated to be directly related to the job.* It is applied primarily when the job the employer is trying to fill requires that an individual perform under an extreme amount of stress, such as law enforcement or security, but it has also been used in some sales and marketing positions.

The interviewer may try to introduce stress into the interview artificially by making you wait a considerable amount of time for the interview to start, act rudely, ask questions so quickly that you don't have time to answer each one. Another interviewer trying to introduce stress may respond to a candidate's answers with silence. The interviewer may also ask weird questions, not to determine what the job candidate answers, but how he/she responds.

To handle this type of interview, you should first "recognize that you're in the situation." After you realize what's happening, it's much easier to stay calm because you can mentally reframe the situation. Then you have two choices: play along or refuse to be treated so poorly. If you do play along, you should later find out if the reason for conducting a stress interview is legitimate. That will determine if this is a company for which you want to work. Chapter 15 discusses how do deal with inappropriate or illegal interview questions.

Second and Third Follow-ups

When job seekers are invited back after they have passed the first initial selection interview, middle- or senior-level management generally conducts the second and third interviews. You can expect more in-depth questions, and the employer will be expecting a greater level of preparation on the part of the candidates. You should continue to research the employer after the first interview and be prepared to use any information gained through the previous interview to your advantage.

PRE-EMPLOYMENT EXAMINATION/TESTING

Some companies use pre-employment tests to help in making decisions. Various types of assessments (commonly referred to as tests or inventories) may be used to determine if you are a likely fit. Among these are

- **Position-based competency** (i.e., computer skills, language proficiency, technical knowledge)
- **Psychological**—includes personality inventory and career interest tests
- **Aptitude**—assesses skills and abilities in certain skill areas
- **Intelligence**—consists of logic problems, word problems, pattern identification and/or other kinds of questions (Employers will use intelligence tests in conjunction with other types of tests.)
- **Combination instruments**—combines any of the four preceding tests
- **Honesty**—predicts truthfulness and integrity
- **Simulations**—role-plays where you might be asked to do one or more of the following: sort through an in-box, meet with your boss, meet with your subordinates, meet with your peers, deal with customers, or give a presentation

Special Test Circumstances

- **Drugs/Alcohol**. An employer may include questionnaires and blood, urine, or hair analysis testing. If you are turned down because of a positive drug test, you can ask if a validation test was done.
- **Medical Examination**. After a job offer is made and prior to the starting of employment duties, an employer may require that an applicant take a medical examination if everyone who will be working in the job category must also take the examination. The employer may condition the job offer on the results of the medical examination.

However, if an individual is not hired because a medical examination reveals the existence of a disability, the employer must be able to show that the reasons for exclusion are job related and necessary for the conduct of business. The employer also must be able to show that there was no reasonable accommodation that would have made it possible for the individual to perform the essential job functions.

If you are turned down because of the results of a medical exam, you can ask why and if the reason is related to the essential functions of the job. If you believe that the medical exam results are being used to discriminate against you, refer to Chapter 17 on the steps you can take to address discrimination in the hiring process.

INTERVIEW-SPECIFIC RESEARCH

Martita Mestey recommended that "once an interview is scheduled, it is critical that you perform additional research and due diligence to properly prepare for the interview. To be viewed as an ideal candidate, your preparation for the interview must extend the knowledge of your résumé and past experience. Understanding the company's core methodologies, products, or brands will also be crucial to the success of the interview. If the employer is a consumer products company, you should know what brands they make or sell, even if it is not related to the position you are interviewing for."

Company and Position Review

Martin Castro, a partner at Sonnenschein, Nath, and Rosenthal in Chicago, tells this story about the value of company research. "My law school professor told us to send out résumés at Thanksgiving and ask for an interview. I mailed 200 letters and received 196 rejections. Baker McKenzie invited me to come for lunch. I discovered how naïve I was about the job search process after talking with a friend. She said 'Marty, they are going to interview you.' 'No, it's for lunch.' She asked, 'What time is the lunch?' I told her that I was supposed to arrive at 10 A.M., and lunch would be at noon. My friend said they would interview me for two hours before lunch. She then asked, 'What do you know about the firm?' I responded, 'Nothing?' She said 'Marty, it is the largest firm in the country. You need to prepare.' I went to do research and was prepared for the interview and was offered the position. I was always prepared after that experience."

Some of the information you should research before the interview follows:

- Size of the company
- Nature of the products and/or services offered
- Target markets
- General company history
- Company competitors (for some positions)
- Specific information about the department
- Company workplace environment and culture
- Recent news about the company

■ Information from the company prospectus or annual report

■ As many details about the position as possible

Listed in Appendix G are suggested resources for company research.

Questions to Ask Before the Interview

In addition to the traditional pre-interview research, you might want to ask general and Latino-specific questions of people in your professional and personal network. The best contacts will be the people who referred you to the position, internal Latino employee network, Latino professional associations in your field, and most diversity search engine customer support services.

■ What do the interviewers look for in general and Latino candidates?

■ How do you test for Spanish speaking and writing proficiency?

■ Should I bring my career portfolio to the interview? What should it contain?

■ Do you have other recommendations for preparing for the interview in general and about discussing my cultural and/or language expertise?

■ What is the work environment for Latinos?

■ How many Latinos are in the company? At what levels? How many Latinos work in the department for which you are interviewing?

■ What characteristics do the successful Latinos in this company seem to share?

■ What support systems does your company have for new Latino employees (orientation, training, mentors)?

■ What support systems does your company have for the retention, development, and advancement of Latino employees (ongoing training, educational benefits, special rotations, employee networks)?

■ What is the retention rate of Latinos versus others in the position for which I am interviewing?

Research: Finding Out What to Expect in a Specific Interview

If you can learn the details on how the interview is conducted and a little about the person(s) who will be interviewing you, you'll be miles ahead of the game. You will want to determine what interview formats will be used for the position and the characteristics the interviewers are looking for in a candidate for this position. Try to find out one or two things about each interviewer's accomplishments, history with the organization, outside interests—anything that will help you break the ice and speak to him/her about their interests.

For help in how to get the inside scoop on the interview and interviewer, try some of these techniques:

■ Ask people in your professional and personal network what they know. Again, the best contacts will be the people who referred you to the position, the internal Latino employee network, the Latino professional associations in your field, and most diversity search engine customer support services.

- Conduct a search on the Internet using the company name and interviewer's name.

- Read the company's Web site to learn about the company's directions and goals, including those that might involve the interviewer's department. Some company sites and literature discuss their hiring process.

- Call organizations like the chamber of commerce, professional associations, and community groups that you think the hiring manager might belong to.

PREPARATION: UNDERSTAND, PLAN, DEAL WITH ANXIETY, PRACTICE

The Keys to Powerful Communication

The first step in preparing for the interview is to understand how effective communication works. After you recognize the process of persuasive communication, then you can overcome any traditional, cultural, or English-as-a-second-language fears or other issues you may have in job interviewing.

Communication can be defined as the transference and understanding of meaning, the way that people exchange information in order to achieve common goals. The importance of this transference of understanding cannot be underestimated. It overcomes issues of race, gender, national origin, speaking accents, language dominance, height, weight, and other factors that can affect the receiver's perception of you.

Ten Essential Interpersonal Skills

- **Effective communication:** Ability and willingness to communicate and establish a rapport with all types of people

- **Good listening habits:** Ability and willingness to listen by giving your undivided attention and not interrupting (One of Stephen Covey's *Seven Habits of Highly Effective People* is "seek to understand before you seek to be understood," which works in this context.)

- **Tact and diplomacy:** Ability and willingness to exercise a fair amount of discretion as needed

- **Consideration of others:** Ability and willingness to demonstrate empathy for those with whom one may interact (An adaptation of the Golden Rule applies here—"treat others as they expect to be treated," which requires an understanding of the individual's culture and the customs of the workplace.)

- **Persuasiveness:** Ability and willingness to convince others why a certain viewpoint is valuable (Sometimes this means to present ideas in a manner that is easiest for the other party to understand.)

- **Professionalism:** Ability and willingness to exhibit poise, self-assurance, and confidence based upon the knowledge and experience gained in one's chosen field

- **Tolerance and objectivity:** *Ability and willingness to consider alternate points of view*

- **Cooperation:** Ability and willingness to contribute constructive ideas and support to the team
- **Constructive feedback:** Ability and willingness to assess situations and offer suggestions for improvement; conversely to openly receive authentic feedback
- **Positive mental outlook:** Ability and willingness to exude a positive attitude about yourself and your job

Effective Communication

Two standards provide the framework for clear communication in an interview:

1. Effective transfer of information
2. Persuasiveness

Effective transfer of information is

Efficient: Information must be presented so the interviewer understands and retains it as quickly as possible.

Concise: Your message is no longer than it needs to be to accomplish the stated purpose.

Organized: Clarity can be achieved by using coherent phrasing and organizing your communication so that it flows smoothly and achieves intent.

Objective: Statements should appear nonbiased and based on facts.

Tactful: Professional consideration and careful word choice should make all of your messages diplomatic.

Effective: The communication should accomplish its stated purpose, in that it answers the interviewer's question(s) by supplying needed information.

Persuasiveness is achieved when

Coherent: The interview answers are logically connected from beginning to end.

Credible: The interviewer must be convinced that the information communicated is accurate.

Thorough: Key pertinent facts are discussed and supporting references are provided.

Compelling: Your message must appeal to the interviewer's hiring motivators.

More on Active Listening

Active listening benefits the process of effective communication. It is critical to having a successful interview. Active listening means listening with intensity to make sure that the message is received correctly and completely. It also means listening with empathy to one another, which validates the interpersonal exchange of information. Active listening may be achieved by verbal inquiries and sustained eye contact. Repeating information back to the other person and asking questions for clarification also indicates you are actively listening. You should avoid distracting behaviors such as looking at your watch or finger tapping that will break concentration or interrupt verbalization.

Maximizing Your Verbal Communication Skills

The Spoken Word

Verbal communication is represented by the spoken word. What is said is often not as important as how it is said. We are going to focus on the four considerations that go along with using your voice in verbal communication: pitch, volume, tone, and pace.

■ Pitch refers to whether a sound is "high" or "low."

■ Tone, on the other hand, is the pitch of a word or string of words often used to determine its meaning or to distinguish differences in meaning.

■ Volume refers to whether the sound of your voice is loud or soft.

■ Pace is the rate of speech or how quickly or how slowly you speak.

Three recurring challenges have been identified regarding the use of our voices:

■ Monotone

■ Speaking too fast or too slow

■ Speaking too loud or too soft

Monotone

Monotone is the uninterrupted repetition of the same tone. Most monotone voices are caused by anxiety. As the speaker tenses up, the muscles in the chest and throat become less flexible, and airflow is restricted. When this happens, the voice loses its natural animation. The key then is to practice relaxing during delivery. Videotaping, audiotaping, or rehearsing with a friend will let you know if you require improvement in this area.

Speaking Too Fast or Too Slow

The average rate of speech during conversation is approximately 125 words per minute. Anxiety will usually increase the rate of speech. An increased rate of speech may not necessarily be a problem if your articulation, enunciation, and diction are good.

A sure indicator that you are speaking too fast is if you trip over your words. You should practice listening to yourself as you complete verbal sentences to make sure you slow down where a period, comma, or other punctuation mark would be in a written document. Pausing during an answer can be an effective device to allow the interviewer to focus on important points.

Just as speaking too fast will "turn off" interviewers because they can't keep up with your statements, speaking too slow will have a similar effect. If your speech seems to drag on and on, you will definitely lose the interviewers' interest. They will invariably become distracted and bored. Even worse, they may begin to yawn, check their watches, or start their own conversations. Therefore, picking up the pace of the answers is essential to communicating your information.

Speaking Too Loud or Too Soft

Being aware of the volume of your voice is important because it can make or break an otherwise good interview. To find out if you have a problem with the volume of your voice, practice with someone.

In summary, you want to ensure that you project your voice; pronounce your words carefully, pause whenever necessary, and vary the pace of longer answers or presentations. It is also suggested that you modulate the tone, emphasize certain parts, and repeat keywords.

Maximizing Your Nonverbal Communication Skills

Body Language

Nonverbal communication includes the body signals we employ whether or not we are aware of them and to which we respond, consciously or subconsciously. Research shows that nonverbal communication is the most significant. Nonverbal communication has been estimated to represent between 70 and 80 percent of the messages that get through to others, as compared to only 10 to 20 percent of verbal communication. The following are some of the more common aspects of nonverbal communication that may be observed in others.

- **Arm barriers:** Folded arms across the chest can suggest a defensive action. The folded arms say, "I don't want to know" or "I'm feeling vulnerable."

  Tip: Videotape yourself or practice interviewing in front of a mirror to become aware of your arm movements. If this is a problem, then try using a notepad to keep your arms open and hands occupied.

- **Hand gestures:** Tapping fingers on the table can indicate frustration or impatience. Tightly clenched fists or wringing hands are clues that a person is under pressure or extremely angry. If the fists are clenched, this is interpreted as displaying a hostile or aggressive attitude.

  Tip: If this is a problem, try using a notepad to keep your hands occupied.

- **Handshaking:** Shaking another's hand indicates that you are willing to make body contact and therefore willing to interact. A "vertical" handshake is a firm grasp of the hand so that both hands are vertical.

  Tip: Practice shaking hands with your career *familia* and then others until you feel comfortable.

- **Eye Signals:** The obvious example of this gesture is looking or not looking at the person to whom you are speaking. Avoidance generally suggests unease, lying, or fear. The more frequent the eye contact, the more open the relationship may be. Eye contact definitely opens a channel of communication between people.

  Tip: If making eye contact with the interviewer is difficult for you, try looking somewhere else on the person's face, like their nose or forehead. We call this looking at the interviewer's third eye.

  Evelyn Salvador, president of Career Catalyst and business leader, told the following story: "During my own upbringing, I was raised that one must always respect authority and the phrase 'what will the neighbors (or others) think?' I didn't make eye contact and if I reciprocated with a handshake at all, it was weak. It took some time for me to realize that I must show confidence in myself to advance in my career. Upon this realization, I made an important decision. . . . From there on in and no matter how difficult (and believe me, it was!), I would look everyone in the eye, give them a firm handshake, and address them with the level of formality that they preferred. I had to role-play it out each time until it became second nature. It probably took about fifty to seventy-five times till the stomach-wrenching stopped."

A more detailed chart of how body language can affect an interview follows.

INTERVIEWEE'S BODY LANGUAGE

Body Language	Possible Interpretations
Eye contact with occasional, natural breaks in the stare	Focused and curious
Crossed arms	You are closed off or defensive You don't want to listen or know You are feeling vulnerable
Fidgeting, running tongue along teeth, playing with hair or jewelry, or tapping feet	Nervous or bored
Leaning back	Uncomfortable
Clasping hands behind head while leaning back	Looking to gain power
Leaning forward	Interested in the conversation
Smiling or attempting to be humorous	Friendly
Nodding while listening	Attentive and alert
Open palms	Approachable and trusting
Gesturing with hands while talking	Genuinely involved in the conversation

INTERVIEWER'S BODY LANGUAGE

Body Language	Possible Interpretations
Crossed arms	Very defensive or reserved mood
Crossed arms and legs	Very reserved or suspicious
Open arms and hands	Person is open and receptive
Standing with hands in pockets	Feels unsure or suspicious
Sitting, shaking one leg	Feels nervous and uncomfortable
Eyes downcast, faced turned away	Uninterested in what you're saying
Palm of hand holding or stroking chin	An evaluating position and being critical
Clasping hands behind head while leaning back	In an analytical mood, but in a position of superiority
Rubbing or touching nose while answering question	Not telling the whole truth
Maintains eye contact, relaxed smile	Receptive to you
Rubbing back of head/neck	Uninterested in conversation
Moves into position with feet and body pointing toward door	Wants to end conversation and leave

Nonverbal Cues

Nonverbal cues are very significant. When communicating with interviewers, nonverbal messages play an important role. Here are some suggestions for effective nonverbal communication:

■ Face the person with whom you are interacting; this indicates that you like and respect people.

■ Posture is a measure of tenseness or relaxation and provides clues to feelings; good posture is associated with confidence and enthusiasm.

■ Facial expressions can belie true feelings. Some people mask their emotions by not using facial expressions while others overexaggerate.

■ Frequent eye contact communicates interest and confidence.

■ Distance between the communicators can be significant. If offered a choice of seats for an interview, select the one closest to the interviewer.

■ Personal appearance is also important. People tend to respond better when individuals are appropriately dressed for the interview. Avoid clothing or accessories that may distract the interviewer's attention.

Prepare Your S.T.A.R. Stories

A key strategy for preparing for your interview is to use the S.T.A.R. technique—situation, task, action, and result. (This technique is often referred to as the CAR, PAR, or SAR technique.)

S **Situation:** Define the situation or "set the stage."

Example: "Assigned as an account manager in an underperforming sales territory—number 92 out of 100 districts."

T **Task:** Identify the task/project performed.

Example: "To increase same store sales by 20 percent and boost commercial customer base by 10 percent."

A **Action:** Describe the action that you took/initiated. This response should illustrate the specific skills you used in completing the task.

Example: "Conducted a competitive market analysis and customer service survey; developed a business plan that included value-added service, sales incentives, and referral bonus program that benefits our business customers; and rolled out a three-level marketing strategy to implement the plan."

R **Result:** Summarize the outcome.

Example: "District became number 9 in the region in first year; same store sales rose by 37 percent; net profit margin per sale improved by 7 percent; commercial customer base grew by 18 percent. My business plan was adapted for use by all account managers in the region. Earned Account Manager of the Year Award."

Note: In your résumé, use percentages instead of actual dollar figures when it is necessary to protect the former employer's proprietary or confidential financial information.

Remember to be specific! Employers claim that many job seekers provide vague information and indefinite responses in their interviews. For example, if you claim that you have strong leadership skills, demonstrate them by citing some actual "stories" from your experiences similar to the preceding one. Be prepared to provide more specifics only if asked.

Prepare Your One- to Two-Minute Introduction

Your one- to two-minute introduction is usually in response to the dreaded question "Tell me about yourself." Essentially, you are creating an infomercial that convincingly communicates your personal career brand. A well-crafted introduction not only establishes a great first impression but can also direct the interviewer's line of questioning to incorporate key "selling points" you have brought to their attention.

- Prepare your master infomercial to
  - ❑ Include a brief summary of your recent career history, relevant education, and credentials
  - ❑ Incorporate your personal career branding statement
  - ❑ Focus on a few job-related accomplishments
  - ❑ Include three to five key competencies and job-related personal attributes
  - ❑ Provide closure by tying it into the needs of the hiring organization
- Make sure the content is authentic so that you are comfortable delivering the message.
- Tailor your introduction to the specific interview.
- Practice so that your delivery is natural and more like a dialogue.

Deal with Interview Anxiety

Being nervous about job interviewing is normal. Fear of the unknown, rejection, or failing is behind most job seekers' interview anxieties. But by managing the interview process, you can control your fears.

Be Prepared for Your Interview

The key to reducing your anxiety is in being well prepared for the interview. If you are not prepared for the interview, you are not in control of your career. You are giving up your power. The benefit of preparing is that you will be more relaxed during the interview. The more relaxed you are, the more in control you will feel.

Use Relaxation Techniques

If you practice some of the following five-minute relaxation techniques on a regular basis, on the day of the interview you will naturally apply them when needed.

1. Focus on Your Breathing

Learn how to breathe deeply. Practice while seated. Inhale through your nose, until you feel your stomach expand. Hold your breath for a few seconds, then slowly exhale through your mouth. After performing this exercise a few times, leave your arms limp and spread your toes; close your eyes and imagine that you are inhaling cleansing air; next exhale the stress through your mouth, fingers, and toes. Try this slowly several times. Then open your eyes, and you should feel a sense of relaxation.

> Tip: During the interview, breathe slowly and deeply. Keep your feet planted on the floor and feel the chair supporting you. This will calm you and lessen your fear. You can draw several deep breaths without distracting the interviewer. To gain time, ask a question that requires a lengthy response.

2. Use the Power of Visualization

Visualization is a form of guided daydreaming. Many top athletes use visualization techniques to reduce anxiety, improve concentration, and enhance athletic performance. As in sporting events, when interviewing for a job, a high level of performance is required for a short period. Thus, using visualization techniques can help build confidence and reduce anxiety. The trick is to remember successful interviews or imagine/see yourself actually performing great in an interview. Practice this technique daily, and you will learn to use it automatically and effortlessly.

> Tip: Just like top athletes, use visualization shortly before an interview. When actually interviewing, you'll feel a sense of deja vu, as though you had the experience before.

3. Progressive Muscle Relaxation and Self-Massage

The following two techniques smooth away stress, pain, and headaches resulting from tensed muscles. They also help increase blood flow to the areas and soothe the nerves, sending calming signals to the brain. And it feels good, too!

> **Progressive muscle relaxation:** While sitting or lying in a relaxed position, tense the muscles of your feet as much as you can; then relax them and notice the difference in feeling. Tense and relax the muscles in your legs, arms, stomach, back, neck, and head and squint your eyes, one area at a time. When finished, remain in a state of relaxation for a few minutes.

> **Self-massage:** Sit with your shoulders relaxed. Use your right hand to massage your left shoulder and neck, working your way up to your scalp. Repeat using your left hand to the right shoulder. Repeat both for five minutes. This will relax the area known as the stress triangle.

> Tip: Do these exercises in your car or somewhere before you enter the building where you are interviewing.

4. Self-Talk

Replace negative mental responses to anxiety and stress such as "I cannot do this" with positive ones such as "I *am* good at interviewing." Your affirmation must be in the present tense for your brain to believe what you are silently telling yourself. Saying I *will* be good at interviewing does not work. You must say I *am*. Repeat self-talk daily.

Tip: Use self-talk as you enter the interview room. You will feel reassured, and it can also trigger an instantaneous fast-forward of your visualization.

5. Meditation

Close your eyes and mentally follow your breathing. As you exhale mentally, repeat a simple word (such as "peace") with each breath. Or visualize a peaceful scene. Do this for at least five minutes, or for more benefit up to thirty minutes.

Tip: If you are anxious, meditate in your car or before you enter the building where your interview is to be held. If you are still anxious, briefly recall the peaceful scene to help you relax.

6. During the Interview

Look at the interviewer—Scan the person's face and decide which feature you like the most. Then, without staring, mentally focus on that characteristic. This technique will help you to feel more positive about the interviewer and lower your anxiety.

Connect with your present surroundings—Mentally label items within your field of vision. For example, you might see and think to yourself, "blue suit, brown desk, gold picture frame." This activates the area of the brain that strengthens logical, linear thinking, enabling you to focus on the interviewer and be present in the conversation.

Practice the Interview

After you have prepared for every aspect of your interview, the next step is to practice, practice, and practice some more until you are comfortable. Your work will pay off at interview time. Here are some tips:

- Practice as often as possible to become comfortable with interviewing.

- Practice several times as if it is a real interview with your interview attire, résumé, and interview portfolio, if you have one.

- Practice with a friend, peer, mentor, and/or career coach who will serve as the interviewer and provide constructive feedback. Also try using your campus or alumni career center.

- Videotape your rehearsal. Watch the playback, and have others view it and critique your performance.

- Incorporate any changes you feel are required.

- Use the visualization technique discussed in this chapter.

- Practice again alone and with members of your career *familia*.

INTERVIEWING—PART 2: THE TWENTY-FIRST-CENTURY JOB INTERVIEW CHECKLIST

I am aware of the purpose and preparation for different types of interview situations.

- Informational Interviews
    - ❑ Telephone
    - ❑ Formal One-on-one
    - ❑ Recruitment events
- Screening Interviews
    - ❑ Telephone
    - ❑ Video conference
    - ❑ Face-to-face or one-on-one
    - ❑ Group
    - ❑ Computer
    - ❑ Campus
- Selection Interviews
    - ❑ One-on-one
    - ❑ Sequential
    - ❑ Serial
    - ❑ Panel
    - ❑ Group
- Questioning Formats
    - ❑ Traditional
    - ❑ Behavioral or competency-based interview
    - ❑ Performance interview
    - ❑ Case interview
    - ❑ Direct, indirect, and patterned interviews
    - ❑ Stress interview
    - ❑ Second/follow-up—third/follow-up
- Pre-employment Examination/Testing
    - ❑ Position-based competency
    - ❑ Psychological
    - ❑ Aptitude
    - ❑ Intelligence
    - ❑ Combination instruments
    - ❑ Honesty
    - ❑ Simulations

- Special Testing Circumstances
  - ❑ Drugs/alcohol
  - ❑ Medical examination
- Interview-Specific Research
  - ❑ Company and position review
  - ❑ Questions to ask before the interview
  - ❑ Research: Finding out what to expect in a specific interview
- Preparation: Understand the Keys to Powerful Communication
  - ❑ Ten essential interpersonal skills
  - ❑ Two standards provide the framework for clear communication in an interview: effective transfer of information and persuasiveness
  - ❑ Active listening
  - ❑ Maximizing your verbal communication skills
  - ❑ Maximizing your nonverbal communication skills
  - ❑ Body language
  - ❑ Nonverbal cues
- Preparation: Plan, Deal with Anxiety, Practice
  - ❑ Prepare your S.T.A.R. stories: situation, task, action, and result
  - ❑ Prepare your one- to two-minute introduction
  - ❑ Deal with interview anxiety
  - ❑ Be prepared for your interview
  - ❑ Use relaxation techniques
  - ❑ Practice the interview

Chapter 14

Interviewing

Part 3: Executing the Twenty-first-Century Job Interview

Myth: There is little I can do to stand out in an employment interview because the interviewer determines the format, decides which questions will be asked, and controls the session. Additionally, an interviewer's personal biases and perceptions cannot be overcome in a single meeting.

Truth: You have the *power* to influence the direction of the interview by how you present yourself and answer questions, proving you can do the job.

Reality 1: When you project your personal career brand from the moment you arrive at the interview, you make that critical first impression that gives an employer a reason to *consider* hiring you. By connecting your personal career brand to the interviewer's buying motivators, you give the employer the reasons to *hire* you.

Reality 2: Executing a successful interview requires thorough preparation, practicing until you are comfortable, presenting your personal career brand, using the power of R.E.S.P.E.C.T., and demonstrating that you can perform the job.

In this chapter, we will cover the following topics for successfully executing the twenty-first-century job interview.

- Interview strategies that work
- Answering common and difficult interview questions/sample responses
- Questions often asked of Latinos/sample responses
- Questions you can ask at the interview
- Navigating behavioral and competency-based interview formats
- Background checks
- Telephone interviewing checklists

INTERVIEW STRATEGIES THAT WORK

Susan Britton Whitcomb, president of Career Master's Institute and author of *Interview Magic*, coaches her clients to adapt a model she calls the "Four C's" to be successful in almost any interview format:

Phase 1: Connect with the interviewer to enhance chemistry.

Phase 2: Clarify the primary deliverables of the job (that you can do what needs to be done).

Phase 3: Collaborate on how you would do the job.

Phase 4: Close in a respectful manner that indicates your desire for the position and commitment to the company.

Phase 1: Connect

- Clear the first thirty-second hurdle with a positive halo effect during which most employers make their critical and dominant first impression of you.

- Share something in common based on your observation of some personal item that you notice in the interviewer's office or that you discovered during your pre-interview research.

- Respect the interviewer by showing consideration for the interviewer's position, time, and needs. When you show respect, you gain respect.

- Support the interviewer by focusing your conversation on the employer's needs and how you can meet them.

- Listen with laser accuracy using your ears and eyes to gain full understanding of the interviewer's intent. Demonstrate the listening techniques we discussed in Chapter 13 to create a connection magnet with the interviewer.

- Communicate exceptionally by determining the interviewer's personality and values and formulating your responses to how the interviewer will best "hear" you.

Phase 2: Clarify

- Identify the employer's top two or three deliverables.

- When responding to the interviewer's questions, use S.T.A.R. stories to tie your related competencies to the employer's needs (see Chapter 13). After you have demonstrated your value, the interviewer will be more open to being asked clarifying questions.

- Ask questions to determine the interviewer's needs or to confirm the deliverables you identified in your pre-interview research. Move forward methodically with your questions to help keep the interview focused and directed to the "picture" of how you meet the company's needs.

- Early on in the interview or if you have a difficult question, you may wish to solicit permission to ask a question.

Phase 3: Collaborate

■ After you understand what needs to be done, then you can ask more specific questions such as "What is working well?" or "What is not working well?" or "What would you like to see more of?"

■ Connect additional S.T.A.R. stories to the employer's needs. You might start out by saying, "We had a similar situation at XYZ Company . . ."

■ A good time to introduce supporting documents from your interviewing portfolio (see Chapter 4) is after a relevant S.T.A.R. story. Ask if the interviewer would like to see the material.

■ Show how you would do the job by way of making suggestions, collaborating on a problem, delivering a presentation, or asking if you can demonstrate specific skills.

Phase 4: Close

■ This is the C in our R.E.S.P.E.C.T. model for interviewing (see Chapter 12).

  ❏ State your interest in the position.
  ❏ Summarize why you are qualified for the job and close any gaps that the employer might perceive.
  ❏ Ask for feedback—"May I ask what you see as my greatest strength for the position?" or "Are you satisfied that I meet the needs of the position?"
  ❏ Clarify the remainder of the hiring decision process. "What are the next steps?"

■ To keep up the momentum and demonstrate your interest, ask if you could leave behind a relevant document from your interviewing portfolio.

■ Send a performance-based thank-you/follow-up letter (see Figure 8.10).

To best convey how to execute twenty-first-century interview strategies, we have placed the Master Interview Checklist below.

MASTER INTERVIEW CHECKLIST

Before the Interview

☐ Confirm the time, date, place, and details of the interview.

☐ You will need to know the full company address and directions, no matter what form of transport you use.

☐ Take a practice run to the location where you are having the interview. Try it at the same time of day so that you get a better idea of how long it will really take to get there.

☐ The night before, lay out your clothes and all items you are bringing with you.

☐ Make sure you get a good night's rest before the big day.

Attire

☐ Dress and adjust your attitude for success.

☐ Dress the part for the job, the company, and the industry.

Example: People who are seeking employment in an office usually wear suits or dresses to an interview, and those seeking construction work should wear work clothes that are clean.

☐ Do err on the side of conservatism.

☐ All interview clothing should be neat and clean. Shoes should be polished.

☐ Do not wear anything that will distract the interviewer's attention. Avoid excessive jewelry, makeup, and cologne or perfume.

☐ Be well groomed. Make sure your hair is neat and styled nicely, fingernails are clean and trimmed, and for men face is shaven or beard is trimmed.

☐ Do not have gum, candy, or cigarettes visible.

☐ Give yourself a second "once-over" before you arrive at the interview.

Bring with You

☐ Appointment book, PDA

☐ Quality folder or small briefcase

☐ Clean 8½″ × 11″ notepad

☐ Your interview portfolios or
  ❏ Birth certificate
  ❏ Social Security card
  ❏ Driver's license (copy)
  ❏ Any other licenses (including business, professional, and technical)
  ❏ Work authorization papers
  ❏ Passport/citizenship papers
  ❏ Additional personal information needed to complete employment applications and hiring documents (i.e., emergency contacts, physician information, medical insurance)
  ❏ Correspondence sent to and received from the employer
  ❏ Job posting and research on the position
  ❏ Company research
  ❏ Résumé—with notations related to the position (Your résumé may be used by the interviewer as a basis for asking some questions.)
  ❏ Interview specific S.T.A.R. stories (see Chapters 8 and 13)
  ❏ Your two-minute verbal biography and personal career brand statement tailored for the interview (see Chapter 13)

- ❑ Responses to questions you expect to be asked (see Chapter 13)
- ❑ Questions you have prepared to ask at the interview (see Chapter 13)
- ❑ Documentation of achievements listed in your résumé that are related to the position you are being interviewed for (see master portfolio checklist for types of documentation)—Do not use proprietary documents. You can fictionalize some of your work product.
- ❑ Performance reviews
- ❑ Writing samples
- ❑ Salary history (if requested)
- ❑ Photocopies of related diplomas, certificates, CEUs, licenses
- ❑ References—targeted reference list (see Chapter 8), master reference list and each reference on an individual page (you can select based on information gathered during your interview)
- ❑ Letters of recommendation
- ❑ Additional information to complete applications and other employment-related documents

Arrival

- ☐ Arrive fifteen to thirty minutes before your interview.
- ☐ Go to the interview alone. You don't want the employer to think you need hand-holding.
- ☐ Find a bathroom to freshen up, and *never* skip this step. You'd be amazed at what the mirror reveals, just in the nick of time. Use a restroom on a different floor from your appointment because you don't want to meet your interviewer there first.
- ☐ Use a breath mint, even if you don't think you need one.
- ☐ If you arrive more than fifteen minutes before the appointment, wait standing in the lobby—it implies energy. While waiting, read awards, posters, and company information, searching for topics of conversation, and check out the employees.
- ☐ Make sure you arrive at the interview floor fifteen minutes early.
    - ❑ Review your notes and résumé.
    - ❑ Read pertinent company literature that is available in the waiting area.
    - ❑ Take a few deep breaths, relax, and visualize.
    - ❑ Make sure you are not too cluttered and are able to stand up without having to fuss with your coat and personal items.
    - ❑ Turn off your cell phone.
- ☐ Realize that your interview starts the minute you arrive.
- ☐ Everyone you meet, from the receptionist to the hiring manager, will form an impression of you. To ensure the impression is positive, remember that your words and mannerisms will affect the image. Interviewers often ask for feedback from the receptionist.

☐ Being late is usually unacceptable. If you are running late, have the professional courtesy to call the office. You might just salvage your chance to be considered for the position.

Making a Good First Impression

☐ When greeting the interviewer, smile immediately.

☐ Make eye contact with your interviewer. It has a magical ability to build rapport.

☐ Offer a firm confident handshake. The right amount of tension in your grip is important—not too tight, not too limp.

☐ Introduce yourself, and say something like "I'm pleased to meet you" or "I've been looking forward to talking with you." Be sincere and avoid informal greetings you might use to say hello to your friends. Take the polite, conservative route.

☐ Wait to be told to take a seat or ask if you may, then say thank you. If you are offered a choice, select a chair closest to the interviewer's desk. Without making a commotion, scoot your chair a little closer to the interviewer's desk like you're ready to dive right in. This shows interest and confidence. Remember not to invade the interviewer's personal space and keep a distance of about two feet by U.S. standards.

☐ Be aware of your good posture while seated. Make sure that it shows you're alert and focused. Avoid negative body language.

☐ Don't eat, drink, chew gum, or smoke, or ask if it's okay to indulge in these activities. If the interviewer offers coffee or other beverages, while it's okay to accept, it is probably better to graciously say "I appreciate the offer, but I am fine thank you" (unless you're at an interview meal). This way you avoid any possible mishaps.

☐ Read the mood. If the interviewer is formal, then you probably should be, too. If the interviewer is casual, then follow along while remaining courteous and professional. In either case, try to appear to be relaxed, but not too relaxed.

☐ Observe the interviewer's office to see if there are personal or business items on display that you can use as a basis to establish rapport with the interviewer.

☐ Breathe deeply and relax. Speak slowly, clearly, and with purpose.

☐ Confirm the interviewer's name and the position you are being screened for. Request the correct spelling and pronunciation of the interviewer's name.

☐ Ask, "how much time will we have for this interview?" This will help you determine how to respond to the interviewer's questions and demonstrate a respect for his/her time.

Establish Rapport

☐ Share something in common based on your observation of some personal item that you saw in the interviewer's office or that you discovered during your pre-interview research.

☐ Use the personality matching or mirroring technique to make a connection. The idea is to match the interviewer's speaking rate, volume, tone, and pitch; physical characteristics, body language and mannerisms; and personality. Remember to stay within your personality range, but venture toward that portion of your range that most closely matches that of your interviewer.

☐ If you were referred by someone the interviewer knows or have a mutual acquaintance, be sure to mention the person's name at the beginning of the conversation.

Answer Questions

☐ Use the R.E.S.P.E.C.T. interviewing model to boost your interviewing power.

☐ Embrace your value!

☐ Manage your stress or anxiety.

☐ Be aware of your body language and that of the interviewer.

☐ Know your résumé. It may be used by the interviewer as a guide for questioning.

☐ Know your interview portfolio.

☐ Remember to focus on the employer's needs.

☐ Use the power of the Four C's to manage the direction of the interview.

☐ Use your interviewer's name when you answer a question.

☐ Use your two-minute prepared opening to communicate your personal career brand and create a great impression.

☐ Listen carefully to everything the interviewer says and ask questions when you don't understand something. Understanding each question will help you formulate the best response.

☐ Answer questions honestly. Answer questions truthfully, frankly, and succinctly. Do not overanswer questions.

☐ Answer questions with an appropriate balance of confidence and modesty. Do not be overly aggressive.

☐ Refer to your prepared interview notes when needed. Take notes during the interview and refer back to them.

☐ Show that you have researched the position, company, and industry when responding to questions.

☐ Respond with S.T.A.R. stories where appropriate to establish your competency and fit with the employer's needs. Remember to weave your stories into the answers of pertinent questions.

   ❏ Situation: Define the situation or "set the stage."

   ❏ Task: Identify the task/project performed.

   ❏ Action: Describe the action that you took/initiated. This response should illustrate the specific skills you used in completing the task.

   ❏ Result: Summarize the outcome. Use numbers, percentages, tangible outcomes, and comments made by customers or supervisors.

☐ Once in a while, answer a question by saying what somebody else has said about you.

   Example: "My supervisor always used to say, I can always count on Marisol to resolve customer issues."

☐ It is okay to be quiet for a moment before you answer a question. It'll help you gather your ideas and give a good answer. The employer will appreciate the fact that you're thoughtful.

☐ Ask questions to better answer the questions the interviewer asks you, for clarifying purposes. Withhold the bulk of your questions until the interviewer asks if you have any, which is typically toward the end of the interview.

☐ Avoid asking frivolous questions just because interviewers expect you to have questions. Instead, ask about important matters, such as job duties, management style, and the financial health of the company.

☐ Never say anything negative about former colleagues, supervisors, or employers.

☐ Try not to answer questions with a simple "yes" or "no." Explain whenever possible. Describe those things about yourself that showcase your talents, skills, and determination. Give examples.

☐ Typically, you'll negotiate salary, benefits, perks, and such in a follow-up interview. Regardless, don't bring it up until asked, yet be ready to discuss it at any time. It's not a good idea to ask questions about vacation, sick days, lunch breaks, and so on, until the interviewer brings up the subject.

Answering Common and Difficult Interview Questions/Sample Responses

The following are typical questions that might be asked during an interview and general guidelines as to how to answer them. We used and adapted this model with our colleague Norberto Kogan, president of TBK Career Management Services and The Kogan Group. We also recommend that you refer to *Resume Magic*, Barron's books on interviewing and other books identified in Appendix G. We suggest you rehearse with someone before interviewing.

1. **Tell me about yourself.**
   Be concise and limit your response to one or two minutes. Explain how your experience relates to the job opening and competencies required. Let the interviewer ask specific questions after the monologue. Showcase your personal career brand and related competencies (i.e., leadership, persistence).

2. **What do you know about our organization?**
   Be prepared to discuss products, services, and other details gleaned during your research on the company. Think of a specific improvement in product or service.

3. **What can you do for us? What can you do better than your competitors?**
   Focus on experience that meets employers' needs and solves bottom-line problems. Share a S.T.A.R. story. Show personal preference for product or service.

4. **Why should we hire you?**
   Provide examples of bottom-line contributions in previous jobs. Link your transferable skills (maturity, problem solving, communication, etc.) to specific company needs. "My unique skills and experience can drive your business. I add value!"

5. **What do you look for in a job?**
   In your own words—challenge, growth, and fair treatment.

6. **What do you know about this job?**
   Loosely define what you know about the position and competencies. Clarify job specifications.

7. **How long would it take you to make a meaningful contribution to our firm?**
   It takes three to six months for employers to get a return on their investment in a new employee. Be realistic. Do not promise more than you can deliver. Ask the interviewer their idea of a reasonable period.

8. **How long would you stay with us?**
   In your own words—as long as I am challenged, have an opportunity to grow, and am treated fairly.

9. **You may be overqualified or too experienced for the position.**
   The position probably pays less than what you need. If you want the job, explain how you can get up to speed quickly; how your experience will generate a faster return on their investment, and that you can relate to their staff better because of your maturity.

10. **Are you or could you become a good supervisor? Give an example. Why do you feel you have management potential?**
    Relate previous experiences. If you have not been a supervisor, describe activity on task forces or leadership in outside activities that reinforce your supervisory skills.

11. **Did you ever fire anyone? If so, what were the reasons and how did you handle it?**
    Describe the circumstance.

12. **What do you see as the most difficult task in being a supervisor?**
    Getting things done with and through people.

13. **Why are you leaving your present job?**
    You have achieved all of your goals and are looking forward to the challenges of (list specifics of the position and the needs of the company) the new position. If you have been downsized, remember to highlight your activity and reputation as a key producer.

14. **How has your educational experience prepared you for this position?**
    Focus on the academic, work, and volunteer experiences directly, and indirectly relate to the position and the interviewer's buying motivators.

15. **Describe what you feel to be an ideal working environment.**
    An environment where you are challenged, have an opportunity to grow as a person and an employee, and are treated fairly. Relate how these also meet the employer's needs.

16. **How would you evaluate your present employer?**
    Do not relate any negative feelings about your previous employers. The prospective employer is seeking to learn about your attitude.

17. **Have you helped increase sales or profits? Have you helped reduce costs? How much money did you account for? Did you supervise people on your last job?**
    Describe accomplishments. Use specific percentages, dollars, and staffing numbers. (Authors Note: Be careful of proprietory concerns if using dollar amounts.)

18. **Do you like working with figures more than words?**
    Try to illustrate a balance since communication is a vital aspect of most positions.

19. **What do your coworkers think of you?**
    Describe your interaction with peers and subordinates. List group projects. You should have a coworker as part of your reference list.

20. **In your current or last position, what features did you like the most? Least?**
    Describe some of your satisfiers and dissatisfiers (and how you manage them). Be careful, some of the items may be characteristics of the position. Be careful that related to dissatisfiers you found a growth opportunity.

21. **In your current or last position, what are or were your five most significant accomplishments? In your career so far?**
    Try to prepare for this question by prioritizing some of your accomplishments in order of your perceived significance.

22. **Identify activities and transferable skills that you developed or used during a break.**

23. **Describe a few situations in which your work was criticized.**
    Pick a situation and describe briefly. Explain that you were able to improve the situation quickly with your boss's guidance.

24. **If I spoke with your previous boss, what would he say are your greatest strengths and weaknesses?**
    Describe a few of your strengths. Try to identify a weakness that can be turned into a positive—"I tend to pay a lot of attention to detail; however, I do not want to make a serious or costly mistake."

25. **Have you worked under the pressure of a deadline? If so, how were you able to meet it.**
    Have a S.T.A.R. story prepared for this question.

26. **In your present position, what problems have you identified that had previously been overlooked.**
    Cite an accomplishment.

27. **Don't you feel you might be better off in a different size company? Different type of company?**
    This is an indication that the interviewer may not feel that you will fit into the company. Try to give the impression that you are looking for the challenges of the new environment and that your experiences and skills are transferable. Search for a life experience that is related to the situation.

28. **If you had your choice of jobs and companies, where would you go?**
    You are interviewing this company because you feel that the environment is for you and that you can make a contribution to the company's future.

29. **Why aren't you earning more at your age?**
    Be acquainted with the differences in pay scales between industries and companies within an industry.

30. **What do you feel this position should pay? How much do you expect and what kind of salary are you worth?**
    Research the range of salaries for comparable positions. This information is available from industry associations, professional societies, and the chamber of commerce offices. Know about benefit package before interviewing. Do not discuss benefits until after an offer. Mention your desire to be compensated at "market value" for the value you will bring to the job.

31. **Any objections to psychological tests?**
    More companies are using tests to qualify applicants because of the inability to gain information from references and the tendency for some to exaggerate on résumés.

32. **Why do you want to work for us?**
    Explain your desire to be part of their culture projects or challenges that you know the company is involved in.

33. **What other types of jobs or companies are you considering?**
    You do not have to name other firms. Explain that you are looking at firms with a challenge and career opportunity and that is why you are interviewing with their company.

34. **Have you kept up in your field? How?**
    Describe the workshops and seminars that are listed in your résumé. Try to relate to the activities of the new company.

35. **What was the last book you read? Movie you saw? Sporting event you attended?**
    This question is not asked frequently. The interviewer is interested in "fit" or chemistry.

36. **Are you creative? Give examples.**
    Cite accomplishment.

37. **How would you describe your own personality?**
    Use the traits you identified in your self-evaluation and relate to their expected competencies.

38. **Are you a leader? Give examples.**
    Cite accomplishments. Describe outside activities, people skills, and sensitivity. "I am adaptable."

39. **What are your goals?**
    Relate how this position fits into your overall career goals.

40. What are your strong points?
Cite strengths.

41. What are your weak points?
Prepare to discuss a weakness briefly. Turn a weakness into a positive (e.g., "my impatience to get the job done has made me pay attention to details to avoid mistakes).

42. How did you do in school?
Summarize first with as favorable and straightforward an approach as possible. If there were circumstances that interfered with studies, describe these briefly. These could include outside work to support education, the involvement in extracurricular activities, and the participation in sports.

43. How do you feel about people from minority groups?
You are committed to diversity and relate to the organizational objectives. See Chapter 15 on handling illegal questions.

44. Would you object to working for a woman/man?
You should have no objection.

45. What are your objectives? Long-range (five or more years)? Short range (one to three years)?
There is no certainty in the workplace. Information is changing very rapidly. Most companies are not guaranteeing job security. You should express the desire to grow in your profession and hope that the company will support your efforts to continue with your education and professional growth.

46. What are you doing or what have you done to reach those objectives?
Cite experiences and professional activities.

47. If you could start again, what would you do differently?
Explain that what you have learned from past experiences has made you a better employee. Give a positive example.

48. According to your definition of success, how successful have you been so far?
You should indicate a high degree of success according to your own definition.

49. How would you restructure this job?
It is too early to describe changes. Indicate that you would like a brief period of time to review the problem, learn the company policies, and understand the boss's expectations. If changes are needed, you would provide recommendations within several weeks after joining the company. Most often keep your comments broad (e.g., strategic) and not specific about the job unless you are very knowledgeable and comfortable.

50. What kind of hours are you used to working?
Whatever it takes to get the job done.

Questions Often Asked of Latinos/Sample Responses

Legal questions asked of Latinos are based on the essential functions of the job and should be asked of all applicants for the position. Refer to Chapter 15 if you feel that you are being asked questions that are illegal or inappropriate.

If you are applying for a position that requires Spanish language skills, you might expect to have a bilingual interview. You also might be given a test to assess your Spanish proficiency. In general, you may be asked some of the following questions:

1. Can you describe how you have read, spoken, written, and/or translated Spanish in your previous positions?
2. Can you describe other settings where you have read, spoken, written, or translated Spanish as is required in this position?
3. Are you proficient in Spanish technical terminology used in this position (i.e., medical, accounting, computer, engineering)?
4. Can you document your Spanish language proficiency?

This is a great opportunity to introduce targeted S.T.A.R. stories and appropriate portions of your bilingual portfolio.

- Résumé in Spanish
- Spanish, Portuguese, and other language career-marketing letters
- Documentation of achievements listed in your résumé that are related to the position
- Writing samples in English and Spanish (Do not use proprietary documents. You can fictionalize some of your work product.)
- Listing of how, when, and where you have used bilingual skills in work, academic, or volunteer settings
- Listing of Spanish coursework, training, and formal assessments of your language proficiencies
- Performance evaluations covering your use of bilingual skills
- Documentation of bilingual special pay or related compensation
- Letters of recommendation regarding your bilingual skills

If you are applying for positions that work with Latino markets, you may also be asked the following questions:

1. Describe your knowledge and experience in our industry as it applies to Latino markets?
2. Tell me about a time when you had to deal with a Latino customer service issue? How did you handle it?
3. Describe a time when you went through a series of steps to penetrate the Latino market with a product or service?
4. Describe a situation in which you developed an effective win–win relationship with a Latino client. How did you go about building the relationship?
5. Describe a situation in which you acted as an advocate within your company for your client's needs where there was some organizational resistance to be overcome?

Again, this is a great opportunity to introduce targeted S.T.A.R. stories and appropriate portions of your interviewing portfolio.

- Documentation of achievements listed in your résumé that are related to the position
- Selective performance reviews
- Selective writing samples
- Salary history (if requested)
- Photocopies of related diplomas, certificates, CEUs, licenses
- References list
- Letters of recommendation

QUESTIONS YOU CAN ASK AT THE INTERVIEW

Interviewers expect you to ask questions. As we mentioned in Chapter 13, interviews are an exchange of information between two or more people about you, the job, and the employer. You should prepare your own questions to achieve the following:

- Gather information you need to make your career decision
- Show that you understand the basics of the job you seek
- Demonstrate your level of commitment, interest, and abilities

Most interviewers will respect and even admire your efforts to obtain a full picture of the opportunity at hand. After all, you share a common goal: to identify whether you're the right person for the job. The more you can contribute in finding the answer to this question, the better off you both will be.

It's a professional courtesy to withhold the bulk of your questions until the interviewer asks if you have any. Interviewers typically ask toward the end of an interview or near the conclusion of each phase. Of course, it's okay to ask a few questions, to identify the employer's preferences, clarify matters, and steer topics, as the interview progresses. On the other hand, if the interview seems to be drawing to a close before the employer inquires if you have questions, inquire if you can ask some questions.

It is not appropriate to inquire about salary, benefits, and related issues until after a job offer is made. In many cases, your research will have collected much of this information and put you in a better position to discuss the total compensation package. Instead, try to determine how closely the position aligns with your professional needs and expectations. Remember, you are also choosing the next step in your career, as well as where you will be spending much of your waking hours for at least a while.

It is appropriate for you to have written down your prepared questions and refer to them during the interview. It shows that you're organized and interested enough in the job to have thought them through in advance.

The following is a discussion of five key questions you may wish to choose from to ask the employer.

1. Can you describe an ideal employee for this position?
   It is good to ask this question early in the interview to help you tailor your answers to the employer's inquiries and to select which S.T.A.R. stories to use. Addition-

ally, most companies have certain key competencies and traits they value in their employees based on their line of business and corporate culture. If you're looking to grow professionally, make sure you possess the qualities a prospective employer finds most important before accepting an offer.

2. **Please describe the primary duties in this position in a typical day.**
   This is another question you can ask early in the interview to assist you in controlling the content of your responses. Also, a position that sounds fabulous in theory may be less than satisfactory when it comes down to your daily routine. Likewise, a job that sounds initially overwhelming may appear more manageable once you've been provided the details. While understanding your overall function in the organization is important, knowing what's in store on a daily basis can be equally valuable.

3. **How do you define successful performance in this position?**
   You will also want to know how that performance is measured and reviewed. This is an opportunity to evaluate if descriptions of the employer's workplace culture are actually practiced.

4. **What growth and professional development opportunities exist for people in this position?**
   Look for specifics with this question. Is it the firm's general policy to promote from within? Is the company expanding so more opportunities are likely to become available? To which positions did other people in this job advance? Strong growth potential can be more beneficial than additional compensation in the long run, so learn what the prospects are early on.

5. **Can you explain how this position fits in your company's organizational structure?**
   This answer provides a road map of how many rungs you are from the top of the corporate ladder and indicates how much responsibility the job entails. It also clarifies who would be supervising you, who manages that person, who you may be supervising, and the number of people in the chain of command—information that shouldn't come as a surprise your first day on the job.

Some additional questions you might want to choose from follow.

About the Job

■ Can you tell me about the competencies necessary to perform this job?

■ Can you describe the best and worst aspects of this job?

■ How long do people usually stay in this job?

■ Can you tell me why the person(s) previously in this position left?

About the Department

■ How many employees are in this department?

■ How does this unit's objectives contribute to the overall company goals?

- What are the strengths of this department? Are there any weaknesses in the department that you're working to improve?

- Will I be able to meet the immediate supervisor for this position?

About the Company

- Where does this position fit in the organization?

- How would you describe the workplace culture?

- What steps is the company taking to be competitive in the twenty-first-century marketplace?

- Can you describe the company's primary objectives for the next couple of years?

NAVIGATING BEHAVIORAL AND COMPETENCY-BASED INTERVIEW FORMATS

Linda Matias, president of CareerStrides and Long Island Outplacement, recommends that interviewees comb the job descriptions and prepare stories to navigate behavioral and competency-based interviewing formats successfully.

Step 1: Comb Job Descriptions

Most companies spell out exactly what they want in the job description. Take the time to scrutinize job descriptions, not just of the company you are interested in, but also their competitors. You will find that the postings usually have a nice balance between general and industry-specific competencies. Take note of the recurring themes, and prepare for behavioral interviews based on the information you gathered.

For example, if the job description states that the company is looking for a team player, you can expect the interviewer to ask the following type of questions (or a variation of) during a behavioral interview:

- What was your role in your department's most recent success?

- Tell me about a time when you had to adjust to a colleague's working style in order to complete a project successfully.

- Describe a situation when working with others produced more successful results than if you had completed the project on your own.

As you can see, behavioral-based interviews can be challenging. However, knowing what the company is looking for sets the foundation to start preparing for the interview. After you have a grasp of the core competencies interviewers are likely to address, it will be easier to predict the kind of questions they will ask.

Step 2: Prepare Stories

For every competency that you have identified, write a story that supports each one. As in any good story, yours should focus on the following: the who, what, where, when, why, and how. As an example of how you should answer behavioral-based questions, let's address the first question mentioned in Step 1: "What was your role in your department's most recent success?"

Here's a possible response using a S.T.A.R. story:

Situation: "At my current employer, The Widget Center, the sales and customer service departments work collaboratively to win and retain accounts. The sales team negotiates the deal and as a customer service manager my role is to ensure that the customer is satisfied with their purchase and handle any glitches that may arise."

Task: "In one particular case, I resolved a potentially damaging situation with a key client when the $1.5 million database system they had purchased began faltering a week after it was installed. Needless to say the customer was not pleased and demanded that all the monies be refunded."

Action: "After I listened to the customer's concern, I immediately dispatched technical support."

Result: "The problem was resolved within one business day with little loss of productivity on the part of the client. In the end, the customer upgraded all the database systems in all four locations."

Linda Matias said, "As a Latina I learned from my family that storytelling is an excellent method of explaining so everyone understands. In the case of the above situation, the interviewee's response has the makings of a classic story—a damsel in distress, a hero coming to the rescue, and a 'they lived happily ever after' ending."

Marcia Perez, a chemical engineer for Exelon Corporation, and Mary Devo, customer service help desk representative for Walgreen's Pharmacy computer services unit, both used this strategy to secure their positions. Marcia read Robin Ryan's 60 Seconds and You're Hired *and has been recommending it to job seekers she knows. Mary learned this strategy from us at the Hispanic Alliance for Career Enhancement's Career Help Center.*

BACKGROUND CHECKS

Background Screening

Following is the general guidance we provide to employers to obtain background information without trampling on an applicants' privacy rights:

- Get applicants to sign a form verifying that they have been informed that a reference/background check will be conducted. Safer: Have applicants sign consent forms that give former employers permission to release employment-related information.

- Let applicants know what kind of information you're gathering and why.

- Make sure trained human resources personnel, the hiring supervisor, or an outside reference-checking agency conducts all reference/background checks.

- Only seek out factual, job-related information.

- Make sure the information you gather on each applicant is kept confidential, with access given only to those with a legitimate, business need-to-know.

Credit Checks

There are two areas of legal concern besides the Fair Credit Reporting Act (FCRA) of 1994 when an applicant is denied employment based in part on information in his/her credit report.

1. **The Bankruptcy Act**: If a credit check indicates that the individual has declared bankruptcy, the employer must comply with the provisions of the federal Bankruptcy Act. Under this act, it's unlawful to terminate an employee or to discriminate in the hiring of an employee solely because that person has sought the protection of the Bankruptcy Act, has been insolvent before seeking protection under the act, or has not paid a debt that is dischargeable under the act.
2. **Title VII**: Rejection of applicants because of poor credit ratings has a disparate impact on minority groups and has been found unlawful by the Equal Employment Opportunity Commission (EEOC) unless business necessity can be shown.

To be on the safe side, many companies reserve credit checks for fiduciary positions or other jobs in which bad credit may have a negative effect. Otherwise, the FCRA (1994) oversees the proper use of credit checking in hiring. Employers have to beware when conducting credit checks these days because of substantial changes to FCRA requirements. It used to be that an employer who denied an applicant employment based in part on information in a credit report was required under the FCRA to notify the applicant that the report played a part in the denial and to give the applicant the name and address of the reporting agency so that the individual could correct any errors.

Employers' obligations under the FCRA are now stricter. Now they must notify applicants before requesting their credit reports and obtain written acknowledgment of the notification. Not only that, employers who use credit reports in the hiring process must give applicants the name and telephone number of the reporting agency and a statement of their rights to dispute the accuracy of those credit reports. If an employer relies on a credit report for an adverse action, it must give the individual a pre-adverse action disclosure that includes a copy of the individual's credit report and a statement of the employee's rights under the FCRA prior to taking the adverse action.

References

It is best to ask applicants to sign a consent form releasing previous employers from liability when providing a reference. This release can be sent to the human resources department of the previous workplace along with your reference form or prior to calling. Former employers and references should be specific to the candidate's ability to perform the essential functions of the position in question.

School Records

Under federal law and the law of some states, educational records—including transcripts, recommendations, and financial information—are confidential. Because of these laws, most schools will not release records without the consent of the student. Some schools will only release records directly to the student.

Workers' Compensation Records

An employer may use the information contained in the public record from a Workers' Compensation Appeal only if the injury in question might interfere with the applicant's or worker's ability to perform required duties.

TELEPHONE INTERVIEWING CHECKLIST

Here are the keys to successful phone interviewing. If you follow these simple rules, you should achieve success in this important phase of job hunting.

Information to Provide to Potential Employers

Provide accurate and detailed telephone contact information in your résumé and cover letter so your interviewers can easily connect with you.

☐ In certain circumstances it may be important to supply additional contact information. A college student going on spring break during the contact interval after submitting a letter and résumé might choose to include an explanation.

Example: "From March 17 to March 29, I will be out of the state/out of the country on spring break. During that time I can be reached at this number/I will be unreachable/I will be unreachable by phone but plan to check my email daily."

☐ An applicant who cannot be contacted during work hours might include the following information.

Example: "Although I prefer to receive messages at my home number, I check messages frequently throughout the day and can usually return calls during breaks."

☐ If you are relocating, include "until" dates with your phone, email, mailing information, and new contact information.

Prepare Your Voice Mail, Answering Machine, and Household Member Message Taking

☐ During your job search, keep a simple professional-sounding greeting on your answering machine or voicemail.

☐ Make sure that your message has at least one simple identifier that you are comfortable with, so that the employers know that they have reached the correct number.

Examples: "You've reached the Tobias Family. Please leave a detailed message at the tone and we will return your call as soon as possible" or "You've reached Andres and Maria Elena. Please leave a message" or "You've reached 949-000-000. Please leave a message." Again, each job seeker must determine what is comfortable. Don't change your message if you feel uncomfortable about having this information on your outgoing greeting.

☐ If the position you are applying for requires bilingual skills, then repeating your message in Spanish demonstrates proficiency in both languages.

☐ Ensure that household members understand the importance of taking detailed phone messages during your job search.

Prepare Your Telephone Interview Space

☐ If possible, dedicate space at home for your telephone interview. This spot should be quiet, ideally have a door that closes, and be somewhere you can easily talk on the phone. You will need to read notes, take notes, and concentrate.

☐ Keep your résumé in view of the phone. It will be there for the call and will be a constant reminder of your job search.

☐ Create a small file for each position you apply for within easy reach of the phone. The file should include

❑ The job posting and specific company research (with highlighted key points)

❑ A copy of the résumé you sent in (if it was modified for the position)

❑ Your three to five strengths and position-related accomplishments for the position

❑ S.T.A.R. note cards and stories

❑ Specific questions you want to ask the employer

☐ Have paper and pen handy to take notes. Do not take notes on a computer unless your keyboard is silent.

☐ Have your calendar or PDA available to schedule an in-person interview.

☐ Be sure to use a high-quality phone, handset, or headset when participating in a phone interview. To ensure that you are communicating clearly, do not use a speakerphone or a cell phone.

☐ If you are using a portable phone, make sure your unit has fresh batteries and that you stay within range.

☐ Place a mirror where you can see the image you are projecting. It comes across in your voice.

If the Phone Interview Will Occur at a Set Time

☐ Warm up your voice while waiting for the call.

☐ Review your notes.

☐ Place a "Do Not Disturb" note on your door.

☐ Turn off your stereo, TV, and any other potential distraction.

☐ Have a glass of water handy, in case you need to wet your mouth.

☐ Speaking of breaks, if your phone interview is at a set time, make sure you use the restroom earlier.

☐ Turn off call waiting on your phone.

Practice Your Telephone Interview Techniques

☐ Have members of your career *familia* call you to conduct a mock phone interview so that you gain the experience of being interviewed over the phone. The calls can be scheduled and unscheduled to help you prepare for both types.

☐ If possible, tape record the practice interview so that you can hear yourself.

☐ If the position requires Spanish language skills, practice in both languages.

☐ Practice sufficiently so that your responses do not sound scripted and you do not fumble over important points.

Try These Winning Telephone Interview Techniques

If your phone interview is scheduled for the early morning, change out of your pajamas, take a shower, and have a cup of coffee or tea to clear your voice.

☐ **Dress nicely**. You will actually project a more professional image than if you were wearing sweats. Dressing better helps you act as if you are at an in-person interview. It can improve your confidence.

☐ **Stand during the phone interview**. Many experts say that it improves your telephone presence and sounds more professional. It gets your blood flowing, improves your posture, speeds your response time, and makes your voice stronger. Standing and even a little pacing back and forth helps give an action perspective to an otherwise passive activity.

☐ **Look in the mirror regularly and smile**. Smiling improves your telephone voice. You will find yourself coming across much friendlier, more interested, and more alert. Seeing yourself as you are speaking on the phone lets you know if you need to change your phone attitude to project a more positive presence.

☐ **Match the interviewer's phone personality**. Try to use the same speaking rate, tone, and pitch as the interviewer, as much as you are comfortable with. Hearing the familiar speaking style helps the recruiter to feel more connected to you. It is an excellent way to establish rapport quickly over distance and phone lines.

When a Recruiter Calls Unexpectedly

☐ If you receive an unexpected call from a recruiter and he/she expects to interview you right then and there, your first step is to be calm! Say something to buy a little time.

Examples: "Terrific! Could you give me a moment to go to a room where we won't be interrupted?" or "Could you give me just a moment to close the door?"

When they agree, cover the voice piece on the phone and go to your quiet area where you have all of your job search material prepared, take two or three deep breaths, and then continue.

☐ If you are genuinely unable to devote enough time to an unscheduled phone interview or are not ready to continue with the interview, politely ask the recruiter for an alternate time. It is preferable to proceed with the interview, if possible, because you might not get a call back. If you must reschedule, offer to be the one who calls back at a scheduled time.

Conducting the Phone Interview

☐ Breathe deeply and relax. Speak slowly, clearly, and with purpose. Remember that your initial goal is to create a great first impression.

☐ Confirm the interviewer's name and the position you are being screened for. Request the correct spelling and pronunciation of the interviewer's name.

☐ Ask how much time will be allotted for this interview. This will help you determine how to respond to the recruiter's questions.

☐ Take notes. You might hear something important about the position or company that you could refer to later. They will also be invaluable in preparing for the face-to-face meeting.

☐ Listen carefully to the interviewer's questions to understand the intent of the questions. Because telephone interviews are time-limited, you then will be able to provide your best responses.

☐ Use the technique of repeating or rephrasing questions. It tells the caller that you listened carefully and gives you time to think about your answer.

☐ Avoid a simple yes or no answer; add selling points at every opportunity.

☐ Be brief when answering your questions. You want to be thorough and keep up your end of the conversation, but you also don't want to ramble.

☐ Support your statements with detailed examples of accomplishments when possible. It is easy for someone to get distracted on a phone call, so paint a vivid picture to keep the interviewer interested.

☐ Use your talking points list of related skills and accomplishments; cross them off as you work them into the conversation. At the end, if you have some uncrossed items that are relevant to the interviewer, you might want to bring these items to light.

Example: "I thought you might be interested to know I coordinated the Hispanic market development project, quite similar to what you are planning. I managed a $50,000 budget for Latino Friendly Company, Inc. and increased our customer base by 30 percent."

☐ Use the interviewer's last name occasionally (only use a first name if the recruiter asks you to), and refer to the company by name a few times.

☐ Do not feel you have to fill in the silences. If you've completed a response, but the interviewer hasn't asked his/her next question, don't start babbling just to fill in airtime. Instead, ask a question of your own related to your last response.

☐ If you hear anything about the company or position that is particularly interesting or attractive, say so. Remarks like "That sounds exciting," "What a great opportunity," or "I worked on a very similar project with my last company and loved it" can convey your interest in the position and the company, which could help increase your chances of being invited to the face-to-face interview.

☐ Deliver a strong finish to your phone interview with thoughtful questions.

☐ Avoid sniffling, sneezing, or coughing. If you can't prevent these actions, say "excuse me."

☐ No gum chewing, eating, or drinking except for a little water, if needed, to keep your voice clear.

Closing the Interview

☐ Show you're interested. When it feels right and it sounds like the interview is wrapping up, ask for a date to meet for a face-to-face interview.

Example: "This sounds like a great position and I know I could step in and contribute. I would love the opportunity to sit down with you in person and discuss this even further. When could we meet for an interview?"

☐ If the interviewer hedges or says "I'll call you," try to politely probe a little further. Ask "When might I likely hear back from you?"

☐ If you are invited for the face-to-face interview, be certain to thank the interviewer and get the important details—when, where, with whom you are interviewing, the format of the interview or process (length and how many interviews are normally undertaken), and whether there is anything in particular you need to bring. Repeat the key details to make sure your notes are accurate.

☐ Remember to thank the interviewer for the opportunity and his/her time.

☐ Do not hang up until the interviewer has hung up.

After the Call

☐ Immediately after the call, add to your notes about what you were asked and how you answered.

☐ Next, write a short thank-you note. The wording for a thank-you for a phone interview follows.

Example: "Thank you for spending time with me on the phone today talking about the enrollment management position. I enjoyed the conversation and have a better understanding of the job. I'd be interested in an on-site interview and would welcome the opportunity to further discuss my candidacy."

Chapter 15

How to T.R.I.U.M.P.H. over Illegal Interview Questions

Myth: Interviewers control the entire process; there is nothing you can do if you encounter an interviewer who is biased.

Truth: Not every interviewer is trained in performing interviews, particularly in smaller companies. Oftentimes when an interviewer asks an illegal question, he/she is doing it inadvertently.

Reality 1: Part of the preparation you do for an interview requires that you be prepared and knowledgeable about legal and illegal questions. This way you will feel confident and can take control if such a situation arises.

Reality 2: If an interviewer is biased and asks illegal or inappropriate questions, you have several alternatives on how to handle the situation including filing a charge of discrimination. The important point is to address it so that future applicants will not face similar treatment.

ILLEGAL INTERVIEW QUESTION SCENARIOS

Your interview is going just as you envisioned and prepared for. You think you have nailed it. Then you are blindsided with an illegal, inappropriate, or offensive question.

So what do you do if it happens to you? In our experience, illegal questions are most often asked in one of four different situations. If you are able to determine which of these scenarios is at work, it may have an impact on your decision as to how to react. We'll discuss the scenarios first and then provide possible responses.

Scenario 1: Small Talk

Many topics appropriate for personal and social discussions are illegal or inappropriate during an interview. This is why illegal questions are often asked during the first few minutes of ice breaking or after the formal interview is over.

Example: During an informal conversation after the interview, you mention the community fair you attended the day before. The interviewer asks, "Oh, do you have kids? How old are your kids? How many kids do you have?" While these questions may be fine at a party, they are not appropriate or legal in an interview.

Scenario 2: Résumé Follow-up

An interviewer may be reviewing your résumé and asking questions about information listed on your résumé. Some of these questions are inappropriate.

Example: Your résumé mentions that you are "Fluent in Spanish." The interviewer says, "I see you are fluent in Spanish." Okay and legal so far. Then the interviewer follows up with, "Are you a native Spanish speaker?" or "Did you learn Spanish at home from your parents or in a class at school?" These kinds of questions are illegal.

Another example: You have listed on your résumé "Vice President, Latino Student Association." The interviewer asks, "I see you are VP of the Latino student organization. What country is your family from and how long have they been in the United States?" Again, these are illegal questions.

Now there is something of a fine line here. It is not illegal per se for interviewers to ask about your involvement in student organizations if you have listed them on your résumé. An organization referenced on your résumé is fair game, and the employer will assume you want to talk about it. It is perfectly appropriate for an interviewer to ask about leadership skills you are developing as vice president of the organization or what events the group will be holding this year. But the interviewer cannot use these kinds of leading questions to ask about your ethnicity or national origin.

Scenario 3: Legitimate Purpose—Question

Sometimes there is an arguably legitimate question underlying an illegal question.

Example: The interviewer asks, "Are you married, and if so what does your spouse do?"

This question has all sorts of illegal implications—it potentially touches on marital status or even sexual orientation. Why would an interviewer ask such a blatantly inappropriate question? The interviewer may be inquiring because he/she is concerned about retention. The interviewer may also want to determine whether you are "attached" to anyone who may work in a high-turnover industry or who may be transferred to another city next year and take you along. But the question is still inappropriate.

Scenario 4: Bias

Sadly, one of the reasons that interviewers may ask illegal questions is the most obvious. It may be a red flag that your interviewer is insensitive to diversity issues and perhaps be even downright discriminatory.

Example: In this day and age our clients still encounter interviewers who ask job seekers if they are Mexican or Puerto Rican; who make derogatory remarks about one group or the other; who comment that "these are the only Latino jobs we have at our company"; who question if Latinas can work with white male supervisors; or who make a point of mentioning that the employer frowns on speaking Spanish on the company property, playing loud Spanish music, and partying in employee break areas and parking lots. Unfortunately the list goes on and on.

T.R.I.U.M.P.H. over Illegal Interview Questions

What if your gut tells you that this is not a totally insensitive, discriminatory interviewer, but that the interviewer slipped up in the phrasing of the question. Perhaps you are truly interested in this company and have sensed that the interviewer's insensitivity or inappropriateness may not be representative of the company as a whole. On the other hand, you may believe that the interview does reflect the company's treatment of minorities and women.

It is important to note that handling this delicate situation is a balancing act. We recommend that you choose to address illegal, inappropriate, and insensitive questions in a manner that supports your best interest in securing a job that fits your values and goals.

What Can You Do?

Remember that you *prepared* for this possibility. Even though you can't control the questions that are asked, you do control how you T.R.I.U.M.P.H. over illegal interview questions.

The seven T.R.I.U.M.P.H. approaches are:

Take a step back; evaluate the question and the situation.

Respond to the question directly.

Identify the intent behind the question and respond indirectly with an answer that relates to the requirements of the position.

Upstage and ignore the question by redirecting the conversation.

Mention the error diplomatically.

Politely refuse to answer the question.

Hit the road. Gracefully and professionally excuse yourself.

Let's look at these seven approaches in more depth.

1. Take a Step Back

Perhaps the question did not come out as the interviewer intended. If the interviewer is given a chance to think about it, he/she might quickly recognize their error. Ask yourself these questions:

- How uncomfortable does this question make you feel?

- Does the interviewer seem unaware that the question is illegal?

- Does your gut feeling tell you that this illegal question is an interviewer's mistake, or does it indicate deeper problems with the company?

- Is this interviewer going to be your boss?

- If you believe the questions reflect the culture of the company, is this a place you want to work?

Tactfully ask for a clarification to give the interviewer enough time to pause and rephrase or strike the question.

Example:

Their Question: *"Are you from Central America?"*

Your Question: *"Could you elaborate on your question as it relates to the job so that I can be sure to provide all the information you need?"*

If Their Answer Is: *Repeating the same inappropriate question*

or

"The person we hire for this position will service our customers in Central America. Can you tell us what sales and marketing experience you have in this region?"

Then respond in a way that you prepared for and is comfortable for you.

2. Respond to the Question Directly

There's no rule saying that you can't respond directly to an illegal question, if you are comfortable with it. There is only a rule saying that the employer shouldn't ask the question. Maybe your company research or instincts tell you that answering will help you land the job.

The following considerations may be useful in assessing whether you want to answer a non-job-related question directly:

■ If you determine that it's okay to disclose information and you do not believe the question will harm your candidacy.

❑ Preferably, reply to it briefly, and then move on to something else.

   or

❑ Elaborate on your response, if you have assessed that that the question was asked so you could link your qualifications to the employers' needs. Be careful here.

■ By replying to the question, you may actually improve your chances of getting the job, particularly if you provide the "right" answer or response the interviewer is looking for.

■ If you choose to do so, realize that you are giving information that is not job related. You can also harm your candidacy by giving the "wrong" answer.

3. Identify the Intent and Respond Indirectly

Maybe the interviewer is asking a question such as "are you married?" because he or she is worried that you will not be able to travel or work long hours. If you are a Latina, this kind of question might signal gender bias and Hispana stereotyping.

Another common illegal question is asking for your immigration status. The interviewer may be concerned about whether you can be lawfully hired, how long you will be able to work for the company, and whether you are going to ask for sponsorship. In some cases, they may assume you are not familiar with U.S. business practices.

Example:

Their Question: *What country are you from and what is your specific immigration status?*

Your Answer: *I am authorized to work in the United States. As my résumé and portfolio show, I have extensive experience successfully working with your products and customers. I would be more than happy to demonstrate my expertise for you.*

4. Upstage and Ignore the Question by Redirecting the Conversation

Courteously overlook the question by not giving the information requested. You won't have to sacrifice your principles while you avoid offending or embarrassing the employer.

Example:

Their Question: *"Are you married?"*

Your Answer: *"If you are asking whether I will be able to meet the work schedule or time requirements of the position, the answer is yes. Yours is an excellent company, and I believe I will be an asset to you because . . . "*

5. Mention the Error Diplomatically

Example:

Their Question: *"Are you a U.S. citizen?"*

Your Answer: *"Yes, I am. I hope you do not mind, but you may not be aware that the question as worded is unlawful. I believe it is appropriate to ask applicants if they are authorized to work in the United States."*

or

Their Question: *"Do you have children?"*

Your Answer: *"I know we're not really supposed to talk about these types of things in an interview setting, but I have one child."*

These responses should keep the interviewer from going any further with inappropriate lines of inquiry. It also shows the interviewer that you are knowledgeable about the law and able to quickly compromise and solve problems.

6. Politely Refuse to Answer the Question

You have the right to refuse to answer an illegal question. It is understandable that you would refuse to do so. But bear in mind that there is a fair chance that you will not get the job if you decline to answer. You may or may not.

A flat refusal to answer may harm your chances of being hired for a position if the interviewer sees you as an uncooperative or stubborn person.

By selecting this option, you'll be within your rights, but you'll also run the risk of coming off as uncooperative, stubborn, or confrontational—hardly the words an employer would use to describe the "ideal" candidate.

Example: *If the interviewer repeats the same illegal question after you tactfully ask for a clarification as to the job relatedness of the question.*

Their Question: *"You have one child; are you planning to have more?"*

Your Answer: *"I do not feel comfortable answering this question because it is not related to the requirements of the job or my ability to perform them."*

Start Taking Notes: *At this point your should openly take notes including the specific question, the context surrounding the question, date, time, location, interviewer's name, witnesses (if any), business unit, and the company.*

Most employers will realize the potential consequences when you start documenting your discussion, and it is unlikely that the interviewer will pursue the issue further.

7. *Hit the Road.*

If the idea of working for an employer who condones the asking of inappropriate or illegal questions turns you off, and you know that you would not want to work for this company, then you may want to end the interview.

Example:

Their Question: *"What does a smart cute chica like you think it takes to be successful in this job?"*

Your Answer: *"Excuse me? What do you mean by this question?"*

Their Reply: *"You know what I mean. We have several well-qualified applicants for this job. What can you offer me that they can't?"*

Your Response: *"I think I am ending this interview right now. It is not appropriate or professional of you to call me a 'smart cute chica.' I am offended by the implication that I have to offer you anything to get this job beside my skills and qualifications."*

Next, immediately go somewhere and write down everything that transpired. In addition to following the guidelines that follow, be sure to read Chapter 17.

What to Do If You Think You Have Been Discriminated Against at the Interview

Please review Chapter 17 to determine whether EEOC and state and local regulatory agencies have jurisdiction over illegal questions and interviewer actions. Also check company policies.

There are several actions you can take if you have been a victim of a discriminatory interview:

- Most colleges have strict no-tolerance policies for any type of discrimination by recruiters and employers. Contact the career placement office to inform them of the discriminatory interview that took place. You may also be asked to submit a letter detailing your specific experience.

- Notify your referral sources, career *familia*, and the professional associations you belong to.

- Contact the company Latino employee group, office of diversity, and/or the EEO/AA office.

- File a complaint with federal, state, and/or local EEO enforcement agency.

What If You Want to Bring Up a Sensitive Issue?

What if the interviewer hasn't asked you anything touching on these topics, but you want to talk about it?

You may want to know about the company's Latino workforce, or whether there is a company Latino employees group. What are the company's policies on flex-time, family leave, and professional development programs? These are the types of questions that may be very important to you.

You should feel free to ask these questions and a savvy, well-prepared interviewer should be ready and able to answer them openly. But be mindful of how you introduce the topic. Sensitive interviewers know they can't ask questions that seek to illicit information about you regarding these areas. So if (in the process of asking your question) you offer information that identifies yourself as a parent, a married person, a certain national origin, you may see your interviewer visibly squirm. But that doesn't mean that you can't ask about issues you care about.

It is a matter of how you ask. Remember your questions demonstrate your professionalism. You are a Latino professional, and your profession is not perceived solely as Latina or Latino.

Example: *What is the difference between these two questions?*

Generic Question: *"Can you tell me a little bit about your firm's corporate culture and policies relating to diverse employee groups?"*

as opposed to

Specific Question: *"I have two kids. What can you tell me about your family-friendly policies?"*

Do you see the subtle yet very important difference? In one situation, you self-identified, but in the other you did not.

How to Determine If an Interview Question Is Illegal

Federal, state, and local equal employment opportunity laws narrowly interpret what can and cannot be asked at an employment interview. Basically, interview questions must be directly related to the essential functions of the job—the legal term is bona fide occupational qualifications (BFOQ). These questions must be asked of all applicants. Although some questions may seem harmless enough and are perfectly acceptable outside of the United States, they are forbidden in this country.

A chart of frequently asked illegal interview questions (and the legal equivalents, if any) follows.

Samples of Acceptable and Unacceptable Interview Questions

Interview questions must be asked of all applicants.

Age

Acceptable: None.
The exception is when the employer can prove that age is BFOQ—Is it necessary to perform the job?

Example:
Compliance with child labor laws.
Others are usually difficult or impossible to prove.
A pre-employment application may request the applicant's age or date of birth as long as it will not be used in any employment decision.

Unacceptable: Any question designed to discover someone's age.

Examples:
How old are you?
What's your birth date?
When did you graduate from high school?

Arrest

Acceptable: None.
Exceptions: Law enforcement agencies are exempt from this restriction. Some positions covered under the Homeland Security Act.

Unacceptable: Any inquiry relating to arrests. Because, under our judicial system, you are presumed innocent until proven guilty, records of arrests without conviction are meaningless.

Availability for weekend work (religious discrimination)

Acceptable: The employer may want to know about an applicant's availability for Saturday or Sunday work. Even if the applicant's religious observance makes him or her unavailable for weekend shifts, this fact cannot be used in a hiring decision.

Title VII requires employers to make *"reasonable accommodation"* for a *"prospective employee's religious observance"* unless it causes *"undue hardship."*

Unacceptable: Any inquiry relating to religious observance.

Citizenship

Acceptable: Whether the applicant is prevented from lawfully becoming employed in this country because of visa or immigration status.

Whether the applicant can provide proof of citizenship, visa, or alien registration number after being hired.

Unacceptable: Whether applicant is a citizen. Any requirement that the applicant present birth, naturalization, or baptismal certificate before being hired.

Convictions

Acceptable: It is permissible to inquire about an applicant's conviction record for "security-sensitive" jobs or jobs where the conviction is directly related to the job duties—such as a child abuse conviction for a day care worker—since it has been shown that people with high conviction rates are poor risks for these jobs.

Security-sensitive jobs include not only the obvious—treasurer, cashier, etc.—but peripheral positions as well—janitor, typist, trucker, or other jobs where the employee would be working in or near a security-sensitive area.

Example:
Under these circumstances, the interviewer may ask:
"Have you ever been convicted of . . . ?"

Unacceptable: Questions about conviction unrelated to job requirements.

Example:
Inquiries about gambling arrests for the job of pipe fitter.

Credit inquiries

Acceptable: None.

Unacceptable: Inquiries about charge accounts, bank accounts, etc.

Disabilities

Acceptable: An applicant can be asked about his/her ability to perform essential functions of the job, as long as the questions are not phrased in terms of disability and if the interviewer has thoroughly described the job.

An applicant can be asked to demonstrate how, with or without reasonable accommodation, he/she will perform job-related functions.

These questions must be asked of all applicants for the position.

Unacceptable: Note: The Americans with Disabilities Act requires that individuals with disabilities be afforded the same access to the employment process as applicants without disabilities.

Examples:
"Do you have any disabilities?"
Questions about a visible disability.
Please answer the following questions about your medical history . . . ?
How's your family's health? (often raised by concerns that you will have to take time off to care for a family member)
Do you need an accommodation to perform the job? (This question can be asked only after a job offer has been made.)

Drug testing

Acceptable: The Americans with Disabilities Act *does not* prohibit employers from testing applicants or employees for *current illegal drug use*, or from making employment decisions based on verifiable results.

Unacceptable: If the drug testing is applied inconsistently or inequitably.

Education

Acceptable: Inquiry to check if the individual has the specific education or training required for the specific job.

Unacceptable: General questions about high school or college degrees unless the educational degree inquired about is necessary to perform the job.

Family status

Acceptable: Whether applicant has any activities, commitments, or responsibilities that might prevent him/her from meeting work schedules or attendance requirements.

Note: It is unlawful to ask this only of women or only of men.

Unacceptable: Whether the applicant is married or single, number and age of children, spouse's job, with whom do you live, spouse's or applicant's family responsibilities, child care arrangements.

Any question asked only of one sex.

Financial status

Acceptable: None.

Unacceptable: Inquiries about an applicant's financial condition. This has been found to result in discrimination against minorities because more nonwhites than whites are below the poverty level.

Questions about home ownership or car ownership (unless owning or renting a car is required for the job).

Height and weight

Acceptable: Inquiries about ability to perform the job (without mentioning the person's height or weight).

Unacceptable: Any inquiry about height or weight not based on the actual job requirements, in which the employer must be able to prove that a specific minimum or maximum height or weight is required to perform the job.

Medical exams

Acceptable: Medical exams *can only be required after a legitimate job offer is made* and prior to the commencement of employment duties, if everyone who will be working in the job category must also take the examination. The employer may condition the job offer on the results of the medical exam.

Unacceptable: If a medical examination reveals a job-related disability, an employer must be able to show that there was no reasonable accommodation that would have made it possible for the individual to perform the job-essential functions.

Marital status	**Acceptable:** None.
	Unacceptable: Whether the applicant is married, single, divorced, separated, engaged, or widowed.

Military status	**Acceptable:** Inquiries about education, training, or work experience gained in U.S. armed forces.
	Unacceptable: Type or condition of military discharge.
	Experience in other than U.S. armed forces.
	Request for discharge papers.

National origin	**Acceptable:** Inquiries into applicant's ability to read, write, and speak English or foreign languages when required to performance for a specific job.
	Example: What languages do you read, speak, and write? What is the level of fluency for each.
	Unacceptable: Questions about an applicant's lineage, ancestry, national origin, descent, place of birth, mother tongue, or national origin of applicant's parents or spouse.
	Example: How applicant acquired ability to read, write, or speak a foreign language?

Organizations/ affiliations	**Acceptable:** Inquiries about membership in professional organizations related to the job.
	Example: List any professional or trade groups or other organizations that you belong to that you consider relevant to your ability to perform this job.
	Unacceptable: Inquiries about community groups, clubs, fraternal organizations, not-for-profit associations, professional/trade organizations (not related to the job), social groups, sports activities.

Personal information	**Acceptable:** Whether the applicant has ever worked for the organization.
	Whether the applicant has ever worked for the organization under another name.
	Names of character references.
	Unacceptable: General inquiries about change of name through application in court or marriage.

Pregnancy

Acceptable: Inquiries about the applicant's anticipated duration of stay on the job or anticipated absences—only if both male and female applicants are asked the same question.

Unacceptable: Any question relating to pregnancy or medical history concerning pregnancy.

Note: the EEOC has ruled that to refuse to hire a female solely because she is pregnant amounts to sex discrimination.

Race or color

Acceptable: None.

Unacceptable: Any questions about race or color.

Relatives

Acceptable: Name of any relative already employed by the organization or competitor.

(This inquiry becomes unlawful when hiring preference is given to relatives or other employees when minorities are underrepresented in the organization's workforce.)

Unacceptable: Requests for the names and addresses of any relatives other than those already working for the organization.

Residence

Acceptable: Inquiries about the applicant's address needed for future contact with the applicant.

Unacceptable: Whether the applicant owns or rents own home (denotes economic status).

Names or relationships of persons with whom the applicant resides.

Religion or creed

Acceptable: None.

Except for very specific positions in religious organizations.

Unacceptable: Questions about applicant's religious denomination, religious affiliation, church or parish, pastor, or religious holidays observed.

Sex

Acceptable: None.

Unacceptable: Any question.

HOW TO T.R.I.U.M.P.H. OVER ILLEGAL INTERVIEW QUESTIONS CHECKLIST

☐ Be prepared to respond by using one or more of the options of how to T.R.I.U.M.P.H. over illegal or inappropriate interview questions.

☐ Take a step back, evaluate the question and the situation.

☐ Respond to the question directly, if you feel comfortable and believe it will not harm you.

☐ Identify the intent behind the question and respond indirectly with an answer that relates to the requirements of the position.

☐ Upstage and ignore the question by redirecting the conversation.

☐ Mention the error diplomatically.

☐ Politely refuse to answer the question.

☐ Hit the road. Gracefully and professionally excuse yourself.

☐ It is okay if you want to bring up a sensitive issue.

☐ If you feel you have been discriminated against, contact the proper authority.

☐ Review the samples of acceptable and unacceptable interview questions to determine if an interview question is illegal.

Chapter 16

Temporary and Part-time Employment

Myth: Temporary and Part-time work is only for people who cannot find a "real" job.

Truth: The American Staffing Association (ASA) reports that 45 percent of temporary employees prefer working part-time or on temporary assignment over traditional employment.

Reality 1: Two million people per day are employed by staffing companies, and 1 million new jobs have been created by staffing companies over the past eight years.

Reality 2: Seventy-nine percent of temporary employees work full-time, virtually the same as the rest of the workforce.

TEMPORARY EMPLOYMENT

Temporary and part-time employment is taking on a whole new connotation with the changes in the economy and the aging of the baby boomer generation. What used to be looked on as simply a transitory stop in your career is now becoming a career destination itself.

The flexibility offered by temporary employment is particularly attractive to working mothers, students, and retirees. The keyword in this employment option is *flexibility*. The ASA reports that 64 percent of temporary employees say flexible work time is important to them. Working mothers may only want to work a few hours a week in order to have more time to spend with their families, students may need flexibility to accommodate their class schedule, and retirees may not want to work full-time. With temping you get to choose you assignments and the hours you want to work and gain varied experience by working for different companies.

Temporary work can also provide you with an opportunity to learn about careers. Earlier in this book we spoke about the need to follow your passion to a successful career. But what if you don't know what your particular passion may be? This uncertainty not only pertains to college students but can affect anyone at any time in his/her career. Using temporary and part-time work can help you find that passion.

Herminia Ibarra in her book *Working Identity: Unconventional Strategies for Reinventing Your Career* described the concept of developing a "working identity." She advised, "consider your professional career as a work in progress. This allows you to explore as many options as you can and as actively as you can. If you have an interest that you would like to explore you can try it part-time, or work on a special project." Temping allows you to try out a new profession to see if it is something you would like to do and is a good fit.

You can also use this option to investigate a prospective employer. Even though you can always leave a bad situation or employer, it is always best if you can find out early on if the company is a good match for you.

If you are in a specialized niche of professions, temporary employment can also provide you with options for your career growth. Consider the opportunities available in the healthcare profession.

A client recently spent considerable time in a hospital. She expressed amazement that most of the nurses in the intensive care unit that she dealt with were involved in temporary travel assignments. They had used a temporary agency as a way to accompany their husbands who were in school or to take the opportunity to travel to a new city while still earning a paycheck. The multiple healthcare staffing agencies advertise sign-on bonuses for a variety of healthcare facilities in the United States and Virgin Islands in addition to health and dental insurance.

Finally, temporary and part-time employment is a good way to bridge your way into full-time employment. In this chapter we will give you

- The rules for temporary employment

- The pros and cons of contractual work

- Strategies you need to move from temporary and part-time work to full-time employment

THE RULES FOR TEMPORARY EMPLOYMENT

Working for a staffing company no longer means that you are relegated to do the boring work that no one else wants to do. Temporary positions range from clerical to factory to sales and marketing jobs to professional work and even CEO. The fastest growth is occurring in the professional and technical occupations.

The competition for good temp help is keen. There are more than 7,000 staffing agencies nationwide, and you need to maximize your opportunities and align yourself with the best company, one that provides an entryway to top employers and offers the services and benefits you want.

The following rules for temporary employment can guide you to successful temping.

1. **Research the staffing company before signing on**. Bennett Santana, owner and president of Business Systems of America, a staffing firm in the technical support area, advised, "Review the length of time the company has been in business, their reputation, and their Web site. You want to make sure their client list has placements in the industry and companies that you are interested in."

2. **Register with as many agencies as you can**. Increased visibility means increased opportunities for placements.

3. **Look for agencies that provide good pay and benefits**. Staffing services offer highly competitive wages and benefits. The average temporary or contract employee earns more than $10 per hour, and some earn more than their permanent counterparts. Most staffing companies offer health insurance and vacation and holiday pay, and many offer retirement plans.

   Note: Be wary of any firm that makes you wait until they get paid by the employer before paying you.

4. **Take advantage of training opportunities**. Staffing firms automatically test your skills when you sign on with them. Ninety percent of staffing companies offer free training to their temporary employees. Specialized niche staffing agencies offer more specialized training options.

5. **Be flexible**. Let your staffing company know what your objective is, whether it's flexibility or permanent placement. Be willing to accept different placements at different work settings, and use each one as a learning experience.

6. **Be prepared for the ups and downs**. Even good temp agencies run into dry spells. Keep your skills up to date, and leave a good reputation behind. A valued employee is worth supporting.

SPECIALIZED JOB RESOURCES

If the prospect of working for a temporary staffing company appeals to you, you can find more information by visiting the following Web sites.

American Staffing Association
www.staffingtoday.net

National Association of Personnel Services
www.napsweb.org

The National Association of Alternative Staffing
www.naas-net.org

Temping.com
www.temping.com

The following are examples of niche agencies in healthcare, accounting, professional services, and information technology.

Preferred Healthcare Staffing
www.preferredhealthcarestaffing.com

Professional Nursing Services
www.professionalnursingservices.com

Accountemps
www.accountemps.com

Mentor 4, Inc.
www.mentor4inc.com

Business Systems of America, Inc.
www.bussysam.com

PART-TIME EMPLOYMENT

In speaking with clients, one of the most asked-about areas is part-time employment. Just like temporary employment, part-time jobs can give you flexibility to fit in the other activities that you consider important. The major difference is that in most part-time jobs, you are locked into a regular schedule with set working hours. The benefit is that, with set hours, you can organize your activities around your job.

Many employers like to use part-time workers because it allows them to gain the services of a trained employee without the added expenses of a full-time staff position. The down side for the employee is that part-time employment often comes without benefits. But, if benefits are not essential to you, and you like the idea of dependable, scheduled hours, then part-time work can be the answer for you.

Part-time jobs have always been a boon to students and women with children as a route to bring in extra income while accommodating their school or home schedule. It is gaining increasing popularity among the baby boomer generation. Many people have retired or taken an early retirement and are looking for new challenges without the day-in and day-out grind of full-time employment. Chronological diversity is destined to be the next wave of social change in the workplace since more than 50 percent of the workforce is already over the age of 40. According to a survey by the American Association of Retired Persons (AARP), more than half of the baby boomer generation intends to work part-time after retirement.

So whichever group you fall into, part-time employment is a valid opportunity for you.

Another benefit of part-time work is that it is a natural bridge to full-time employment. It gives you an opportunity to show your skills and gain valuable insider information on the company.

CONTRACT AND FREELANCE EMPLOYMENT

The concept of actually working for a company full-time was ingrained into our psyche with industrialization when many of our ancestors were recruited into the United States to work in the factories, railroads, and steel mills. Until then we were largely self-employed, earning our living as contractors, tradespeople, craftspeople, farmers, and small business owners. This entrepreneurial spirit is at the base of contractual and free-lance employment.

As a contractual or freelance worker, you get the benefit of independence. You are free to set your own schedule and, in many instances, to determine how you will accomplish the task that you are assigned. Training may be provided, but you do not report directly to a supervisor, and the time you are allotted to accomplish the task is left up to you or settled contractually. The opportunity to set your own schedule again makes this an ideal situation for those who want flexible work schedules. The downside for the employee is the lack of benefits, but it can be ideal for those who have another means of covering their insurance needs.

Domingo took an early retirement from his position at the State Board of Education after thirty years of service. Prior to his retirement, he shared his plans for retirement and interest in keeping involved while using his expertise to help local school districts with his career network. His proactive networking netted him a contractual position

231

as an auditor for a local school district, working on average three days a week and earning $50 an hour.

Building your career from part-time or consulting positions is more challenging than looking for a regular job. The best place to find these jobs is in small companies that need the assistance but are not able to commit to hiring you on a permanent basis. The key here is to learn about the company, their issues, and their problems and to position yourself as the answer. You must learn to showcase your skills and abilities in relation to the employer's needs. (See how to sell yourself in an interview in Chapter 13). You can market your talents to a variety of companies and build up a client base for yourself. Many freelancers wind up starting their own companies and building a consulting business from their experience.

Freelancing is not for everyone due to its uncertainty, but it can provide valuable rewards monetarily, increase your self-confidence, and offer a variety of experience that can propel your career forward.

PROS AND CONS OF TEMPORARY, PART-TIME, AND CONTRACTUAL EMPLOYEE STATUS

As you look into the possibilities of temporary, part-time, and contractual employment, you need to examine which would be best for you to pursue. The following chart compares some of the opportunities and benefits each represent.

PROS AND CONS OF TEMPORARY, PART-TIME, AND CONTRACTUAL EMPLOYMENT

Issues	Temporary	Part-time	Contractual and Freelance
Length of employment	Uncertainty of employment	Guaranteed	Prearranged contract length
Benefits	Benefits available after a length of time	Usually no benefits	No benefits
Salary	Can be above average	General salary range	Can be above average
Flexible schedule	Flexible	Fixed hours	Flexible
Training	Temp agencies offer free training	Employer-provided training	Employer-provided training
Status	Temporary hired help	Employee status	Hired expert
Variety	Work with a variety of companies and people	One employer	Work with a variety of companies and people

STRATEGIES TO DEVELOP TEMPORARY/PART-TIME WORK INTO FULL-TIME WORK

For many people reading this book, the road to temporary, part-time, and contractual work is simply a stop on the way to full-time employment. As discussed, these options offer many benefits, not the least of which is the ability to demonstrate to a potential employer your brand and skills and eventually to work your way into a job offer. The ASA reports that 72 percent of temporary employees obtain permanent jobs while working for a staffing company.

The following strategies show you how to make your brand shine and turn part-time into full-time employment.

1. **Pinpoint the industry that you are interested in.** The same is true here as everywhere else: if you know where you want to go, the rest follows. By pinpointing the industry, you can then choose the right temp agency or pursue the company on your own.

2. **Request the assignments and companies that you want.** Even though you may not get into the company you want at first try, keep your perspective and persistence and look for the opportunity to move into your target area.

3. **Keep good rapport with your staffing company.** The staffing company agents are the ones who can look out for you and who have the ability to get you into the great companies. They can be the key to your dream job.

4. **Do an excellent job.** Build a reputation as a conscientious, hardworking employee and let Brand You emerge.

5. **Learn the business.** Check out their Web site. Once inside, study the company, its products, services, market, and competitors. Impress your supervisor with the fact that you know the company better than most employees. This will also prepare you for that important interview.

6. **Send thank-you notes to company supervisors when you leave.** If you have been at a company for an extended period of time, let them know how good your experience was there. It will make you stand out from the crowd.

7. **Don't forget to ask for a job.** After you have built your reputation, express your interest in a full-time position. If one is not immediately available, you can place yourself at the top of the list for the next one.

These strategies work; just ask Maria Enriquez-Iniguez.

Maria was working part-time doing contract work with Navistar, now International Truck and Engine Corporation, while she was finishing her bachelor's degree in business administration from DePaul University. She had been employed for almost two years. She learned about the full-time opening when a coworker announced she was ready to move into another position. Although she was not finished with her degree (she had two months to go), the vice president and the manager of finance gave her an opportunity to interview. She began the job as financial asset analyst before her graduation day. Maria said, "my time in the company gave me the information I needed to present myself as a winner in my interview."

TEMPORARY AND PART-TIME EMPLOYMENT CHECKLIST

Benefits of Temporary Employment

- ☐ Flexibility is the key benefit of temporary employment.
- ☐ It gives you the opportunity to learn about different career fields.
- ☐ You get to choose among assignments and hours.
- ☐ It is a good way to gain experience.
- ☐ You can use the opportunity to investigate a prospective employer.
- ☐ The employer gets to know you.

Before Signing on with a Temporary Agency

- ☐ Research the company to see if they have a good reputation.
- ☐ Look for an agency that has good pay and benefits.
- ☐ See if they offer training.
- ☐ Consider registering with more than one agency to increase employment options.
- ☐ Investigate to see if your temp agency offers benefits.

Part-time, Contractual, Freelance

- ☐ The flexibility of this type of employment is attractive to students, retirees, and others.
- ☐ Part-time employment provides stability in income and scheduled work hours.
- ☐ Contractual and freelance work provides independence.
- ☐ Salary can be above average.
- ☐ They provide a variety of experience.

Remember the Strategies for Developing Temporary/Part-time Employment into Full-Time Employment

- ☐ Pinpoint the industry you are interested in.
- ☐ Request the assignments and companies that you want.
- ☐ Keep good rapport with staffing agency staff.
- ☐ Do an excellent job.
- ☐ Take the opportunity to learn the prospective employer's business.
- ☐ Ask for the job.

Chapter 17

Dealing with Job Search and Workplace Discrimination

Among individuals as among nations, the respect to other people's rights is peace.

Benito Juarez

The road to career success is not an easy one. Each stage—from preparing your résumé to researching the marketplace and employers, conducting your job search, interviewing, and networking—requires concentrated effort on your part to be successful. Yet, in each step, you control the action. One of the disheartening things about discrimination is that there is nothing you can do to control another person's bias and prejudice. You have done nothing wrong. However, there are steps you can take to confront it both informally and formally. In this chapter, we will discuss

- Job search and workplace discrimination
- Key employment discrimination laws
- Strategies to deal with discrimination
- How to file a charge of discrimination

Myth: I cannot fight discrimination because I am only a job seeker. As a Latino I will not be taken seriously and may or may not be a U.S. citizen. It is not worth complaining about discrimination because probably nothing will come of it. I may be retaliated against, and my legal status to work may be questioned.

Truth: Unfortunately, job search and workplace discrimination is alive and well. Fortunately, there are protections in place to safeguard our rights. The law, courts, and government employment rights enforcement agencies are making great strides in addressing legal discrimination.

Reality 1: Our personal and collective powers as Latinos have expanded the available informal options that can be used to address discrimination. Many employers have company policies, programs, diversity operations, training, and specific individuals that will protect your rights. Even smaller employers are more willing to address discrimination informally due to small business antidiscrimination outreach programs and the fear of the costs of fighting formal charges of discrimination.

Reality 2: Job seekers are protected against unlawful discrimination committed by employers. It is illegal to retaliate against an individual for informally or formally raising an issue of employment discrimination if you have legal authorization to work. In some states, undocumented employees can also file a charge of discrimination. If you seek quality advice (free or paid), you can be more successful and speed up the process.

Most regulatory agencies offer a free pre-investigation mediation program, which can resolve a complaint within a month or two.

BIAS, PREJUDICE, AND ILLEGAL DISCRIMINATION

Even as Latinos are becoming integral parts of the fabric of American culture, discrimination is still a problem that affects many Latinos according to a national survey conducted by the Washington, D.C.–based Pew Hispanic Center. They found that 31 percent of the approximately 3,000 Hispanics polled reported that they or someone close to them had suffered job discrimination in the past five years because of their racial or ethnic background. Another 14 percent reported that they had experienced employment discrimination personally, including not being hired for a job or not being promoted because of race or ethnicity. Eight-two percent responded that discrimination is a problem that keeps them from succeeding in general. It is a difficult reality for many of us to face in this modern age.

But as the survey shows, discrimination still exists. In this chapter, we will share some of our own experience of facing discrimination. Luckily, not everyone has experienced the shock of discrimination. Sometimes it is hidden and we do not recognize it; even we the authors have had that experience. Several years ago I, Rose Mary, a recent college graduate, applied for a position as the assistant director of a research project at a local not-for-profit agency. After a dynamite interview, I was offered the job, but at a lesser salary than advertised. When I questioned the interviewer, he said the reason I was offered less was that as a single female I did not have a family to support and did not need the higher salary. I was inexperienced and naive and accepted the smaller amount. I felt the injustice, but at the time I did not know I had the right to request the full advertised salary.

The moral of this story is that it is important to know your rights under the law. How you proceed after that is up to you.

Our combined experience in civil rights has given us a first-hand view of the ugliness and trauma of discrimination. Still, one of the most difficult things we have had to do is clarify to people what is and is not illegal discrimination, especially if someone feels they have been wronged. The concept that not all discrimination is illegal is not easy to understand. Put simply, if the boss is a *bruto* (brute) to all employees, then a charge of discrimination may not stand. Coincidentally, unfair labor practices are not necessarily discriminatory either. To gain a better understanding, we need to first look at the three basic concepts of prejudice, bias, and discrimination.

- *Bias* is an attitude that clouds impartiality of a question, issue, or person. A bias can be favorable or unfavorable and does not always carry the negative implication of prejudice.

- *Prejudice* encompasses unreasonable feelings, opinions, or attitudes frequently of a hostile nature against a racial, religious, or ethnic group different from your own. These feelings can be based on stereotypes or another irrational basis. Prejudice is often the precursor of discrimination.

- *Discrimination* is the act of treating a person differently on the basis of some characteristic of the group or class to which the person belongs.

So, you can be biased, prejudiced, and even in some cases discriminate without breaking the law. Discrimination is illegal when it has a negative impact against an individual or individuals in a class protected under the law that can be proven.

Illegal discriminatory acts are categorized as disparate treatment or disparate impact.

Disparate treatment is intentional discrimination. This occurs when you as a protected class member are treated differently than another employee/employees who are not Latino. Proof of illegal discrimination can be done by direct or indirect means. This type of discrimination usually has a direct impact on an individual. The following court case was filed in California by a coalition of four organizations:

Example: Juan had applied to work as a salesperson at a national clothing retailer that markets to young adults, teenagers, and children. He was hired but only on a temporary basis and then was shortly dismissed. He filed a charge of discrimination claiming that Latinos and other people of color were hired only to work in the stock room and overnight shift positions, not as salespeople. He charged that the minority applicants did not fit the company's "appearance policy." Juan's original claim has turned into a class action lawsuit against the major retailer.

Disparate impact occurs when a supposedly neutral employment practice has a discriminatory impact on a protected class member. In this instance, it is up to the employer to defend and show that the employment practice in question is a necessary, job-related practice, or bona fide occupational qualification. Proof of this type of discrimination is commonly done by inference using a statistical comparison. The following Illinois court case illustrates the point.

Example: Local Hispanic law enforcement personnel had noted the distinct lack of Latino state police officers working on the state's highways. Although many had applied, very few made it past the height requirements set for state troopers. A charge of discrimination was filed charging that the height restriction was not a BFOQ and was discriminatory toward Latinos and others. The court ruled that the height restriction was not a bona fide occupational qualification and indirectly discriminated against Latinos, Asians, and women who often did not meet the height requirements.

Both types of discrimination can have an impact on your job search. It is important to understand the concepts of disparate impact and disparate treatment in order to be alert to potential issues for yourself or others.

KEY EMPLOYMENT DISCRIMINATION LEGISLATION

Title VII of the Civil Rights Act of 1964 is the primary law prohibiting employment discrimination. It prohibits discrimination in employment on the basis of race, sex, national origin, and religion. The law also makes it unlawful for the employer to take retaliatory action against an individual for filing a charge of discrimination or for testifying or assisting in any investigation or proceeding. The Equal Employment Opportunity Commission enforces Title VII against private employers.

National origin is the most common basis for a charge of employment discrimination filed by a Latino. National origin not only means your place of birth but also includes the following characteristics:

- Birthplace

- Ancestry

- Culture—Traits or characteristics associated with one's nation of origin; examples: styles of dress or types of food one eats

- Linguistic characteristics, including accents

- Marriage or association with persons in a national origin group

- Membership or association with a specific ethnic promotion group

- Attendance or participation in school, churches, temples, or mosques associated with a national origin group

- Surname associated with a national origin group

In Chapter 18 we will cover the enforcement of national origin protections under the Immigration Reform and Control Act (IRCA) by the Office of Special Counsel at the Department of Justice. It is important to note that each enforcement agency has its own rules regarding the size of the employer, time lines for filing, remedies, and so on. To understand the guidelines and protections offered, review the chart on the next page, which compares the national origin protections offered under IRCA, Title VII of the Civil Rights Act, and an example of a state statute, the Illinois Human Rights Act (IHRA).

Latinos often cite other discrimination roadblocks such as ancestry, sexual harassment, and retaliation as major obstacles. Each one of these can be a basis for a charge of discrimination.

- *Ancestry* even if you are not foreign born but if your parents or grandparents are from a country that is in a protected class group.

- *Sexual harassment* is a behavior of a sexual nature that is unwelcome, offensive, intimidating, or threatening. It includes pressure for sexual favors or dates, unwanted touching, and sexual teasing, jokes, or questions. It also includes a hostile work environment where the sexual behavior adversely impacts your ability to do the job.

- *Retaliation* is any adverse employment action against the person who filed the charge in order to intimidate, harass, or punish the complainant. The retaliation provision also covers the witnesses or persons used as comparatives in the charge.

Other legislation prohibiting discrimination in employment under different basis include:

- *Age Discrimination in Employment Act of 1967 (ADEA)* prohibits discrimination in employment on the basis of age with respect to individuals who are 40 years of age or older.

- *Title I of the Americans with Disabilities Act (ADA)* prohibits discrimination in employment against a qualified individual with a disability. It also makes it illegal to retaliate against any individual for filing a charge of discrimination or testifying or assisting in an investigation or hearing under the ADA.

- *Equal Pay Act of 1963* prohibits sex-based wage discrimination between men and women in the same establishment who are performing under similar working conditions and require equal skill, effort, and responsibility.

COMPARISON OF NATIONAL ORIGIN PROTECTIONS UNDER IRCA AND TITLE VII

Issue	IRCA	Title VII	Illinois Human Rights Acts
Enforcement agency	Office of Special Counsel	EEOC	Illinois Human Rights Act
Filing time limit	180 days from date of discriminatory acts	300 days from date of discriminatory acts	180 days from date of discriminatory acts
Type of claim	National origin (IRCA also covers citizenship discrimination)	National origin (Title VII) also covers race, color, religion, and sex discrimination	National Origin Ancestry (IHRA also covers race, color, religion, and sex harassment, citizenship discrimination)
Size of business	4–14 employees	15 or more employees	15 or more employees; 1 employee for retaliation, sexual harassment, and if the company has government contracts
Who is protected?	U.S. citizens, nationals, and aliens with work authorization	All persons (including aliens) in the United States	All persons (including aliens) if violation occurred in Illinois
Actions covered	Hiring; firing; recruitment or referral for a fee; retaliation	Hiring, firing, recruitment, promotion, pay and fringe benefits, all other terms and conditions of employment, retaliation	Hiring, firing, recruitment, promotion, pay and fringe benefits, all other terms and conditions of employment, retaliation
Possible relief	Hiring; reinstatement; back pay; attorney's fees; OSC can educate personnel, correct job files, lift restrictions on work assignments; fines paid to government	Hiring, reinstatement, back pay, attorney's fees, promotion and other steps to put you in the position you would have had	Hiring, reinstatement, back pay, attorney's fees for prevailing CP, lost benefits, emotional distress damages, other damages such as interest

STATE AND LOCAL LAWS

State and local laws are key resources in dealing with job search and workplace discrimination. Most states have a human rights or civil rights statute as do some counties and local city governments. In many instances, the basis for discrimination covered under state and local statutes are broader and more encompassing than the federal legislation (see comparison of national origin chart). For example, sexual orientation, weight, marital status, and other areas are sometimes covered under state and local law but not federal law. Local enforcement agencies might also cover smaller workplaces with fewer employees. Most important, the U.S. Supreme Court has ruled that state and local laws take precedence over more stringent federal laws.

Each agency has regulations and distinct timelines for filing a charge. The EEOC allows a charge of discrimination to be filed 300 days from the date of the discriminatory act, while the state statute may allow only 180 days. Another difference is the time it takes to have a charge of discrimination investigated and processed. It can take a long time, even years for a charge of discrimination to be investigated and a hearing held in some agencies. When contemplating filing a charge of discrimination, you should call the local and state agencies to find out their rules, coverage areas, and average processing times.

STRATEGIES TO OVERCOME BIAS, PREJUDICE, AND ILLEGAL DISCRIMINATION

The move to embrace diversity in the workplace promotes the ideal of recognizing and valuing each other's differences. But for some individuals, the differences become the major focus and lead to stereotyping, bias, prejudice, and discrimination. These issues can manifest themselves in various stages of your job search.

As your search begins: Job vacancies may only be advertised by word of mouth within the network of current employees, or advertising will be placed in selected newspapers that have limited Latino readership. Lack of access to certain clubs and organizations may hinder networking opportunities.

Recruitment: Recruiters may focus solely on Ivy League schools or universities with small Latino enrollment. College career placement offices may not effectively reach out to Latinos students, thereby denying them access to recruitment and employment opportunities.

During the interview: The interviewer may be biased, prejudiced, and/or poorly trained, resulting in an unfair interview process.

Assessment: Company policies may unintentionally and unfairly inhibit the selection of Latino candidates. Latino candidates may intentionally be screened out due to foreign sounding last names.

As an employee: Lack of company training opportunities and staff development strategies may have a negative impact on retention and promotion of Latino employees.

Each of these roadblocks can be overcome as we discussed in Chapters 6 and 15. Yet, there are situations that require more direct action.

If you think you have been treated unfairly and were the target of discrimination, you can address the situation either formally or informally.

Informal Strategies

You've gone through the interview process and the interviewer asked you an illegal question which you addressed as described by the T.R.I.U.M.P.H. method. But you question whether you have placed yourself out of the running. Or you learn your résumé was discarded because of your last name or when the employer heard your accent or some other questionable action.

Use your internal network: Now is the time to professionally and tactfully notify your internal network at the employer in question. Most employers would prefer not to have to face a discrimination complaint. The diversity manager, EEO/AA officer, and members of the company affinity group all have a stake in the issue and are a good source for airing your concerns. They or other employees in the company may be able to help you traverse the landmines informally. You may be able to resolve the issue or at least ensure that no other Latino/Latina is subjected to similar tactics.

Use community resources: Contact local community-based organizations or professional associations and advise them of the problem. Many of these organizations have relationships with employers and employer groups that can serve as a conduit for information and potentially help resolve the issue.

One such organization is the Latino Committee on the Media (LCOM). Mary Gonzalez Koenig, president, said, "We have served as the oversight entity and the Latino voice of accountability on the media in the Chicago land area. Often we have had to confront management and decision makers to ensure that Latinos are treated fairly and equitably in the employment process." The point is to take positive action against discrimination and not let yourself be a victim.

Formal Strategies

When Cesar Chavez founded the Farm Workers Association in California (later the United Farm Workers of America), no one gave much credence to the ability of the fledgling organization to make an impact on the plight of farm workers. But under Chavez's fearless leadership, the union made historic achievements on behalf of the workers. It was not an easy fight, but his *Sí se puede* (Yes, we can) message led the movement. The fight against discrimination and injustice continues today. As you contemplate formal action against discrimination, you continue the tradition forged by Latino leaders and other groups that have been historically oppressed and denied their right and place in U.S. society.

Filing a formal discrimination complaint with the company EEO office, union, or other company authority: The employer should have an established procedure for the handling of discrimination charges. If you are unsure of the process, contact the EEO officer, diversity office, union steward, or human resource/personnel office for information. (*It is important to note that you do not have to be an employee of the company to register a complaint.*) If the illegal action took place before, during, or after the interview process, you have the right to file a charge.

Employers want to avoid a formal complaint through the EEOC or other enforcement agency and would prefer to resolve the issue internally. So, the opportunity to resolve the complaint is good during this process. In most cases, it is beneficial to proceed through the internal administrative remedies available first because if you still proceed and file a charge with EEOC and other such organizations, the company cannot excuse its actions alleging they were unaware of the issue and did not have a chance to remedy the situation.

Whichever method you use to register a discrimination complaint, there are inherent consequences that you must evaluate before moving forward. In many cases, there is an administrative backlog, and the time it takes to work through the system is lengthy. Although employer retaliation for filing a complaint is illegal, there may be subtle or not so subtle reactions to the filing. Last but not least, you may lose the complaint, and if you are still employed at the company, you may be labeled as a troublemaker. It is a difficult decision, but it is yours to make.

Remember all of the social breakthroughs that have resulted from protest, challenge, and legal resolutions. America has a history of individuals fighting against and overcoming injustice. Each of us has the power to change that which is evil and wrong.

Filling a formal charge of discrimination with the EEOC or other state or local enforcement agency is free and can be managed by yourself with guidance and does not have to be overwhelming. It requires a substantial amount of time to collect the information necessary, line up witnesses, and in some instances hire the services of a lawyer. The process itself can last a very long time as the case proceeds through the system. Patricia Mendoza, civil rights bureau manager at the Illinois attorney general's office and former Mexican-American Legal Defense Fund regional counsel, said, "The wisest thing you can do is to consult an employment lawyer who will conduct an assessment of your case and advise you if you have a meritorious case and if you have enough evidence to prevail in court." She also advises that there are free legal services available such as law schools with free clinics or legal aid offices that can be accessed for those who cannot afford an attorney. She explained, "I do not want to discourage anyone who feels they have been discriminated against from following through because it is their personal experience. But you must have your ducks in order."

The average process for filing a charge has seven major steps with different variations per jurisdiction. Figure 17.1 illustrates the usual path of a charge through an administrative agency.

KEY ISSUES IN FILING A CHARGE

Collect your data. Raquel Guerra, intake division manager at the Illinois Department of Human Rights, advised that very often Latinos come to the department unprepared. They lack documentation such as correct name and address for the employer and cannot verify the dates and times of specific instances of discriminatory acts. She said the complainants often think that the administrative agency is representing their case, but the agency is actually a neutral body. So it is imperative that you be prepared if you wish to file a charge of discrimination. When you go to file a charge, be prepared with the following data:

- Name and address of employer
- Number of employees at the company
- Dates and times of discriminatory actions
- Name of supervisor or other staff involved in the incident
- Comparatives with other employees who were treated differently

Make sure that you are within the timelines for filing a charge.

Keep good notes. Note taking is extremely important when filing a charge. The process of documenting discrimination should begin as soon as possible. If the incident occurs during the interview, jot down notes during the interview, as you leave, or as soon as possible. We encourage keeping a diary of events to document harassment, retaliation or other ongoing discrimination. Remember that the dates and times do not have to be exact; they just need to be to the best of your recollection.

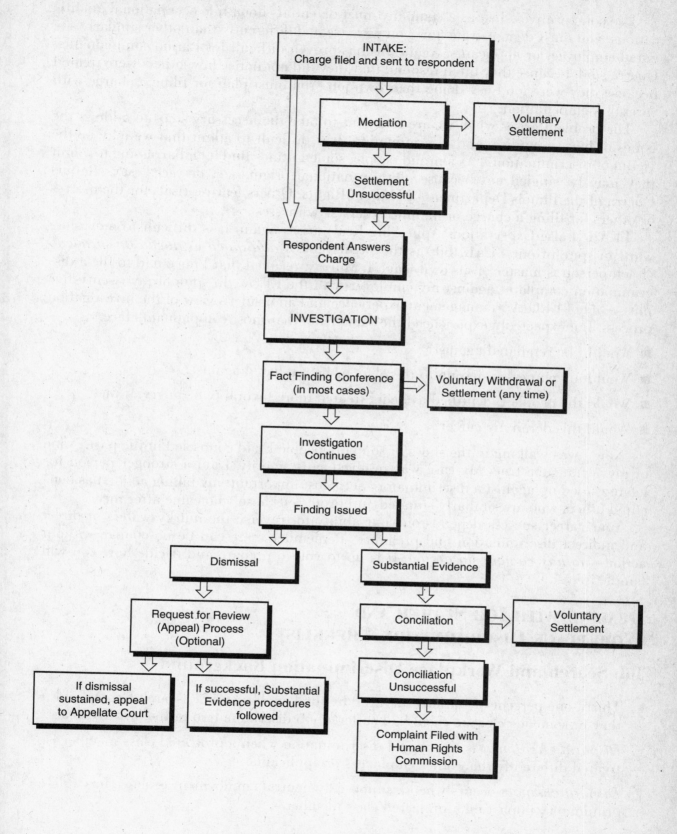

Figure 17.1 Path of a charge.

Use comparatives. Just as a company must defend its bona fide occupational qualifications, you must demonstrate how you were treated differently than other similarly situated employees or applicants. Again this has proven difficult for Latino complainants, Guerra said, because they often respond that they did not notice how others were treated because they were too busy doing their own job. You must plan for filing a charge with careful documentation.

The problem arises when we are reluctant to take the necessary steps to address the issues of bias, prejudice, and discrimination. It is difficult to admit that we may be the victim of discrimination. "As a proud people, some Latinos find it embarrassing to admit they may be singled out because of their national origin, sex, or race," says Raquel Guerra of the Illinois Department of Human Rights. Others fear reprisals for themselves or others for filing a charge or naming others as witnesses.

FEAR (False Expectations Appearing Real) arises again. It is difficult to move forward in spite of our FEAR, but as the saying goes *Cada quién es dueno de su miedo* (Each person is master of his own fear). I, Murray, recalled that I once had to file a discrimination complaint against my employer with the EEOC. In spite of my twenty-five plus years of EEO/AA management experience and an insider's view of the investigation process, I unexpectedly experienced the same fears that most complainants face:

■ Would I be retaliated against?

■ Would my witnesses step up to the plate or be retaliated against?

■ Would the people I identified as being treated more favorably be angry at me?

■ Would this derail my career?

Now I was walking in the shoes of so many people I had counseled in the past. None of my fears came true. My case was resolved satisfactorily. I am a stronger person for having stood up against a discriminatory act. Most important, my taking action has benefited others who are similarly situated and protected those who came after me.

Your career success depends on your ability to traverse the murky waters of direct and indirect discrimination and prejudice. Remember there can be no change without action—*no hay cambio sin acción*. It is up to you to prepare and decide how you will handle it.

DEALING WITH JOB SEARCH AND WORKPLACE DISCRIMINATION CHECKLIST

Job Search and Workplace Discrimination Background

☐ Thirty-one percent of Latinos surveyed by the Pew Hispanic Research Center said they or someone close to them had suffered job discrimination in the last five years.

☐ *Disparate treatment* is intentional discrimination when a protected class member is treated differently than other employees or applicants.

☐ *Disparate impact* occurs when a supposedly neutral employment practice has a discriminatory impact on a protected class member.

Key Employment Discrimination Legislation

☐ Title VII of the Civil Rights Act of 1964 prohibits discrimination on the basis of race, sex, national origin, or religion.

☐ The Age Discrimination in Employment Act of 1967 prohibits discrimination in employment on the basis of age for people over 40.

☐ Title I of the Americans with Disabilities Act prohibits discrimination in employment against a qualified person with a disability.

☐ The Equal Pay Act of 1963 prohibits sex-based wage discrimination between men and women.

☐ The Equal Employment Opportunity Commission enforces all these acts.

☐ Although the average timeline for filing a charge of discrimination is 300 days after the discriminatory act, some legislation only allows 180 days. Companies covered can range from one employee to companies with at least fifteen employees.

☐ State and local laws may cover additional areas of employment discrimination.

Informal Strategies

☐ Use your internal network to advise them of any discriminatory action and solicit their help in correcting any issues.

☐ The diversity manager, EEO/AA officer, and affinity group members all have a stake in avoiding discrimination complaints.

☐ Use community-based organizations or professional associations to intercede on your behalf.

Filing a Charge of Discrimination

☐ Check with the enforcement agency for their guidelines and timelines for filing charges of discrimination.

☐ You do not have to be an employee to file a charge of discrimination.

☐ As soon as a discriminatory act or statement is made, take notes and list the date of the incident, what happened, and any witnesses.

☐ Use the internal process at the company to file a charge.

☐ You may file with the company internally and with the EEOC or local or state enforcement agency at the same time.

When you go to file a charge, be sure to have the following data:

1. Name and address of employer

2. Number of employees at the company

3. Dates and times of discriminatory actions

4. Name of supervisor or other staff involved in the incident

5. Comparatives with other employees who were treated differently

☐ Keep within the timelines for filing a charge.

☐ You do not need a lawyer to file a charge of discrimination.

☐ Retaliation is prohibited under the law.

☐ National origin is the most common basis for a charge of employment discrimination by a Latino or Latina. National origin encompasses more than your birthplace.

☐ Ancestry, even if you are not foreign-born, includes your parents or grandparents.

☐ Culture.

☐ Language includes accents or limited English-speaking ability.

☐ Marriage with a person of a particular national origin group.

☐ Membership or association with a specific ethnic promotion group.

☐ Attendance or participation in schools and churches or temples or mosques associated with a national origin group.

☐ Last name identified with a national origin group.

Chapter 18

Immigration

U.S. immigration, both permanent and temporary, has become increasingly more difficult, complicated, and increasingly filled with land mines, particularly since the tragic events of 9/11. All matters involving U.S. borders and security have, in virtually all areas, been infused with heightened concern and stricter regulation and enforcement. However, employers and prospective foreign-born employees should not despair. Even though no particular visa should be considered as a "piece of cake" or "just filling out a form," using a knowledgeable and experienced professional attorney or the services of a licensed non-profit immigration service can ensure that the complicated processing of visas and immigration status will be achieved as quickly or smoothly as possible, under the circumstances of the case and given the strict regulatory and enforcement environment.

Because this chapter is written by the authors' counsel, Barbara A. Susman, an attorney specializing in worldwide immigration law for over twenty years, it is incumbent to mention that the following should not be relied upon in any particular case without seeking the particularized advice of a licensed immigration attorney.

Certain challenging realities exist now that Congress recently reduced by one half the number of H-1B professional/specialty worker visas available during each fiscal year. However, there are creative and resourceful methods of applying for alternative visa categories, thus alleviating somewhat the impact of this reduction in one of the most useful temporary working visa categories.

In this chapter we will discuss

■ Federal immigration law

■ Documentation required to work in the United States

■ Visa strategies

■ Illegal discrimination under the Immigration Act

■ Remedies

Myth: Immigrants are not welcome in the United States at this time, cannot get work permits, and face discrimination.

Truth: The process for obtaining employment authorization is not always fast or easy, but the number of employers and immigrants applying for immigration and working visas is increasing and serves as a testament to the fact that immigrant talent is becoming more important as a labor force.

Reality 1: Temporary and permanent visas continue to be readily available, particularly to the especially talented or highly educated. Nonetheless, aliens with some skills or training are also eligible for labor certification and thus permanent residence if they have a bona fide offer of permanent employment from a qualified employer.

Reality 2: Planning and good professional advice are fundamental to avoiding the many pitfalls and availing yourself of all the opportunities.

Reality 3: The Immigration and Nationality Act (INA) prohibits employers with four or more employees from discriminating against U.S. citizens, U.S. nationals, and authorized aliens due to national origin or citizenship status. Title VII of the Civil Rights Act prohibits national origin discrimination by employers of fifteen or more employees.

FEDERAL IMMIGRATION LAW

The laws relating to residency, citizenship, and naturalization are all federal laws. The two primary areas of the law that govern in this area are immigration and citizenship/naturalization.

- Immigration laws are the rules and requirements that permit foreign-born nationals to reside or work in the United States on a temporary or permanent basis.

- U.S. citizenship and naturalization laws are rules that govern how citizenship is determined.

- Naturalization laws govern the procedures and requirements permitting foreign-born nationals to acquire U.S. nationality. These rules also govern the ability of U.S. citizens to acquire other nationalities and to retain or lose their own nationality.

DOCUMENTATION REQUIRED TO WORK IN THE UNITED STATES

Every person working in the United States—whether a U.S. citizen, permanent resident, or nonnational—must present proof of employment eligibility to his/her employer. Those who are not native-born U.S. citizens must have special documentation to be employed or work in the United States.

Although this has always generally been the case, it was not until the Immigration Reform and Control Act of 1986 (IRCA) that such a comprehensive legislative scheme of corresponding enforcement systems and penalties existed. Employers are obligated to verify the working status of all employees, U.S. citizens and noncitizens alike. Every newly hired employee, within seventy-two hours of hire, must produce evidence of his/her ability to work legally. The employer must complete and sign an I-9 form for each new employee. Both the employer and employee must attest to their statements on the I-9 form under penalty of perjury.

Employers who knowingly hire unauthorized aliens face numerous penalties ranging from paperwork violations to pattern and practice in the hiring of unauthorized alien workers. In addition to hiring, IRCA also regulates the recruitment or referral for a fee of any person for employment.

DOCUMENTS APPROVED FOR EMPLOYMENT ELIGIBILITY VERIFICATION

All new hires must produce any document or combination of documents as approved by the U.S. Citizenship and Immigration Services to their employer. The employment verification may be based upon the employee's presentation and the employer's verification of documents from nonexclusive lists provided by law:

- One document from List A (documents that establish both identity and employment eligibility)

or

- One document from List B (documents that establish identity) and one document from List C (documents that establish employment eligibility).

DOCUMENTS APPROVED TO ESTABLISH
IDENTITY AND EMPLOYMENT ELIGIBILITY

List A	List B	List C
Documents that establish both identity and employment eligibility.	Documents that establish identity	Documents that establish employment eligibility
U.S. passport (unexpired or expired)	Driver's license or ID card issued by a state or outlying possession of the United States provided it contains a photograph or information such as name, date of birth, sex, height, eye color, and address	U.S. Social Security card issued by the Social Security Administration (other than a card stating it is not valid for employment)
Certificate of U.S. Citizenship (INS Form N-560 or N-561)		Certification of Birth Abroad issued by the Department of State (Form FS-545 or Form DS-1350)
Certificate of Naturalization (INS Form N-550 or N-570)	ID card issued by federal, state, or local government agencies or entities provided it contains a photograph or information such as name, date of birth, sex, height, eye color, and address	Original or certified copy of a birth certificate issued by a state, county, municipal authority or outlying possession of the United States bearing an official seal
Unexpired foreign passport, with I-551 stamp or attached INS Form I-94 indicating unexpired employment authorization		
Alien Registration Receipt Card with photograph (INS Form I-151 or I-551)	School ID card with a photograph	Native American tribal document
Unexpired Temporary Resident Card (INS Form I-688) **OR**	Voter's registration card	U.S. Citizen ID card (INS Form I-197)
	U.S. military card or draft record **AND**	
Unexpired Employment Authorization Card (INS Form I-688A)	Military dependent's ID card	ID card for use of Resident Citizen in the United States (INS Form I-179)
Unexpired Reentry Permit (INS Form I-327)	U.S. Coast Guard Merchant Mariner card	Unexpired employment authorization document issued by the INS (other than those listed under List A)
Unexpired Refugee Travel Document (INS Form I-571)	Native American tribal document	
Unexpired Employment Authorization Document issued by the INS which contains a photograph (INS Form I-688B)	Driver's license issued by a Canadian government authority	
	For persons under age 18 who are unable to present a document listed above:	
	School record or report card	
	Clinic, doctor, or hospital record	
	Day-care or nursery school record	

The employer is required to examine the documents, and if they reasonably appear to be genuine and properly belong to the employee, then the employer is to accept them. Otherwise the employer could be subject to an unfair immigration-related employment practice. It must be noted that the designated lists *are not exclusive*, meaning there may be other documentation not listed that may prove identity and employment eligibility. Employers should be careful when rejecting candidates based on their perceived employment eligibility.

Sergio Vasquez was born in the United States but raised in Mexico until he finished high school. Sergio was having trouble getting employed because employers did not believe he was a U.S. citizen because English was his second language. Even though he provided his U.S. birth certificate and other acceptable documents, companies insisted that he produce a "green card." Sergio contacted a local civil rights enforcement agency for help. The agency informally called the employer to advise them that they were potentially violating Sergio's rights under federal and state law. He was immediately hired.

Employers are required to reverify the employment eligibility of persons who have provided proof of only temporary work authorization, upon the expiration of their temporary employment authorization. Documents must be original and *unexpired*, based on current law. So, an original *expired* U.S. passport would not be acceptable documentation.

Visa Strategies

H-1B Visa

The H-1B (Temporary Worker) visa is a popular nonimmigrant working visa granted to foreigners who will be employed as professionals or specialty workers. The category has traditionally included the professions but has been expanded over the years in case law and in the Immigration Act of 1990 to cover "specialty workers" reflecting the expanding range of white-collar jobs that require a college degree as a reasonable minimum requirement to enter the field. Some of the qualifying professions include engineers, lawyers, accountants, and architects, among others. Under this category a maximum stay of six years is permitted.

The H-1B visa might be seen as recently coming under attack since Congress lowered the number of visas, commonly known as the "cap" on this visa category. In 2000, propelled by the technology boom, Congress raised the number of available H-1B visas to as high as 195,000; in 2003 it more than halved the cap to 65,000. The cap for fiscal year 2005 was reached in October 2004, the first month of the new fiscal year.

Applicants and employers must seek innovative and creative ways to seek visas for professionals they had otherwise sponsored under the H-1B category. The category reopens in October every year. Immigration advocates say a cap has never been set that reflects the real need in our economy. Even though the cap has been reached a few times in the past, Fiscal Year 2005 was the fastest time ever that H-1B visas have run out. Sensitivity about exporting American jobs overseas, protecting domestic jobs, and reacting to the shift in the economy, including the slump in the once hot technology field, have led to Congressional reluctance to raising the cap again.

In view of the shortage of H-1B visas, there are various alternative visa categories that employers may turn to, including

- F-1 visa students with employment authorization

- Curricular or Optional Practical Training

- O extraordinary visas

- NAFTA and the TN classification

- Exchange visitor visas under an L-1 visa program

- E Treaty visas

Better and more sophisticated visa planning—for employers and prospective employees—is key to maximizing employment opportunities for immigrants seeking work in the United States.

Students and employers may get relief from a legislative proposal being promoted by Senator Saxby Chambliss (R–Georgia), and Representative Lamar Smith (R–Texas). They are proposing that foreign students graduating from masters or doctoral programs at U.S. universities not be counted against the H-1B limit. This would allow such graduate-level students to receive H-1B visas outside of the quantitative numerical system. Such highly educated students are often recruited by U.S. businesses and could end up working for global competitors if H1-B visas are unavailable.

Student, Graduate, and Training Visas

Despite all of the restrictions that have been placed (and continue to be tightened, particularly in the area of student visas), the F-1 student visa is still one of the best and simplest ways to obtain nonimmigrant (temporary) employment authorization.

The student visa category continues to present an extraordinary opportunity to be employed in the United States. After one year of full-time studies (12 credit hours) a foreign-born student pursuing studies in the United States may

- Obtain employment authorization for up to twenty hours per week

- Obtain full-time employment during holiday and school vacation periods

Foreign students may also receive similar employment authorization to work even in his/her first year of study, but only for on-campus employment. After the first year, students may obtain work authorization for any type of employment, whether on or off campus.

Another truly extraordinary employment authorization opportunity is found in Optional Practical Training, a route available to immediate postgraduate students who seek to work in their fields following graduation.

- Optional practical training (OPT) is intended to provide the graduate with one year of employment experience in his/her own field.

- OPT is not employer-specific.

- The OPT recipient cannot only work for any employer, but there is no restriction on the kind of employment that is acceptable, which in effect allows the recipient to work anywhere in any position.

If you are interested in pursuing this authorization, it is best to file the OPT work authorization application with your school as early as possible before graduation, to allow for processing time, if you plan on staying and working in the United States after graduation.

Other Training Visas

The H-3 Non-Immigrant Trainee visa requires the employer to create and maintain a training program that does not involve excessive on-the-job training.

- The company must show a need to train an alien worker in a field related to his/her education and employment background on a temporary basis.
- The alien must show that he/she cannot receive this particular type of training in his/her country.
- The H-3 visa is employer-specific (unlike OPT).
- The H-3 visa requires a relatively major commitment by the employer to put into place a program of practical training (if it does not yet have one).
- It must be intended, in the case of the H-3 training visa, that the foreign worker will return to his/her country after the training is completed.
- The visa covers an eighteen-month special education training program, or up to two years for other trainee programs.

O Extraordinary Worker Visas

The O visa is designed specifically to cover the highly talented or acclaimed foreign-born who may not qualify under the other designations. The O extraordinary worker visa is a useful and flexible alternative to the H-1B visa program, with particularly contrasting benefits:

- There is no wage maintenance feature, no overall limit on time in classification, and no cap.
- The employer's extra "perk" in hiring professionals qualifying for the O-1 visa includes the assurance that these professionals are truly considered to possess extraordinary ability and have distinguished themselves because of the extensive evidence of achievements and awards they have demonstrated to qualify for the O-1 visa to show "sustained national or international acclaim."
- The O visa holder has demonstrated "a level of expertise indicating that the person is one of the small percentages who have risen to the very top of the field of endeavor."

Professionals who qualify for the O worker visa include the following:

- Nobel Prize winners
- Those who make original scientific, scholarly, or business-related contributions of major significance
- Those who participate on a panel or judge the work of others in the same or allied field
- Those who have current or previous employment in a critical or essential capacity for organizations and have a distinguished reputation

NAFTA and the TN Classification

Yet another temporary working visa strategy available to Canadian and Mexican professionals is the TN classification, a category created under the North American Free Trade Agreement (NAFTA). This visa classification avoids the H-1B quantitative limitations and other requirements coincident with the H-1B visa, such as labor department filings and minimum preliminary wage requirements, and has no overall limitation on duration. The TN visa may be obtained for one-year increments continuously with no limitation or cap on the number of years the recipient may remain in that category.

Even when other visas are foreclosed for one reason or another, NAFTA offers nonimmigrant working visas to nationals of Canada or Mexico whose profession is within the scope of the sixty-three professions enumerated in NAFTA.

The TN visa can be particularly useful for certain professions which otherwise would not qualify for H-1B visa treatment, such as nursing. For example, Mexican and Canadian nurses are eligible for the TN visa category because nurses may not generally qualify for an H-1B visa (except for some exceptional cases).

L-1 Intracompany Transferees and E Treaty Visas

The L Nonimmigrant visa category can be used as a means to seek employment in the United States with advance planning. The L-1 visa is available to international companies (both large and small) needing to transfer employees from the overseas employer to the U.S. company. Qualifying affiliations may include parent–subsidiary corporate relationships, U.S. divisions of foreign companies or foreign divisions of U.S. companies, affiliated sister companies owned by the same parent, and similarly qualifying corporate relationships based upon ownership and control.

■ The L visa holder must have worked for the organization abroad at least one year during the last three years.

■ An employee would need to work abroad for one year before he/she is eligible for transfer to the United States in the L visa category.

■ A foreign-born graduate student or foreign-born worker may be immediately eligible for the L visa category if he/she has already worked abroad for the same multinational company within the last three years.

■ Start career planning as early as possible from an immigration law standpoint if you are interested in the L-1 visa.

The E Nonimmigrant visa category is a similarly useful tool available to nationals of the transferring foreign company, who, like L nonimmigrants, need to be employed in the capacity of manager, director, or worker possessing specialized knowledge. Particular to the case of the E visas:

■ There must exist as a prerequisite the appropriate treaty providing for the E "treaty visa" between the United States and the intending foreign candidate's foreign (home) country, and

■ The foreign-affiliated company must possess the same nationality as the individual wishing to be hired and transferred to the United States under the E visa. Unlike the L-1 visa, there is no one-year work abroad requirement as a prerequisite to hiring and transferring the E visa holder.

Categories of Immigrant (Permanent) Work Visas

In addition to the temporary visa options described previously, the foreign-born job seeker also has a variety of permanent visa options available. Acquisition of U.S. permanent residence conveys the "green card" status (although the "cards" are no longer green). It should not be confused with U.S. citizenship, which can be sought later through the naturalization process, three to five years after receiving the green card, depending upon the basis on which the green card was obtained.

Permanent employment-based immigration applicants should avoid the labor certification process and quotas if at all possible. Labor certification is generally required unless a special exemption applies. The labor certification proves legally that there are no qualified U.S. legal permanent resident or citizen candidates ready, willing, and able to take the job offered. In general, it requires a testing of the labor market through advertisements and job postings. The foreign-born job seeker is well advised to seek an alternative to the labor certification process, if one can be found to apply. Generally, exceptions are made for exceptional or specialized professional position/qualification (e.g., extraordinary researchers and scholars, nurses, doctors, and religious workers), certain advanced level degrees, intracompany managerial positions (transferees), extraordinary and exceptional prominence in the field, and other similar qualifications.

As in the temporary visa categories, permanent visas are also allocated on a per year quantitative basis per country, currently a total of at least 140,000 visa numbers annually. Should a visa category be filled, the individual must find another visa category or an exception to the quota system. One such exemption is the "national interest waiver," which is a difficult waiver to obtain because, to qualify, the foreigner's immigration must be judged to be in the "national interest" based on certain specified guidelines. Other visa strategies may include resorting to nonemployment relative petitions, such as asylum and special legislation or amnesty.

STRATEGIES FOR CREATING EMPLOYMENT OPPORTUNITIES AND WORKING WITH YOUR IMMIGRANT STATUS

Question: So how do you go about getting your foot in the door when the immigration issue accompanies your résumé?

Answer: Put your best foot forward, shore up your value, and make yourself needed.

Being from another culture can actually be a "plus" or feature for certain positions. These may be positions that can benefit greatly by virtue of your language skills, multicultural background, or business experience abroad. On the other hand, some positions are incompatible with your value added as a foreigner. Knowing the difference is quite important for the foreign-born job seeker. Part and parcel of "shoring up your value" is evaluating and discerning the employers who might be interested in or need your "value added" and unique branding and features as a foreign national. You should be spending more of your time and efforts pursuing these leads. (Review Chapter 3.)

Question: Why would employers want to hire a foreign national?

Answer: The global economy combined with increased recognition of the expanding diversity of the consumer market in the United States has prompted many firms to broaden their view of the qualifications they seek in new employees.

The following is a nonexclusive list of desirable characteristics and reasons why employers may wish to hire a foreign national:

- Foreign language ability
- Employment or other experience abroad
- The "image" the employee brings to the job
- The intent to redeploy foreign worker abroad after service or training in the United States
- The desire to expand foreign market(s), which may be well known to the foreign worker
- The applicant's unique training or abilities, which are not easily attained or are not available domestically
- The employer's inability to fill the position immediately or in a timely manner with available U.S. workers

Of course, as in all negotiations, the value of what you are offering or contributing will always have a correlation to what the employer is willing to pay or finance. Thus, if you are perceived as needed and valuable, your "stock goes up."

One way of shoring up your value is making yourself needed and indispensable.

Question: How do you "make yourself needed"?

Answer: Internships. Sometimes you can find "internships," which are often volunteer positions, in which case you will need to weigh whether the potential opportunity may be worth giving up a salary for an interim period. Keep in mind that you may never again be in a better position to explore job opportunities than early upon your graduation, before you have fully launched your career. You will be able to check out different fields or employers, and certainly give them an opportunity to check you out. Moreover, this is simply a great way to "get your foot in the door"!

- Consider creating your own "perfect internship." Research the possible employment opportunities carefully, and then put together a "personal business plan" or outline for your desired internship to be presented to a potential employer of your choice. You may be able to persuade a prospective employer of your initiative and ability and at the same time influence the kind of internship experience you will receive at the employer's business. This situation is not a bad combination and is definitely worth the extra effort.

- You should also think of seeking the help of global human resources consultants, who can help position or "brand" you using your own unique foreign background.

- Do your homework: research which employers are sponsoring and for what positions.

- Always "go the extra mile"; it will always pay off. Even if the employer does not hire you, in the long-term, going the extra mile will score intangible value points with your employer, manager(s), and peers. Your employer may become your best reference or even your best recruiter—they may even refer you to your next and better job opportunity! By your having gone the extra mile, you will have set into place a professional habit of doing so and benefit from this in innumerable ways. By doing better than your mere best, you will learn what your capabilities are and what type of work product or results you are capable of producing.

- Find ways that you can uniquely benefit the employer's market, international sources or clientele, ability to do business abroad, or any other aspects of the business that your unique life or educational experiences can make a value-added contribution to.

- We would be remiss here to fail to mention the benefits of "networking," which is not just exchanging cards and shaking hands but going to the next level of networking—value-added networking. Latinos are comfortable, from a cultural standpoint, in meeting others at important career building, educational, political, or other events, meetings, and programs. The distinguishing point of value-added net-working is making important connections in which you attempt to engage or person-ally connect at some level with the people you meet on a personal, common-interest, professional, spiritual, or other transcending basis, that would tend to distinguish that contact and connection for the longer term. The balance in doing this is to be authentic and have self-respect (see Chapter 3) and to show professionalism. We do not need to be the same, or even alike, to share a sense of engagement or connection with one another.

The history of Lisseth Sesatty, outlined in Chapter 3, highlights living proof of the effective use of internships by someone who went the extra mile and who clearly rose higher and higher based on the work reputation she established, and on her talent and visibility. She demonstrates how she made herself indispensable to her employers, result-ing in multimillion-dollar savings and improvements in teamwork, operational changes, increased productivity and efficiency, and enhanced product quality. Finally, Ms. Sesatty's profile also highlights the key role that networking has played in her success, and that she continues networking today.

Question: How do you approach an employer regarding sponsorships or assistance?

Answer: No matter how you approach it or view it, if you do not have work author-ization, you will need your employer's assistance via sponsorship for employment. Even if you have work authorization and will not need employer sponsorship for a year, be aware that you cannot raise the sponsorship issue with an employer too early after being hired. Many foreign graduates have joined employers as an intern on their one-year practical training authorization, only to find all too late that the employer is unwilling to sponsor them for an employment-based visa toward the end of their internship. Be prepared. We recommend that you raise the sponsorship issue early. At the time of your internship interview, the employer's willingness to sponsor you for an employment-based visa (likely an H-1B) should be a part of your internship deci-sion, if it is your intention to continue working in the United States following your internship.

Question: How should you discuss your I status? When should you start?

Answer: The issue of "immigration" should not be a focal point in your discussions with your prospective employer. (If it has, then you should have been prepared.) The I status issue should arise for the first time when the employer extends you a job offer or immediately thereafter. If, after you receive a job offer, you and your employer have not yet discussed your immigration status, now is the time for you to raise the issue as delicately, yet with as much preparation and confidence, as possible.

We recommend conferring or consulting with an experienced legal professional in the field so that you are prepared to explain the concept and procedures needed in hiring a foreign worker or, if necessary and appropriate, to direct the employer to speak with your lawyer, who would already be familiar with your case.

You should also be careful to be and appear to be as truthful and straightforward as possible. The possibility exists that if the issue of immigration (work authorization) arises late in the interviewing process, the employer may blame you for not having raised it earlier. Although you cannot be evasive or obscure about anything with the prospective employer, including your immigration status, you are not obligated to raise the issue if the employer does not inquire into it. Keep in mind that, nevertheless, this may result in a sensitive moment and discussion that you should also be prepared for. You should be clear that it was not discussed because the employer had not yet raised it. You may wish to decide in advance whether you will simply raise the issue in the interview or wait for the employer to do so. In either case, you can also be prepared to inform the employer that you have already sought professional legal advice, that you are qualified for employment authorization in the position, and that it will not be inordinately difficult to obtain.

When discussing this issue with your employer, wording may be important. It may be easier to discuss the issue in terms of "employment authorization" rather than "immigration status." The latter may be perceived as a problem or situation relating only to you. The former, employment authorization, is mutual as both the employer and employee are involved in the employment authorization process. If the employer wishes to hire you, then the employer and you need to verify your status on the I-9 form. If you do not already have a status that authorizes you to work, the employer will need to sponsor you for a visa. There are several issues and alternative reactions that you need to be prepared for:

■ You must be prepared and well informed regarding your status, and you should be well advised as to the steps that your employer will need to take, if any, in order for you to work.

■ If you are not well prepared in these areas, even if you have been extended an offer of employment, "all bets could be off" and the employer might quickly revoke the offer.

■ The employer may also be reluctant or unwilling to wait very long for the immigration process. It is common for employers to extend a job offer and expect the candidate to begin within two weeks (and often the need is immediate).

■ The challenge to the candidate who still needs to pursue immigration action based on the job offer is to be well prepared and ready to get the process in motion immediately.

Of course, if the employer and you had a clear understanding throughout the interviewing process that your hire carries an immigration step, then many of the preceding concerns do not affect you, presumably because the employer extended an offer knowing that immigration procedures would be necessary. Nevertheless, issues of delay or uncertainty can always be of concern to any employer. Being well prepared on all of these issues can substantially reduce delay and uncertainty—to the employer as well as to you.

Question: Who selects the immigration counsel?

Answer: Increasingly, it seems that companies are more flexible in allowing, or even suggesting, that the new hire select outside counsel to handle the immigration case. Once again, being prepared from the outset will help greatly, including having the opportunity to choose your own lawyer. There are obvious benefits to having your own counsel: the immigration process will be more transparent to you, and you will generally have the opportunity to be better and more closely apprised of developments in your case. If the corporation uses its own immigration counsel, then having conferred with your own attorney you will already know what to expect.

Question: Who pays for and who retains immigration counsel?

Answer: Assuming that you do need the employer to sponsor you and cooperate in the immigration process, immigration counsel will be necessary and there are related legal and INS (CIS) fees. The question arises as to who will pay these fees?

Many corporate employers cover all of the immigration law fees and expenses. On the other hand, depending upon the company, this may be a negotiable item. Other companies do not cover any of the immigration legal expenses. If the company does not have a policy that allows for payment of INS and legal fees, you can negotiate that as part of your compensation; or perhaps you can negotiate a 50–50 arrangement, in which you and the company share the fees. In the case of the H-1B nonimmigrant visa, the employer is by regulation supposed to pay the INS (CIS) fee. Even though larger companies are more likely to cover the INS and attorney's fees than smaller companies, they also tend to be less flexible in terms of hiring of aliens. Smaller companies are often able to support a position that uniquely benefits both the company and the alien that effectively utilizes the new hire's particular background and skills.

Question: What should I look for in an Immigration Counsel?

Answer: Look for an experienced immigration counsel. Speaking engagements and authorship of books or articles tend to be good signs of professional knowledge and involvement. Make sure the attorney has handled this type of case before. If it is employment-based, corporate immigration, make sure that is a large part of the attorney's practice. The attorney should be able to answer your questions and be responsive. Make sure the attorney is able to give your case the individual attention it deserves. The American Immigration Lawyers Association (AILA) is a good source of information in this regard. (See Appendix U for immigration and naturalization resources.)

ILLEGAL DISCRIMINATION UNDER THE IMMIGRATION ACT AND RELATED STATE LAWS

Federal Laws—Homeland Security, INA, IRCA

Under the Immigration Reform and Control Act of 1986, individuals are protected from national origin discrimination, and "protected individuals" from citizenship discrimination. Protected individuals include citizens and nationals of the United States, legal permanent residents, temporary residents, and refugees and asylees, *unless* the person failed to apply for naturalization within six months of the date he/she is first eligible and unless he/she became a U.S. citizen within two years thereafter or is actively pursuing U.S. citizenship. INS processing time is not counted in this calculation for "intending citizens."

Employers, with four or more employees, may not discriminate against U.S. citizens, U.S. nationals, and authorized aliens due to national origin. Nor may they discriminate due to citizenship status against U.S. citizens, U.S. nationals, and the following classes of aliens with work authorization:

- Permanent residents
- Temporary residents (individuals who have gone through the legalization program)
- Refugees and asylees

Case law extends unfair immigration-related employment practices to include persons or entities not in a position to hire the applicant, but who "interfered with the individual's employment opportunities with another employer." Note there are some legal exceptions to the antidiscrimination laws that allow an employer to require U.S. citizenship for some positions and to give preference to a U.S. citizen over an alien if *both are equally qualified*. In general, however, an employer's policy to hire only U.S. citizens would be in violation of the law.

The Immigration Reform and Control Act of 1986 prohibits discrimination on the basis of citizenship status and document abuse, in addition to expanding protection against national origin discrimination. The Equal Employment Opportunity Commission and the Department of Justice, Civil Rights Division, Office of the Special Counsel for Immigration Related Unfair Employment Practices (Special Counsel) issued a joint Memorandum of Understanding (MOU) to clarify respective agency roles and to avoid overlap and promote efficiency.

Valentin Obregon, senior community liaison for the U.S. Department of Homeland Security's Office of U.S. Citizenship and Immigration Services (USCIS), encourages immigrants to seek assistance if they are facing unlawful discrimination. Obregon stressed that "The U.S. is a nation of laws, and unless you follow through with the sources that can help you, nothing can be done to address any discrimination that you are facing. It is important to stand up for your rights." He added, "You do not have to do it alone. You can contact government agencies designated to protect immigrant rights, community-based advocacy organizations, or a good attorney."

The Special Counsel, which was created under Section 274B of the Immigration and Naturalization Act, has jurisdiction to process charges alleging an individual act or a pattern or practice of employment discrimination on the basis of any of the following:

- National origin
- Citizenship status
- Unfair document practices
- Intimidation or retaliation

"Document abuse" as it has come to be called, is an illegal practice by some employers in fulfilling the I-9 verification requirements by requesting more documents than required, or rejecting acceptable documents. An employer may not specify which document(s) from the approved employment authorization lists the employee must present. The Immigration Act of 1990 (IMMACT 90) sought to address this practice by making such requests a violation of IRCA's antidiscrimination provisions. (Note Sergio Vasquez's story earlier in this chapter.) Amendments to the law do require proof that the employer's discrimination was intentional.

State Laws—IDHR Example

Congress is known to and must draw "bright lines," which it does where it deems appropriate. These bright lines are intended to provide clarity in the oftentimes murky language of legislation. In the case of green card holders (or others within the "protected class" who are protected from discrimination *before* they are U.S. citizens), Congress has drawn that line by designating the group to be protected as "intending citizens."

If you are considering action on an immigration discrimination complaint, you may wish to consider reviewing your own state law that often has broader and more flexible enforcement power. Under state law, the issue of citizenship is not always an impediment.

Raymundo Luna, chief legal counsel for the Illinois Department of Human Rights, recommended that you check your state laws as they relate to discrimination and immigration issues. "The Illinois Human Rights Act was enacted to protect all people in Illinois from illegal discrimination, regardless of national origin or citizenship status. The department does not ask or consider an individual's immigration status when they file a charge of discrimination."

IMMIGRATION DOCUMENTATION AND VISA STRATEGIES CHECKLIST

Federal Immigration Law

- ☐ The laws relating to residency, citizenship, and naturalization are all federal laws.
- ☐ Immigration laws involve the rules and requirement to permit foreign-born nationals to reside or work in the United States on a permanent or temporary basis.
- ☐ U.S. citizenship and naturalization laws are rules that govern how citizenship is determined.

☐ Naturalization laws govern the procedures and requirements permitting foreign-born nationals to acquire U.S. nationality.

Documentation Required to Work in the United States

☐ Everyone working in the United States, whether a citizen, permanent resident, or nonnational must present proof of employment eligibility to his/her employer.

☐ The Immigration Reform and Control Act of 1986 requires employers to verify the working status of all employees.

☐ A newly hired employee must produce evidence of his/her ability to work legally within seventy-two hours of being hired.

☐ The employers must complete and sign an I-9 form for every new employee.

☐ Employers face numerous penalties for knowingly hiring unauthorized aliens.

☐ The list of approved documents is contained in the chapter. (The list is included in the Appendix AA in Spanish.)

☐ Employers are to accept the documentation provided they reasonably appear genuine and properly belong to the employee.

H-1B Visa

☐ The H-1B visa is a nonimmigrant working visa granted to foreigners who are to be employed as professionals or specialty workers.

☐ The specialty worker category covers positions that require a college degree, including engineers, lawyers, accountants, and architects, among others.

☐ The H-1B visa has a cap on availability set by Congress.

Student, Graduate, and Training Visas

☐ The F-1 student visa allows students after one year of full time studies to work for up to twenty hours per week.

☐ The F-1 visa holders can obtain work authorization for any type of employment whether on or off campus after their first year in full-time student status.

☐ Some employment authorizations may be available even in the first year, but only for on-campus employment.

☐ The OPT visa is a status extending one year of employment authorization to graduated students.

☐ The OPT visa is not employer-specific, allowing the graduate to work anywhere in any position.

☐ The OPT work authorization must be filed with your school, preferably before graduation.

☐ The H-3 nonimmigrant trainee visa requires the employer to create and maintain a training program that does not involve excessive on-the-job training.

☐ The H-3 program requires the employer to show a need to train an alien worker in a field related to their education and employment background on a temporary basis.

☐ The training must not be available to the person in his/her own country.

☐ The H-3 program is employer-specific.

☐ The H-3 visa covers an eighteen-month training program, or up to two years for other trainee programs.

O Extraordinary Worker Visas

☐ The O-1 visa is designed to cover the highly talented or acclaimed foreign-born who may not qualify under other designations.

☐ Persons who qualify for the O-1 visa are Nobel Prize winners; those with scientific, scholarly, or business-related contributions of major significance; or those with other significant or critical abilities.

North America Free Trade TN Classification

☐ The NAFTA TN classification is available to Canadian and Mexican professionals.

☐ The TN category does not count toward the H-1B cap.

☐ The visa can be obtained for one-year increments continuously with no cap on the number of renewals.

☐ There are sixty-three professions approved under the TN visa.

L-1 Intracompany Transfers and E Treaty Visas

☐ The L-1 visa is available to international companies that need to transfer employees from their overseas employer to the U.S. company.

☐ The visa holder must have worked for the company for at least one year out of the last three.

☐ A graduate student could become immediately eligible if the student worked for the same hiring company in its out-of-the-country affiliate in one of the last three years.

☐ The E nonimmigrant visa is used for nationals of the transferring foreign country who are to be employed as managers, directors, or workers possessing specialized knowledge.

☐ There must be an appropriate treaty providing for E treaty visas between the United States and the foreign candidate's home country.

Immigrant Permanent Work Visas

☐ The permanent visa categories are allocated in a per-year quantitative basis per country.

☐ The permanent residence category allows for employment, but should not be confused with citizenship.

☐ One exception to the quota system is if the applicant's immigration is said to be in the national interest.

Strategies for Creating Employment Opportunities for Immigrants

☐ Put your best foot forward.

☐ Recognize the value that you add to the employer (especially certain employers) with your foreign language skills and multicultural experience.

☐ Look for employers who are multinational in scope or have an interest in expanding their foreign markets both in the United States and elsewhere.

☐ Consider an unpaid internship as a way to make you necessary to the company.

☐ Go the extra mile in performing your job.

☐ Find a way that you can uniquely benefit the employer's market.

Strategies for How to Broach the Immigration Issue with the Employer

☐ There is no need to disclose your immigration status during your employment interview process.

☐ When the issue is raised, be prepared to discuss the issue confidently.

☐ Make sure to consult a knowledgeable and experienced professional attorney or the services of a licensed immigration service to help you understand the work authorization process. (Do this early in the process.)

☐ If a job offer has been made, then you must raise the issue with the employer.

☐ Using the words "work authorization" instead of "immigration status" is often easier for the employer to understand.

☐ Be truthful and straightforward and indicate your preparation and ability to get the process in motion immediately.

Chapter 19

Evaluating a Job Offer

If you have ever browsed through the self-help section of the bookstore you will find numerous books on finding the perfect mate. The first chapter usually covers how to go about finding a life partner, where to look, and how to attract attention. Then the book points out what qualities to look for, how to compare your values to those of your potential mate, and how to evaluate if this is the right one for you. Well, we are not matchmakers, but the process of looking for a job can be compared to finding a love match. In previous chapters, we have covered how to prepare yourself for the search, where to look, and how to present yourself in the interview (courtship) stage. Now that you have made a connection and the offer is made, do you accept or not?

In this chapter, we will discuss how to evaluate a job offer not just in terms of salary but also in conjunction with your goals, aspirations, and value-added benefits. Just as we would not recommend jumping into a personal relationship without looking ahead, we do not recommend jumping into a job without taking the time to evaluate it.

Myth: A bird in the hand is worth two in the bush. I need to take the first job offered to me because I cannot count on getting another one.

Truth: In terms of career growth, not every job offer is a good one. A bad fit can set you back years in your career path by sidetracking you onto a road that leads you nowhere.

Reality 1: Jumping at a salary without looking at total job satisfaction quotients is a mistake. A 1998 study by William M. Mercer, Inc., found that in companies with low turnover, 40 percent of employees said emotional factors such as work satisfaction and good relationships with managers and other employees kept them on the job as compared to only 21 percent who cited salary and benefits.

Reality 2: Economic circumstances may dictate taking a job outside of your target area when you are attending school or other emergency situations. But don't get locked in. Keep your eye on your career strategy, and keep your persistence up. Success is not achieved in a day.

CAREER PLAN REVIEW

Felicidades! All your hard work has paid off. You have been selected and offered a new position. But before you take the leap into your new venture, you need to take the time to evaluate the position and see if it is the right move for you. There are many issues to consider, including the organization, the job, the people, the salary and benefits, and the fit into your career goals, among others.

Fortunately, most employers will not expect you to respond to a job offer immediately. You did your research on the company and the job before the interview, but now you need to examine it even further. First and foremost is the job itself. You are excited about being chosen, but are the job responsibilities really ones you will find challenging and provide you with an opportunity to learn and grow? How does the position fit into your career goals? As you go through the list, put a checkmark by the items that are most important for you and then compare your offer with your ideal. Let's look at some of these items step by step.

The Job

Nature of the Work

- What are the day-to-day responsibilities of the position?
- Ask for a copy of the job description, if you do not have one already.
- What are the required competencies of the job?
- Do the responsibilities play to your strengths and not your weaknesses?
- Will you be learning new skills?

The Position

- Where does the job fit into the organization?
- How will you contribute to the overall company objectives?
- Who in the company will be your customer?

Commute

- Where is the company located?
- How long will your commute be to and from work?
- Is public transportation available?

Hours

- What are the normal working hours?
- Will you be required to work weekends, holidays, or overtime?
- How will this fit into your personal schedule?

Travel

- How much travel is required?
- Are you comfortable with the areas of travel?
- What about the countries that you may be required to visit?

Evaluating a Job Offer

The Supervisor

- Have you met your supervisor?
- Can you get along with this person?
- What do you know about his/her management style?

Coworkers

- Have you met your coworkers?
- How long have they been employed with the company?
- Do they seem friendly and happy?
- What is your compatibility quotient?
- Where is the previous position holder?
- What do former employees say about the company?

Promotional Prospects

- How long do most people stay with the company?
- What are the promotional opportunities?

Career

- Will this job enhance my skills?
- How will it look on my résumé?

Make sure that you ask your prospective employer a full range of questions during the interview and afterward. If you have not gotten a copy of the job description, now is the time. Be sure to call on your inside sources to get more detailed information about the position. Current employees and former employees are the best sources for the real picture about the organization.

Isaias Zamarripa, director of experienced staffing and diversity at General Mills, recalled that when he was offered his position, he called his inside source and got the names of two former employees and cold called them for information. He said he asked them about the company and why they left. Zamarripa said he used that information to help him make his decision to accept the offer.

The Company

The next issue is the company itself. Is it a good fit with your values, attitudes, and goals? You want to feel proud of where you work and the work of the organization. The company culture should be one that is attractive to you. If you hate dressing up and prefer working in a casual environment, then you need to know that before accepting a position in the banking industry, for example. You can always adapt to a new environment, but going against your nature and values are not conducive to a happy work life. Again, compare your ideal to the offer.

Company Stability

- How old is the company?
- What is its financial condition?
- Will you be helping to create a new company?
- Is working in a more stable, established environment better for you?

Corporate Philosophy

- Is the company employee-friendly?
- Does it have a competitive culture?
- What are the company's mission and vision statements?
- Is there a value statement?
- What are the average stress levels?
- Is it a place you would be proud to work?

Company Product

- Does the company product or business appeal to you?
- Does it match your interests?

Size of the Organization

- Do you prefer working for large or small companies?
- Larger companies may be more highly structured; smaller ones may offer broader authority and responsibility.

Work Environment

- Is the company family-friendly?
- Is it a flexible workplace in terms of emergencies?
- How will this position alter my lifestyle?

Diversity

- Does the company embrace diversity?
- Does it value a Latino perspective?
- Is there a Latinos affinity or employee organization?
- What support does it get from management?
- Is diversity apparent throughout the organizational structure?
- Which are the minority leadership positions? Are there any?

Management Style

- What is the management style of the company leadership?
- What is your boss's management style?
- Is it compatible with your style of leadership?
- Will you be allowed a certain level of autonomy?

Training Opportunities

- What types of training opportunities are available?
- Is there a professional development plan for employees?
- Will the company support involvement in professional associations and organizations?

Security

- What type of building security is available?
- What security access is required?
- Are there security arrangements for travel status?

The company's annual report will have most of the information on its corporate philosophy, history, products or services, goals, and financial status. The company Web site, if one is available, often lists the mission and diversity information, plus any related affinity or minority supplier groups. Don't forget to review press releases, company newsletters, recruitment brochures, and magazine articles for a broad perspective on the organization. And as mentioned earlier, speak to current and ex-employees to get their point of view.

Examining the job and the organization will give you an answer as to whether the position and company are a "fit" for you. You will also be able to determine if the position fits into your career plan. Is this job a stage in your learning curve or is it an opportunity for autonomy and advancement? Both fits are important.

"We spend way too many years of our life working to not enjoy what we do," observed Pat Smith-Pierce, Ph.D., president of Power Speaking Consultants, a firm that specializes in communication skills. She added, "Salary and benefits are important. But remember it is equally important to know with whom you are working. If there is not fit, then you will be miserable." So, let's look at the financial benefits.

Salary and Benefits

The issue of salary usually does not come up until the actual job offer is made. So be sure to wait until the employer brings it up before you do. But after the offer is laid on the table, then there are various options for you to consider. Is the salary at market level? How often is salary reviewed? Yet, salary is only one part of the package. Benefit packages can add thousands to your overall compensation. How does the benefit package compare to your needs? Is there an ability to pick and choose benefits (cafeteria plan)? The following list outlines some of the issues to be evaluated. Review and rank them according to your needs, and then do your comparison.

Salary

- Will you be paid the going rate for a position, commensurate with your title and industry standard?
- Would taking this position create an economic hardship?
- How are salary increases determined?
- How often are salary reviews done?

Bonuses

- Are there bonuses available for peak performance?
- How are they determined?
- Is there a sign-on bonus? (If not, you can ask for it as part of your salary negotiations and use it to play off more benefits.)

Vacation

- How many weeks of vacation are you eligible for?

Holidays

- The average is ten paid holidays per year.
- What about your birthday?

Medical Insurance

- Does the employer pay all or part of the premiums on the medical insurance policy?
- Is the plan an HMO, preferred provider, or other type of plan?
- Is there an employee cost for routine physicals and prescriptions?
- What about coverage for family members?

Retirement

- Does the company offer a 401K?
- Does the company match your contributions?
- What other pension plan is available? How long does it take to get vested?

Stock Options

- Are stock options available?
- Are they available below market value or with employer contributions?

Life and Disability Insurance

- Are life and disability insurance plans available?
- Can you buy added coverage at a low cost?

Tuition Assistance

- What is the company's tuition assistance program?
- Does the company pay all or part of employment-related classes?

Child Care

- Are there on-site facilities for child care?
- Are there any after-school programs?
- Does the company pay any cost or offer a pre-tax program?

Remember, taking a job simply for the salary is a bad idea. As the saying goes, money cannot buy happiness. Your career plan encompasses the entire progression of your career including position, job satisfaction, promotion, salary, personal values, and lifestyle—your passion. Tipping the scale in any one direction will upset the balance needed to create a complete you.

Gabriel Najera, managing partner of the Management Development Group noted that "When I graduated from college I had thirteen job offers and took the one with the lowest salary. I wanted a job that included travel and still be able to live in my home city. I had my picture of my ideal. I started at under $18,000, but in one year my salary had already increased by 25 percent because I was passionate about my work."

Another example:

Robert Bard, publisher of Latina Style Magazine, *had a job in corporate America. He hated it. On Sunday night he would become sick to his stomach, dreading going to work the next day. He decided to leave the $72,000 job he hated for an $18,000 job doing what he loved in publishing. Bard advised, "Don't just follow the money. Follow your passions and your dreams. You can make money at what you love. Too many of us get stuck with the burdens of a mortgage, etc., that we cannot escape and are unhappy."*

HOW TO RESPOND TO A JOB OFFER

You've done your research, examined the company, and compared the job offer to your career goals and are ready to make your decision. Whether your answer is "yes" or "no," it is important to remember to handle this part of the process with respect for yourself, the employer, and the job offer. You want to keep open good lines of communication for the future.

Don't Jump into It

Remember that there is no reason to accept an offer immediately. Most employers will usually give you some time to consider the offer. You will want to take some time to review the various aspects of the offer and determine its fit. You may need to research some questions about the salary and benefit package. Or perhaps you are still waiting for a second job offer to come through. Whatever the reason, you can ask for some time to carefully think about your decision.

Express Your Appreciation

Whether you decide to accept or reject the job offer, be sure to express your appreciation to the employer. Your response will set the tone for further discussion if you are preparing for salary negotiations, or if you opt to decline the current offer, it will leave the door open for future employment opportunities.

Need More Time, Ask for It

As is sometimes the case, your empty job basket suddenly becomes full. You get an offer while you are waiting for another job to come through. What should you do? Your best bet is to contact the other potential employer and ask if the timeline for the employment decision can be made sooner. With both offers in hand you can then decide which is best for you.

Another approach would be to contact the first employer and ask for more time. Understandably the employer is anxious to fill their position, but asking for a short delay of four to seven days is not unreasonable. Remember that the employer wants you for the position. Again, thank the employer for the job offer, and be sure to get back to them within the allotted time frame. It is best not to mention the potential second offer, if possible. You do not want the company to question your interest in the job.

A recent client of ours had a similar situation occur to her. Maria received a job offer from a major retailer in a management training position. Her real interest lay in a pending offer from another major retailer on the computer help desk. Her quandary: should she accept one or wait for the other? After review, Maria opted to begin the lengthy orientation process with the first employer. In this way, Maria got to experience firsthand the climate and job responsibilities of the company. When the second offer came in, she was able to honestly say that the first offer was not a good fit.

We do not recommend backing out of any job offer you may have accepted. However, if you find in the first few days that the offer is not the right one for you, then make your decision on whether to stay or leave as soon as possible before the company invests more time and money in orientation and training. It is a serious decision that handled poorly can cloud your prospects at the company in the future.

Do It in Writing

Whether accepting or declining an offer, be sure to follow up in writing. When accepting an offer the company should follow up with a letter advising you of the offer. If you do not receive one, ask for it. The importance of detailing the offer in writing is to avoid any misunderstandings later on.

Evaluating a Job Offer

If you decide to decline the offer, you should again do this in writing. It is always a good idea to say something positive about the company and express your gratitude for the offer. It is important to leave a good impression with the employer for any potential prospects.

The following are sample letters for accepting or declining an offer.

Example of an Acceptance Letter

Mr. Martinez:

I am very pleased and excited to accept your job offer for the position of Sales Marketing Manager. I believe I will be able to do an excellent job for Marketing, Inc., and I look forward to our working together. I would appreciate it if you would confirm your offer in writing so I may have it for my files.

Thank you again for your confidence in me. I will work diligently to become an asset to the company and help build Marketing, Inc., together.

Sincerely,

Example of a Letter Declining the Offer

Dear Mr. Terronez:

I regret to inform you that I have decided not to accept your offer of the position of Accounts Manager. Latino, Inc., is a dynamic company with an outstanding reputation. However, due to several personal reasons, I have decided not to accept your offer. I thank you for your offer and hope that we can keep in contact in the future.

Sincerely,

NEGOTIATING SALARY AND BENEFITS

Salary negotiation is a process that makes many people feel uncomfortable because we are taught that it is unmannered or *mal educado* to discuss money. The paradox is that unless you position yourself and learn to value your abilities, strengths, and vision, you may not gain your true worth in the job market. As you move toward your career goal, achieving your financial objective is a major part of it.

Salary negotiations get underway after the job offer. You should avoid getting into any discussion of salary before then. Starting earlier can be used as a screening process to eliminate you from the pack, because companies do not want to waste their time talking to applicants who are out of their budget parameters. Starting too early can also hinder your negotiating stance later if you have already been boxed into a salary range. So try to avoid answering the salary question until later. We will provide you with some negotiation hints to help you come out the winner.

Researching Your Value

The first step in negotiating your salary is determining your value. Along with the attributes that you bring to the table, you should have some indication of the average market salary for the position for which you have applied. If you are not familiar with the job market rate, you can research this by either job title, industry, or job responsibilities. The Internet is a good place to conduct your research because it will more likely provide up-to-date data.

Keep in mind that if you have language and writing skills in another language, and the job may need those skills, use your unique language skills as a bargaining chip in negotiations. It is worth money.

Some good sites to look into follow:

- Bureau of Labor Statistics Career Information Home Page
  www.bls.gov

- Job Web
  www.jobweb.com

- Wage Web
  www.wageweb.com

- JobStar.com
  www.jobstar.org

- Salary.com
  www.salary.com

- Wall Street Journal
  www.careerjournal.com

Another excellent source for salary information is trade and professional associations that offer salary information on their industry. College and university career centers can also be a good resource for salary comparison data.

Negotiating Do's and Don'ts

The advantage of doing your research ahead of time is that it can give you a realistic picture of the value placed on the job for which you are applying. Now you are ready to begin negotiating. We've already warned you about sharing your salary expectations too soon.

Christine Eddick, president of A Career Coach for You and a board member of Career Masters Institute, indicated that she tells her clients that the first person who talks money loses. Why? A salary that is judged too high or too low can put you out of the game. So what do you do when the employer starts the interview and asks you for your salary? Instead of answering directly, Eddick recommended responding like this: "What I would really like to do is discuss the job opportunity you have available in your company in more detail to see if there is a fit for me. After we have established that, I'm sure you would offer me a salary that would be fair and commensurate with my background and skills."

Eddick suggested that other ways to respond to the salary question might be:

"What is the range you have for the position?" When the employer responds with a range, you say, "I think we are in the same range for the position."

or

"I really prefer to talk about the fair market value of the position. I believe we can come to an agreement along those lines."

An exception to the nondisclosure guideline is when you are dealing with a recruiter, as they will often require that you provide your salary at the beginning. The same is true of employment agencies. If you are placed in a position where you must disclose your salary, speak of it in broad terms.

"My salary requirements are negotiable. I am looking for a range in the high twenties to low thirties for a start."

or

"My salary with my next promotion would bring me to the range of the high forties."

Practice your negotiation skills with a friend or colleague. Keep in mind that the company has extended you an offer. They want you on board. If you do not negotiate a good package now, it probably will not happen again once you become an employee.

Don't be afraid to say you are disappointed with an offer. Eddick recommended letting a little silence speak for your disappointment and see if they show any movement. Remember, too, that future salary increases and other benefits can sometimes be used to sweeten the package.

The following chart sums up our recommendations.

Do's	Don'ts
Do your research	Don't talk about salary too soon
Do ask for a salary range	Don't give out your salary first
Do aim for the top of the range	Don't lie about your current salary
Do negotiate salary increases	Don't be afraid to ask for more
Do include benefits	Don't negotiate by telephone
Do express flexibility	Don't create hostility

Finally, when you do reach an agreement, do not forget to *get it in writing*. You need to make sure that you and your employer are both clear on what you have agreed to. It will avoid a lot of misunderstandings later.

EVALUATING A JOB OFFER CHECKLIST

The Job

- [ ] How does the position fit into your career goals?

Nature of the Work

- [ ] What are the day-to-day responsibilities of the position?
- [ ] Ask for a copy of the job description, if you do not have one already.
- [ ] Do the responsibilities play to your strengths and not your weaknesses?
- [ ] Will you be learning new skills?

Status of the Position

- [ ] Where does the job fit into the organization?
- [ ] How will you contribute to the overall company objectives?

Commute

- [ ] Where is the company located?
- [ ] How long will your commute be to and from work?
- [ ] Is public transportation available?

Hours

- [ ] What are the normal working hours?
- [ ] Will you be required to work weekends, holidays, or overtime?
- [ ] How will this fit into your personal schedule?

Travel

- [ ] How much travel is required?
- [ ] Are you comfortable with the areas of travel?
- [ ] What about the countries that you may be required to visit?

The Boss

- [ ] Have you met your supervisor?
- [ ] Can you get along with this person?
- [ ] What do you know about his/her management style?

Evaluating a Job Offer

Coworkers

☐ Have you met your coworkers?

☐ How long have they been employed with the company?

☐ Do they seem friendly and happy?

☐ What is your compatibility quotient?

Promotional Prospects

☐ How long do most people stay with the company?

☐ What are the promotional opportunities?

The Company

☐ Is the company a good fit with your values, attitudes, and goals?

Company Stability

☐ How old is the company?

☐ What is its financial condition?

☐ Will you be helping to create a new company?

☐ Is working in a more stable, established environment better for you?

Corporate Philosophy

☐ Is the company employee-friendly?

☐ What is its workplace philosophy?

☐ What are the average stress levels?

☐ Is it a place you would be proud to work?

Company Product

☐ Does the company product or business appeal to you?

☐ Does it match your interests?

Size of the Organization

☐ Do you prefer working for large or small companies?

☐ Larger companies may be more highly structured; smaller ones may offer broader authority and responsibility.

Work Environment

☐ Is the company family-friendly?

☐ Is there flexibility for emergencies?

☐ How will this position alter my lifestyle?

Diversity

☐ Does the company embrace diversity?

☐ What are the diversity employment statistics at all levels of the organization?

☐ Does it value a Latino perspective?

☐ Is there a formal Latino employee group organization?

☐ What support does it get from management?

Management Style

☐ What is the management style of the company leadership?

☐ Is it compatible with your style of leadership?

☐ Will you be allowed a certain level of autonomy?

Training Opportunities

☐ What types of training opportunities are available?

☐ Is there a professional development plan for employees?

☐ Will the company support involvement in professional associations and organizations?

Security

☐ What type of building security is available?

☐ What security access is required?

☐ Are there security arrangements for travel status?

Salary and Benefits

☐ Is the combined salary and benefits package at market level?

☐ Does the benefits package meet your needs?

☐ How often is salary reviewed?

Evaluating a Job Offer

Salary

☐ Will you be paid the going rate for a position, commensurate with your title and industry standard?

☐ Would taking this position create an economic hardship?

☐ How are salary increases determined?

☐ How often are salary reviews done?

Bonuses

☐ Are there bonuses available for peak performance?

☐ How are they determined?

Vacation

☐ How many weeks of vacation are you eligible for?

Holidays

☐ The average is ten paid holidays per year.

☐ What about your birthday?

Medical Insurance

☐ Does the employer pay all or part of the premiums on the medical insurance policy?

☐ Is the plan an HMO, preferred provider, or other type of plan?

☐ Is there an employee cost for routine physicals and prescriptions?

☐ What about coverage for family members?

Retirement

☐ Does the company offer a 401K?

☐ Does the company match your contributions?

☐ What other pension plan is available? How long does it take to get vested?

Stock Options

☐ Are stock options available?

☐ Are the available below market value or with employer contributions?

Life and Disability Insurance

☐ Are life and disability insurance plans available?

☐ Can you buy added coverage at a low cost?

Tuition Assistance

☐ What is the company's tuition assistance program?

☐ Does the company pay all or part of employment-related classes?

Child Care

☐ Are there on-site facilities for child care?

☐ Are there any after-school programs?

☐ Does the company pay any cost or offer a pre-tax program?

Chapter 20

Building Your Career Management Plan

Myths: The way to build a career is to do a good job, keep out of trouble, and stay at your job until you retire.

Truths: The unpredictability of today's work environment factored in with the move by employers to do more with less has negatively affected the career paths that worked in the past. You can no longer depend on the employer to provide you with a job that will last your entire career.

Reality 1: You need to be proactive and take the steps necessary to develop new pathways for your career growth.

Reality 2: The development of a career management plan requires reflection and assessment of your personal and professional goals in order to develop a comprehensive plan that satisfies all aspects of your life.

The Complete Job Search Guide for Latinos provides you with the road maps, the skills, and language of a successful job search and allows you to garner tips from experienced professionals, educators, and others who have shared the wealth of their experience. Now is the time to put that information together, mold it to your own agenda, and create your own career management plan.

GETTING YOUR HOUSE IN ORDER

Unless you lay the proper foundation, your job search and career can easily flounder and crumble under the weight of the ups and downs of life's unexpected turns. Keep in mind the following building blocks to a successful job search that are discussed in this book:

■ Design your blueprint: customize your plans and goals.

■ Lay the proper foundation: create a strong you by means of the twelve characteristics of successful Latinos.

■ Use the correct tools and materials: prepare yourself with a strong and compelling career portfolio, résumé, and cover letter.

■ Build a valuable product: create a brand that embodies your unique values and strengths and that lets you stand out from the others.

■ Market your brand: use your contacts both old and new to network yourself into new opportunities and challenges.

■ Complete the process: do not forget to ask for the job and take the time to evaluate the offer.

After you have completed these steps, you will be on your way to securing a position that will lead you to a successful career. When you began this journey in Chapter 1, we asked you to take the MI CASA survey to see how well you understood the impact and value of culture in your job search. We invite you to take it again now to see if the skills and information you have gained by reading this book has helped you grow in your own self awareness. Keep in mind that there are no right or wrong answers. Remember too that the process of self-assessment and reflection is an ongoing process that should be repeated throughout your career.

THE LATINO CAREER BUSINESS PLAN: BUILDING YOUR CAREER MANAGEMENT TOOLKIT

The next step in developing your career management plan includes taking some time to further reflect on your goals, skills, and expectations. To help you in that process we have prepared a Career Management Toolkit.

Each tool was selected to help you further define your goals and aspirations while laying the groundwork for your job search. Use the toolkit as an added element to help you in your self-assessment.

It is an exciting time to be Latino in the work environment as the nation awakens to the beat of our growing, vibrant community. Take advantage of it, and give yourself the power to succeed.

Your Career Management Toolkit includes the following:

How to write a personal mission statement—A personal mission statement forces you to think about your life and clarify what is really important to you. This checklist outlines the steps necessary to come up with a comprehensive mission statement that will apply to all aspects of your life.

MI CASA survey—MI CASA is a comprehensive survey covering all phases of the career management process. It is designed to provide you with insight on your current career management know-how. This assessment tool serves as a foundation from which you can identify developmental needs and strategies you may wish to pursue.

Career Management Toolkit: general questionnaire—The general questionnaire allows you to examine your career in a step-by-step process by focusing on your career achievements and goals. The questionnaire and its answers provide the material you will need to develop your career portfolio, résumé, and other marketing tools.

Career Management Toolkit: college questionnaire—The questionnaire for college students helps you translate your educational experience into skills that will assist you in your job search. What are your career aspirations? What awards, recognition, or leadership experience will bolster your career brand? Completion of the questionnaire will give you new insight into your own achievements.

Career marketing material development worksheet: Example for retail management—The targeted Career Management Toolkit (our example is retail) is an invaluable tool that will help you analyze your career in any professional area. As you pinpoint your areas of expertise, develop the keywords needed to give your résumé a higher profile, and highlight your achievements, you are laying a solid foundation for your job search.

S.T.A.R. power questionnaire—The S.T.A.R. technique is a key strategy for preparing your career portfolio, marketing documents, branding, networking, and interview strategies.

Use the results from the Career Management Toolkit to build your job search material. Then as you review the material, search for the pattern of your success, your strengths. Coupling these strengths with work that inspires you will propel you forward.

CAREER MANAGEMENT TOOLKIT

Writing a Personal Mission Statement

In Chapter 2, we discussed the importance of where you are going, which requires developing a career road map. Many people chart a course to the next move(s) in their career without making sure that the professional direction is aligned with values and personal goals; this requires a career compass.

Stephen Covey, author of *The Seven Habits of Highly Effective People*, refers to crafting a mission statement as "connecting with your own unique purpose and the profound satisfaction that comes in fulfilling it." It gives you a foundation for defining all of your activities, who you are, and what you are about.

The Career-Altering Purpose of Writing a Personal Mission Statement

Thinking about and writing a personal mission statement

- Forces you to think deeply about *your* life, clarify the purpose of your life, and identify what is really important to you.

- Prompts you to clarify and express succinctly your deepest values and aspirations.

- Imprints your values and purposes firmly in your mind to become a part of you rather than something you thought about once.

- Drives how you live in your personal and professional life.

Five Elements of a Good Mission Statement

A personal mission statement should be

- Comprehensive—apply to all aspects of your life
- No more than one or two sentences long
- Easily understood by everyone
- Repeatable to anyone, at any time, and under any circumstances
- An authentic connection to you

Evaluating Your Mission Statement

Consider the following when writing or reviewing your personal mission statement:

- Is your mission based upon timeless proven principles? Which ones?
- Do you feel this mission statement represents the best that is within you?

- Do you feel direction, purpose, challenge, and motivation when you review this statement?

- Are you practicing the strategies and skills that will help you accomplish what you have written?

Sample Personal Mission Statements

"To enable people and organizations to follow their own path."
—Murray Mann, president of Global Career Strategies and ResumeCompass.com

"To live an extraordinary life that embraces love of God and the nurture and support of family, friends, and community."
—Rose Mary Bombela-Tobias

"To uphold, discover, and uphold trust, honesty, and integrity in all relationships."
—Labor relations specialist at a Fortune 500 company

"To contribute to the health and well-being of people."
—Director of Hispanic markets for a multinational insurance company

The MI CASA™ Survey

MI CASA™ is designed to provide you with insight on your current career management know-how. This assessment tool serves as a foundation from which you can identify developmental needs and strategies you may wish to pursue.

MI CASA™ is personal survey. It is important to note that you should review the completed survey in the context of your life; not all items will be applicable or appropriate to your specific career management needs.

If you are a college student, please complete the assessment in terms of your academic work product, projects, internships, and part-time employment.

There is no formal score. For each statement, circle the number that best describes your level of agreement (1 = low, 5 = high).

Career Direction and Alignment

- I have explored who I am as a person, assessing my values, interests, personality, talents, and skills.
    1   2   3   4   5

- I know my strengths and weaknesses.
    1   2   3   4   5

- I have linked my self-assessment to job-related tasks and activities that I find most enjoyable, interesting, and challenging.
    1   2   3   4   5

- I have created my own definition of success.
    1   2   3   4   5

Building Your Career Management Plan

■ I have written a personal/professional life mission statement so I can follow my own calling, not someone else's goals.
  1   2   3   4   5

■ I have clearly visualized myself at the height of my career.
  1   2   3   4   5

■ I have linked my personal values with my career goals.
  1   2   3   4   5

■ I have clear short- and long-term career goals.
  1   2   3   4   5

■ I have evolved a personal career brand that is a combination of my authentic strengths and values, work reputation, and unique promise of value to employers.
  1   2   3   4   5

■ I have created an action or business plan to implement my career goals.
  1   2   3   4   5

■ I am implementing my career action or business plan.
  1   2   3   4   5

■ I am the most powerful person influencing my career direction.
  1   2   3   4   5

■ My overall career direction and alignment is excellent.
  1   2   3   4   5

Behavioral Characteristics

■ I believe in myself as someone with something special/unique to give.
  1   2   3   4   5

■ I am aware of my biological, psychological, and cultural programming and the impact they have on my attitude, behavior, and the results that I am getting in my life.
  1   2   3   4   5

■ I know my dominant workplace behavioral styles (director, relater, socializer, thinker, passive).
  1   2   3   4   5

■ I know my main conflict management style (competitor, accommodator, avoider, compromiser, conciliator).
  1   2   3   4   5

■ My boss/colleagues/customers would currently rate my workplace attitude as very positive.
  1   2   3   4   5

■ My current enthusiasm toward my job and life is great.
  1   2   3   4   5

- I adapt well to changes in the workplace and/or help make changes without complaints.
    1   2   3   4   5

- I practice techniques that help reduce anxiety and stress.
    1   2   3   4   5

- I work well under stress.
    1   2   3   4   5

- I see problems as challenges and opportunities.
    1   2   3   4   5

- I am willing to take risks to accomplish tasks and/or advance my career.
    1   2   3   4   5

- I am the most powerful person influencing career behaviors.
    1   2   3   4   5

Communication

- I have good verbal communication skills.
    1   2   3   4   5

- I have good writing skills.
    1   2   3   4   5

- I would do well on a test for Spanish verbal communication skills.
    1   2   3   4   5

- I would do well on a test for Spanish writing skills.
    1   2   3   4   5

- I am aware of the messages I send through nonverbal communication (body language, eye contact).
    1   2   3   4   5

- I am good at reading the nonverbal cues of others.
    1   2   3   4   5

- I am an active listener (understand the facts presented, not judgmental, not defensive, not thinking of what I am going to say next).
    1   2   3   4   5

- I am skilled at providing helpful feedback.
    1   2   3   4   5

- When receiving negative feedback, I handle it in a constructive and positive manner.
    1   2   3   4   5

- I am comfortable speaking one-on-one with my coworkers.
    1   2   3   4   5

- I am comfortable speaking one-on-one with my boss.
    1   2   3   4   5

■ I am comfortable speaking one-on-one with my customers.

    1   2   3   4   5

■ I have strong presentation skills to a group.

    1   2   3   4   5

■ Diplomacy is one of my greatest strengths.

    1   2   3   4   5

■ I have good problem solving skills.

    1   2   3   4   5

■ I deliver excellent customer service.

    1   2   3   4   5

■ I am comfortable in one-on-one negotiations.

    1   2   3   4   5

■ I am skilled in group negotiations.

    1   2   3   4   5

■ When I speak, people pay attention to my ideas and opinions, and I see them later used or implemented.

    1   2   3   4   5

■ When it is appropriate, I don't have a problem with expressing a viewpoint different from management's.

    1   2   3   4   5

■ I am the most powerful person influencing my communication skills.

    1   2   3   4   5

■ I rate my overall communication skills as excellent.

    1   2   3   4   5

Job Skills and Performance

■ I am knowledgeable and skilled at performing my job.

    1   2   3   4   5

■ I have a clear understanding of my supervisor's expectations for my performance.

    1   2   3   4   5

■ I am willing to sign my name on any task I complete.

    1   2   3   4   5

■ I deliver a high-quality and timely work product.

    1   2   3   4   5

■ I have feelings of ownership with respect to my company's welfare and output.

    1   2   3   4   5

■ I display a strong work ethic with high energy, focus, dedication, and purpose.

    1   2   3   4   5

- My boss knows that I can be counted on to "pitch in."
  1   2   3   4   5

- I am a team player; I contribute to the team through actions and words.
  1   2   3   4   5

- I effectively use workplace resources (people and information) to improve my knowledge, skills, and performance.
  1   2   3   4   5

- I communicate well with coworkers of different backgrounds.
  1   2   3   4   5

- I understand the four basic types of power and how and when to use each (personal, position, knowledge, perceived).
  1   2   3   4   5

- I have good time management skills.
  1   2   3   4   5

- I know how to get and have achieved career-advancement visibility in my organization.
  1   2   3   4   5

- My bilingual skills are an asset to the company.
  1   2   3   4   5

- My cultural background and experiences are assets to my employer.
  1   2   3   4   5

- I am the most powerful person influencing my job performance.
  1   2   3   4   5

- I rate my current overall job performance as excellent.
  1   2   3   4   5

Corporate Culture

- I know the organization's customs and values.
  1   2   3   4   5

- I practice workplace behaviors, style, and communication expected by my company.
  1   2   3   4   5

- I am aware of the unwritten rules of the organization.
  1   2   3   4   5

- I deal well with office politics.
  1   2   3   4   5

- I know what management characteristics are valued in my company.
  1   2   3   4   5

- I understand the dynamics of my being (ethnicity/culture/gender) in my place of work.
  1   2   3   4   5

■ I know how to manage the process by which my background (ethnicity/culture/gender) is evaluated.

    1   2   3   4   5

■ I know the issues and concerns that are key to my organization's success.

    1   2   3   4   5

■ I am the most powerful person influencing my ability and success to navigate the workplace environment and culture.

    1   2   3   4   5

■ My overall skills at navigating the workplace culture are excellent.

    1   2   3   4   5

Networking

■ I have a personal network (or support system).

    1   2   3   4   5

■ I have a strong professional network.

    1   2   3   4   5

■ I have a strong workplace network.

    1   2   3   4   5

■ I effectively network with people of my background (ethnicity/culture/sex) in the workplace.

    1   2   3   4   5

■ I effectively network with people of a different background (ethnicity/culture/sex) in the workplace.

    1   2   3   4   5

■ I have a good mentor(s) with a background (ethnicity/culture/sex) similar to my own.

    1   2   3   4   5

■ I have a good mentor(s) with a background (ethnicity/culture/sex) different from mine.

    1   2   3   4   5

■ I know and fulfill my responsibilities as a mentee.

    1   2   3   4   5

■ I am a good mentor to someone.

    1   2   3   4   5

■ I have colleagues in positions similar to mine in other divisions within my company, or at other companies, with whom I regularly interact to exchange ideas and keep abreast of issues pertinent to my job.

    1   2   3   4   5

■ I belong to in-house and external professional organizations and attend their meetings with enough regularity to know the other members.

    1   2   3   4   5

■ I share my knowledge and experience with others.

    1   2   3   4   5

■ I keep in touch with my network contacts through notes, phone calls, lunches, and planned meetings.

    1   2   3   4   5

■ I am the most powerful person in making my networking a success.

    1   2   3   4   5

■ I rate my overall networking skills as excellent.

    1   2   3   4   5

Dealing with Stereotypes, Discrimination, Racism, and Sexual Harassment

■ I understand my own prejudices and stereotypes.

    1   2   3   4   5

■ I have strong cross-cultural communication and management skills.

    1   2   3   4   5

■ I am effective at managing the prejudicial behavior of others.

    1   2   3   4   5

■ I build bridges that link work and personal cultures that allow me to be authentic in both worlds and help educate others.

    1   2   3   4   5

■ I know my company's nondiscrimination policies and procedures.

    1   2   3   4   5

■ I know the workplace discrimination legal protections afforded me and how to exercise my rights.

    1   2   3   4   5

■ I know the antidiscrimination legal protections under immigration employment laws and regulations afforded me.

    1   2   3   4   5

■ I rate my overall knowledge of and willingness to exercise my antidiscrimination rights on the job as excellent.

    1   2   3   4   5

Job Search Management

■ I know what steps are necessary to conduct a successful job search.

    1   2   3   4   5

■ I am comfortable marketing my skills and abilities to employers.

    1   2   3   4   5

■ I know how to market the value of my skills and abilities.

    1   2   3   4   5

Building Your Career Management Plan

■ I know how to market the value of being a (my ethnicity/culture/gender).
    1   2   3   4   5

■ I have a high-quality current résumé available for job search, promotions, or career assignment opportunities.
    1   2   3   4   5

■ I have high-quality cover letters and career marketing letters available for job search, promotions, or career assignment opportunities.
    1   2   3   4   5

■ I maintain a career portfolio that documents my accomplishments, contributions, and work products.
    1   2   3   4   5

■ I know how to research industries and companies.
    1   2   3   4   5

■ I know how to tap into the "hidden" job market.
    1   2   3   4   5

■ I know the steps for successful job search networking and am willing to network myself into a job.
    1   2   3   4   5

■ I know how to work with the college/alumni career offices and professional association employment services.
    1   2   3   4   5

■ I know how to work with recruiters and headhunters.
    1   2   3   4   5

■ I know how to market myself to employers in ways that will get me an interview.
    1   2   3   4   5

■ I know how to tap into Latino professional associations and Latino-friendly sources as part of my job search.
    1   2   3   4   5

■ I know how to use the Internet in my job search.
    1   2   3   4   5

■ I know how to use traditional and diversity career fairs in my job search.
    1   2   3   4   5

■ I know the types of job interviews and how they work.
    1   2   3   4   5

■ I know how to conduct pre–job interview research on companies and specific jobs.
    1   2   3   4   5

■ I understand the interview process, including types of interviews, testing, and background checks.
    1   2   3   4   5

- I know how to prepare for a successful job interview.
    1   2   3   4   5

- I am comfortable marketing myself (skills, abilities, contributions) during a job interview.
    1   2   3   4   5

- I know how to deal with interview anxiety.
    1   2   3   4   5

- I know how to execute my interview plan to get the employer to call me back/hire me.
    1   2   3   4   5

- I know how to make a great first impression and manage my body language.
    1   2   3   4   5

- I know how to "read" the interviewer and respond accordingly.
    1   2   3   4   5

- I know how to close the interview and ask for the job.
    1   2   3   4   5

- I know how to follow up after a job interview.
    1   2   3   4   5

- I know how to prepare my references.
    1   2   3   4   5

- I know how to accept, negotiate, or reject a job offer.
    1   2   3   4   5

- I actively pursue my own continuing education, training, and development.
    1   2   3   4   5

- I actively participate in company-sponsored training and development.
    1   2   3   4   5

- I am assertive with my employer regarding training, development, and career-advancing work assignments.
    1   2   3   4   5

- I am the most powerful person in my job search.
    1   2   3   4   5

- I rate my overall job search skills as excellent.
    1   2   3   4   5

MI CASA™ Follow-up

- I will review and reflect on my MI CASA™ survey answers.
    1   2   3   4   5

- I will complete the MI CASA™ survey periodically throughout my career.
    1   2   3   4   5

GENERAL CAREER MARKETING DOCUMENTS DEVELOPMENT WORKSHEET

Note: This form can be downloaded from *www.JobSearchGuideforLatinos.com*.

Personal Information

Name:

Address:

City:

State:

Zip:

Home phone:

Office phone:

Cellular phone:

Pager/beeper:

Fax:

Work fax:

Email:

Objective/Job Target

What position will you be holding when you are at the top of your career, or what do you want to be when you grow up?

What jobs will you be applying for in the next step of your career?

Key Industry Terms

Please list keywords that are industry/job-specific. To identify the most effective keywords, pull three to five detailed job postings from Internet job search engines, including major portals, industry-specific sites, and/or Latino-focused engines. (See Directories G and I for listings of job search engines.)

Keyword:	Synonym:	Synonym:
Keyword:	Synonym:	Synonym:
Keyword:	Synonym:	Synonym:
Keyword:	Synonym:	Synonym:
Keyword:	Synonym:	Synonym:

Keyword:	Synonym:	Synonym:
Keyword:	Synonym:	Synonym:
Keyword:	Synonym:	Synonym:
Keyword:	Synonym:	Synonym:
Keyword:	Synonym:	Synonym:
Keyword:	Synonym:	Synonym:

Briefly summarize, in one paragraph or less, what you believe your strengths are. Identify both hard and soft skills. Use these questions as a guide. Why should a prospective employer hire you? Why does your present employer like you? What is your personal career brand?

Memory Jogger

If you were walking into a merit pay review meeting, what contributions, achievements, productivity, or other results would you mention as justification for your merit pay increase? Refer to these questions to help probe your memory:

- Did you save your company money? Describe in detail how you made this happen.
- How did you save or improve time, payroll hours, overall efficiencies for yourself or your team?
- Did you meet an impossible deadline through your effort? Describe the situation.
- Did you bring a major project in ahead of schedule or under budget? What were the details?
- Did you suggest and/or help launch a new product or program? What was your involvement? Why were you selected?
- Did you take on any new responsibilities that weren't part of your job? Please provide details.
- Did you help increase sales?
- Did you generate new business or create/strengthen affiliations?
- What difference have you made being bicultural and/or bilingual? Explain with specific examples.
- What special skills/experiences/expertise have you developed or gained while working in this position?

Remember, just refer to these questions to assist you in identifying your accomplishments. Place an asterisk next to the accomplishments that rank among your top ten.

Professional Experience

List the following information for each job held. For military service, list branch of service, rank, and relevant experience (include full job description if relevant to job target).

Company name:

City and state:

Description of company: What does this company do? Size? Type of products/ services? Is it national, regional, or local?

Job title:

Dates:

Key responsibilities:

Key accomplishments: Please refer to the "Memory Jogger" questions to help you come up with your greatest accomplishments in this position or things you did that you are most proud of. Make sure that you provide detailed information. What did you do? Back it up by explaining how you did it. Be specific. Think of savings, productivity, or methods of improvements, new ideas, and so on.

Special recognition: Did you receive any special recognition awards, certificates, or letters from your supervisor or customers? What sets you apart from the others who do the same thing as you do?

Education and Training

List the following information for each school attended.

Name of school:

City and state:

Degree:

Major:

Dates attended:

GPA:

Honors:

Recent graduates, please list relevant coursework:

Activities:

Activities

List the folowing information for each activity.

Professional development/training/seminars/continuing education/military/personal development (even if not career-related):

Name of course, conference, or workshop:

Presented by (school, company, professional association, organization, or other):

Dates attended:

City, state, and country:

Grades (if any):

Continuing education units:

Licenses, credentials, or certifications earned (if any):

Special Skills

Licenses:

Credentials:

Certifications:

Computer skills:

Office software:

Operating systems:

Programming languages:

Protocols/networking:

Job-specific skills (include job-related techniques, tools, and technologies):

Spoken and Written Languages

Use the following criteria to list your level of proficiency in speaking, reading, writing, and translating: (1) Highly proficient, excellent at all business levels; (2) Very good at specific business levels; (3) Working knowledge for everyday communications; (4) General conversational or understanding; (5) Some knowledge, exposure to the language and courtesy phrases.

Volunteer Activities, Publishing Credits, Awards

List the following information for each activity. Include dates and positions held.

Affiliations/memberships:

Volunteer activities:

Publishing credits:

Speeches/conferences:

Awards:

References

List as many references as you can. Choose people who know how you work and are not just personal friends or family members. List the following information for each reference.

Name:

Address:

City:

State:

Zip:

Home phone:

Office phone:

Cellular phone:

Pager/beeper:

Fax:

Work fax:

Email:

Relationship to you:

What would this person say about you in a letter of reference?

Career Marketing Documents Development Worksheet: Additional Questions for Recent College Graduates and Students

List the following information for each high school, college, or university attended:

Name of school:

City and state:

Degree:

Major:

Dates attended:

GPA:

Were you on the Dean's List? If so, which semesters?

Honors: Please describe in detail each award, what activity you engaged in to win the award, how competitive the award was and when you received it:

1. Please provide a list of courses you completed that were part of your major curriculum and/or related to the type of position you are currently seeking.

    List work product, related S.T.A.R. stories, grades, and written instructor comments that you can add to your career portfolio, including key

    Research papers
    Hands-on practicum
    Case studies
    Business simulations
    Presentations
    Senior thesis
    Publications
    Student abroad programs
    (on team projects, identify your role)

2. What was your academic experience like?

    What are you most proud of?

    Courses you liked best? Why?

    Courses you liked least? Why?

    How did you manage your time between course work, extracurricular activities, work, and personal needs?

    What did you learn from your college experience that you will carry into the workplace? Give specific examples or S.T.A.R. stories.

3. Describe your college experience from the perspective of being bilingual and/or bicultural. Include positive and negative experiences, how you handled them, and the benefits of going through them. Be specific and/or use S.T.A.R. stories.

4. Did you receive any scholarships? If so, please list name of each scholarship, when awarded, selection criteria, and amount.

5. Did you participate in any internships, paid or unpaid? If so, how many hours per week for each internship? Include detailed responsibilities, special projects, contributions, and accomplishments.

6. Have you taken graduate qualifying exams? If so, which ones? What are your plans for graduate school?

7. Were you a teaching, research, or lab assistant? If yes, how many hours per week? Include details, responsibilities, special projects, contributions, or accomplishments.

8. Did you work during the academic year? If yes, how many hours per week by academic year? Did you receive any honors or awards? Provide details.

9. Did you participate in a cooperative education program? If yes, how many hours per week for each experience? Include detailed responsibilities, special projects, contributions, or accomplishments.

10. Did you participate in a formal work study program? If yes, how many hours per week for each experience? Include details of responsibilities, special projects, contributions, or any other accomplishments on your General Career Marketing Documents Development Worksheet.

11. Did you participate in any community service, college service, or volunteer programs? What programs? When? Any honors or awards for these efforts? Include details, responsibilities, special projects, contributions, or any accomplishments on your General Career Marketing Documents Development Worksheet.

12. What clubs, associations, fraternities, or sororities do you belong to? Did you have any leadership roles, formal assignments, or informal responsibilities within these organizations? Did you manage any special events or projects? Can you provide a list of the skills you developed in each position? How do these skills relate to your current career objectives? Can you highlight any notable achievements or contributions? Include details, responsibilities, special projects, contributions, or accomplishments.

13. Are you a member of any community or professional organizations outside of college? Did you have any leadership roles, formal assignments, or informal responsibilities within these organizations? Did you manage any special events or projects? Can you provide a list of the skills you developed in each position? How do these skills relate to your current career objectives? Can you highlight any notable achievements or contributions? Include details, responsibilities, special projects, contributions, and accomplishments.

14. Did you play competitive sports, either formally with your college, intramural, or through some other organization? What sport and for how long? Any leadership positions? Did you win any athletic honors or awards?

15. List any references from all of the above:

Name:

Address:

City:

State:

Zip:

Home phone:

Office phone:

Cellular phone:

Pager/beeper:

Fax:

Work fax:

Email:

Relationship to you:

What would this person say about you in a letter of recommendation?

Career Marketing Material Development Worksheet: Retail Management

This worksheet is based on a worksheet that was contributed by Evelyn V. Salvador, principal partner, Creative Image Builders, Inc., and Career Catapult.)

Sample Position Titles

Assistant manager
Assistant store manager
Back end supervisor
Deli manager
Department manager
District manager
Front end supervisor
Front end manager
Frozen foods manager
Grocery store manager
Hardlines manager
Homelines manager
Night store manager
Retail manager
Shift supervisor
Softlines manager
Store operations manager
Store manager

Building Your Career Management Plan

Areas of Expertise

Instructions: Review the list of keywords and check off all skill areas in which you have knowledge. Double-check those skills in which you are highly proficient and directly target your résumé toward the positions for which you are applying.

Note: Keywords are critical components of your résumé, especially for firms that use scanning software to look for these words and determine whether to screen your résumé in or out based on their presence or nonpresence. Keywords are also important because they qualify your expertise.

Account servicing
Account management
Ad development
Audits
Bank reconciliations
Big box retail/warehouse superstores
Budget development
Business development
Cash control
Client needs assessment
Client relations
Cold calling
Community relations
Competitive analysis
Conversion of customer desires
    into needs
Costing/budgeting
Creative sales techniques
Cross-selling
Customer satisfaction
Customer shopper client base
Data collection
Demographic analysis
Direct mail
Employee suggestions
Exceptional customer service
Financial management
General store operations
Hardlines
High-gross item promotion
High referral base
Human resources management
Increased sales/profits
Internet marketing
Inventory control
Inventory management

Lead/develop sales
Low-gross item liquidation
Low staff turnover
Maintaining account base
Marketing identification/capturing
Marketing
Market penetration
Market research
Maximizing employee potential
Media analysis
Merchandise assessments
Merchandising/set-ups
Negotiations
Networking
New business development
New merchandise implementation
New product launches
Open lines of communication
Organizational development
OSHA safety standards
Payroll
Permanent markdown prevention
Planogram design
Planogram implementation
Policy and procedure development
Presentations
Printing coordination
Proactive retail management
Product implementation
Product knowledge
Product management
Productivity improvement
Productivity quality standards
Profit/loss responsibilities
Profit contributions improvement
Promotions/campaigns

Purchasing
Quality assurance
Receipts/disbursements
Recruiting
Relationship building
Repeat business
Resolving client concerns
Retail management
Revenue growth
Sales
Sales forecasting
Sales management
Sales planning

Sales training
Scheduling
Softlines
Special events coordination
Staff supervision
Strategic planning
Strategizing client needs
Team builder
Team player
Territory development
Trade shows
Training/development
USDA sanitation standards

Personal Attributes

Instructions: Check off those attributes that you believe come closest to who you are. Then review each checked item and determine which attributes help you the most in your profession. Underline those.

Note: items marked with an asterisk are deemed critical for management personnel.

Accommodating
*Action-driven leadership
Ambitious
*Approachable/nonthreatening
Articulate
Assertive
Autonomous
Balanced
Calm/level-headed
*Candid
Client-focused
*Command presence
Communicative
*Composure
Confident
*Conflict management
Competitive
Convincing
Creative
Credible
Cultivator
Customer-focused
Customer service oriented
*Dealing with ambiguity
*Decisive

*Delegation
*Developing loyalty in staff
Diplomatic/tactful
Directing high-producing teams
Diversity management
Dynamic
Easy to get along with
*Employee retention
Empowered
Empowering
Energetic/vital
*Ethics/values
Enthusiastic
Exhibits conviction
Expressive
Flexible/versatile
Follow-up
Focused
Friendly
Genuine
Goal-driven
Good listener
Help others solve problems
Honest
Independent

Influencing
Initiative
Initiator
*Innovative
Inquisitive
Insightful
*Inspires team
Inspiring
Interpersonal skills
Intuitive
*Leadership abilities
*Listening skills
Look forward to challenges
*Mentoring
*Morale building
Motivated
Motivator
Negotiator/mediator
Observant
Open to change
Optimistic
Outcome-focused
Outgoing
*Overcoming adversity
*Overcoming boundaries
Persistent
Personable
Persuasive
People-oriented
*Planning/conceptualizing
Positive attitude
Presenter

Problem solver
Productive
Promoter
*Profit-conscious
Provide direction
Quick learner
Rapport builder
*Relationship building
Reliable
Resilient
Resourceful
Respected by others
Responsive
Results-oriented
*Revenue growth
Self-directed
Self-motivated
Self-starter
*Straightforward
Success-driven
*Tackling challenges/obstacles
Tactful
Tactical action plans
*Team builder/team leader
Team-oriented
*Think outside the box
Troubleshooter
Trusted by others
Visionary
Willing to try new things
Work well under pressure

Achievement Questions

1. What type of retail store/store department do you manage or supervise?

   Type of store:

   Chain store?:

   Type of products:

   Department(s)/unit(s):

   Annual sales volume—company-wide: $ _____

   Annual sales volume—your store: $ _____

   Annual sales volume—your department(s)/unit(s): $ _____

   Store square footage:

Department square footage:

Employees—company-wide:

Employees—store-wide:

Employees—your department:

Store payroll: $ _____

Department payroll: $ _____

Overtime: $ _____

Customers serviced on an average day:

Customers serviced on a peak day:

2. What aspects of the store's daily operations do you manage/oversee?

( ) New store opening
( ) Volume purchasing/buying/merchandising
( ) Front end/back end
( ) Hardlines/softlines/homelines
( ) Sales development
( ) Customer service/customer relations
( ) Window merchandising
( ) Inventory control/management
( ) Vendor relations
( ) Cash controls/cash flow management
( ) Automated payroll
( ) Planogram implementation/maintenance
( ) Store display set-ups
( ) Store opening/closing procedures
( ) Loss prevention
( ) Customer shopper client base
( ) Billing
( ) Staff training and development
( ) Freight
( ) Sales/budget forecasting
( ) Shipping and receiving
( ) Store and personnel safety/security
( ) Price change maintenance
( ) Merchandising ordering
( ) Staff recruitment
( ) Store staff training/development
( ) Staff scheduling
( ) Profit/loss responsibility
( ) Stockroom/warehouse

(   ) Store expenses/expense control
(   ) Payroll/attendance records
(   ) Store budget: $ _____
(   ) Store safety/security
(   ) Store maintenance/repairs
(   ) Advertising
(   ) Office administration
(   ) Overall store performance
(   ) Establishing productivity goals
(   ) Establishing sales goals
(   ) Monitoring sales goals
(   ) Petty cash
(   ) Store supplies
(   ) Other:

3. What areas of the department/unit do you manage/supervise?

(   ) Planogram implementation
(   ) Merchandise stocking
(   ) Flush and filling
(   ) Inventory management and control
(   ) Sales
(   ) Customer assistance, service, and follow-up
(   ) Commissioned retail sales
(   ) Department budget: $_____
(   ) Product installations
(   ) Department staff training/development
(   ) Special order merchandise
(   ) Department display set-ups
(   ) Staff scheduling/coverage
(   ) Receipts/disbursements
(   ) Inventory control
(   ) Customer inquiries and complaints
(   ) Supervise incoming deliveries
(   ) Placing product orders with vendors
(   ) Oversee packing out of products onto shelves
(   ) Other:

4. Have you increased annual sales for your store/department?

By how much? Percentage: _____ %

From $ _____ to $ _____

In what period of time?

What primary methods do you use which resulted in increased sales?

( ) Stock rotation
( ) Display merchandise in designated "sell" areas
( ) Complete timely layouts
( ) Display new merchandise as soon as it arrives
( ) Perform major resets
( ) Ensure all merchandise is signed with correct pricing
( ) Maintain correct signage
( ) "Stack it high to let it fly" method
( ) Intensive staff training
( ) Maintain rotation and dating policies on perishables
( ) Cut inventory class levels
( ) Implement all planograms in a timely manner
( ) Increase saleable merchandise
( ) Encourage cross-selling of higher priced items
( ) Improved in-stock conditions
( ) Promote add-on sales of service contracts
( ) Increased cashier performance
( ) Promote a consumer-sensitive approach
( ) Heightened customer satisfaction
( ) Appeasing dissatisfied customers
( ) Convert customer desires into needs
( ) Enforcing appropriate store standards
( ) Maintain tight control on planograms
( ) Assisting customers with buying decisions
( ) Remerchandising items based on demographic expectations
( ) Promote sale of coordinating products and/or accessories
( ) Maintain open line of communication with planners, merchandisers, and buyers
( ) Keep sales items and general merchandise fully stocked and/or fresh
( ) Conduct competitive shopping and adjust pricing accordingly
( ) Other:

5. If you transitioned from a previous store manager or department supervisor, did you feel the need to change the store/department routine in any way?

If so, what did you change?

How were you able to effectively do so without affecting employee morale?

What were the results of your efforts?

6. How do you accurately assess merchandise to promote high-gross items, liquidate lesser ones, and prevent permanent markdowns? What are the results?

7. What do you do to ensure that your store/unit runs efficiently? (Examples: proper staffing and scheduling, impromptu register openings, walking the floor, improving staff morale, employee suggestion box, innovative problem-solving, etc.) What are the results?

8. What is your employee turnover percentage for your store or the departments you manage/supervise? _____% Have you decreased turnover? _____ What was it prior? _____%

9. How do you minimize turnover and maximize employee potential and in what ways have you increased employee morale and/or staff loyalty?

   ( ) Successful morale building
   ( ) Proactive hiring and training policies
   ( ) Open-door policy
   ( ) Promoting an ongoing spirit of friendly competition
   ( ) Encouraging employee input
   ( ) Ensuring all sales people make their quotas
   ( ) Treat all employees fairly
   ( ) Recognition of strengths and weaknesses
   ( ) Offer praise when due
   ( ) Develop reachable but challenging goals
   ( ) Enforce company guidelines
   ( ) Provide equal opportunity for promotion
   ( ) Other:

10. Have you decreased store costs or losses?

    If so, by how much? _____%

    (From $ _____ to $ _____)

    In what areas have you decreased store costs or losses?

    ( ) Payroll expenses
    ( ) Training costs
    ( ) Shortages
    ( ) Shrinkage
    ( ) Shoplifting
    ( ) Attempted Fraud
    ( ) Other:

    How did you accomplish this? (Such as by cross-training employees; timely returning to vendors damaged merchandise that previously was being sold at a loss, etc.)

11. In what ways have you helped increase customer loyalty or satisfaction and/or gained repeat business or referrals?

12. What type of proactive business development/marketing initiatives have you spearheaded? Through what means? What were the results?

13. Have you helped increase saleable merchandise?

    If so, from what to what?

    From $ _____ to $ _____

    What was the annual sales projection for the store? $ _____

    If you surpassed sales projections, how did you accomplish this?

14. Have you helped reduce or eliminate store penalties from the pulling center?

    By how much? ____%

    (From $ _____ to $ _____)

    How did you accomplish this?

15. What do you do to plan for upcoming ad sets, ensure all planograms are implemented correctly, and ensure all merchandise is in stock, correctly signed, and flows to the right locations?

16. Were you selected to manage/comanage a store or a department? Why were you selected and what was the result? (Example: helped turn around out-of-stock conditions, clean up the store, boost employee morale and productivity, improve sales, etc.)

17. In what ways have you increased total store margins? From what percentage to what percentage? _____% to _____%

18. What do you do to maximize close rates and add-on sales (e.g., work closely with sales staff, assure that sales floor product mix is appropriate for community and current trends)?

19. In what areas do you conduct staff training and development (e.g., on developing merchandising strategies, on the features and benefits of all new merchandise, on sales techniques that maximize commissions and store margins)?

20. Have you reduced employee turnover?

    If so, by how much? _____%

    How did you accomplish this?

21. Have you increased customer service levels?

    From what percentage to what percent? ____% to ____%

    How did you accomplish this?

22. What do you do to increase customer satisfaction, referrals, and repeat business (e.g., remerchandise and reorganize inventory so everything is easier to locate, ensure adequate coverage at all times, especially during peak periods, cross-train staff to fill in for others, act as a role model to staff and exhibit excellent customer service skills daily, ensure customers always depart happy)?

23. Have you reduced shrinkage?

    If so, by what percentage? _____%

    How did you accomplish this?

24. Have you increased inventory levels?

    If so, by how many points?

    From _____ to _____

    How did you accomplish this (e.g., by over-ordering high-demand items at sale prices to increase revenues)? What was the end result/department benefit?

25. Have you saved the store money in lost product costs? How did you accomplish this?

26. Have you increased the average dollar transaction?

    If so, from what amount to what amount per customer?

    From $_____ to $ _____

    How did you accomplish this?

27. In what ways have you streamlined operations (e.g., by restructuring stocking areas, by aiding work flow of stock-to-floor replenishment)?

28. Have you improved store safety in any way? How did you accomplish this? What was the result?

Use Your S.T.A.R. Power

A key strategy for preparing your career portfolio, marketing documents, branding, networking, and interviewing is to use the S.T.A.R. technique, as outlined here. (This technique is often referred to as the CAR, PAR, or SAR technique.)

Situation: Define the situation or "set the stage."

Example: "Assigned as an account manager to an underperforming sales territory—number 92 out of 100 districts.

Task: Identify the task/project performed.

Example: "To increase same store sales by 20 percent and boost commercial customer base by 10 percent."

Action: Describe the action that you took/initiated. This response should illustrate the specific skills you used in completing the task.

Example: "Conducted a competitive market analysis and customer service survey; developed a business plan that included value-added service, sales incentives, and referral bonus program that benefits our business customers; and rolled out a three-level marketing strategy to implement the plan."

Result: Summarize the outcome.

Example: District became number 9 in the region in the first year; same store sales rose by 37 percent; net profit margin per sale improved by 7 percent; commercial customer base grew by 18 percent. My business plan was adapted for use by all account managers in the region. Earned Account Manager of the Year Award."

Note: In your résumé, use percentages instead of actual dollar figures to protect the former employer's proprietary/confidential financial information.

Remember to be specific! Employers claim that many job seekers provide vague information and indefinite responses in their career marketing documents or interviews. For example, if you claim that you have strong leadership skills, demonstrate them by citing some actual "stories" from your experiences like the preceding one. Be prepared to provide more specifics only if asked.

The S.T.A.R. Technique Worksheet Example

S = Situation   T = Task   A = Actions you took   R = Results delivered

Example: What was the most difficult problem you had to overcome in your last position? How did you cope with it? _____

Situation: Select a problem that is significant for you; otherwise, your positive results won't have much impact. Identify a problem that you surmounted by using one or more of your strengths. If possible, the situation should be related to the position you are applying for.

Example: "Our department exceeded its operating budget by 10 percent."

One problem I had to overcome was _____

Task: Specify a specific task that you successfully handled to resolve the situation. This allows you to keep your answers focused and to the point.

Example: "I identified unnecessary inventory in our warehouse."

One specific issue I addressed was: _____

Action: Make it as specific as you can.

Example: "I met with the manager and explained what exactly had happened. I then provided two recommendations for reducing our inventory costs, including . . ."

To solve the problem, I _____

Results: If possible, describe the results in concrete, numerical terms or measurable outcome.

Example: "Reduced inventory by 15 percent, saving XXX dollars."

The end result was: _____

Building Your Career Management Plan

The S.T.A.R. Technique Worksheet

S = Situation   T = Task   A = Actions you took   R = Results delivered

Situation: One problem I had to overcome was

_____

_____

_____

_____

_____

Task: One specific issue I addressed was

_____

_____

_____

_____

_____

Action: To solve the problem, I

_____

_____

_____

_____

_____

Results: The end result was

_____

_____

_____

_____

_____

Appendix A

Directory of Latino Student Associations

This directory includes general and industry-specific Latino student associations and organizations. We have also listed a few examples of student organizations from different universities. We were not able to list all the student organizations so you should check on your own campus to see if there is a local chapter of any of these organizations, student chapters of various national professional associations, or others that may interest you.

If any of these organizations interest you, we recommend that you

- Become a member.

- Network with members and faculty advisors.

- Attend the organization's national meetings.

- Take on a project with the organization.

- Become an officer.

- Network with external supporters of the organization.

- Let your brand become your image.

Use this listing as just one of several resources for you to use in your job search.

This directory of Latino student associations is presented in alphabetical order.

A&M Texas Hispanic Graduate Student Association
www.tamu.edu/hgsa/

An educational organization committed to the recruitment, retention, and academic/professional development of Hispanic and Latin American graduate students at Texas A&M University.

AMAS: University of Texas at Arlington
www2.uta.edu/amas/

The Association of Mexican-American Students (AMAS) is an organization at the University of Texas at Arlington dedicated to the preservation and advancement of the Mexican-American culture and to serve as a support network for students of Mexican and Hispanic descent.

El Centro Chicano
www.stanford.edu/group/centro/

Chicano center at Stanford University, including various groups, events, and news.

Estudiantes Contemporáneos del Norte
www.unm.edu/~ecdn/
   Chicano nationalist organization at the University of New Mexico.

Hispanic Business Student Association
www.acs.ohio-state.edu/students/hbsa
   The Hispanic Business Student Association (HBSA) promotes the educational and professional careers of its members with an emphasis on the Hispanic minority population.

Hispanic Scholarship Fund
www.hsf.net/
   The Hispanic Scholarship Fund (HSF) is the nation's leading organization supporting Hispanic higher education.

La Unión Chicana por Aztlán at MIT
mexico2.mit.edu/
   Chicano student organization at the Massachusetts Institute of Technology.

Latin American Law Students Association
www.columbia.edu/cu/lalsa/
   We endeavor to strengthen the presence of Latinos in the legal profession, encourage the attendance of more Latino students at Columbia Law School, and support the Latino community outside of the legal profession.

Latin American Student Communication Organization
www2.uic.edu/stud_orgs/prof/lasco/
   The purpose of the Latin American Student Communication Organization (LASCO) is to establish networks and an academic supportive foundation for all Latin American students in communication, journalism (radio, television, print media, cyber-media), and English, both internally and externally within their professional environments.

Latinas Unidas
www.latinas-unidas.org
   Student-run organization that is dedicated to the welfare and promotion of the Latin cultures.

Latino Student Organization
www.sru.edu/pages/6601.asp
   The Latino Student Organization will strive to encourage all students to foster better social relations and cultural harmony within the university.

Latino Student Union
www.bgsu.edu/studentlife/organizations/lsu/main.html
   Latino student organization at Bowling Green State University in Ohio.

MEChA
www.nationalmecha.org/

The purpose of MEChA is to respond to the social, political, cultural, and educational needs of the Chicano/Latino community and to promote and publicize these needs to the Stanford community at large.

MEChA at Yale University
www.yale.edu/mecha/

Chicano student organization at Yale University.

Midwest Association of Hispanic Accountants, DePaul University Chapter
condor.depaul.edu/~maha/home.htm

A professional and student organization dedicated to increasing awareness and sharing accounting and finance information among Hispanic students at DePaul University.

National Association of Latino Fraternal Organizations
www.nalfo.org/

The purpose of the National Association of Latino Fraternal Organizations (NALFO) is to promote and foster positive interfraternal relations, communication, and development of all Latino fraternal organizations through mutual respect, leadership, honesty, professionalism, and education.

National Council of Latin American Students of Architecture (CLEAUSA)
www.geocities.com/~cleausa/elea2000eng/introeng/introeng.htm

Latino students of architecture are establishing an organization that will in the future, work for the benefit of all architecture students of our nation.

National Network of Latin American Medical Students
www2.uic.edu/stud_orgs/cultures/hola/index.html

Founded to represent, support, educate, and unify U.S. Latino/a medical students.

Organization for Multicultural Publications
www.acs.ohio-state.edu/students/omp/

Based in the Ohio State University, the Organization for Multicultural Publications (OMP) works to unite the various ethnic organizations on campus.

Puerto Rican Student Association
www2.uic.edu/stud_orgs/cultures/prsa/

The mission of the Puerto Rican Student Association is to provide an atmosphere where Puerto Ricans and other Latinos can come together and feel part of a community at the university level.

Rafael Cintrón Ortíz Latino Cultural Center at UIC
www.uic.edu/depts/lcc/

The mission of the Latino cultural center is to create a positive atmosphere, through the development of educational, cultural, and social programs, which will lead to a greater retention and advancement of Latino students.

Rice University: Hispanic Association for Cultural Enrichment at Rice
www.ruf.rice.edu/~hacer/

The Hispanic Association for Cultural Enrichment at Rice (HACER) is the most visible organization for Hispanics on campus. However, we also offer many opportunities for all members of the Rice community to enjoy such as cultural, educational, political, service, outreach, and social activities.

Strategic Alliance of Latino Student Associations
www.ushli.com/salsa.asp

The mission of the Strategic Alliance of Latino Student Associations (SALSA) is to create a network of over 100 colleges and universities to empower Latino student leaders and develop the potential of their respective organizations.

Student Alliance for Latino Solidarity and Achievement
www.salsanj.org/

Offers fellowship information, forums, newsletter, and links.

The Health-Oriented Latino Association
www2.uic.edu/stud_orgs/cultures/hola/index.html

The Health-Oriented Latino Association was established in 1981 at the University of Illinois at Chicago to provide a source of encouragement and assistance to students of Latino and non-Latino origins interested in achieving a career in the health sciences.

The Mexican-American Alumni Association
www.usc.edu/student-affairs/MAAA-Web/

The Mexican-American Alumni Association (MAAA) was founded in 1973 to develop programs that provide tuition assistance grants to Mexican American/Hispanic/Latino students attending USC.

UCLA Latino Alumni Association
clnet.sscnet.ucla.edu/community/alumni.html

The purpose of the UCLA Latino Alumni Association (LAA) is to organize Latino Alumni and other friends of UCLA for the benefit and advancement of the Latino community, alumni, students, faculty, and staff.

University of California, Berkeley: TRENZA
www.trenza.org/

TRENZA is an academic and social support group for Chicana/Latina women.

University of California, Riverside: La Unión Estudiantil de la Raza (UER)
www.uer-inc.com/history.htm

La Unión Estudiantil de la Raza (UER) Chicano-Latino/Indigenous organization promoting community service, academic achievement, and cultural awareness.

University of Chicago Latin American Business Group
gsbwww.uchicago.edu/student/labg/

Business students with interests in Latin America. Helping GSB students and Latin American recruiters establish a connection, organizing social events to strengthen our network, and leveraging our faculty to learn about the ways we can help Latin America prosper.

U.S. Student Association
www.usstudents.org

The U.S. Student Association (USSA) is the country's oldest and largest national student organization, representing millions of students. Founded in 1947, USSA is the recognized voice for students on Capitol Hill, in the White House, and in the Department of Education. USSA believes education is a right and works on building grassroots power among students to win concrete victories that expand access to education at the federal, state, and campus level.

Wichita State University: Hispanic American Leadership Organization
webs.wichita.edu/halo/

The Hispanic American Leadership Organization (HALO) was established for the purpose of better serving our people, community, and fellow students.

Wichita State University CULMA: College of Urban, Labor, and Metropolitan Affairs
www.culma.wayne.edu/cbs/Latino%20Student%20Org.htm

The mission of the Center for Chicano-Boricua Studies (CBS) is to transform the university, and ultimately society, by providing equitable access to a quality university education, and by enhancing the environment of diversity on the campus.

Appendix B

Directory of Latino Sororities and Fraternities

This directory includes a list of Latino sororities and fraternities. If you have an interest in a sorority or fraternity, you can contact the National Association of Latino Fraternal Organizations for information on chapters in your school or the student services center on your campus.

If you are interested in any of these organizations, we recommend that you

■ Become a member.

■ Network with members and faculty advisors.

■ Contact the alumni of the organization for career information.

■ Become an officer.

■ Use the organization to develop and showcase your leadership skills.

■ Let your brand become your image.

■ Participate in national meetings of the organization.

National Association of Latino Fraternal Organizations (NALFO)
www.nalfo.org/
Stated purpose is to promote and foster positive interfraternal relations, communication, and development of all Latino fraternal organizations through mutual respect, leadership, honesty, professionalism, and education.

Alpha Psi Lambda
www.alpha-psi-lambda.org
Promote continued personal and collective growth of our membership, success and unity through education, leadership, cultural awareness and community service.

Gamma Phi Omega
www.gammaphiomega.org/
A Latina-oriented organization that unites women through sisterhood. As an organization of professional young women, they strive both to excel academically, serve our community, raise cultural awareness, and promote sisterhood.

Hermandad de Sigma Iota Alpha Inc.
www.hermandad-sia.org/

Strives to travel through new channels of involvement in the Latino community while reinforcing our commitment to our philanthropies.

Lambda Alpha Upsilon Fraternity, Inc.
wings.buffalo.edu/student-life/greeks/lau/

Stated mission is to support each other personally and academically and to establish a network of professionals.

Lambda Theta Phi Latin Fraternity, Inc.
www.lambda1975.org/default.asp

Stated goals are to promote scholarship, Latin unity, respect for all cultures and brotherhood.

Lambda Upsilon Lambda (La Unidad Latina)
greeklife.drexel.edu/lul/

Primarily seeks to take a leadership role in meeting the needs of the Latino community through cultural awareness, community service, and promotion of the Latino culture and people.

Omega Phi Beta Sorority, Inc.
www.omegaphibeta.org/

Provides its diverse membership with a strong sisterhood and the opportunity to develop, practice, and exhibit many leadership skills through community service and outreach.

Phi Beta Sigma
www.pbs1914.org/main.htm

Reaffirms and maintains a strong commitment to brotherhood, scholarship, and service. Ensure that the Fraternity programs are focused and committed to serving humanity. Create an environment that respects the dignity and worth of each brother.

Sigma Lambda Alpha
www.geocities.com/slanational/

Stated mission is to unite women in Hispanic cultures through community service involvement and academic achievement.

Sigma Lambda Beta
www.sigmalambdabeta.com/

With community service being one of the principles on which the fraternity was founded, involvement in the community is one commitment that Sigma Lambda Beta takes great pride in.

Sigma Lambda Gamma National Sorority
www.sigmalambdagamma.com/
　An academic, cultural, service, and social organization dedicated to promoting the empowerment of women in higher education.

Sigma Lambda Upsilon (Soñoritas Latinas Unidad Sorority, Inc.)
www.sigmalambdaupsilon.org
　A nonprofit Greek-lettered organization dedicated to the success and achievement of Latinas and the Latino community.

Sigma Pi Alpha
www.sigmapialpha.org/
　Network of Chicanas/Latinas who want to make a difference in their communities by starting with themselves.

Appendix C

Directory of Education Resources

This listing includes books and online resources that will assist you in researching colleges and universities as you determine which school to attend. The listing also includes information on scholarships particularly focused on the Hispanic student.

As you prepare to do your research on colleges and universities, we recommend that you include the following suggestions in your search:

■ Speak with your high school counselor.

■ Network with friends and colleagues to find out about their experiences.

■ Do online research.

■ Look over college brochures.

■ Visit the campus.

■ Speak with current and former students of the school you are interested in attending.

■ Look over some of the Web sites and references listed here.

Financial Assistance

Federal Student Aid
www.studentaid.ed.gov

The U.S. Department of Education's Federal Student Aid (FSA) programs are the largest source of student aid in America, providing nearly 70 percent of all student financial aid. Help is available to make education beyond high school financially possible for you or your child. The information provided is designed to assist you in your college planning. It provides you with access to and information about the products and services that you will need throughout the financial aid process

The 2005 Hispanic Scholarship Directory: Over 1,000 Ways to Finance Your Education
Paperback, WPR Pub, 2004

The directory contains over 1,200 funding sources including 758 new or updated listings, an introduction by noted actor and activist Edward James Olmos, and an informative financial aid calendar.

TheKey2: An Interactive Guide to the Top Colleges and Universities for Hispanics
Ember Media

TheKey2 is a free interactive resource designed to help students and parents with the college admissions process. The CD-ROM features profiles of over 200 schools, useful Web links, tutorials on writing essays and filling out college applications, financial aid tips, and exclusive access to SAT and ACT online test preparation. This guide also features bilingual content as well as video clips from famous Hispanic graduates. Available through *www.thekey2.com.*

Scholarships for Hispanic Students (*Getting Money for College*)
Petersons, 2003

This reference provides information on thousands of scholarships that are geared specifically for Hispanic American college students.

College and University Research Resources
College Board, 2005
The College Handbook 2005: All New 42nd Edition

This invaluable reference book should be available to all students considering a college education. *The College Handbook* outlines in detail study programs, degrees, admission requirements, locations, facilities, expenses, financial aid available and almost any facet of college life on which a student or parent may have a question. This book is available from College Board Publications, Dept. S62, Box 886, New York, NY 10101-0886.

Hispanic Magazine
www.hispanic.com

Hispanic Magazine publishes a listing of the 100 best colleges for Latinos and 50 best MBA schools annually.

U.S. News & World Report Magazine
www.usnews.com

U.S. News & World Report publishes a listing of The Best Colleges, The Best Graduate Schools, and E Learning Schools annually. Available in bookstores and online.

Kiplinger Magazine
www.kiplinger.com

Kiplinger Magazine publishes a listing of 100 Best Values in Public Colleges and Best Values in Private Colleges annually.

Education and Social Science Library
University of Illinois, Champaign
222.library.uic.edu/edx/rankgen.htm

The purpose of the rankings site is to draw together and provide context for various online sources of information on the ranking of institutions of higher education. The site tries to only provide links to stable sites offering original information. These sites rank colleges with criteria ranging from the academic to the spiritual. Some are serious, while others are intended more for entertainment. Because not all ranking services have the same goal, recognizing the criteria and methodology used by any individual ranking service is a key step in ensuring that it is used properly.

The Princeton Review
www.princetonreview.com

    The Princeton Review helps students, parents, and educators deal responsibly with the increasingly competitive and complex process of admissions to college and graduate school as well as the growing pressures of accountability. The information on colleges is available online and in book form.

Appendix D

Directory of Latino Education Organizations

This directory includes general Latino educational organizations with a (primarily) national focus. Some of these organizations have state or local chapters. You can check the Internet for other organizations that we were not able to include in this appendix.

If any of the organizations interest you, we recommend that you

- Review the organization's Web site for further information.
- Sign up for the group's e-newsletter, and add your name to its mailing list.
- Identify a local chapter or subgroup in your area.
- Establish a networking relationship with appropriate staff contacts and members.
- Participate in the organizations message board for information gathering and networking.
- Volunteer if you can.

Use this listing as just one of several resources in your job search.

The Directory of Latino Education Organizations is presented in alphabetical order.

ASPIRA
www.aspira.org

Provides leadership training, career and college counseling, financial aid, scholarship assistance, educational advocacy, cultural activities, and community action projects for Latino youth.

Hispanic Association of Colleges and Universities (HACU)
www.hacu.net

Represents more than 300 colleges and universities committed to Hispanic higher education success in the United States, Puerto Rico, Latin America, and Spain. Supports an internship program with nearly 700 interns annually.

Hispanic Council for Reform and Educational Options (HCREO)
www.hcreo.org

Stated mission is to improve educational outcomes for Hispanic children by empowering families through parental choice in education.

Hispanic Scholarship Fund (HSF)

www.hsf.net

Nation's leading organization supporting Hispanic higher education.

National Association for Chicana and Chicano Studies (NACCS)

www.naccs.org

The academic organization that serves academic programs, departments, and research centers that focus on issues pertaining to Mexican Americans, Chicana/os, and Latina/os.

National Association of Latino Elected and Appointed Officials (NALEO) Educational Fund

www.naleo.org

Leading organization that empowers Latinos to participate fully in the America political process, from citizenship to public service.

National Hispanic University

www.nhu.edu

Enables Hispanics, other minorities, women, and others to acquire an undergraduate degree or certificate using a multicultural educational experience to obtain a professional career in business, education, or technology

Project 00

mati.eas.asu.edu

A national project devoted to helping underrepresented minorities apply to graduate school. Academic advisors for the program are bilingual in Spanish and English and are there to answer any questions about where to apply, what to do on an application to increase your chance of being accepted, how to apply for financial aid, and so on.

Note: These two directories provide information on scholarships available to Hispanic college students.

The 2005 Hispanic Scholarship Directory: Over 1,000 Ways to Finance Your Education

Paperback, WPR Pub, 2004

More than 1,200 funding sources including 758 new or updated listings, an introduction by noted actor and activist Edward James Olmos, and an informative financial aid calendar.

Scholarships for Hispanic Students (Getting Money for College)

Petersons, 2003

Information on thousands of scholarships that are geared specifically for Hispanic-American college students.

Appendix E

Building Your Career Portfolio and E-Folio Resources

INTERNET CAREER PORTFOLIO RESOURCES

CareerFolios™
www.CareerFolios.com
 Attractive, multifunctional Web résumé with ASCII download, URL, and six months of online hosting.

eResume IQ
www.eresumeiq.com
 Provides eResume articles, links to Web résumé resources, and subscription to newsletter, eResume Terms, and Web résumé gallery.

Jump Start Your Job Search
jumpstartyourjobsearch.com
 Contains several articles on electronic career portfolios.

Quintessential Careers
www.quintcareers.com
 Search this site using keywords "career portfolio" to retrieve ten articles on career portfolios.

CAREER PORTFOLIOS

Barron's e-Resumes
by Pat Criscito, Barron's Educational Series, Inc., 3rd edition, 2004

Building Your Career Portfolio
by Carol A. Poore, Delmar Learning, 1st edition, May 1, 2001

The Career Portfolio Workbook: Using the Newest Tool in Your Job-Hunting Arsenal to Impress Employers and Land a Great Job!
by Frank Satterthwaite and Gary D'Orsi, McGraw-Hill, 1st edition, December 24, 2002

Creating Your Career Portfolio: At a Glance Guide for Students
by Anna Graf Williams and Karen J. Hall, Prentice Hall, 3rd edition, 2004

Creating Your Career Portfolio Practical Exercises
by Anna Graf Williams, Karen J. Hall, and David E. Morrow, Learnovation LLC,
February 2003

Creating Your Skills Portfolio: Show Your Accomplishments
(Crisp Fifty-Minute Series)
by Carrie Straub, Crisp Publications, April 1997

Career Portfolio Sampler
by Martin Kimeldorf, SearchInc, April 2003

eResumes: Everything You Need to Know
by Susan Britton Whitcomb and Pat Kendall, McGraw-Hill, 2001

Portfolio Power, The Creative Way to Showcase Your Job Skills and Experience
by Martin Kimeldorf, Digital, April 2003

Appendix F

Find Résumé Writing, Cover Letter, and Career Coach Resources

Global Career Strategies
www.globalcareerstrategies.com and *www.resumecompass.com*

Global Career Strategies (GCS) is an international professional organization dedicated to creating personal marketing solutions that empower career success. GCS's deep belief in a highly consultative client partnership is vitally important to your satisfaction. GCS alleviates the struggle of developing career marketing materials that open doors to professional possibilities.

Advanced Résumé Concepts
www.reslady.com

Principal Pat Kendall is a nationally certified résumé writer (NCRW), certified job and career transition coach, and former president of The National Résumé Writers' Association (NRWA). Pat has created résumés and personal marketing tools for 10,000+ traditional and online job seekers over the past two decades. She is coauthor of *eResumes: Everything You Need to Know* (McGraw-Hill) and author of *Jumpstart Your Online Job Search in a Weekend* (Prima Publishing).

National Résumé Writers Association
www.nrwaweb.com

The National Résumé Writers' Association (NRWA) is the only not-for-profit professional association of résumé writers in the United States. Click on **Find A Consultant** to locate a NRWA member who will best meet your needs.

Career Masters Institute
www.cminstitute.com

Career Masters Institute (CMI) is a professional association dedicated to building and strengthening the professional competencies and expertise of its members—career coaches, career counselors, résumé writers, outplacement consultants, and other career–industry professionals nationwide. To find a top-flight career professional to help you with your job search and career development, visit *www.cminstitute.com* and click on **Find A Career Expert**.

LIST OF RÉSUMÉ AND COVER LETTER REFERENCE BOOKS

Note: The following reference books are recommended by the National Résumé Writers Association.

Résumé Writing

America's Top Résumés for America's Top Jobs
by J. Michael Farr with Louise M. Kursmark, JIST Works, 2nd edition, 2002

Asher's Bible of Executive Résumés and How to Write Them
by Donald Asher, Ten Speed Press, 1996

Best Résumés for $100,000+ Jobs
by Wendy S. Enelow, Impact Publications, 2nd edition, 2002

Blue Collar & Beyond: Résumés for Skilled Trades & Services
by Yana Parker, Ten Speed Press, 1995

Designing the Perfect Résumé
by Pat Criscito, Barron's Educational Series, Inc., 2nd edition, 2000

Expert Résumés for Computer and Web Jobs
by Wendy S. Enelow and Louise M. Kursmark, JIST Publishing, 2001

Expert Résumés for Manufacturing Careers
by Wendy S. Enelow and Louise M. Kursmark, JIST Works, 2002

Expert Résumés for Teachers and Educators
by Wendy S. Enelow and Louise M. Kursmark, JIST Publishing, 2001

Gallery of Best Résumés: A Collection of Quality Résumés
by Profssional Résumé Writers
by David F. Noble, Ph.D., JIST Works, 3rd edition, 2004

Gallery of Best Résumés for People Without a Four-Year Degree
by David F. Noble, Ph.D., JIST Works, 3rd edition, 2004

Professional Résumés for Executives, Managers, and Other Administrators
by David F. Noble, Ph.D., JIST Works, 1998

Sales and Marketing Résumés for $100,000 Careers
by Louise Kursmark, JIST Publishing, 2nd edition, 2004

Federal Résumé Guidebook
by Kathryn Kroemer Troutman, JIST Works, 3rd edition, 2004

Appendices

Résumés in Cyberspace: Your Complete Guide to a Computerized Job Search
by Pat Criscito, Barron's Educational Series, Inc., 2nd edition, 2001

Résumés and Job Search Letters for Transitional Military Personnel
by Carl Savino and Ronald L. Krannich, Impact Publications, 1997

More Résumé Books

1500+ KeyWords for $100,000+ Jobs
by Wendy S. Enelow, Impact Publications, 1998

The Complete Idiot's Guide to the Perfect Résumé
by Susan Ireland, Penguin Putnam, 3rd edition, 2003

The Everything Resume Book
by Steven Graber and Mark Lipsman, Adams Media Corporation, 2000

How to Write Better Resumes and Cover Letters
by Pat Criscito, Barron's Educational Series, Inc., 2003

The Resume Kit, 3rd edition
by Richard H. Beatty, John Wiley and Sons, Inc., 1995

Résumé Magic: Trade Secrets of a Professional Résumé Writer
by Susan Britton Whitcomb, JIST Works, 2nd edition, 2003

Résumé Power: Selling Yourself on Paper in the New Millennium
by Tom Washington, Mount Vernon Press, 7th edition, 2003

Résumés for Dummies
by Joyce Lain Kennedy, For Dummies, 4th edition, 2002

Résumés That Will Get You the Job You Want
by Andrea Kay, Betterway Books, 1st edition, 1997

Strategic Résumés: Writing for Results
by Marci Mahoney, Crisp Publications, 1993

Winning Resumes for Computer Personnel
by Anne Hart, Barron's Educational Series, Inc., 2nd edition, 1998

Your First Résumé: For Students and Anyone Preparing to Enter Today's Tough Job Market
by Ronald Fry, Thomson Delmar Learning, 5th edition, 2001

Cover Letter Books

Cover Letters! Cover Letters! Cover Letters!
by Richard Fein, Thomson Delmar Learning, 2nd edition, 1996

Cover Letter Magic
by Wendy S. Enelow and Louise M. Kursmark, JIST Publishing, 2nd edition, 2004

Cover Letters for Dummies
by Joyce Lain Kennedy, For Dummies, 2nd edition, 2000

Cover Letters That Knock 'Em Dead
by Martin Yate, Adams Media Corporation, 6 Rev. edition, 2004

Cover Letters That Will Get You the Job You Want
by Stan Wynett, Betterway Books, 1993

How to Write Better Résumés and Cover Letters
by Pat Criscito, Barron's Educational Series, Inc., 2003

The Perfect Cover Letter
by Richard Beatty, John Wiley and Sons, 3rd edition, 2003

Appendix G

General Career and Job Search Information Resources

RESOURCES ON THE INTERNET

Jumpstart Your Job Search (author's affiliate site)
www.jumpstartyourjobsearch.com

A–Z information index where job seekers can quickly find job search information and advice. The user-friendly site provides practical do-it-yourself instructions, comprehensive job search links, and job search strategies to jumpstart your job search.

America's Career InfoNet
www.acinet.org/acinet/

Contains wages and employment trends, occupational requirements, state-by-state labor market conditions, millions of employer contacts nationwide, and the most extensive career resource library online.

Career Journal
www.CareerJournal.com

The Wall Street Journal career site includes job-hunting advice, career management columns, salary and hiring information, and discussion boards. Additionally, the site lists management and professional positions available in many industries, with emphasis on sales, marketing, finance, and technology.

Job Hunters Bible
www.JobHuntersBible.com

Designed as a supplement to the 2005 edition of *What Color Is Your Parachute? A Practical Manual for Job-Hunters and Career-Changers.* This Net Guide is a carefully selected collection of information and resources to guide you in doing part of your job hunt on the Internet. The Parachute Library, an extensive library of articles written by Richard Bolles, Bob Rosner, Peter Weddle, and others, is organized into easy-to-navigate categories.

Occupational Outlook Handbook

www.bls.gov/oco/home.htm

A nationally recognized source of career information, designed to provide valuable assistance to individuals making decisions about their future work lives. Revised every two years, the *Handbook* describes what workers do on the job, working conditions, the training and education needed, earnings, and expected job prospects in a wide range of occupations.

Occupational Outlook Quarterly

stats.bls.gov/opub/ooq

Provides practical information on jobs and careers. Articles are written in straightforward, non-technical language and cover a wide variety of career and work-related topics such as new and emerging occupations, training opportunities, salary trends, and results of new studies from the Bureau of Labor Statistics.

Quintessential Careers

www.quintcareers.com

Offers more than 2,000 pages of free college, career, and job-search content to empower your success in life with cover letters, résumés, networking, interviewing, and salary negotiation. Take career tests and quizzes.

Job-Hunt.org

www.Job-hunt.org

A guide to more that 3,000 online career and job hunting resources.

Salary.com

www.salary.com

Free average salary and benefits by position title in your local area. Fee-based personalized data and advice for a win–win salary negotiation.

Vault

vault.com

Job seekers may browse jobs and sign up to receive e-mail notification of matching jobs. Provides an excellent resource for researching companies (history, goals, how to get hired) and a water-cooler/gossip message board to get the inside scoop from current or former employees. Weddle's.com Users Choice Awardee.

WetFeet

WetFeet.com

Award-winning career Web sites that provides comprehensive company research and career-related information to help make better career decisions, as well as for the latest job and internship opportunities for college-educated talent.

The Riley Guide

www.rileyguide.com/

A well organized, user-friendly index of the job-hunting resources on the Internet, with extras like a wonderful summary of databases and job search guides.

LIST OF REFERENCE BOOKS ON JOB SEARCH

Recommended by the National Résumé Writer's Association.

Change Your Job, Change Your Life: High Impact Strategies for Finding Great Jobs in the Decade Ahead, 7th edition, by Ronald Krannich, Impact Publications, 1999

Don't Send a Résumé: And Other Contrarian Rules to Help Land a Great Job by Jeffrey J. Fox, Hyperion, 2001

Guide to Careers in Federal Law Enforcement: Profiles of 225 High-powered Positions and Surefire Tactics for Getting Hired by Thomas H. Ackerman, Hamilton Burrows, 2001

Headhunters Revealed! Career Secrets for Choosing and Using Professional Recruiters by Darrell W. Gurney, Hunted Arts Publishing, 2000

Interview Strategies That Will Get You the Job You Want by Andrea Kay, Betterway Books, 1996

Rites of Passage at $100,000 to $1 Million+: Your Insider's Lifetime Guide to Executive Job-Changing and Faster Career Progress in the 21st Century by John Lucht, Viceroy Press, 2000

Seven Steps to Getting a Job Fast by Michael Farr, JIST Works, 2002

What Color Is Your Parachute: A Practical Manual for Job-Hunters or Career-Changers by Richard Bolles, Mark Emery Bolles, Ten Speed Press, Rev. and Updated Edition, 2004

Winning Interviews for $100,000+ Jobs by Wendy S. Enelow, Impact Publications, 1999

Appendix H

Directory of Online Diversity Career Resources

Affirmative Action Register
www.aar-eeo.com/
   The national EEO recruitment publication directed to females, minorities, veterans, and disabled persons as well as to all other employment candidates.

Diversity Employment Solutions
www.my-des.com
   A diversity career portal specializing in connecting corporations with diverse talent.

Diversity Job Fairs
diversityjobfairs.jobexpo.com
   Source for diversity job fairs, professional sales, marketing, management, finance, telecommunication, healthcare, customer service, information technology, and administration employment exchange! Site provides job search functions, job postings, a résumé builder, articles, and so on.

DiversityInc.com Career Center
www.diversityinc.com/public/department33.cfm
   Provides information about career opportunities with companies and organizations that truly value diversity in the workplace. Offers a confidential, searchable database of jobs and provides the opportunity for resume posting.

Diversity Working
www.diversityworking.com
   Largest diversity job board with more than 220,000 active, nonduplicated job opportunities. Also hosts online career fairs.

Equal Opportunity Publications
www.eop.com
   Equal Opportunity Publications, Inc. (EOP) publishes *Hispanic Career World* and offers the publication at no charge to qualified Hispanic students and professionals. Summer/Fall and Winter/Spring editions are published each year. The site also maintains a résumé database and career fair information.

IMDiversity

IMDiversity.com

Dedicated to providing career and self-development information to all minorities, specifically African Americans, Asian Americans, Hispanic Americans, Native Americans, and women. The goal of IMDiversity.com is to provide you with access to the largest database of equal opportunity employers committed to workplace diversity. This site has a dedicated Hispanic-American Village.

Multicultural Advantage

multiculturaladvantage.com

An excellent source of current career articles, job postings, career development resources, and links to fellowships and awards, as well as recommended companies and executive lists.

Workplace Diversity

www.workplacediversity.com

A Web-based community that enables experienced diversity talent (1) to find open positions at companies that support diversity and (2) to get information and resources that will help them attain their career goals.

ONLINE CAREER ASSESSMENT TOOLS

Quintessential Careers

www.quintcareers.com/online_assessment_review.html
www.quintcareers.com/online_assessment.html

Provides reviews and ratings of the major online career assessment tools for job seekers.

Appendix I

Directory of Latino Internet Research Sites

This directory includes Internet sites that serve as resources for information on the Latino community, organizations, and employment. These sites can be used to supplement the information contained in the job search sites listed in the Appendices G and J.

We recommend that you

- Review the organization's Web site thoroughly for free services.

- Participate in the organizations message boards for information gathering.

- Keep the sites on file for future research needs.

Hispanic Online
www.hispaniconline.com
Provides articles and recruitment information.

Internet Resources for Latin America
lib.nmsu.edu/subject/bord/laguia/index.html#lists
Molly Molloy's guide to Latin America resources on the Web, as seen in *Latin Trade* magazine.

LANIC
lanic.utexas.edu
A University of Texas project; a big collection of Latin America links.

PEW Hispanic Center
www.pewhispanic.org
Stated mission is to improve understanding of the diverse Hispanic population in the United States and to chronicle Latinos' growing impact on the nation. The center strives to inform debate on critical issues through dissemination of its research to policymakers, business leaders, academic institutions, and the media.

Tomas Rivera Policy Institute
www.trpi.org
Conducts and disseminates policy-relevant research and its implications to decision makers on key issues affecting Latino communities.

Appendix J

Directory of Latino Job Search Engines

Included in the listing are some of the most popular Latino job search engines. The Latino search engines are an excellent resource for identifying job listings targeted to Latino and minority candidates. Companies that list vacancies on these job sites tend to be Latino-friendly.

When using one of these sites be sure to

- Use Latino-based keywords.
- Highlight your bilingual skills, if applicable.
- Identify potential employment opportunities.
- Submit or post your résumé.
- Follow up with the employer.
- Use the site's resources if you need help with your résumé and job search.
- Note the companies that advertise on the site for follow-up on future vacancies.
- Refresh your profile and résumé every thirty days.
- Do not respond to job postings that you do not qualify for, as you may be blacklisted.

Hirediversity.com

A job search engine that features separate news channels for different populations with employment listings combined in one job bank.

iHispano.com

This leading career site for Hispanic and bilingual professionals has job listings, career advice, networking events, and an e-newsletter.

Telemundo.com/empleos

This is a career site for Hispanics/Latinos with job listings and career advice.

Joblatino.com

This job search engine allows job seekers to post their résumés, provides interview tips, and provides job postings by state.

LatPro.com

One of the largest Hispanic and bilingual job sites and diversity career boards in the Americas.

Saludos.com

Primarily lists bilingual/bicultural positions. The site offers a Career Pavilion for researching career fields, mentor profiles, career guides, job search information, résumé posting, job search agent, job fairs, and career links.

336

Appendix K

Directory of Latino Professional Associations

This directory includes general and industry-specific Latino professional associations that have a primarily national focus. Several of these organizations have state, local, and student chapters. You can also search the Internet for the numerous state and local Latino professional organizations we were unable to include in this appendix.

If any of the associations are of interest to you, we recommend that you

- Review the organization's Web site thoroughly for free services and member benefits.
- Identify a chapter in your local area.
- Sign up for the group's electronic newsletters, eList, and mailing list (check privacy policies).
- Search current job postings and check out companies that support the association.
- Submit your résumé to the organization's résumé database or job-matching system (check privacy policies).
- Establish a networking relationship with appropriate staff contacts and members.
- Participate in the organizations message boards for information gathering and networking.
- Attend on-site or participate in online organization events, professional development activities, mentorship programs, and career conferences.
- Volunteer if you can.

Use this listing as just one of several resources for your job search.

The Directory of Latino Professional Associations is presented in alphabetical order.

Association of Hispanic Arts, Inc. (AHA)
www.latinoarts.org

A not-for-profit organization dedicated to the advancement of Latino arts, artists, and arts organizations as an integral part of the cultural life of the nation.

Association of Latina and Latino Anthropologists (ALLA)
www.aaalla.org

The goals of ALLA are to promote research and distribute information on Latinos in the United States. It will stimulate dialogue in academic and other circles about Latino community objectives and realities encouraging respect for indigenous and insider views, encouraging the participation of community leaders, non-academic anthropologists and others, and in the process, provide information to the public about these objectives, and form affiliations and coalitions with other other professional groups with similar interests.

Association of Hispanic Healthcare Executives (AHHE)
www.ahhe.org

A national organization seeking to foster programs and policies to increase the presence of Hispanics in health administration professions. AHHE is the first organization devoted exclusively to Hispanic healthcare executives and to the education of the healthcare industry about the Hispanic healthcare marketplace.

Association of Latino Information Technology Professionals (ALITP)
www.alitp.org

An organization geared toward the advancement of Latinos in information technology. It offers opportunities for leadership and education, provides information on relevant information technology issues, and offers forums for networking with experienced peers and other information technology professionals.

Association of Latino Professionals in Finance and Accounting (ALPFA)
www.alpfa.org

Stated mission is to be the leading Latino professional association dedicated to enhancing opportunities for CPAs, accountants, finance professionals, and students, while expanding Latino leadership in the global workforce.

California Chicano News Media Association (CCNMA)
www.ccnma.org

Stated mission is to promote diversity in the news media by providing encouragement, scholarships, and educational programs for Latinos pursuing careers in the news media; to foster an accurate and fair portrayal of Latinos in the news media; and to promote the social, economic, and professional advancement of Latino journalists.

California Hispanic Professional Association (ChispPA)
www.chisppa.net

Stated mission is to spark and empower advancement of its members and the Hispanic community by providing value-added services and programs in the areas of professional, educational, and community development.

Center for the Advancement of Hispanic and Science and Engineering Education (CAHSEE)
www.cahsee.org

An organization created by Latino engineers and scientists dedicated to the advancement of Hispanics in science and engineering.

Coalition of Hispanic Police Associations (CHAPA)
www.lasculturas.com

A not-for-profit corporation dedicated to providing a national perspective and definitive voice on issues facing Hispanics in law enforcement.

Cuban-American Certified Public Accountants Association, Inc.
www.cacpa.org

A nonprofit organization of certified public accountants united in common heritage and interest, sharing a commitment to the highest standards of professional and ethical conduct.

Federal Hispanic Law Enforcement Officers Association (FHLEOA)
www.fhleoa.org

Networking with over 20,000 Hispanic law enforcement professionals from around the world to provide the opportunity to both acquire and share information. A collective voice and representation to address law enforcement concerns before legislative bodies, regulatory agencies, and the courts.

Hispanic Alliance for Career Enhancement (HACE)
www.hace-usa.org

Stated mission is to strengthen the foundation for the professional and economic advancement of the Hispanic community. Provides career conference, Latino recruitment series, job posting, professional development workshops, mentorship program, networking events, and college student support programs.

Hispanic American Police Command Officers Association (HAPCOA)
www.hapcoa.com

Composed of command-level officers from local, county, state, and federal law enforcement agencies throughout the United States and Puerto Rico.

Hispanic Bankers Association (HBA)
hbachicago.org
www.dfwhba.org

Serves the needs and interests of Hispanics employed in the banking and financial services industry. Nationwide chapters are located in Albuquerque, NM; Chicago, IL; Dallas/Fort Worth, TX; Hackensack, NJ; Los Angeles, CA; Miami, FL; Phoenix, AZ; San Diego, CA; and San Francisco, CA.

Hispanic Bar Association of the District of Columbia
www.hbadc.org

Organization of several hundred lawyers practicing in Washington, DC; Maryland; and Virginia. Includes Latino students attending local law schools and other non-lawyers who join as associate members.

Hispanic Dental Association
www.hdassoc.org

Dedicated to promoting the oral health of the Hispanic community through improved prevention, treatment, and education. Fosters research and knowledge concerning Hispanic oral health problems. Stimulates interest and encourages entry of Hispanics into oral health.

Hispanic Designers (HDI)
www.hispanicdesigners.org

Dedicated to highlighting Hispanic talent and cultural contributions in the design industry; provides a national focus on positive contributions by Hispanics in the United States by showcasing Hispanic excellence, works to create educational and employment opportunities and build public awareness about major issues affecting education, health and overall well-being of Hispanic Americans.

Hispanic Employment Program Managers
www.hepm.org

Established to focus specific attention on the needs of Hispanic Americans in all areas of federal employment.

Hispanic Foundation of Silicon Valley
www.hispanicfoundation-sv.org

Engages leadership and bridges resources to invest in a thriving Hispanic community. Resources are directed toward educational achievement, economic advancement, and leadership development to create opportunities for Hispanic children and families.

Hispanics in Information Technology and Telecommunications (HITT)
www.hittglobal.org

Stated mission is to put together a network of Hispanic technology and communications professionals who will be able to assist and engage each other whenever necessary.

Hispanics in Philanthropy (HIP)
www.hiponline.org

Provides individual members with numerous opportunities for professional development. Members are offered opportunities for engagement and learning at the local, regional, national, and international level. Members also receive weekly job listings of open positions within philanthropic organizations.

Hispanic Marketing and Communication Association (HMCA)
www.hmca.org

Promotes excellence in Hispanic marketing.

Hispanic National Bar Association (HNBA)
www.hnba.com

Dedicated to the advancement of Hispanics in the legal profession.

Hispanic National Law Enforcement Association
www.angelfire.com/md2/hnlea

Site for professionals who are involved in the administration of justice and dedicated to the advancement of Hispanics' interests in law enforcement.

Hispanic Professional Network
www.hpnct.org

A nonprofit organization aimed to serve as a unifying source of information, communication, and cultural enrichment for the Hispanic community.

Hispanic Public Relations Association
www.hprala.org

A nonprofit organization dedicated to establishing a network of Hispanics employed in the public relations profession in Southern California.

Hispanic Organization of Latin Actors (HOLA)
www.hellohola.org

Dedicated to expanding the presence of Hispanic actors in both the Latino and mainstream entertainment and communications media by facilitating industry access to employing professional and emerging Hispanic actors.

Interaamerican College of Physicians and Surgeons, Inc. (ICPS)
www.icps.org

Meets the changing needs of today's healthcare environment and promotes cooperation among Hispanic physicians to advance their professional and educational needs. Reaches a vast majority of the Hispanic medical community in the United States and Puerto Rico . . . over 39,000 physicians and a growing number of health professionals in Mexico, the Caribbean, Central and South America, and Spain through its publication, conference, and links to Hispanic medical societies.

International Association of Hispanic Meeting Professionals
www.hispanicmeetingprofessionals.com

Promotes excellence in education, professional development, and networking opportunities. Past attendees have included meeting planners, suppliers, corporate representatives, business leaders, exhibitors, job recruiters, and students.

Latino Professional Network (LPN)
www.lpnonline.com

Stated mission is to empower Latino professionals by providing them with the tools they need to succeed in their professional lives and by surrounding them with an expansive support group of over 12,000 Latino professionals.

Latino Social Workers Organization (LSWO)
www.lswo.org

An online organization for social workers to participate in professional development, networking, employment opportunities and advocacy. Local affiliates hold meetings.

Latino Speakers Bureau (LSB)
www.latinospeakersbureau.com

Provides training, seminars, and conferences in English and Spanish. Represents fifty successful Latinos in many areas. Multicultural, financial, leadership, management, sales psychology, negotiation, team building, peak performance, and communication improvement are some of the topics they cover.

Mexican American Engineers and Scientists (MAES)
www.maes-natl.org

Promotes excellence in engineering, science, and mathematics while cultivating the value of cultural diversity.

MEXPRO—Association of Mexican Professionals of Silicon Valley
www.mexpro.org

Ser el enlace entre asociaciones, instituciones y profesionistas de México y Estados Unidos, ademas de proveer un foro para el intercambio de ideas.

Minorities in Medicine
www.aamc.org/students/minorities/start.htm

Provides resources for minorities considering a career in medicine.

National Association of Hispanic Federal Executives (NAHFE)
www.nahfe.org

Stated mission is to enhance the excellence and professionalism of the federal workforce while assuring the fair and equitable delivery of services to the Hispanic American community in housing, justice, economic development, health, and employment opportunities.

National Association of Hispanic Firefighters (NAHF)
www.nahf.org

Committed to the recruitment, retention, and advancement of the Hispanic firefighter as well as the formation of coalitions and the establishment of strategic partners in the support and realizations of a more responsive, productive, and diverse workforce within the fire service.

National Association of Hispanic Investment Bankers and Advisors (NAHIBA)
neta.com/~1stbooks/nahiba.htm

Promoes quality and excellence among Hispanic professionals in investment banking and asset management including Hispanic-owned broker/dealers, investment advisory firms, registered representatives, attorneys associated with the investment industry, banks, trusts, financial, consultants, and pension administrators and trustees.

National Association of Hispanic Journalists (NAHJ)
www.nahj.org/home/home.shtml

Dedicated to the recognition and professional advancement of Hispanics in the news industry. Established in April 1984, NAHJ created a national voice and unified vision for all Hispanic journalists.

National Association of Hispanic Nurses (NAHN)
www.thehispanicnurses.org

Promotes Hispanic nurses to improve the health of our communities.

The National Association of Hispanic Priests
www.ansh.org

Asociacion Nacional de Sacerdotes Hispanos, EE.UU.

A priestly fraternity and support for Hispanic Priests in the United States.

National Association of Hispanic Public Administrators
www.netside.net/jalera/nahpa.htm

The National Association of Hispanic Public Administrators has worked closely with local officials to establish training and internship programs that help promote the career development of public administrators and public sector employees who want to become public administrators.

National Association of Hispanic Real Estate Professionals (NAHREP)
www.nahrep.org

To increase the Hispanic home ownership rate by empowering the real estate professionals that serve Hispanic consumers.

National Association of Latino Independent Producers (NALIP)
www.nalip.org

NALIP promotes the advancement, development, and funding of Latino/a films and media arts.

National Association of Puerto Rican and Hispanic Social Workers (NAPRHSW)
www.naprrhs.org

The NAPRHS is dedicated to the interest of the community as well as promoting members' professional growth.

National Hispanic Corporate Achievers, Inc.
www.hispanicachievers.com

As corporate leaders we promote the advancement of diversity in Corporate America. We will achieve this by: hiring, promoting and retaining Hispanics; highlighting Hispanic role models; sharing knowledge and best practices between corporations

National Hispanic Employee Association
www.nhea.com

Recruitment, mentoring, networking, and more aimed at Hispanic upward mobility.

National Hispanic Medical Association (NHMAMD)
www.nhmamd.org

History, conferences, and summer programs. If you're a Latino physician, you can add your contact information to their database.

National Hispanic Medical Association (NHMA)
www.nhmamd.org

Provides policy makers and healthcare providers with expert information and support to strengthen health service delivery to Hispanic communities across the nation. Provides policy makers and healthcare providers with expert information and support in strengthening health service delivery to Hispanic communities across the nation.

National Image, Inc.

www.nationalimageinc.org

National Image is committed to disseminating the most current information to the Hispanic community.

National Latina/o Psychological Association

nlpa.web.arizona.edu/bodyindex.htm

Supports the employment, professional development and advancement of Latina/o psychologists and graduate students.

National Latino Peace Officers Association (NLPOA)

www.nlpoa.org

Promote professionalism in law enforcement and to create a fraternal/professional association that provides its members and members of the community with career training; conferences and workshops to promote education and career advancement; mentoring; and a strong commitment to community service.

National Society for Hispanic Professionals (NSHP)

www.nshp.org

NSHP empowers Hispanic professionals with networking and leadership opportunities and information on education, careers, and entrepreneurship.

National Society of Hispanic MBAs (NSHMBA)

www.nshmba.org

NSHMBA's vision is to be the premier Hispanic MBA professional business network for economic and philanthropic advancement.

Professional Hispanics in Energy

www.phie.org

PHIE maintains a resource repository for energy and environmentally related education, training and employment opportunities for Hispanics, create an industry forum for the exhange of information and innovative ideas regarding energy and environmental issues among Hispanics in energy and environment-related professions.

REFORMA

www.reforma.org

A national network of librarians, library trustees, community and library school students with mutual concerns; and programs and workshops that focus on serving Latinos.

Society for the Advancement of Chicanos and Native Americans in Science (SCANAS)

www.sacnas.org

SACNAS focuses on encouraging not only students but also on science education through featuring innovative workshops for pre-college (K-12) science teachers. SACNAS encourages Chicano/Latino and Native American students to pursue graduate education and obtain the advanced degrees necessary for research careers and science teaching professions at all levels.

Society of Mexican American Engineers and Scientists (MAES)
www.maes-natl.org

A organization with a national membership representing all the engineering and scientific disciplines of the Mexican American community.

Spanish Association on Accounting and Business Administration
www.aeca.es

Actively contributes to the development of studies and research in the Business Studies field with the aim of improving management techniques and levels of information in business organizations.

The Society of Hispanic Professional Engineers (SHPE)
www.shpe.org

SHPE promotes the development of Hispanics in engineering, science and other technical professions to achieve educational excellence, economic opportunity and social equity. SHPE has 140 college chapters, and 27 professional chapters in the United States and Puerto Rico.

TODOS Network of Hispanic Practitioners in Occupational Therapy
todos.freehosting.net

TODOS is a network and a professional community of occupational therapy practitioners and students who have as their mission to support employment.

Appendix L

Directory of Latino Health-Related Organizations

This directory includes general and industry-specific Latino health-related organizations that have primarily a national focus. We suggest that you search the Internet for the state and local health organizations that we were unable to include in this appendix.

If any of these associations interests you, we recommend that you

- Review the organization's Web site thoroughly for free services and member benefits.
- Sign up for the group's electronic newsletters, eList, and mailing list (check privacy policies).
- Identify career exploration opportunities.
- Search for internship, mentoring, scholarship, and job-posting opportunities.
- Establish a networking relationship with appropriate staff contacts and members.
- Attend on-site or participate in online organization events, professional development activities, and career conferences.

Use this listing as just one of several resources in your job search.

The Directory of Latino Health-Related Organizations is listed alphabetically.

Interaamerican College of Physicians and Surgeons, Inc. (ICPS)
www.icps.org

Meets the changing needs of today's healthcare environment and promotes cooperation among Hispanic physicians to advance their professional and educational needs. The ICPS reaches a vast majority of the Hispanic medical community in the United States and Puerto Rico . . . over 39,000 physicians and a growing number of health professionals in Mexico, the Caribbean, Central and South America, and Spain through its publication, conference, and links to Hispanic medical societies.

Minorities in Medicine
www.aamc.org/students/minorities/start.htm

Resources for minorities considering a career in medicine. The Association of American Medical Colleges (AAMC) has a commitment to increasing the number of underrepresented minorities in medical education.

National Alliance for Hispanic Health
www.hispanichealth.org

The nation's oldest organization focusing on the health, mental health, and human services needs of the diverse Hispanic communities, as well as connecting communities and creating change to improve the health and well being of Hispanics in the United States (formerly known as COSSMHO).

National Hispanic Medical Association (NHMA)
www.nhmamd.org

Provides policymakers and healthcare providers with expert information and support in strengthening health service delivery to Hispanic communities across the nation.

Appendix M

Directory of Latino Business and Entrepreneurial Associations

This directory includes information on Latino organizations that have a primary focus on business and entrepreneurial development for its membership. Several of these organizations have state and local chapters (i.e., Chambers of Commerce). You may find them in your local community directories. You can also search the Internet for other organizations that we were not able to include in this appendix.

If any of the associations interest you, we recommend that you

- Review the organization's Web site thoroughly to learn about free services and member benefits.

- Identify a chapter in your local area.

- Sign up for the group's electronic newsletters, eList, and mailing list (check privacy policies).

- Search for internship, job postings, and companies that support the organization.

- Develop networking contacts within the organization.

- Attend on-site or participate in online organization events, professional development activities, and mentorship programs.

- Volunteer if you can.

- Use this opportunity to explore a profession in business or self-employment.

Use this listing as just one of several resources in your job search.

The Directory of Latino Professional Associations is presented in alphabetical order.

Association of Bi-National Commerce in South Florida (ABiCC)
www.abicc.org

Stated mission is to promote, foster, articulate, and advance the common interests of all binational chambers of commerce in Florida.

Global Business Opportunities
www.musashicorp.org

A nonprofit virtual organization dedicated to promoting world trade on a global scale for the betterment of local communities and economic progress in developing countries.

Hispanic Business Women's Association
www.hispanicbizwomen.com

Stated mission is to encourage women to develop their business and professional endeavors by promoting business growth through education, mutual support, the sharing of information, business referrals, and networking.

Hispanic Business Women's Alliance
www.hbwa.net

An online community that enables you to do business, share information and ideas, and collaborate with other Hispanic women in North America, Latin America, the Caribbean, and Spain.

Internet Resources for Latin America
lib.nmsu.edu/subject/bord/laguia/index.html#lists

Molly Molloy's guide to Latin America resources on the Web, as seen in *Latin Trade* magazine.

Las Vegas Latin Chamber of Commerce
www.lasvegaslatincc.com

Stated mission is "to develop, advance, and promote Hispanics and small businesses and to enhance the economic, political, social, educational, and cultural interests of Hispanics in Nevada."

Latin Business Association
www.lbausa.com

The primary and simple purpose is to grow Latino-owned businesses by generating opportunities that impact the bottom line, by providing educational workshops and by formulating effective advocacy programs.

The Latin Business Association Institute
www.lbainstitute.com

A nonprofit educational, research, and economic development organization that provides technical assistance and enhanced business opportunities to the Latino business community.

National Association of Women Business Owners (NAWBO)
www.nawbo.org

An organization that works to strengthen the wealth-creating capacity of its members; promote economic development; create innovative and effective changes in the business culture; build strategic alliances, coalitions, and affiliations; transform public policy; and influence opinion.

National Hispanic Corporate Achievers
www.hispanicachievers.com

Association of corporate leaders who promote the advancement of diversity in corporate America.

National Hispanic Corporate Council
www.nhcc-hq.org
    Advocates for increased employment, leadership, and business opportunities for Hispanics in corporate America.

New America Alliance
www.naaonline.org
    An organization of American Latino business leaders united to promote the advancement of the American-Latino community.

Texas Association of Mexican American Chambers of Commerce
www.tamacc.org
    Formed to encourage opportunities in commerce and to organize local programs to improve the overall economic conditions of the Hispanic business population in Texas.

United States Hispanic Chamber of Commerce (USHCC)
www.ushcc.com
    Organization working toward bringing the issues and concerns of the nations more than one million Hispanic-owned businesses to the forefront of the national economic agenda.

Appendix N

Directory of Latina Organizations

This directory of Latina organizations includes national organizations that focus on the empowerment of Latinas through economic development, leadership development, and advocacy. Several of these organizations have state and local chapters. You can also search the Internet for numerous state and local based organizations for Latinas that we were unable to include in this appendix.

If any of the organizations interest you, we recommend that you

■ Review the organization's Web site thoroughly for free services and member benefits.

■ Identify a chapter in your local area.

■ Sign up for the group's electronic newsletters, eList, and mailing list (check privacy policies).

■ Establish a networking relationship with appropriate staff contacts and members.

■ Participate in online organization events, professional development activities, mentorship programs, and career conferences.

Use this listing as just one of several resources for your job search.

The Directory of Latina Organizations is presented in alphabetical order.

Hispanic Business Women's Alliance
www.hbwa.net

An online community that enables you to do business, share information and ideas, and collaborate with others.

Hispanic Business Women's Association
www.hispanicbizwomen.com

Stated mission is to encourage women to develop their business and professional endeavors by promoting business growth through education, mutual support, the sharing of information, business referrals, and networking.

MANA: A National Latina Organization
www.hermana.org

Stated mission is to empower Latinas through leadership development, community service, and advocacy.

National Association of Women Business Owners (NAWBO)

www.nawbo.org

An organization that works to strengthen the wealth-creating capacity of its members; promote economic development; create innovative and effective changes in the business culture; build strategic alliances, coalitions, and affiliations; transform public policy; and influence opinion.

National Conference of Puerto Rican Women (NACOPRW)

www.nacoprw.org

Dedicated to the leadership development of the Puerto Rican woman.

National Hispana Leadership Institute

www.nhli.org

Stated mission is to develop Hispanas as ethical leaders through training, professional development, relationship building, and community and world activism.

National Latina/o Lesbian, Gay, Bisexual and Transgender Organization (LLEGÓ)

www.llego.org

The only national nonprofit organization devoted to representing Latina/o lesbian, gay, bisexual, and transgender (LGBT) communities and addressing their growing needs regarding an array of social issues ranging from civil rights and social justice to health and human services.

Appendix O

Directory of Latino Career Development Associations

This directory provides an overview of the career development associations that can be found on both a national and local level. These organizations offer professional development, organized networking, job posting, and training opportunities with strong support from business, education, and government agencies. You can search the Internet for the numerous other state and local professional and career development organizations we were unable to include in this appendix.

If any of these organizations interest you, we recommend that you

- Review the organization's Web site for free services and member benefits.

- Identify a chapter in your local area.

- Sign up for the group's electronic newsletters, eList, and mailing list (check privacy policies).

- Search current job postings and check out companies that support the association.

- Submit your résumé to the organization's résumé database or job-matching system (check privacy policies).

- Establish a networking relationship with appropriate staff contacts and members.

- Attend on-site or participate in online organization events, professional development activities, mentorship programs, and career conference.

Use this listing as just one of several resources in your job search.

The Directory of Latino Career Development Associations is presented in alphabetical order.

Hispanic Alliance for Career Enhancement
www.hace-usa.org

Stated mission is to strengthen the foundation for the professional and economic advancement of the Hispanic community.

Hispanic Online Career Center
www.hispaniconline.com/cc

Provides articles and recruitment information.

Hispanic Professional Network (HPN)
www.hpnct.org

A nonprofit organization aimed at serving as a unifying source of information, communication, and cultural enrichment for the Hispanic community.

Latino Professional Network (LPN)
www.lpnonline.com

Stated mission is to empower Latino professionals by providing them with the tools they need to succeed in their professional lives and by surrounding them with an expansive support group of over 12,000 Latino professionals.

National Hispanic Business Association
www.nhba.org

A national network of students and alumni whose mission is to promote the development of undergraduate Hispanic business students through educational, professional, and networking opportunities to foster diversity, higher education, and the improvement of the Hispanic community.

National Hispanic Employee Association
www.nhea.com

Provides recruitment, mentoring, networking, and more aimed at Hispanic upward mobility.

SER—Jobs for Progress National, Inc.
ser.masterlink.com

Nonprofit corporation with special emphasis on addressing the needs of Hispanics in the areas of education, job skill training, literacy, and employment opportunities.

Note: We recommend you review the Latino Job Search and Professional Association listings in Appendices G, J, and K as well.

Appendix P

Directory of Latino Publications

This directory includes several national publications that focus on the Latino market. The publications were selected due to their focus on issues affecting the Latino community, and particular focus on economics and employment trends for Latinos.

You can also search the Internet for other magazines and publications that cover areas of your particular career interest.

We recommend you read these publications to

- Keep an eye on the latest trends that could affect your job search.

- Read career-specific articles.

- Review each publication's Web site for free services and other online services.

- Look at the companies that advertise in the magazine.

- Read company-specific articles.

- Review the listing of best companies for Latinos.

Use this listing as just one of the resources for your job search.

The Directory of Latino Publications is presented in alphabetical order.

AmericaEconomia
www.americaeconomia.com

AmericaEconomia is published biweekly in Spanish and Portuguese and is recognized as Latin America's most authoritative publication. The multinational editors are based in Latin America and provide valuable insights and in-depth analysis into the region's dynamic economy.

Catalina Magazine
www.catalinamagazine.com

Catalina is a bimonthly English-language, national lifestyle magazine targeting Hispanic American women, ages 24 and older.

Hispanic Magazine
www.hispanicmagazine.com

Founded in 1987, *Hispanic Magazine* has an ABC-audited circulation of 280,000, reaching upwardly mobile Hispanic professionals, corporate executives, entrepreneurs, opinion leaders, members of Hispanic organizations, and students. *Hispanic*'s editorial focus is on business, career, politics, and culture, with upbeat, informative, and timely stories on people and issues of interest to Hispanics.

Hispanic Business Magazine
www.hispanicbusiness.com

Hispanic Business is a gateway to the Hispanic business community all over the United States with a collective brochure of all Latino entrepreneurs trying to do business with major corporations.

Hispanic Journal of Behavioral Sciences
hjb.sagepub.com

The *Hispanic Journal of Behavioral Sciences* publishes research articles, case histories, critical reviews, and scholarly notes that are of theoretical interest or deal with methodological issues related to Hispanic populations.

Hispanic Trends
www.hispaniconline.com/trends

Hispanic Trends is not about trends but aims to provide readers with the tools and information needed to attain their business and professional goals.

Journal of Hispanic Higher Education
jhh.sagepub.com

The *Journal of Hispanic Higher Education* is a quarterly international journal devoted to the advancement of knowledge and understanding of issues at Hispanic-serving institutions.

Latina Style
www.latinastyle.com

Latina Style magazine broke new ground in 1994 by launching the first national magazine dedicated to the needs and concerns of the contemporary Latina business owner and the Latina professional working woman in the United States. With a national circulation of 150,000 and a readership of nearly 600,000, *Latana Style* is unique in its ability to reach the seasoned professional and the young Latina entering the workforce.

National Association of Hispanic Publications (NAHP)
www.nahp.org

NAHP's primary objective is to promote Hispanic print as the most effective means of reaching the Hispanic community.

National Federation of Hispanic Owned Newspapers (NFHON)
www.hispanicprwire.com

NFHON is an educational organization created to promote the highest standards of the Hispanic media and the understanding of diverse Hispanic cultures.

Saludos Hispanos Magazine
www.saludos.com/saludosmagazine

Saludos Hispanos Magazine is a bilingual career and education publication dedicated to encouraging Hispanic youth to strive for excellence in both career and academic pursuits. Our publication is distributed to colleges and universities nationwide. *Saludos Hispanos* can also be found in the offices of state, county, and city officials; state boards of education; career placement centers; and other organizations that champion the causes of workplace diversity, Hispanic recruitment, and supplier diversity.

Today's Latino News!
www.overweight-teen-solutions.com/latinonews.html

Today's Latino News! contains sophisticated technology that continually scours the Internet to capture breaking news from more than 5,000 qualified, handpicked sources of information on Latino issues.

Appendix Q

Directory of Latino Media Associations

This directory includes a sampling of the Latino media associations on both a national and state level. Several of these organizations have state, local, and student chapters. You can also search the Internet for other industry-specific state and local Latino media associations not included in this appendix.

The media associations were broken out from the professional associations due to their importance in advocating for Latino representation in the mainstream media.

If any of these organizations interest you, we recommend that you

- Review the organization's Web site thoroughly for free services and member benefits.

- Identify a chapter in your local area.

- Use the organization for career exploration opportunities.

- Sign up for the organization's newsletter and mailing list.

- Search current job postings and check out internship and mentoring opportunities.

- Submit your resume to the organization's resume database or job matching system (check privacy policies).

- Establish a networking relationship with appropriate staff contacts and members.

- Participate in the organization's message boards for information gathering and networking.

This listing is just one of several resources available to use in your job search.

The Directory of Latino Media Associations is listed alphabetically.

Association of Hispanic Advertising Agencies
www.ahaa.org/index.htm

The mission of AHAA is "to grow, strengthen and protect the Hispanic marketing and advertising industry by providing leadership in raising awareness of the value of the Hispanic market opportunities and enhancing the professionalism of the industry."

The California Chicano News Media Association (CCNMA)
www.ccnma.org

CCNMA's mission is to promote diversity in the news media by providing encouragement, scholarships, and educational programs for Latinos pursuing careers in the news media.

Hispanic Broadcasting Corporation
www.hispanicbroadcasting.com

The Hispanic Broadcasting Corporation is the largest Spanish-language radio broadcasting company in the United States and currently owns or programs sixty-three radio stations in fifteen of the top twenty U.S. Hispanic markets.

Hispanic Marketing and Communication Association (HMCA)
www.hmca.org

HMCA's stated mission is to promote excellence in Hispanic marketing.

Interamerican Press Association
www.sipiapa.org

The Interamerican Press Association is a nonprofit organization dedicated to defending freedom of expression and the press throughout the Americas.

Latinos/Hispanos en Estados Unidos
www.webspawner.com/users/jeanniebelgrave/index.htm

This database includes women, men, students, and professionals interested or working in the field of video/film making.

National Association of Latino Independent Producers (NALIP)
www.nalip.org

NALIP promotes the advancement, development, and funding of Latino/a films and media arts.

National Hispanic Media Coalition
www.nhmc.org

The National Hispanic Media Coalition's goals are (1) to improve the image of Hispanic-Americans as portrayed by the media and (2) to increase the number of Hispanic-Americans employed in all facets of the media industry.

Appendix R

Directory of Unions

This directory of unions lists the AFL-CIO, the nation's largest union, and its sixty affiliate members. A small sampling of unions not affiliated with the AFL-CIO is included. The largest of these is the National Education Association.

Further information on all unions can be obtained on their Web sites.

AFL-CIO
www.aflcio.org

As the federation of America's unions, the AFL-CIO includes more than 13 million of America's workers in sixty member unions working in virtually every part of the economy. The AFL-CIO's mission is to bring social and economic justice to our nation by enabling working people to have a voice on the job, in government, in a changing global economy, and in their communities. We are teachers and teamsters, musicians and miners, firefighters and farm workers, bakers and bottlers, engineers and editors, pilots and public employees, doctors and nurses, painters and laborers, and more.

Labor Council for Latin American Advancement (LCLAA)
www.lclaa.org

The LCLAA is the official Latino constituency group of the AFL-CIO. LCLAA is the first national organization to represent the views of not only Latino trade unionists but all Latino workers seeking justice at the workplace.

LCLAA was founded in 1972 by local Latino trade union committees to promote participation by Hispanic trade unionists in a more responsive labor movement. LCLAA builds political empowerment of the Latino family, supports economic and social justice for all workers, and promotes greater cultural diversity at the workplace.

UNIONS AFFILIATED WITH THE AFL-CIO

Actors and Artists of America, Associated (4As)
Actors' Equity Association (AEA)
American Federation of Television and Radio Artists (AFTRA)
American Guild of Musical Artists (AGMA)
American Guild of Variety Artists (AGVA)
Hebrew Actors' Union, Inc.
The Guild of Italian American Actors
Screen Actors Guild (SAG)
Air Line Pilots Association (ALPA)

Amalgamated Transit Union (ATU)

American Federation of Government Employees (AFGE)

American Federation of Musicians of the United States and Canada (AFM)

American Federation of School Administrators (AFSA)

American Federation of State, County, and Municipal Employees (AFSCME)

American Federation of Teachers (AFT)

American Postal Workers Union (APWU)

American Radio Association (ARA)

American Train Dispatchers Department (ATDD)

Association of Flight Attendants (AFA)

Bakery, Confectionery, Tobacco Workers and Grain Millers International Union (BCTGM)

Brotherhood of Locomotive Engineers (BLE)

Brotherhood of Maintenance of Way Employees (BMWE)

Brotherhood of Railroad Signalmen (BRS)

California School Employees Association (CSEA)

Communications Workers of America (CWA)

Federation of Professional Athletes

Glass, Molders, Pottery, Plastics and Allied Workers International Union (GMP)

Graphic Communications International Union (GCIU)

International Alliance of Theatrical Stage Employees (IATSE)

International Association of Bridge, Structural, Ornamental and Reinforcing Iron Workers

International Association of Fire Fighters (IAFF)

International Association of Heat and Frost Insulators and Asbestos Workers (AWIU)

International Association of Machinists and Aerospace Workers (IAM)

International Brotherhood of Boilermakers, Iron Ship Builders, Blacksmiths, Forgers and Helpers (IBB)

International Brotherhood of Electrical Workers (IBEW)

International Brotherhood of Teamsters (IBT)

International Federation of Professional and Technical Engineers (IFPTE)

International Longshore and Warehouse Union (ILWU)

International Longshoremen's Association (ILA)

International Plate Printers, Die Stampers and Engravers Union of North America

International Union of Allied Novelty and Production Workers

International Union of Bricklayers and Allied Craft Workers (BAC)

International Union of Elevator Constructors (IUEC)

International Union of Operating Engineers (IUOE)

International Union of Painters and Allied Trades

International Union of Police Associations (IUPA)

Laborers' International Union of North America (LIUNA)

Marine Engineers' Beneficial Association (MEBA)

National Air Traffic Controllers Association (NATCA)

National Association of Letter Carriers (NALC)

Office and Professional Employees International Union (OPEIU)

Operative Plasterers' and Cement Masons' International Association of the United States and Canada (OP&CMIA)

PACE International Union

Seafarers International Union of North America (SIU)
Service Employees International Union, AFL-CIO (SEIU)
Sheet Metal Workers International Association (SMWIA)
Transportation Communications International Union (TCU)
Transport Workers Union of America (TWU)
UNITE HERE
United American Nurses (UAN)
United Association of Journeymen and Apprentices of the Plumbing, Pipefitting and
    Sprinkler Fitting Industry of the United States and Canada (UA)
United Automobile, Aerospace & Agricultural Implement Workers of America
    International Union (UAW)
United Farm Workers of America, AFL-CIO (UFW)
United Food and Commercial Workers International Union (UFCW)
United Mine Workers of America (UMWA)
United Steelworkers of America (USWA)
United Union of Roofers, Water Roofers and Allied Workers
Utility Workers Union of America (UWUA)
Working America, a community affiliate
Writers Guild of America, East, Inc.

OTHER UNIONS

A sample of unions not affiliated with the AFL-CIO follows.

National Education Association (NEA)
www.nea.org
   The NEA is the nation's largest professional employee organization and is committed to advancing the cause of public education. NEA's 2.7 million members work at every level of education, from preschool to university graduate programs. NEA has affiliate organizations in every state, as well as in more than 14,000 local communities across the United States.

United Transportation Union (UTU)
www.utu.org
   The UTU, headquartered in Cleveland, Ohio, is a broad-based, transportation labor union representing about 125,000 active and retired railroad, bus, and mass transit workers in the United States and Canada. With offices in Ottawa, Ontario, and Washington, D.C., the UTU is the largest railroad operating union in North America, with more than 600 locals. The UTU represents employees on every Class 1 railroad, as well as employees on many regional and shortline railroads. It also represents bus and mass transit employees on approximately forty-five bus and transit systems and has recently grown to include airline pilots, dispatchers, and other airport personnel.

United Brotherhood of Carpenters and Joiners of America
www.carpenters.org
   The UBC has more than 50,000 members in apprentice courses and 19,000 journeymen taking upgrades. They also partner with industries, manufacturers, and government agencies to develop specialized courses and certifications.

Appendix S

100+ Top Employers for Latinos

Hispanic, Latina Style, Diversity Inc., and *Fortune* magazines produce annual lists of top companies for Latinos and minorities to work at. We compared the lists, reviewed the data, and compiled the 100+ companies for this appendix. This directory is just one of several resources for you to use in your job search.

If any of the companies interest you, we recommend that you

■ Review each company's publication's lists from the past few years.

■ Research the employer at *Vault.com, Wetfeet.com,* or Web sites that provide company profiles.

■ Check out the company's Web site.

■ Make contacts with the Latino resources within the organization.

■ Network with industry-related professional associations.

Using these strategies can help you identify employment opportunities, determine that you are comfortable with the corporate culture, secure interviews, and get hired.

How do publications choose which companies are the best employers? Roberto Bard, publisher of *Latina Style,* said that "to select the annual list of 50 Top Companies for Latinas, we use a 140-question comprehensive survey (developed with the assistance of *Catalyst, Working Mothers Magazine,* the U.S. Census, the Department of Labor, and the EEOC), conduct confidential interviews with Latina employees, and verify applicant submissions through additional research. It is a combination of many factors, not just a human resources issue; diversity must translate into all areas of a corporation."

Bard added that "We go to extreme lengths to ensure that the Latina Style 50 is unimpeachable. A company cannot buy its way onto the list. The majority companies that are selected have never advertised with *Latina Style Magazine.*"

The list of 100+ Top Employers for Latinos is presented in alphabetical order.

Abbott Laboratories
100 Abbott Park Road
Abbott Park, IL 60064-6400
847-937-6100
www.abbott.com

AETNA
151 Farmington Avenue
Hartford, CT 06156
860-273-0123
www.aetna.com

AFLAC
1932 Wynnton Road
Columbus, GA 31999
800-99-AFLAC (23522)
www.aflac.com

Alliant Energy
4902 North Biltmore Lane
P.O. Box 77007
Madison, WI 53707-1007
800-255-4268
www.antenergy.com

Allstate
2775 Sanders Road
Northbrook, IL 60062-6127
847-402-5000
www.allstate.com

American Airlines
P.O. Box 619616
Dallas/Ft. Worth Airport, TX 75261-9616
817-963-1234
www.aa.com

American Express
World Financial Center
200 Vesey Street
New York, NY 10285
212-640-2000
www.americanexpress.com

American Family Insurance
6000 American Parkway
Madison, WI 53783-0001
608-249-2111
www.amfam.com

Anheuser-Busch
One Busch Place
St. Louis, MO 63118
314-577-2000
www.hispanicbud.com

Andersen LLP
33 West Monroe Street
Chicago, IL 60603
312-580-0033
www.arthurandersen.com

AOL Time Warner
75 Rockefeller Plaza
New York, NY 10019
212-484-8000
www.timewarner.com

AT&T
295 North Maple Avenue
Basking Ridge, NJ 07920
212-387-5400
www.att.com

Avon Products, Inc.
1345 Avenue of the Americas
New York, NY 10105
212-282-7000
www.avon.com

Bank of America
100 N. Tryon Street
Charlotte, NC 28255-0001
888-279-3457
www.bankofamerica.com

Bank One
100 E. Broad Street
Columbus, OH 43215
800-282-9494
www.bankone.com

Bausch & Lomb
One Bausch & Lomb Place
Rochester, NY 14604-2701
585-338-6000
www.bausch.com

BellSouth
1155 Peachtree Street, NE
Atlanta, GA 30309-3610
404-249-2000
www.southbellcorp.com

Blockbuster Video
1202 Elm Street
Dallas, TX 75270
www.blockbuster.com

The Boeing Company
500 Naches Avenue SW
Renton, WA 98055
425-393-2914
www.boeing.com

Bristol-Myers Squibb Company
345 Park Avenue
New York, NY 10154
212-546-4000
www.bms.com

Burlington Northern
2650 Lou Menk Drive
Ft. Worth, Texas 76131
800-795-2673
www.bnsf.com

Chase Manhattan
270 Park Avenue
New York, NY 10017
212-270-6000
www.chase.com

Chevron-Texaco
575 Market Street
San Francisco, CA 94105
415-894-7700
www.chevron.com

Cingular Wireless
Glenridge Highlands Two
5565 Glenridge Connector
Atlanta, GA 30342
1-866-CINGULAR
www.cingular.com

Cisco Systems
170 West Tasman Drive
San Jose, CA 95134
408-526-4000
www.cisco.com

Citigroup
153 E. 53rd Street
New York, NY 10043
212-559-1000
www.citigroup.com

The Coca-Cola Company
1 Coca-Cola Plaza
Atlanta, GA 30313
404-676-2121
www.thecocacolacompany.com

Colgate-Palmolive
300 Park Avenue
New York, NY 10022
212-310-2000
www.colgate.com

Compaq Computer Corporation
20555 SH 249
Houston, TX 77070-2698
281-370-0670
www.compaq.com

Consolidated Edison Company of New York, Inc.
Cooper Station
P.O. Box 138
New York, NY 10276-0138
212-460-4600
www.coned.com

Continental Airlines
1600 Smith Street
Houston, TX 77002
713-324-5000
www.continental.com

Coors Brewing Company
17735 West 32 Avenue
Golden, CO 80401-0030
303-279-6565
www.coors.com

DaimlerChrysler Corporation
Auburn Hills, MI 48326-2766
248-576-5741
www.daimlerchrysler.com

Dell Computer Corporation
1 Dell Way
Round Rock, TX 78682-2222
512-338-4400
www.dell.com

Deloitte & Touche, LLP
Deloitte Services LP
Two World Financial Center
New York, NY 10281-1414
212-436-2000
www.deloitte.com

Delta Airlines
Hartsfield Atlanta International Airport
Atlanta, GA 30320
404-715-2600
www.delta.com

Denny's
203 E. Main Street
Spartanburg, SC 29319
www.dennys.com

DuPont
1007 Market Street
Wilmington, DE 19898
302-774-1000
www.dupont.com

Eastman Kodak
343 State Street
Rochester, NY 14650
585-724-4000
www.Kodak.com

EDS
5400 Legacy Drive
Plano, TX 75024
972-605-6000
www.eds.com

Eli Lilly
Lilly Corporate Center
Indianapolis, IN 46285
317-276-2000
www.lilly.com

Exxon Mobil
5959 Las Colinas
Irving, TX 75039-2298
972-444-1000
www.exon.mobil.com

Fannie Mae
3900 Wisconsin Avenue NW
Washington, DC 20016
202-752-7000
www.fanniemae.com

Farmers Insurance
4680 Wilshire Boulevard
Los Angeles, CA 90010
323-932-3200
www.farmersinsurance.com

Federated Department Stores
7 W. 7th Street
Cincinnati, OH 45202
513-579-7000
www.federated-fds.com

Ford Motor Company
1 The American Road
Dearborn, MI 48121-1899
313-322-3000
www.ford.com

Freddie Mac
8200 Jones Branch Drive
McLean, VA 22102
703-903-2000
www.freddiemac.com

Gannett Company, Inc.
7950 Jones Branch Drive
McLean, VA 22107
(703) 854-6000
www.gannett.com

General Electric
3135 Easton Turnpike
Fairfield, CT 06431
203-373-2211
www.ge.com

General Mills, Inc.
P.O Box 1113
Minneapolis, MN 55440
1-800-328-1144
www.generalmills.com

General Motors Global Headquarters
300 Renaissance Center
P.O. Box 300
Detroit, MI 48265
www.gm.com

The Gillette Company
Prudential Tower Building
Boston, MA 02199
617-421-7000
www.gillette.com

Hallmark Cards, Inc.
2501 McGee Trafficway
Kansas City, MO 64141
816-274-5111
www.hallmark.com

HEB
646 S. Main Avenue
San Antonio, TX 78283
210-938-8000
www.heb.com

HSBC Bank USA
One HSBC Center
Buffalo, New York 14203
716-841-2424
www.hsbc.com

Hewlett-Packard
3000 Hanover Street
Palo Alto, CA 94304
650-857-1501
www.hp.com

Honda
1919 Torrance Boulevard
Torrance, CA 90501
310-393-4840
www.honda.com

Hyatt Hotels
200 West Madison Street, Suite 3700
Chicago, IL 60606
312-920-2400
www.hyatt.com

IBM
New Orchard Road
Armonk, NY 10504
914-765-1900
www.ibm.com

Intel, Inc.
2200 Mission College Boulevard
P.O. Box 58119
Santa Clara, CA 95052-8119
408-765-8080
www.intel.com

Intercontinental Hotels Group
67 Alma Road
Windsor
Berkshire, United Kingdom
SL 4 3HD
44-0-1753-410100
www.ihgpolc.com

International Truck & Engine
P.O. Box 1488
Warrenville, IL 60555
630-753-5000
www.internationaldelivers.com

JC Penney
6501 Legacy Drive
Plano, TX 75024-3698
972-431-1000
www.jcpenney.com

JP Morgan Chase
270 Park Avenue
New York, NY 10017
212-270-6000
www.jpmorganchase.com

Johnson & Johnson
1 Johnson & Johnson Plaza
New Brunswick, NJ 08933
732-524-0400
www.jnj.com

Kaiser Permanente
1 Kaiser Plaza
Oakland, CA 94612
510-271-5910
www.kaiserpermanente.org

KPMG
345 Park Avenue
New York, NY 10154
212-KPMG-LLP
345-758-9700
www.kpmg.com

Kellogg Company
1 Kellogg Square
P.O. Box 3599
Battle Creek, MI 49016-3599
616-961-2000
www.kellogs.com

Kraft Foods
Kraft Foods Global, Inc.
Three Lakes Drive
Northfield, IL 60093
847-646-2000
www.kraftfoods.com

Lockheed Martin
6801 Rockledge Drive
Bethesda, MD 20817
301-897-6000
www.lockheedmartin.com

Lucent Technologies
600 Mountain Avenue
Murray Hill, NJ 07974-0636
908 582-8500
www.lucent.com

Marriott
10400 Fernwood Road
Bethesda, MD 20817
301-380-2553
www.marriott.com

MasterCard Global Headquarters
2000 Purchase Street
Purchase, NY 10577
914-249-2000
www.mastercard.com

McDonald's Corporation
McDonald's Plaza
2111 McDonald's Drive
Oak Brook, IL 60523
630-623-3000
www.mcdonalds.com

MCI Worldcom
500 Clinton Center Drive
Clinton, MS 39056
601-360-8600
www.worldcom.com

Merck
1 Merck Drive
Whitehouse Station, NJ 08889
908-423-1000
www.merck.com

MetLife
1 Madison Avenue
New York, NY 10010-3690
1-800-438-6382
www.metlife.com

Microsoft
1 Microsoft Way
Redmond, WA 98052-6399
425-882-8080
www.microsoft.com

Morgan Stanley
1585 Broadway
New York, NY 10036
212-761-4000
www.morganstanley.com

Motorola
1303 E. Algonquin Road
Schaumburg, IL 60196
847-576-5000
www.motorola.com

New York Life
51 Madison Avenue
New York, NY 10010
212-576-5151
www.newyorklife.com

New York Times
229 W. 43rd Street
New York, NY 10036
646-728-9200
www.nytimes.com

Nissan North America
P.O. Box 191
Gardena, CA 90248
310-771-5631
www.nissan.com

Nordstrom
500 Pine Street
Seattle, WA 98101
206-628-2111
www.nordstrom.com

Pacific Care Health Systems, Inc.
5995 Plaza Drive
Cypress, CA 90630
www.pacificare.com

Pacific Gas and Electric
1 Market Street
Spear Tower, Suite 2400
San Francisco, CA 94105
415-973-7000
www.pge.com

PepsiCo, Inc.
700 Anderson Hill Road
Purchase, NY 10577
914-253-2000
www.pepsi.com

Pfizer
235 E. 42nd Street
New York, NY 10017-5755
212-573-2323
www.pfizer.com

PG&E Corporation
1 Market Plaza, Suite 2400
Spear Tower
San Fancisco, CA 94105
415-267-7000
www.pgecorp.com

Philip Morris Companies, Inc.
120 Park Avenue
New York, NY 10017
917-663-5000
www.philipmorris.com

Physical Electronics USA (PHI)
Lake Drive East
Chanhassen, MN 55317
952-828-6200
www.phi.com

Pitney Bowes, Inc.
1 Elmcroft Road
Stamford, CT 06926
203-356-5000
www.pitneybowes.com

PricewaterhouseCoopers
75 Varick Street
New York, NY 10013
646-471-5000
www.pwcglobal.com

Procter & Gamble
1 Procter & Gamble Plaza
Cincinnati, OH 45202
513-983-1100
www.pg.com

Prudential Insurance Company of America
751 Broad Street
Newark, NJ 07102
973-802-6000
www.prudential.com

Qwest Communication International
1801 California Street
Denver, CO 80202
800-899-7780
www.qwest.com

Ralston Purina
Checkerboard Square
St. Louis, MO 63164
800-778-7462
www.purina.com

Ryder System
3600 NW 82nd Avenue
Miami, FL 33166
305-500-3726
www.ryder.com

Safeco
Safeco Plaza
Seattle, WA 98185
206-545-5000
www.safeco.com

SBC Communications
175 East Houston Street
San Antonio, TX 78205
210-821-4105
www.sbc.com

S. C. Johnson
1525 Howe Street
Racine, WI 53403-5011
262-260-2000
www.scjohnson.com

Schieffelin & Somerset
2 Park Avenue, 17th Floor
New York, NY 10016
212-251-8200
www.trade-pages.com

Sears & Roebuck Company
3333 Beverly Road
Hoffman Estates, IL 60179
847-286-2500
www.sears.com

Seven Eleven
2711 North Haskell Avenue
Dallas, TX 75204
214-828-7011
www.7-eleven.com

Shell Oil Company
910 Louisiana Street
Houston, TX 77002
713-241-6161
www.shell.com

Sodexho U.S.A.
Corporate Headquarters
9801 Washingtonian Boulevard
Gaithersburg, MD 20878
800-763-3946
www.sodexhousa.com

Southwest Airlines
P.O. Box 36611
Dallas, TX 75235
214-792-4000
www.iflyswa.com

Sprint
2330 Shawnee Mission Parkway
Westwood, KS 66205
913-624-3000
www.sprint.com

Starwood Hotels & Resorts
1111 Westchester Avenue
White Plains, NY 10604
914-640-8100
www.starwoodhotels.com

State Farm
1 State Farm Plaza
Bloomington, IL 61710
309-766-2311
www.statefarm.com

Sun Microsystems
901 San Antonio Road
Palo Alto, CA 94303
650-960-1300
www.sun.com

Texas Instruments
12500 TI Boulevard
Dallas, TX 75243
972-995-2011
www.ti.com

The Principal Financial Group
711 High Street
Des Moines, Iowa 50392
800-986-3343
www.principal.com

TIAA/CREF
730 Third Avenue
New York, NY 10017-3206
212-490-9000
www.tiaa-cref.org

Time Warner
1 Time Warner Center
New York, NY 10019
212-444-8000
www.timewarner.com

Toyota
19001 S. Western Avenue
Torrance, CA 90509
310-618-4000
www.toyota.com

Tri-Con Global
1441 Gardiner Lane
Louisville, KY 40213
502-874-1000
www.triconglobal.com

Union Pacific
1400 Douglas Street
Omaha, NE 68179
888-870-8777
www.up.com

United Airlines Headquarters
P.O Box 66100
Chicago, IL 60666
847-700-4000
www.ual.com

UPS
55 Glenlake Parkway, NE
Atlanta, GA 30328
404-828-7123
www.ups.com

USAA
P.O. Box 659464
San Antonio, TX 78265
877-632-3002
www.usaa.com

U.S. Postal Service
475 L'enfant Plaza SW
Washington, DC 20260
800-275-8777
www.usps.com

Appendices

Valero
One Valero Place
San Antonio, TX 78212-3186
210-370-2000
www.valero.com

Verizon
1095 Avenue of the Americas
New York, NY 10036
800-621-9900
www.verizon.com

Vivendi Universal
375 Park Avenue
New York, NY 10152
212-572-7000
www.vivendi.com

Wal-Mart
702 S.W. 8th Street
Bentonville, AR 72716
501-273-4000
www.wal-mart.com

Washington Mutual
1201 3rd Avenue
Seattle, WA 98101
206-461-2000
www.wamu.com

Wells Fargo
420 Montgomery Street
San Francisco, CA 94163
415-396-3053
www.wellsfargo.com

Xerox
800 Long Ridge Road
Stamford, CT 06904
203-968-3000
www.xerox.com

Appendix T

Directory of Corporate Hispanic Employee/Affinity Groups

This directory provides a sampling of Hispanic Affinity Groups at some of the companies listed as one of the best companies for Latinos. The affinity groups are a good source of information on a company and what it is like to work there. If you are interested in one of the companies listed, contact the company headquarters and ask for the affinity group contact.

When you are searching for an affinity group in a particular corporation,

1. Go to the company Web site.
2. If no diversity site is listed, go to the careers section.
3. After careers, check for employee's sites.
4. This will usually lead you to the diversity site.
5. The diversity site will give information on the affinity group.
6. The affinity group may have a Web site or use the diversity office for contact information.

American Airlines
www.aacareers.com/us/frame_index.htm?http&&&www.aacareers.com/us/index.shtml
Latin Employee Resource Group: Employee resource groups are an important part of American Airlines efforts to foster an inclusive work environment. The employee resource groups create opportunities for employees to have a voice in business, support each other, and share their unique perspectives, cultures, and experiences with employees.

American Family Life Assurance Company (AFLAC)
www.aflac.com/corp_careers/whywork_culture.asp
The Hispanic Association is constantly working to ensure that AFLAC employees have a fair, inclusive, and rewarding work environment. Engaged employees who are given what they need to grow and succeed will ensure that the business is given what it needs to grow and succeed.

Chevron
www.chevrontexaco.com/about/careers/why/#Diversity
SOMOS: In employee network groups, employees collaborate across the company and advance our diversity objectives. Employee networks are formed based on gender, race, age, national origin, disability, or sexual orientation. Activities include sponsoring cultural events, participating in community outreach, suggesting ways to help the company

build an inclusive culture, and partnering with other groups, such as Recruiting, Public Affairs, and Human Resources, to advance the company's diversity objectives.

Citigroup
www.citigroup.com/citigroup/oncampus/homepage/diversity.htm

Hispanic Network: Networks are employee-initiated groups—open to all Citigroup employees—that support the diversity and business goals of the organization and provide members with an opportunity to share common experiences and build awareness of diverse cultures and communities within the company.

Coca-Cola
www2.coca-cola.com/ourcompany/diversity-workplace-iniatives

Latin Employee Forum (LEF): Provides opportunities for continuous learning and development to enhance the personal and professional potential of Latin associates within the company.

Daimler Chrysler
www.career.daimlerchrysler

Hispanic Employee Network: The Chrysler group is committed to creating and maintaining an inclusive work environment that encourages and values teamwork.

Eastman Kodak
www.kodak.com/cluster/global/en/corp/diversity/networks

The Hispanic Organization for Leadership and Advancement (HOLA) is committed to foster excellence and leadership among Hispanics by providing personal growth and development opportunities through networking, informal mentoring, training, and interaction with management.

Fannie Mae
www.fanniemae.com/careers/diversity/employeegrowth.jhtml?p=Careers&s=Diversity&t =Programs&q=Employee+Growth+Opportunities

Hispanic Employee Networking Group: Fannie Mae boasts fifteen employee networking groups (ENGs) that are employee-initiated and employee-managed. Members of the ENGs share common interests based on race, ethnicity, gender, sexual orientation, military service, religion, national origin, and cultural heritage. They meet on a monthly basis to discuss issues and organize community service projects for their areas of interest.

Ford Motor Company
www.mycareer.ford.com/ONTHETEAM.ASP?CID=15

Ford Hispanic Network Group (F-HNG), through service and support, strives to be a positive force in the Hispanic community. The group's vision is to assist the corporate effort to employ, develop, and retain Hispanics in the workforce. Programs include hosted professional development events and sponsoring speakers on diversity initiatives.

General Mills

www.generalmills.com/corporate/commitment/workforce.aspx

General Mills' Employee Networks provide a supportive, positive forum for developing, sharing, and exchanging information and ideas. They support General Mills' strategic workforce objectives by attracting and retaining a highly talented diverse workforce; creating and maintaining an inclusive workforce environment; providing a voice to our leadership regarding barriers and opportunities; and providing a support system and forum for exchanging information and ideas.

JPMorganChase

www.jpmorganchase.com/cm/cs?pagename=Chase/Href&urlname=jpmc/community/diversity/workplace

Hispanic Employee Networking Group: Participation in employee networking group activities is open to all employees. Networks strengthen the diversity culture within the firm by providing support to employees and facilitating a sense of belonging to the company, promoting professional development, offering mentoring opportunities, helping employees understand the JPMorganChase culture, reinforcing JPMorganChase's commitment to inclusiveness and diversity, functioning as a resource to the Corporate Diversity Council, and functioning as a forum to accelerate the pace of change and cultivate an inclusive atmosphere.

Kraft Foods

www.kraftfoods.com/careers/ourCulture/diversity

Hispanic Employee Council: The Diversity Steering Team and Employee Councils oversee and lead specific initiatives in support of the company's commitment to diversity.

Lawrence Livermore Laboratories

www.llnl.gov/aadp/zemploy.html

The Amigo Unidos Hispanic Networking Group (AUHNG) promotes the achievement of professional and personal excellence for all laboratory employees through career development, diversity, and community outreach. The company is committed to educating and mentoring Hispanics to meet the challenges and opportunities at Lawrence Livermore.

Microsoft

www.microsoft.com/mscorp/citizenship/diversity/inside/dac.asp

Grupo Unido Ibero Americano (GUIA): To help foster diversity, Microsoft has a rich community of resource groups that are organized and run by employees. These groups provide support and networking opportunities such as mentoring, recruiting, working in the community, encouraging career development, and assisting with other activities that promote cultural awareness. Their programs include a Women's Conference and Heritage Month celebrations.

PepsiCo

www.pepsico.com

The Hispanic Employee Network was formed in the early 1990s as part of the company's diversity program.

State Farm Insurance
www.statefarminsurance.com
> Hispanic Employee Resource Organization (HERO)

Ryder
www.ryder.com/about_us_dwl_grps.shtml
> Ryder Hispanic Network (RHN) assists Ryder in achieving its corporate goals and objectives by enhancing its position in the Hispanic community from a marketing, social, economic, and community perspective.

SBC Communications, Inc.
www.sbc.com
> The Hispanic Association of Communications Employees (HACEMOS) is an organization open to all SBC employees. Each year, HACEMOS links thousands of students across the country via satellite for High Technology Day, which educates students about technology careers.

Sun Microsystems
www.sun.com/aboutsun/corpdiversity/outreach.html
> Sol@Sun has taken a leadership role in the exchange of information and insights with other regional and national Hispanic focus groups. In fact, they are delivering the diversity message to neighboring corporations and the community at large in addition to all employees here at Sun. The group will host an annual Hispanic Heritage Month and extends an open invitation to learn more about the Hispanic culture.

Visteon
www.visteon.com/about/diversity/emp_res_group/index.shtml#5
> Visteon's Hispanic Network represents Hispanic interests, promotes inclusion, and contributes to the achievement of Visteon's business goals. Its objectives include supporting the attraction, retention, and career development of Hispanic employees; mentoring within Visteon (and affiliated organizations and individuals); promoting participation and involvement; providing a forum for diversity issues; demonstrating good corporate citizenship; and communicating feedback on cultural issues to management.

Xerox
www.xerox.com
> The Hispanic Association for Professional Advancement (HAPA) is an independent employee caucus group that plays an important role at Xerox, advocating self-development, openness, equal opportunity, and inclusion for the entire Xerox community. Groups representing women, blacks, Hispanics, Asians, and gay and lesbian employees provide members with an avenue to improve society via their activities and success.

Appendix U

List of Immigration and Discrimination Referral Agencies

GOVERNMENT AGENCIES

Office of Special Counsel for Immigration Related Unfair Employment Practices (OSC)
www.usdoj.gov/crt/osc
> Immigration discrimination

Equal Employment Opportunity Commission (EEOC)
www.eeoc.gov
> Discrimination complaints

U.S. Citizenship and Immigration Services (USCIS)
www.uscis.gov
> Questions about green card/citizenship

Office of Federal Contract Compliance Programs (OFCCP)
www.dol.gov/esa/ofccp
> Veterans, disability, and discrimination complaints in companies with federal contracts

U.S. Department of Education Office of Civil Rights
www.ed.gov/about/offices/list/ocr
> Discrimination in education

U.S. Department of Housing and Urban Development (HUD)
www.hud.gov
> Discrimination in housing

U.S. Department of Labor (USDOL)
www.dol.gov
> Workers compensation for federal employees, wage and hour division pay disputes, Employee Standards Administration, Family Medical Leave Act

Local & State Human Rights/Human Relations Agencies
> Discrimination in employment

NOT-FOR-PROFIT AGENCIES

National Network for Immigrant and Refugee Rights
www.nnirr.org
> Immigrant and refugee advocacy and resources

American Civil Liberties Union (ACLU)
www.aclu.org
> Constitutional violations

Mexican American Legal Defense and Education Fund (MALDEF)
www.maldef.org/
> Civil rights and immigration violations

Puerto Rican Legal Defense and Education Fund (PRLDEF)
www.prldef.org
> Civil and human rights violations

ATTORNEYS

American Immigration Lawyers Association
www.aila.org
> Advocacy for immigrant populations and referrals to lawyers specializing in immigration law

Susman & Associates
susmanusa@aol.com
> (the authors' immigration counsel)

La Admistración de su Actividad Profesional Individual y Evaluación de la Búsqueda

Mi Casa™

MI CASA™ le ayudará a comprender el mejor modo de administrar su carrera. Esta herramienta de evaluación sirve como base para identificar la necesidad de desarrollo y estrategias que usted desee seguir.

MI CASA™ es una encuesta personal. Es importante mencionar que usted debe examinar la encuesta dentro del contexto de su vida; no todos los artículos serán pertinentes ni apropiados para la administración de su carrera.

Si usted es un estudiante de universidad, complete por favor la evaluación en términos de su trabajo académico, proyectos, prácticas como interno y empleo por horas.

No hay un puntaje formal. Para cada declaración, circule el número que mejor describe su nivel de acuerdo.

Dirección y Alineación de su Profesión (añada "Título" de profesión personal)

- He explorado quién soy como persona, considerando mis valores, intereses, personalidad, talentos y destrezas.

     1   2   3   4   5

- Conozco mis talentos y debilidades.

     1   2   3   4   5

- He enlazado mi autoevaluación a tareas y actividades relacionadas con el empleo que encuentro más agradables, interesante y estimulantes.

     1   2   3   4   5

- He creado mi propia definición del éxito.

     1   2   3   4   5

- He escrito una definición de la misión personal/profesional de mi vida, para seguir mi propio llamado y no las metas de otras personas.

     1   2   3   4   5

■ Me he visualizado claramente en la cima de mi profesión.

    1   2   3   4   5

■ He entrelazado mis valores personales con mis metas profesionales.

    1   2   3   4   5

■ Tengo claras metas profesionales de corto y largo plazo.

    1   2   3   4   5

■ Mi carrera ha logrado una combinación de atributos que incluye virtudes y valores anténticos, reputación profesional y considerables beneficios para mis empleadores.

    1   2   3   4   5

■ He creado un plan de acción o de negocios para mis metas profesionales.

    1   2   3   4   5

■ Estoy implementando mi plan de acción.

    1   2   3   4   5

■ Soy la persona que más influye en la dirección que tome mi carrera.

    1   2   3   4   5

■ La dirección total de mi carrera y su alineación son excelentes.

    1   2   3   4   5

Características de Conducta

■ Tengo fe en ser alguien con algo extraordinario que ofrecer.

    1   2   3   4   5

■ Estoy consciente de mi programación biológica, psicológica y cultural y el impacto que ésta tiene en mi actitud, conducta y en los resultados que obtengo en mi vida.

    1   2   3   4   5

■ Conozco el estilo de conducta que domino en mi sitio de empleo (líder, relacionador, socializador, teórico, pasivo).

    1   2   3   4   5

■ Conozco mi estilo personal en el manejo de conflictos (competidor, acomodador, evasivo, negociador, conciliador).

    1   2   3   4   5

■ Mi jefe/colegas/clientes evaluarían mi actitud en el trabajo, en este preciso momento, como muy positiva.

    1   2   3   4   5

■ En la actualidad, mi entusiasmo en el trabajo y mi vida son estupendos.

    1   2   3   4   5

■ Me adapto bien a cambios en mi sitio de empleo y/o ayudo a hacer cambios sin quejas.

    1   2   3   4   5

■ Practico técnicas que me ayudan a reducir la ansiedad y el estrés.

    1   2   3   4   5

■ Trabajo bien bajo estrés.

    1   2   3   4   5

■ Veo los problemas como estímulos y oportunidades.

    1   2   3   4   5

■ Estoy dispuesto a tomar riesgos para completar mis tareas y/o salir adelante en mi profesión.

    1   2   3   4   5

■ Soy la persona con mayor poder e influencia sobre mi comportamiento profesional.

    1   2   3   4   5

Comunicación

■ Poseo buenas técnicas de comunicación oral.

    1   2   3   4   5

■ Poseo buenas técnicas de comunicación escrita.

    1   2   3   4   5

■ Destacaría en una prueba de comunicación oral en español.

    1   2   3   4   5

■ Destacaría en una prueba en capacidad de redacción en español.

    1   2   3   4   5

■ Estoy consciente de los mensajes que transmito por medio de la comunicación corporal (señales corporales, contacto visual).

    1   2   3   4   5

■ Soy bueno para interpretar las señales no verbales de otros.

    1   2   3   4   5

■ Escucho activamente (entiendo los hechos que se me presentan, no juzgo, no estoy a la defensiva, no pienso en lo próximo que debo decir).

    1   2   3   4   5

■ Poseo la habilidad de responder con información útil.

    1   2   3   4   5

■ Cuando recibo información negativa, la manejo de una manera constructiva y positiva.

    1   2   3   4   5

■ Me siento cómodo hablando de uno a uno con mis compañeros de trabajo.

    1   2   3   4   5

■ Me siento cómodo hablando de uno a uno con mi jefe.

    1   2   3   4   5

■ Me siento cómodo hablando de uno a uno con mis clientes.

    1   2   3   4   5

■ Poseo la habilidad para hacer buenas presentaciones a grupos de personas.

    1   2   3   4   5

■ La diplomacia es una de mis mejores habilidades.

    1   2   3   4   5

■ Poseo la habilidad para resolver problemas.

    1   2   3   4   5

■ Brindo un excelente servicio al cliente.

    1   2   3   4   5

■ Me siento confortable al negociar frente a frente.

    1   2   3   4   5

■ Poseo la habilidad de negociar en grupo.

    1   2   3   4   5

■ Cuando hablo, la gente presta atención a mis ideas y opiniones. Después las veo empleadas o aplicadas.

    1   2   3   4   5

■ Cuando tengo buenas razones, no tengo problema en expresar mi punto de vista aún cuando difiera de la gerencia.

    1   2   3   4   5

■ Soy la persona con más poder e influencia sobre mis habilidades en la comunicación.

    1   2   3   4   5

■ Evaluó mis habilidades de comunicación como excelentes.

    1   2   3   4   5

Capacidad en el Trabajo y Rendimiento

■ Conozco y realizo bien mi trabajo.

    1   2   3   4   5

■ Comprendo claramente las expectativas que mi jefe tiene de mi desempeño.

   1   2   3   4   5

■ Estoy dispuesto a firmar mi nombre en cualquier tarea que completo.

   1   2   3   4   5

■ Entrego un producto de buena calidad a tiempo.

   1   2   3   4   5

■ Me siento como propietario con respecto al bienestar de mi compañía y su rendimiento.

   1   2   3   4   5

■ Mi ética de trabajo se caracteriza por mucha energía, concentración, dedicación y propósito.

   1   2   3   4   5

■ Mi jefe sabe que puede contar conmigo para labores adicionales.

   1   2   3   4   5

■ Soy parte del grupo; contribuyo al equipo por medio de acciones y palabras.

   1   2   3   4   5

■ Uso los recursos de mi sitio de trabajo (personas e información) con eficacia para mejorar mis conocimientos, habilidades y rendimiento.

   1   2   3   4   5

■ Me comunico bien con compañeros de diferentes ambientes.

   1   2   3   4   5

■ Entiendo los cuatro tipos básicos del poder, y cómo y cuándo usarlos (personal, posición, conocimiento, percepción).

   1   2   3   4   5

■ Sé administrar bien mi tiempo.

   1   2   3   4   5

■ Sé cómo obtener y lograr visibilidad para el avance profesional, en mi organización.

   1   2   3   4   5

■ Mis habilidades bilingües son una ventaja para la compañía.

   1   2   3   4   5

■ Mis raíces culturales y experiencias son una ventaja para mi empleador.

   1   2   3   4   5

■ Soy la persona con más poder e influencia sobre mi propio desempeño en el trabajo.

   1   2   3   4   5

■ Evaluó mi rendimiento en mi trabajo como excelente.

   1   2   3   4   5

Cultura Empresarial

■ Conozco las costumbres en la organización y sus valores.

   1   2   3   4   5

■ Mi conducta, estilo y comunicación están de acuerdo con los requeridos por mi compañía.

   1   2   3   4   5

■ Estoy enterado de los reglamentos no escritos de la organización.

   1   2   3   4   5

■ Me llevo bien la política de la empresa.

   1   2   3   4   5

■ Sé cuáles son las características apreciadas por la compañía.

   1   2   3   4   5

■ Comprendo mi dinámica (mi etnicidad/cultura/sexo) en mi lugar de trabajo.

   1   2   3   4   5

■ Sé cómo manejar el proceso por el cual mis caracteristicas (etnicidad/cultura/sexo) son evaluadas.

   1   2   3   4   5

■ Entiendo los temas claves para el éxito de mi empresa.

   1   2   3   4   5

■ Soy la persona más capacitada para influir sobre mi propia navegación por el ambiente y la cultura prevalentes en mi lagar de trabajo.

   1   2   3   4   5

■ Poseo habilidad para navegar por el ambiente cultural que rige en el trabajo.

   1   2   3   4   5

Red de Contactos

■ Tengo una red personal de contactos o de un sistema de apoyo.

   1   2   3   4   5

■ Tengo una sólida red de contactos profesionales.

   1   2   3   4   5

■ Tengo una sólida red de contactos en mi sitio de trabajo.

   1   2   3   4   5

■ Sé como relacionarme con eficacia con personas semejantes a mí (etnicidad/cultura/sexo) en mi sitio de trabajo.

    1   2   3   4   5

■ Sé como relacionarme con eficacia con personas que son distintas a mí (etnicidad/cultura/sexo) en mi sitio de trabajo.

    1   2   3   4   5

■ Tengo un buen consejero cuyas características (etnicidad/cultura/sexo) son similares a las mías.

    1   2   3   4   5

■ Tengo un buen consejero cuyas características (etnicidad/cultura/sexo) son distintas a las mías.

    1   2   3   4   5

■ Sé cuáles son mis obligaciones como aprendiz y cómo cumplirlas.

    1   2   3   4   5

■ Soy un buen consejero para otra persona.

    1   2   3   4   5

■ Tengo a colegas en posiciones semejantes a la mía en otras divisiones dentro de mi propia compañía, o en otras compañías, con quienes interactúo frecuentemente para intercambiar ideas y estar al día de los asuntos pertinentes a mi trabajo.

    1   2   3   4   5

■ Pertenezco a organizaciones internas y externas y asisto a sus reuniones con suficiente regularidad como para conocer a otros miembros.

    1   2   3   4   5

■ Comparto mi conocimiento y experiencias con otros.

    1   2   3   4   5

■ Soy la persona más capacitada para lograr que mis relaciones sean todo un éxito.

    1   2   3   4   5

■ Califico a mi capacidad de lograr una red de contactos como excelente.

    1   2   3   4   5

Relación con Estereotipos, Discriminación, Racismo y Hostigamiento Sexual

■ Comprendo mis propios prejuicios y estereotipos.

    1   2   3   4   5

■ Poseo buena capacidad de comunicación y administración interculturales.

    1   2   3   4   5

- Trato con eficacia los prejuicios de otros.

  1   2   3   4   5

- He creado lazos de unión con los empleados y sus diversas culturas, lo cual mejora mi capacidad de ayndarlos y ayuda a educar a los demas.

  1   2   3   4   5

- Sé las normas antidiscriminatorias de mi compañía y sus procedimientos.

  1   2   3   4   5

- Conozco la protección legal contra discriminación que poseo en mi sitio de empleo y sé cómo ejercer mis derechos.

  1   2   3   4   5

- Conozco la protección legal contra la discriminación que se me otorga bajo las leyes del Departamento de Inmigración.

  1   2   3   4   5

- Califico mi conocimiento e intención de ejercitar mis derechos antidiscriminatorios en el trabajo como excelentes.

  1   2   3   4   5

Manejo de la Búsqueda de Empleo

- Sé los pasos que se deben tomar para una búsqueda de trabajo exitosa.

  1   2   3   4   5

- Me siento cómodo ofreciendo mis conocimientos y habilidades a los empleadores.

  1   2   3   4   5

- Sé cómo lograr la mejor oferta por mis conocimientos y habilidades.

  1   2   3   4   5

- Sé cómo establecer mi valor como . . . (mi etnicidad/cultura/sexo).

  1   2   3   4   5

- Tengo un curriculum actualizado y disponible para la búsqueda de empleo, promociones u oportunidades de asignaciones de carrera.

  1   2   3   4   5

- Tengo cartas de presentación de gran calidad y disponibles para la búsqueda de empleo, promociones u oportunidades de asignaciones de carrera.

  1   2   3   4   5

- Mantengo un portafolio que documenta mis logros, contribuciones y productos de mi trabajo.

  1   2   3   4   5

■ Sé cómo investigar industrias y compañías en búsqueda de empleo.

      1   2   3   4   5

■ Sé cómo penetrar en el mercado de empleo "oculto".

      1   2   3   4   5

■ Sé los pasos para establecer contactos exitosos en la búsqueda de trabajo y estoy dispuesto a ponerlos en práctica para obtener un empleo.

      1   2   3   4   5

■ Sé cómo trabajar con las asociaciones de empleo profesionales y las oficinas de universidades/colegios en la búsqueda de empleo para ex-alumnos.

      1   2   3   4   5

■ Sé cómo trabajar con reclutadores de empleo.

      1   2   3   4   5

■ Sé cómo venderme para obtener una entrevista con los empleadores.

      1   2   3   4   5

■ Sé cómo utilizar las asociaciones profesionales y fuentes de empleo latinas como parte de mi búsqueda.

      1   2   3   4   5

■ Sé cómo usar el internet en mi búsqueda de empleo.

      1   2   3   4   5

■ Sé cómo usar ferias de empleo tradicionales y especializadas en mi búsqueda de empleo.

      1   2   3   4   5

■ Sé los tipos de entrevistas para empleos y cómo funcionan.

      1   2   3   4   5

■ Sé realizar investigación sobre compañías y trabajos específicos antes de acudir a la entrevista. Comprendo el proceso de la entrevista, incluyendo tipos de entrevista, exámenes, verificación de antecedentes.

      1   2   3   4   5

■ Sé cómo prepararme para tener éxito en una entrevista del trabajo.

      1   2   3   4   5

■ Me siento cómodo cuando ofrezco mis conocimientos, destrezas y contribuciones durante una entrevista de trabajo.

      1   2   3   4   5

■ Sé cómo contralar la ansiedad durante las entrevistas.

      1   2   3   4   5

■ Sé cómo ejecutar mi plan de entrevista para lograr que el empleador se comunique nuevamente conmigo/me emplee.

    1   2   3   4   5

■ Sé cómo dejar una buena impresión inicial y manejar mi lenguaje corporal.

    1   2   3   4   5

■ Sé analizar al entrevistador y responder apropiadamente.

    1   2   3   4   5

■ Sé cómo terminar la entrevista y como dejar establecido mi valor.

    1   2   3   4   5

■ Sé cómo mantener el contacto después de la entrevista de trabajo.

    1   2   3   4   5

■ Sé cómo preparar mis referencias.

    1   2   3   4   5

■ Sé cómo aceptar, negociar o rechazar una oferta de trabajo.

    1   2   3   4   5

■ Sigo continuando mi educación, capacitación y desarrollo.

    1   2   3   4   5

■ Participo activamente en los programas de desarrollo profesional patrocinados por la compañía.

    1   2   3   4   5

■ Mantengo una actitud dinámica con mi empleador respecto a mi entrenamiento, desarrollo y todo trabajo que me ayude a avanzar en mi profesión.

    1   2   3   4   5

■ Soy la persona más capacitada para lograr que mi búsqueda de trabajo tenga éxito.

    1   2   3   4   5

■ Califico mi habilidad de búsqueda de trabajo como excelente.

    1   2   3   4   5

Seguimiento con MI CASA™

■ Revisaré y reflexionaré sobre mis respuestas a la encuesta MI CASA™.

    1   2   3   4   5

■ Completaré la encuesta MI CASA™ con regularidad durante mi carrera.

    1   2   3   4   5

Appendix W

Doce Características de Éxito de Carrera para Latinos

TU ERES EL ARQUITECTO DE TU PROPIO DESTINO

■ El éxito en la vida y carrera sólo puede ser definido por sí mismo.

■ Dedique tiempo para desarrollar su definición del éxito es esencial para lograr la satisfacción que busca en su carrera.

Las siguientes son doce características que deben dominar si usted quiere lograr éxito en su carrera y vida.

CONÓZCASE A SÍ MISMO

■ Evalue sus intereses, valores, conocimientos, destrezas, habilidades, contribuciones, logros, su estilo y mérito.

■ Entienda su programación cultural, si existe alguna, y cómo transformar esos factores en ventajas de carrera.

■ Abrace sus atributos, su historia familiar y su cultura.

■ Desarrolle su combinación de atributos para lanzar o hacer crecer su carrera.

DESARROLLE UNA META QUE LE INSPIRE

Desarrolle una visión de lo que usted quiere alcanzar en la vida y su carrera.

■ Despierte su pasión y deseo para tener éxito en cualquier cosa que haga.

■ Permita que sus metas lo impulsen hacia adelante. Sus objetivos no se deben auto-limitar.

■ Asegúrese que sus metas, grandes o pequeñas, ayuden a otros y no soló por sí mismo.

CREA EN SU POTENCIAL PERSONAL

■ Recuerde que es usted la persona a quien más importa su carrera.

■ Abrace su potencial personal para promover su potencial profesional.

■ Despierte su potencial de carrera para estimular su búsqueda de empleo, maneje el proceso para reaccionar positivamente ante los acontecimientos que no puede usted controlar.

- Aprenda a adaptar y transformar cualquier programación autolimitadora en los centros de poder.

Aprenda a Desenvolverse en Ambos Mundos

- Reconozca que su adaptación a la cultura empresarial del empleador no vende ni cambia su identidad cultural.

- Construya un puente cultural que cruce de un ambiente a otro, crúcelo y ayude a otros a cruzar.

- Conozca su cultura y compártala.

Desarrolle Oportunidades y Prepárese para Aprovecharlas

- La iniciativa y el establecer contactos "networking" creen oportunidades.

- La preparación y la práctica a menudo determinan el éxito de la carrera.

- Mantenga su actitud positiva y siéntase afortunado.

- Use estrategias probadas para vencer cualquier "FEAR" (Falsas Expectativas que Parecen Verdaderas) que podrá usted tener.

La Persistencia y el Éxito Viajan Juntos

- Recuerde que no es el candidato más rápido ni el más brillante, sino el candidato mejor preparado y más sensato y persistente el que genera una entrevista y asegura el empleo.

- Reconozca que esos obstáculos en la búsqueda de empleo sólo son desvíos secundarios y que usted puede encontrar una ruta alternativa, o bien esquivarlos o evitarlos por completo.

- Trabaje inteligentemente y use el creciente número de empresas que establecen contactos "networking", enfocados específicamente hacia Latinos que buscan empleo.

Construya su Estilo Profesional para el Mercado

- Si usted no desarrolla un Estilo Profesional para el Mercado, otros lo definirán por su cuenta.

- Pinte un retrato de sí mismo que sea impactante y sincero, y que muestre la especial contribución que usted ofrece a una compañia.

- La construcción de su reputación o Estilo Profesional para el Mercado mejorará su confianza y su potencial durante la búsqueda de empleo.

Haga el Aprendizaje un Proceso que Dure Toda la Vida

- El aprendizaje continuo lo enriquece y mejora sus oportunidades de empleo y superación.

- El desarrollo profesional y personal mejora su potencial, agilidad y disponibilidad en el mercado laboral.

- Su compromiso de desarollo personal y profesional justifica la inversión y su rendimiento (Return on Investment) que el empleador ha hecho en usted.

SEA FLEXIBLE

- Mantenga abiertas sus opciones en la búsqueda de empleo.

- Sea abierto, adáptese y acomódese a enfoques y oportunidades diferentes.

- Mida las ofertas de empleo y oportunidades de carrera para ver cómo se aplican a sus metas de carrera. No se fije solamente en el dinero.

CREE UN SISTEMA SÓLIDO DE APOYO

- Extende su "familia" de carrera, cree una red de personas que estarán allí para usted en varias capacidades que le ayudarán en su búsqueda de empleo.

- Mantenga los contactos en su red, agradézcales su ayuda y devuelva su apoyo cuando se lo pidan a usted.

RECONOZCA CUANDO HA LLEGADO EL MOMENTO DE APARTARSE

- Comprender que ha llegado el tiempo de marcharse no debe interpretarse como algo negativo. Es un paso que puede liberar, estimular, y llevar al éxito de carrera.

- Tal vez aceptó un trabajo que ha resultado ser inadecuado o su situación de trabajo se agravó hasta el punto llegar al colapso. Como sea, sepa seguir adelante.

- Las metas de su trabajo pueden haber cambiado, o quizás usted ve que el enfoque del equipo puede ser más productivo si usted se aparta. En estas y otras situaciones reconozca que es tiempo de irse.

- Aprenda a aceptar sus errores y úselos como experiencias de aprendizaje. Déjelos atrás.

RECUERDE DE DEVOLVER ALGO A NUESTRA COMUNIDAD

- Aprecie a los latinos que fueron los pioneros que dejaron un camino para que usted lo siga.

- Al ayudar a otros colegas latinos o a los latinos que le siguen abre más oportunidades a otros como usted.

- Cuando devuelve a nuestra comunidad, enriquece su propio valor y ayuda a construir su Estilo Profesional para el Mercado.

- Labores de liderazgo y trabajos de voluntario a menudo ofrecen oportunidades únicas de desarrollo profesional que a menudo no están disponibles en el sitio de empleo.

Appendix X

Creación de su Propio Estilo Profesional para el Mercado

Conózcase a sí mismo. Entienda sus valores, personalidad, conocimientos, habilidades, talentos, pasiones, individualidad y lo que usted vale.

Tome una prueba. Hay numerosos medios de evaluación que le ayudarán a identificar su tipo de personalidad, talentos, valores y/o profesión ideal. El apéndice contiene fuentes de pruebas gratuitas y de paga.

Ejemplo: El Keirsey (www.keirsey.com) *o Perfil de Personalidad de Meyer Briggs. El* Mazemaster o Strengths Finder Profile *(Perfil de Búsqueda de Puntos Fuertes). El* MAPP o Motivational Appraisal of Personal Potential Career Análisis *(Análisis Profesional de Evaluación del Potencial Personal). El* Princeton Review Career Quiz *(Prueba Princeton sobre Estudio de Profesiones).*

Haga su propia evaluación.

Ejemplo: Hágase el análisis SWOT—Talentos, Debilidades, Oportunidades y Amenazas (Strengths, Weaknesses, Opportunities, and Threats)—y cómo se relacionan a sus metas profesionales. Lea de nuevo sus evaluaciones de desempeño de los últimos años y pregúntese lo que dicen realmente acerca de usted. ¿Hay adjetivos que se usan constantemente entre todas sus evaluaciones?

Formule una lista de todas las áreas en las que usted sobresale.

Ejemplo: Algunas ideas de su estilo profesional en el mercado incluyen el manejo de conflictos, entrenamiento en ventas, sistemas de mejoras prácticas, mercado para profesionales de servicio y servicio al cliente.

Identifique su mayor interés.

Ejemplo: Usando la lista de áreas en las que usted sobresale, circunde aquéllas que le apasionan. Limite la lista a uno o a dos artículos.

Determine las ventajas de sus cualidades.

Ejemplo: Si usted sobresale en el manejo de conflictos, las ventajas para los empleadores de contar con personas que poseen su estilo profesional quizás sea una mayor cooperacion entre miembros del equipo, lo cual puede llevar a mejorar la productividad, dar nuevas ideas, etc.

Enumere por lo menos tres ventajas claras de su *estilo profesional*.
Enumere sus contribuciones y logros.

Por ejemplo: Use el cuestionario principal e industrial específico de su "Toolkit" para desarrollar sus documentos profesionales de mercadeo.

Valore su reputación.

Por ejemplo: Escuche lo que otros dicen sobre usted. Cuando la gente lo presenta o habla de usted con otros, a menudo hacen algunas declaraciones de su estilo profesional y usan adjetivos calificativos que lo describen claramente. Preste atención la próxima vez que lo presenten.

También, conviértase en un autoobservador y reflexione honestamente sobre las siguientes preguntas.

¿Cómo responde la gente a mi presencia?
¿Le agrada a la gente verme en reuniones o suspiran con alivio cuando me voy?
¿Me escucha la gente?
¿Quieren oír lo que tengo que decir o se alegran cuando dejo de hablar?
¿Qué veo y escucho en conversaciones diarias que me indica quién soy y qué es lo que sienten acerca de mí?

Dése permiso para crear y promover su propio *estilo profesional* en el mercado.

Por ejemplo: Use el poder del modelo "R.E.S.P.E.C.T." para dar mayor ímpetu a su estilo profesional. Para algunos de nosotros esto significa comenzar con la familia, a la cual debe preguntar cuáles son sus talentos y logros. El reconocimiento de sus cualidades refuerza la valoración de sus talentos. Luego diríjase al mundo externo, preguntando a sus amistades, compañeros, supervisores, empleados, amigos, mentores y entrenadores.

Destáguese. Busque oportunidades para hacer que las personas apropiadas adquieran conocimiento de su *estilo profesional*. Hágase notar. El mejor estilo del mundo no significa nada si la gente no lo ve.

Ejemplos: Usted puede hacer notar su nombre tomando parte en reuniones de la compañía o juntas de la asociación, solicitando trabajos en proyectos de gran importancia, sirviendo en proyectos donde será visto por un número de personas (por ejemplo, repartir etiquetas en una exposición de comercio), haciendo copias de correos electrónicos para que el jefe de su jefe se mantenga enterado de correos/memos de importancia y sugiriendo ideas sobre cómo ahorrar tiempo/dinero a su empleador inmediato.

Verifique las oportunidades de empleo que concuerden con su *estilo profesional*. ¿Hay demanda de lo que usted ofrece? ¿Están las compañías empleando en esa área?

Por ejemplo: Verifique mediante su red de contactos o utilice el internet.

Determine la mejor forma de proyectar su *estilo profesional* hacia el mercado.

Por ejemplo: Para demostrar su considerable valor, sea el primero y el mejor en cualquier cosa que realice. ¿Es usted el mejor en crear estrategias de venta de un producto? ¿Es usted el primero en dominar y usar nuevas tecnologías en la oficina? ¿Es usted el profesional en ventas más premiado en su compañía / industria?

Un *estilo profesional* se puede alcanzar por medios verbales y visuales.

Por ejemplo:

❑ Verbalmente incluya una frase breve y concisa un éxito pasado

❑ Visualmente optimice sus acciones, actitud y vestimenta—*¡Viva y Respire su Estilo Profesional Propio!*

Sintetice su *estilo profesional* en un mensaje de venta de tres puntos que transmita sus talentos. Dicho mensaje será una frase breve y concisa.

Por ejemplo: "Sobresalgo en las 3 Rs en ventas: Investigación (research), *relaciones* (relationships) *y ganacias* (revenue)—*investigo minuciosamente las necesidades del cliente, construyo relaciones basadas en mis servicios a esas necesidades y tengo un record de incrementos de las ganancias como resultado".*

Prepare declaraciones breves de su *estilo profesional.* Exprese concisamente su gran valor. Si su promesa es muy complicada para ser expresada en pocas palabras, no será efectiva.

Por ejemplo: Incluya una historia exitosa con frases concisas para crear una pequeña presentación informal de 2 minutos. ¿Leyó el guión de muestra en el capítulo? Considere usar un slogan que ayude a la gente a recordarle de una forma única y favorable, tal como: ¡Mis colegas me llaman "El Sr. FedEx" porque siempre entrego los proyectos a tiempo!

Practique.

Por ejemplo: Ensaye sus frases breves con naturalidad, sin aparentar que lee de un guión de telemercadeo.

Establezca un grupo de apoyo.

Por ejemplo: Reclute a una persona o dos que respetuosa y sinceramente le apoyan en su empresa de formar y mejorar su imagen. Un mentor o un entrenador profesional pueden ser los respaldos ideales.

Con un estilo profesional, reclute a triunfadores.

Por ejemplo: Si su red profesional crece y usted cultiva sus relaciones con ellos, creará una excelente familia de líderes, promotores y personas de mercadeo.

Evalúe periódicamente su *estilo profesional*, asegurándose así que sigue teniendo significado.

Por ejemplo: Use a su familia de profesionales, las revisiones anuales de desempeño y las investigaciones en el área del empleo para evaluar su estilo profesional y asegurarse de que éste continúe siendo relevante en el mercado laboral actual.

Mantenga su estilo profesional

Ejemplos:

❑ Sea consistente en cualquier tarea que usted haga en el trabajo y en su comunicación con cada persona.

❑ Cultive relaciones con compañeros, supervisores, administradores, mentores, otros profesionales y con nuevos contactos.

❑ Asegure la visibilidad de su estilo profesional.

Evolucione.

Ejemplo: Para mantenerse al día con su audiencia, todos los estilos profesionales eficaces evolucionan con el tiempo. Ahora tenemos a AOL Latino *y la revista* People *en* Español. *Si la clientela básica se altera, si la tecnología cambia o surgen oportunidades que requieren habilidades adicionales, usted debe evolucionar con estos acontecimientos.*

Appendix Y

El Poder de R.E.S.P.E.C.T. para Entrevistarse

Use el modelo de entrevista R.E.S.P.E.C.T. para aumentar la fuerza de su entrevista. Reconozca que el concepto de respeto para los latinos es muy poderoso.

■ Respétese, reconociendo sus habilidades, contribuciones y logros.

■ Respete a su familia, aumentando su habilidad de proveer por ella.

■ Respete a la compañía, la cual necesita decidir si usted ofrece lo que la compañía necesita y si es usted la persona adecuada para ese puesto.

Determine quién es usted y qué es lo que le ofrece a la compañía. Desarrolle sus metas y su portafolio de entrevista.

La confianza en sí mismo es necesaria para una buena entrevista. La clave para presentarse con aplomo y confianza en sí mismo es hacer un estimado de todo lo que usted le ofrece a la compañía.

Prepare, planee y practique cada entrevista. Acomode las experiencias exitosas que ha tenido a los intereses de la compañía que lo entrevista. Practique hasta que esté cómodo y su presentación se sienta natural.

Ejecute su plan con aplomo. Observe, escuche y tome sugerencias del ambiente, de la comunicación sin palabras y de las preguntas del entrevistador para poder así comunicar eficazmente sus puntos fuertes.

Al terminar la entrevista, exprese su interés en el cargo ofrecido, resuma sus calificaciones, pida información adicional y clarifique los próximos pasos a seguir en el proceso.

Dé las gracias al entrevistador y a las personas que le ayudaron a llegar allí. El hecho de mandar cartas de agradecimiento comunica su profesionalismo, promueve la buena voluntad y las buenas relaciones.

Aumente su cultura y lenguaje en su búsqueda.

■ Identifique y haga una lista de los beneficios derivados de sus experiencias multiculturales y/o bilingües.

■ Establezca una correspondencia entre su lista y las experiencias positivas que explican cuándo usó usted esos atributos.

■ Conecte estas historias con los requisitos del cargo y con las necesidades del empleador.

Appendix Z

Las Claves para el Éxito en una Feria de Empleo

Su Lista de Verificación para la Feria de Empleo

A continuación aparecen sugerencias para aprovechar al máximo las conferencias sobre empleos, carreras y profesiones. Puede ser que usted sólo tenga tiempo de seguir algunas de estas sugerencias. **LA CLAVE PRINCIPAL es que usted asista a la conferencia y se relacione.**

Pre-Registro

Muchas ferias de empleo son gratis si usted entrega su resumé y completa el formulario de registro antes de comenzar la feria. Esto eliminará la espera en la fila.

Preparación

Investigue a los empleadores que asisten. Encuéntrelos en el internet para aprender más acerca de las compañías, sus productos, servicios, etc.

Prepare una estrategia para trabajar en la feria. Establezca prioridades en sus visitas a empleadores.

Traiga résumés de sobra y versiones preparadas especialmente para esa industria (si los tiene). Vea LOS RÉSUMÉS **H.I.S.P.A.N.I.C.** GENERAN ENTREVISTAS DE EMPLEO para proveer sugerencias en cómo redactar résumé.

Lleve su portafolio profesional si tiene uno. Estos portafolios deben incluir copias de sus resumés, muestras de su mejor trabajo, testimonios, evaluaciones y una lista de referencias. Aunque la mayoría de las entrevistas de ferias de empleo son bastantes cortas, puede haber oportunidades para hablar de su portafolio profesional con un reclutador—en un descanso corto o durante una segunda entrevista en el sitio.

Imprima tarjetas de presentación para relacionarse con información básica en un lado y un mini-resumé en el otro.

Lleve una carpeta, portafolio, un maletín o una cartera para mantener su resumé en orden, con espacio para mantener las tarjetas de presentación, materiales colectados y una libreta de papel u organizador electrónico/PDA para anotar.

Vístase profesionalmente como lo hace cuando va a una entrevista y use zapatos cómodos.

Escriba y practique un diálogo de presentación/**un comercial de promoción personal** de 30 segundos a 2 minutos. Las primeras impresiones son críticas.

Por ejemplo: Entregue al reclutador una copia de su resumé y esté preparado para comentar sobre él rápidamente. Comparta información básica sobre usted y sus intereses profesionales. Por ejemplo: "Buenos días. Mi nombre es Marisol Quiñones. Tengo un Bachiller en Artes (B.A.) en Administración de Empresas con tres años de experiencia progresiva como representante de cuenta con la Corporación XYZ en Nueva York. Me gustaría hablar con usted acerca de las posiciones bilingües altas que su organización necesita. Como usted puede ver en mi resumé, he completado los siguientes cursos profesionales de educación en. . . ."

Prepare preguntas específicas para cada compañía. Hacer buenas preguntas demuestra su interés en trabajar para la compañía.

Ejemplos: ¿Puede decirme usted más acerca de su programa de entrenamiento en administración? ¿Cuáles son los caminos a tomar en su departamento de mercadeo? ¿Cuáles son los pasos en su proceso de entrevista y selección?

Prepare preguntas específicas sobre latinos, minorías o representación femenina para los representantes de compañía. Estas preguntas le ayudarán a evaluar la importancia que el empleador le presta al latino y a otros puntos importantes para usted.

Ejemplos: ¿Tiene usted cierto número de hispanos entre sus empleados? ¿Cuáles son las mejores estrategias que puedo usar para mejorar mis oportunidades de obtener una entrevista? ¿Puedo hablar con alguien en la empresa para obtener información más detallada sobre una posición "x" y sobre oportunidades futuras de empleo? ¿Cuál es el perfil de los candidatos latinos que consiguen el empleo y son retenidos en esa posición?

Tambien puede hacer preguntas más a fondo y recibir respuestas más informativas sobre el empleo. ¿Cuáles son los pasos en su proceso de entrevista y selección? ¿Qué formatos de entrevista usan? (Ejemplos, paneles, entrevista progresiva, de conducta—Vea el capítulo de Entrevistas.)

Duerma bien para estar descansado y lleno de energía para la feria. Aliméntese bien para mantener su energía. Siempre tenga algunas mentas—nada destruye la confianza más rápido que preocuparse por el aliento.

CUANDO USTED LLEGUE

Llegue temprano, regístrese, revise el directorio y el plano del plantel, camine el área de exhibición para sentir el ambiente de la conferencia y revise su estrategia si es necesario.

Tenga confianza, demuestre una actitud positiva y permanezca enfocado.

Visite los puestos del centro de asistencia profesional para obtener sugerencias sobre la mejor manera de redactar su resumé y consejos sobre entrevistas.

DURANTE LA FERIA DE EMPLEO

Comience con sus empleadores prioritarios. Muchas personas se atoran en la estampida a la entrada. Vaya donde haya representantes esperando que alguien se presente.

Sea eficiente. Si usted ve un puesto que tiene mucha gente, no espere su turno para hablar con un reclutador. Simplemente vaya a otro puesto y regrese después u obtenga la tarjeta de presentación del representante y llámele después de la feria de empleo.

Condúzcase profesionalmente. Recuerde que usted puede estar proyectando impresiones cuando se para en la línea o camina por la feria.

No dé por sentado que una compañía no tiene posiciones abiertas en su rama. En cambio, pregunte qué posiciones tienen disponibles ahora y cuáles anticipan en el futuro.

No juzgue un puesto por su apariencia. Algunas de las mejores oportunidades pueden estar en los puestos que no tienen la mejor decoración. Si no hay otros aspirantes de trabajo presentes, ésta es una gran oportunidad para hablar cara a cara con el reclutador. Tiene aquí mayor probabilidad que se acuerden de usted.

Observe a los reclutadores de lejos o mientras espera en línea. Una vez que haya dado un vistazo al recentador, puede prepararse mentalmente para la entrevista o la conversación que está a punto de tener. Observe a los aspirantes de empleo delante de usted y obtendrá algunas ideas sobre lo que puede anticipar.

Haga contactos personales. Acérquese a expositores con una sonrisa al hacer contacto visual y ofrezca un firme apretón de manos. Preséntese tal como practicó anteriormente. Exprese sus interés demostrando conocimiento de la organización. Cuente su potencial, su intereses profesionales y sus experiencias específicamente necesarias para el empleador. Relájese y hable con calma y con seguridad. Escuche detenidamente y haga preguntas pertinentes acerca de la compañía y la posición. Pregunte qué es lo que ellos buscan en un candidato ideal. Este no es el momento de hacer preguntas relacionadas al salario. **Haga una conexión humana**.

Antes de salir del puesto, obtenga información sobre el contacto, pida una tarjeta de presentación y pregunte al representante sobre el próximo paso a tomar.

Tome notas al reverso de la tarjeta de presentación del reclutador en su libreta u organizador electrónico. **Escriba** detalles importantes acerca de la compañía, incluyendo los nombres de personas que no tenían tarjetas de presentación. ¡Tómese unos minutos después de dejar cada mesa y haga estas anotaciones!

Use la feria de empleo para mejorar sus destrezas de entrevista. Ponga atención a las preguntas frecuentes que usted quizás no haya anticipado y prepare respuestas a esas preguntas para entrevistas futuras.

Relaciónese con otros aspirantes de empleo y asociaciones hispanas profesionales. Hable con otros mientras hace la cola para intercambiar ideas sobre estrategias para conseguir empleo, apoyo mutuo e identificación de pistas para obtener empleo.

Visite los puestos del Centro de Ayuda para Profesionales para una crítica del resumé, consejos administrativos, asistencia en la búsqueda de empleo y entrenamiento sobre entrevistas.

Tome un descanso para revisar la literatura que ha recogido e identifique las preguntas adicionales que usted pueda tener.

Antes de salir de la feria de empleo, regrese a los puestos que le fueron interesantes. Recuerde al reclutador que estaba interesado. Dé gracias al reclutador por su tiempo y deje claro que usted estará en contacto pronto. Su contacto de seguimiento demuestra profesionalismo. Hay una buena posibilidad de que haga una impresión duradera que le servirá.

DESPUÉS DE LA FERIA DE EMPLEO

Envíe inmediatamente una nota de agradecimiento y confirme de nuevo su interés en la posición y compañía. Si es posible, conecte las necesidades de la compañía con sus cualidades y exprese su deseo de tener una segunda entrevista.

Envié un o más cartas al Director/EEOO o encargado de Diversidad de la compañía de relaciones hispanas o VP sobre Diversidad, así como también otros contactos que usted ha hecho en la compañía. Adjunte una copia de su resumé y de cualquier nota de agradecimiento que usted envió al Departamento de Personal de la compañía.

Dentro de una semana, dé seguimiento con una llamada telefónica bien ensayada, a menos que se le haya especifcado que no lo haga.

Appendix AA

Oficina del Consejero Especial para Prácticas Injustas Relacionadas a la Condicion de Immigrante (OSC)

¿QUÉ DOCUMENTOS HAY QUE PRESENTAR AL SOLICITAR UN PUESTO DE TRABAJO?

Usted tiene derecho a ESCOGER los documentos a presentar, siempre que muestren que usted está autorizado para trabajar en los Estados Unidos. El patrón NO PUEDE PEDIRLE documentos específicos, como la tarjeta de residencia, y NO PUEDE RECHAZAR los documentos válidos que usted le presente.

Grupo A
Lista de documentos aceptables

Los documentos del Grupo A que comprueban a la vez su identidad y autorización para trabajar son:

Pasaporte de los Estados Unidos (vencido o vigente)

Certificado de ciudadanía de los Estados Unidos (N-560 o N-561)

Certificado de naturalización (N-550 o N-570)

Pasaporte vigente de otro país, con el sello "I-551" o con el formulario "I-94" del Servicio de Inmigración, indicando autorización vigente de trabajo

Tarjeta vigente de residencia permanente, con foto (I-151 o I-551)

Tarjeta vigente de residencia temporal (I-688)

Tarjeta vigente de autorización para trabajar (I-688A)

Permiso vigente de reingreso a los Estados Unidos (I-327)

Documento vigente de viajar para refugiados (I-571)

Documento vigente de autorización para trabajar, expedido por el Servicio de Inmigración, con foto (I-688B)

Grupo B
Documentos de identidad

Tarjeta de conducir o tarjeta de identidad expedida por un estado

Tarjeta de identidad expedida por una agencia del gobierno federal, estatal o local

Tarjeta de identificación estudiantil, con foto

Tarjeta de registro para votar

Tarjeta militar de los Estados Unidos o papeles de reclutamiento

Tarjeta de identidad de un dependiente de militar

Tarjeta de marino mercantil del Servicio de Guardacostas de los Estados Unidos

Documento de identidad de una tribu de indios de los Estados Unidos

Tarjeta de conducir expedida por el gobierno de Canadá

Si usted es menor de 18 años de edad y no tiene ninguno de los documentos del Grupo B, puede presentar al patrón:

Expediente de la escuela, o notas escolares

Informe médico de la clínica, hospital o del doctor

Archivo de guardería

Grupo C
Documentos de autorización para trabajar

Tarjeta de Seguro Social de los Estados Unidos, expedida por la Administración del Seguro Social

Acta de nacimiento de otro país, expedido por el Departamento de Estado (FS-545 o formulario DS-1350)

Original o copia certificada del acta de nacimiento, expedido por un estado, condado, municipio o territorio de los Estados Unidos

Documento de identidad de una tribu de indios de los Estados Unidos

Tarjeta de identidad de ciudadano estadounidense (I-197)

Tarjeta de identidad para uso de ciudadano residente en los Estados Unidos

Autorización vigente para trabajar, expedida por el Servicio de Inmigración (que no aparezca en el Grupo A)

Recuerde: Si usted no tiene ningún documento del Grupo A, puede presentar uno del Grupo B y uno del Grupo C, respectivamente.

Appendix BB

Contributors

The following individuals and organizations made significant contributions to this book. Please feel free to contact these professionals should you require assistance with your job search and career management.

RESUMES, CAREER MARKETING LETTERS AND CAREER WORKSHEETS

Arnold G. Boldt, CPRW, JCTC
Arnold-Smith Associates
625 Panorama Trail, Bldg. 1, #120
Rochester, NY 14625 U.S.
Phone: (585) 383-0350
Fax: (585) 387-0516
E-mail: Arnie@ResumeSOS.com
www.ResumeSOS.com

Pat Criscito
President
ProType, Ltd.
P.O. Box 49552
Colorado Springs, CO 80949
Phone: (800) 446-2408
Phone2: (719) 592-1999
Fax: (719) 598-8918
E-mail: pat@patcriscito.com
www.protypeltd.com

Louise Garver, MA, JCTC, CMP, CPRW,
   MCDP, CEIP
President
Career Directions, LLC
115 Elm Street, Ste 203
Enfield, CT 06082
Phone: (860) 623-9476
Fax: (860) 623-9473
E-mail: TheCareerPro@aol.com
www.careeeredge.com
www.resumeimpact.com

Gay Anne Himebaugh-Rodriguez
President, Seaview Resume Solutions
2855 E. Coast Hwy. #102
Corona del Mar, CA 92625 U.S.
Phone: (949) 673-2400
Fax: (949) 673-2428
E-mail: gayanne@seaviewsecretarial.com

Pat Kendall, NCRW, JCTC
Advanced Resume Concepts
Tigard, OR 97224
Phone: (800) 591-9143
Phone2: (503) 639-6098
Fax: (503) 213-6022
E-mail: pat@reslady.com
www.reslady.com
www.jumpstartyourjobsearch.com

Murray A. Mann, CCM
Principal
Global Career Strategies Group
Phone: 877-825-6566
Fax: 877-264-4628
E-mail: Murray@globalcareerstrategies
   .com
www.globalcareerstrategies.com
www.resumecompass.com
www.globalhrstrategies.com
www.globaldiversitystrategies.com

Linda Matias, NCRW, CIC, JCTC
  Executive Director
CareerStrides and
Long Island Outplacement
80 Davids Drive, Suite One
Hauppauge, NY 11788
Phone: (631) 387-1894
Fax: (631) 382-2425
E-mail: linda@careerstrides.com
www.careerstrides.com
www.lioutplacement.com

Don Orlando, MBA, CPRW, JCTC,
  CCM, CCMC
President
The McLean Group
640 South McDonough Street
Montgomery, AL 36104 U.S.
Phone: (334) 264-2020
Fax: (334) 264-9227
E-mail: yourcareercoach@aol.com

Geralynn Reyes, FJSCT
President
CareersByDesign
Maryland and District of Columbia
Phone: (310) 580-4577
E-mail: careersbydesign@aol.com

Evelyn U. Salvador, NCRW, JCTC
Creative Image Builders Inc.
8 Marla Dr.
Coram, NY 11727
Phone: (631) 698-7777
Fax: (631) 698-0984
E-mail CareerCatapult@aol.com
www.designerresumes.com

John Suarez, MA, CPRW
President
Success Stories, Inc.
132 Kansas Avenue
Belleville, IL 62221 U.S.
Phone: (866) 830-6518
Fax: (618) 233-6436
E-mail: jasuarez@htctech.net

Vivian VanLier, CPRW, JCTC, CEIP,
  CCMC
President
Advantage Resume & Career Services
6701 Murietta Avenue
Valley Glen, CA 91405 U.S.
Phone: (818) 994-6655
Fax: (818) 994-6620
E-mail: vvanlier@aol.com
www.CuttingEdgeResumes.com

CAREER COACHING, COUNSELING AND INTERVIEWING ADVICE

Christine Edick, PCCC, JCTC, CEIP,
  CCMC
President
A Career Coach 4 U
2691 N. Vista Heights Rd.
Orange, CA 92867 U.S.
Phone: (888) 261-4497
Phone2: (714) 974-6220
Fax: (714) 921-4838
E-mail: christine@acareercoach4u.com
www.ACareerCoach4U.com

Sally Gelardin, NCC, Ed.D. in Multicultural
  Education, DCC, CLTC, CDFI
Fellow at the University of San Francisco
  and Career Transition Coach
Phone: (415) 461-4097
Fax: (415) 461-4097
E-mail: sally@askdrsal.com
www.askdrsal.com
www.jobjuggler.net

Deborah Wile-Dib, CCM, NCRW, CPRW,
CEIP, JCTC, CCMC
"America's Executive Power Coach"
President
Advantage Resumes of NY and
Executive Power Coach
77 Buffalo Avenue
Medford, NY 11763 U.S.
Phone: (631) 475-8513
Fax: (501) 421-7790
E-mail: deborah.dib@advantageresumes
.com
www.advantageresumes.com
www.executivepowercoach.com

Norberto Kogan
Chairman & CEO
Kogan Group, Inc. and
TBK Career Management Services
Division
www.kogangroup.com

Lorenzo "Larry" R. Uribe, SPHR
Principal
Partners Solutions Group
Chicago, IL
Phone: (773) 889-4988
E-mail: luribe1111@aol.com
E-mail2: luribe@globalcareerstrategies.com
www.globalcareerstrategies.com

Susan Britton Whitcomb, CCMC, CCM,
NCRW, MRW
President
Career Masters Institute and Career Coach
Academy
757 East Hampton Way
Fresno, CA 93704 U.S.
Phone: (559) 222-7474
Fax: (559) 227-0670
E-mail: SWhitcomb@cminstitute.com
www.cminstitute.com
www.CareerCoachAcademy.com

IMMIGRATION AND LEGAL ADVICE

Barbara A. Susman, Esq.
Principal
Susman and Associates
203 N. Wabash, Suite 1400
Chicago, Illinois 60601
Phone: (312) 444-9600
Fax: (312) 444-9612
E-mail: susmanusa@aol.com
www.lawyers.com/susman

National Organizations of Professional Career Coaches and Resume Writers

These organizations have members throughout the United States and internationally who can deliver a variety of career services for you.

Career Masters Institute
757 East Hampton Way
Fresno, CA 93704
Phone: (800) 513-7439
Fax: (559) 227-0670
www.cminstitute.com

National Resume Writers' Association
P.O. Box 184
Nesconset, NY 11767
Phone: (888) NRWA-444
Phone2: (631) 930-6287
www.nrwaweb.com

Parachute
51 Washington Avenue
Point Richmond, CA 94801
Phone: (510) 232-3700
www.parachute.com (main site)
www.parachuteassociates.com (to find a
    career professional)

Index

Index